FOOD RIOTING IN IRELAND IN THE EIGHTEENTH AND
NINETEENTH CENTURIES

Food rioting in Ireland in the eighteenth and nineteenth centuries

The 'moral economy' and the Irish crowd

JAMES KELLY

FOUR COURTS PRESS

Set in 10.5 pt on 12.5pt MEhrhardt for
FOUR COURTS PRESS
7 Malpas Street, Dublin 8, Ireland
www.fourcourtspress.ie
and in North America for
FOUR COURTS PRESS
c/o ISBS, 920 N.E. 58th Avenue, Suite 300, Portland, OR 97213.

A catalogue record for this title
is available from the British Library.

ISBN 978-1-84682-639-9

Printed in England
by CPI, Chippenham, Wilts.

Contents

Contents

Tables, Maps, Illustrations

TABLES

ILLUSTRATIONS

Abbreviations

b.	born
c.	*circa*
CSO	Chief Secretary's Office
d.	died
DIB	*Dictionary of Irish biography* edited by James McGuire and James Quinn (9 vols, Cambridge, 2009)
(e)	estimate
ed./eds	editor/editors
edn.	edition
EHR	*English Historical Review*
IHS	*Irish Historical Studies*
MS(S)	Manuscript(s)
n.	note
n.d.	no date
n.s.	new series
NAI	National Archives of Ireland
NAI, OP	National Archives of Ireland, Outrage Papers
NLI	National Library of Ireland
NLW	National Library of Wales
no./nos	number/numbers
NUIG	National University of Ireland, Galway
NUIM	National University of Ireland, Maynooth (now Maynooth University)
NYPL	New York Public Library
ODNB	*Oxford dictionary of national biography* (60 vols, Oxford, 2004)
PRONI	Public Record Office of Northern Ireland
QUB	Queen's University, Belfast
rept.	reprint
RIA	Royal Irish Academy
RIA proc.	*Proceedings of the Royal Irish Academy*
TCD	Trinity College Dublin
TNA	The National Archives, Public Record Office
trans	translation
UCC	University College Cork
UCD	University College Dublin
vol.	volume
vols	volumes

Preface

Various encounters with individual food riots (in the eighteenth century mainly) have sustained a fitful and largely unstructured interest in the phenomenon of food protest over many years. This provided the foundation for the more sustained recent engagement with the evidential record – in manuscript and in print – that has permitted this text to be constructed. This then is a further essay in recovery in the mould of previous work on duelling, urban faction, sport and other subjects. It seeks to identify the pattern of food protest in Ireland in order, first, to establish its chronology, geography and its durability; second, to reconstruct the manner in which it was conducted; third, to describe its structure and main features; fourth, to locate it beside the more vigorous tradition of agrarian disquiet once this emerged on the Irish landscape; and fifth, to trace the attitude of the authorities and opinion formers. It aspires also to consider if the pattern of food rioting that can be identified in Ireland conforms to the contested model of a 'moral economy' elaborated by E.P. Thompson several decades ago, and (mis)applied, and not exclusively by anthropologists at whom the charge has been levelled, in a manner 'implying an association with a supracultural implication of justice'.

Whatever the verdict, I wish to acknowledge the assistance of the historians, archivists, librarians, publishers, friends and colleagues who have helped with the preparation of this work. They are not mutually exclusive categories, of course, and were I to list them separately there are many whose name would be repeated. Short of doing this, I wish to express my gratitude for specific guidance as well as general counsel to Raymond Gillespie, David Hayton, David Dickson, Carla King, Donal Moore (for extracts from the council books of the Corporation of Waterford), Martyn Powell, Will Murphy, Ruth MacManus and Susan Hegarty. I am indebted once again to Matthew Stout's cartographic skills, and to Ciarán Mac Murchaidh for observations on the evolving text. I owe a more general intellectual debt to John Bohstedt, Cynthia Bouton, John Cunningham and, of course, to E.P. Thompson, to whose work on food protest I have looked for direction as well as perspective.

I am grateful also to the owners, custodians, trustees and keepers of the manuscripts cited in this work that were consulted in The National Archives (at Kew), the National Archives of Ireland, the National Library of Wales, the British Library, the Public Record Office of Northern Ireland, Waterford City Archives, County Louth Archives Service, the New York Public Library, the Beinecke Library of Yale University and The American Philosophical Society. I wish similarly to extend my appreciation once more to the librarians, library assistants and others in the National Library of Ireland, the Cregan Library of St Patrick's College (now Dublin City University), and the Department of Early Printed Books and Special Collections at Trinity College who facilitated my exploration of the press and printed literature. For assistance with inter-library loans and locating rare texts, it is a pleasure to commend the staff of the Cregan Library and the staff at the National Library. I wish also to express my ongoing gratitude to my colleagues past and present for their fellowship, collegiality and support of historical inquiry. Their commitment was matched by that of the Research Committee of St Patrick's College; this book did not require a signifi- cant financial injection to bring it to completion, but the support that was forth- coming is warmly acknowledged. For their continuing commitment to the publication of elegant and quality academic books it is my pleasure once again to thank the full team at Four Courts Press. Finally, for the combination of for- bearance, indulgence and support that my family provide, a simple acknowl- edgement is insufficient, but its conventionality belies its significance as the preparation of this book was undertaken during a period of time-consuming insti- tutional change.

Dublin, 2017

Introduction

Food related protest possesses a complex and revealing historiography. Conceived of in the wake of its re-discovery by social historians in the 1960s and 1970s as an emblematical pre-modern phenomenon, and an exemplary manifestation of the class conflict that ensued as the emerging market economy collided with the 'customary norms ... and practices' that had hitherto shaped economic relations, this argument was given its classic expression in 1971 in E.P. Thompson's article 'The moral economy of the English crowd in the eighteenth century'.[1] A compelling essay in 'thick description', Thompson's contention 'that during times of high prices ... the crowd ... enforce[d], with robust direct action, protective market-control and the regulation of prices' provided the empirical foundation for the concept of a 'moral economy' in which those who perceived that access to the necessaries of life was diminished or endangered asserted their entitlement by intervention.[2] As an investigation of a hitherto little-appreciated phenomenon, and an explanation of a process, Thompson's argument excited great interest. As well as animating a lively debate in English historiography,[3] its broader interpretative applicability ensured that it was not only embraced by historians whose interest extended beyond eighteenth-century England and the societal impact of industrialization, but also by economists, political scientists and anthropologists. Indeed, the efforts of the poor and marginalized to hold those more powerful and wealthy than themselves to account during times of scarcity by appealing to embedded moral expectations has proved so eminently transferrable that the concept of a 'moral economy' has been applied to a great variety of contexts, while the phenomenon of food protest has been identified in a range of historical contents and locations spanning the Middle Ages to the present.[4] The 'IMF auster-

1 E.P. Thompson, 'The moral economy of the English crowd in the eighteenth century', *Past and Present*, 50 (1971), 76–136. 2 E.P. Thompson, 'The moral economy reviewed' in idem, *Customs in commons* (London, 1991), pp 260–1. 3 See Adrian Randall and Andrew Charlesworth, 'The moral economy: riot, markets and social conflict' in idem (eds), *Markets, market culture and popular protest: crowds, conflict and authority* (Basingstoke, 2000), pp 1–32; John Bohstedt, 'The moral economy and the discipline of historical context', *Journal of Social History*, 26 (1992), 265–84. 4 See, inter alia, Marc Edelman, 'E.P. Thompson and moral economies' in Didier Fassin (ed.), *A companion to moral anthropology* (Oxford, 2012), pp 49–66; Jaime Palomera and Theodora Vetta, 'Moral economy: rethinking a radical concept', *Anthropological Theory*, 16:4 (2016), 413–43; George Karandinos, L.K. Hart, F.M. Castrillo and Phillipe Bourgeois, 'The moral economy of violence in the US inner city', *Current Anthropology*, 55:1 (2014), 2–3; M.T. Davis (ed.), *Crowd actions in Britain and France from the Middle Ages to the modern world* (Basingstoke, 2015), passim.

ity riots' of 1976–91, and the spate of food rioting (in Jordan, Egypt, Morocco, Yemen, Tunisia, Côte d'Ivoire, Cameroon, Senegal, Mauritania and Haiti) in 2007–8 are now conceived of as merely the most striking recent manifestations of an enduring impulse.[5]

Curiously, given the island's familiarity with famine and subsistence crises extending over two millennia, food protest has not featured prominently in mainstream Irish history.[6] The prevailing impression when E.P. Thompson published his seminal article was that Ireland did not possess either 'a tradition of food rioting' or 'a moral economy' because (as John Bohstedt has put it) 'Ireland lacked the legitimizing reciprocity that sustained the political nation and provision politics in England'.[7] Thompson did not refer to Ireland in his 1971 article (and he did not have any reason to do so), but he was content to echo George Rudé, whose pioneering studies of 'the crowd in history' he deemed 'most helpful'; Rudé observed in 1978 that food rioting 'played little part' in Ireland before 1829–31.[8] Thompson sought to account for Irish exceptionalism in 1991 in his combative response to the various critics and commentators who found fault with his original thesis or who were already embarked on the 'analytical slippage in the use of [the term] moral economy' that has accelerated since.[9] Drawing upon an over┆

tions of food rioting during the famine of 1740–1, and a number of other accounts, Thompson acknowledged that 'the "classical" food riot was certainly known to the eighteenth-century Irish' – commenting that it was 'under reported in general histories'.[10] Though the tentativeness of this observation stands in sharp contrast to the robust blows he rained down on his multifarious detractors in the same lengthy essay, Thompson's contention that the failure of food rioting 'to prevent exports and to relieve famine (as in 1740–1) … might account for a weakening of the tradition [in Ireland] as the century wore on' was incautious.[11] His reference to incidents in 1792 and 1793 illustrates that he was aware that

5 See John Walton and David Seddon, *Free markets and food riots: the politics of global adjustment* (Oxford, 1994); John Bohstedt, 'Food riots and the politics of provisions in world history', Institute of Development Studies Working Paper, no. 444 (Brighton, 2014). 6 E. Margaret Crawford (ed.), *Famine – the Irish experience: subsistence crises and famines in Ireland* (Edinburgh, 1989), passim. 7 John Bohstedt, 'Food riots and the politics of provisions in early-modern England and France, the Irish Famine and World War I' in Davis (ed.), *Crowd actions in Britain and France*, p. 110. 8 Thompson, 'The moral economy of the English crowd', p. 78 n. 6; Thompson, 'The moral economy reviewed', p. 295; George Rudé, *Protest and punishment: the story of the social and political protesters transported to Australia* (Oxford, 1978), p. 57; idem, 'English rural and urban disturbances on the eve of the first reform bill, 1830–31' in H.J. Kaye (ed.), *The face of the crowd: selected essays of George Rudé* (Atlantic Highlands, NJ, 1988), pp 168–9. 9 Karandinos et al., 'The moral economy of violence in the US inner city', 2; Edelman, 'E.P. Thompson and moral economies', pp 49–66. 10 Thompson, 'The moral economy reviewed', pp 295–6. The pamphlet cited was *Famine in Ireland, 1740–41* (London, 1847). It was published by the Foreign Office and Irish Office. 11 Thompson, 'The moral economy reviewed', p. 296. Thompson cited food riot references from Samuel Clark and J.S. Donnelly (eds), *Irish peasants: violence and political unrest, 1780–1914* (Manchester, 1983), p. 55; C.H.E. Philpin (ed.), *Nationalism and popular protest in Ireland*

food riots occurred in Ireland beyond the mid-eighteenth century. He did not conceive of them as other than isolated events, however, and appealing to the 'divergent national traditions' interpretation that was/is as integral to the English Marxist narrative on Ireland as it is to Irish nationalist historiography, he offered the conclusion that 'food riots did not "work" in Ireland partly because there was no political space (as in England) within which the plebs could exert pressure on their rulers'. This is an alluring argument. The problem is that it does not sit easily with the record. Moreover, Thompson's elaboration is uncharacteristically hesitant: 'perhaps food rioters had less "political" clout in Ireland [than in England], since they did not threaten in the same direct way the stability and "face" of a resident governing gentry. Nor (in the absence of poor laws) did they stimulate in the same way an apparatus of relief, nor even (despite some examples) of gentry charity.'[12]

Though one might conclude from this that the conceptual vigour of Thompson's interpretation of the history of food rioting in Ireland belies its evidential frailty, its endorsement by John Bohstedt underlines its enduring attraction. It also reflects ill on historians of the crowd in Ireland, who have been slow to engage with the subject of food protest, and disinclined to identify how it related to agrarian protest, which is a subject that has attracted considerable attention since the late 1970s.[13] Indeed, apart from Jim Donnelly's pioneering account of food protest in county Cork in 1846–7, which was published in 1975, there was minimal engagement with either food protest or the idea of a moral economy in Ireland for many years after Thompson's influential intervention.[14] This is the case no longer, as Thomas Bartlett, Sean Connolly, Kevin Whelan, Eoin Magennis, Martyn Powell, Patrick McNally, Roger Wells, Andrès Eiríksson, Michael Huggins and John Cunningham have all invoked the concept

(Cambridge, 1987), p. 196. **12** Thompson, 'The moral economy reviewed', p. 296; H.J. Kaye and Keith McClelland (eds), *E.P. Thompson: critical perspectives* (Philadelphia, 1990), passim. England's exceptional economic trajectory, and the perception that it sustained a pattern of government that was more paternalist than that in France or Ireland, continues to encourage the conclusion that it possessed a unique tradition of food protest. In 2010, John Bohstedt observed: 'But rule by physical force – an Irish or French solution – was repulsive and expensive, so paternalism had also to be palpably acted out' (*The politics of provisions: food riots, moral economy and the market transition in England, c.1550–1850* (Farnham, 2010), p. 3); in 2015 he offered a still more explicit commentary, citing Thompson (and Terry Eagleton), that Ireland's colonial character explains why 'provision politics' failed (Bohstedt, 'Food riots and the politics of provisions in early-modern England and France, the Irish Famine and World War I', pp 110–14). There was, it will be argued here, an identifiably paternalist strand to Irish life also, and to the Irish food protest tradition, but it may be that it is less essential than other factors in explaining food protest than Thompson's concept of a 'moral economy' or Bohstedt's model of 'provision politics' implies. **13** The formative interventions were J.S. Donnelly, 'The Rightboy movement 1785–8', *Studia Hibernica*, 17 and 18 (1977–8), 120–202; idem, 'The Whiteboys, 1761–65', *IHS*, 21 (1978–9), 20–55. **14** J.S. Donnelly, *The land and the people of nineteenth-century Cork: the rural economy and the land question* (London, 1975), pp 87–91. Donnelly identified food protest as a subject which would repay closer study.

of the moral economy as an explanatory paradigm. It has been appealed to variously to highlight its limited applicability (Magennis, McNally); to locate its demise (Bartlett); to embrace houghing, agrarian and other forms of collective protest (Powell, Connolly, Whelan and Huggins), and extended beyond Thompson's temporal frame of reference to account for the prevalence of food rioting in the early nineteenth century (Eiríksson, Cunningham).[15]

Of those just listed, Magennis's account of the 1756–7 subsistence crisis merits particular notice. Guided by Mark Harrison's contention that because 'food riots were comparatively rare' any focus on crowd behaviour that fails to engage with 'the way in which ritual and ceremony in crowd actions actually establish or reinforce consensus between different social groups' is necessarily incomplete, Magennis endorses Thompson's conclusion that the pulse of the moral economy beat weakly in eighteenth-century Ireland.[16] Thomas Bartlett adopted a different approach. In an influential article published in 1983 he maintained that the anti-militia riots of 1793 signalled the end of the Irish moral economy, but since he equated this with the breakdown in the 'tacit understanding between governor and governed' that characterized agrarian protest prior to this episode, he deployed the concept in a manner different to what its author intended. It has, as Thompson pointed out in 1991, 'little to do with my (1971) usage but is concerned with the social dialectic of unequal mutuality ... which lies at the centre of most societies'.[17] By contrast, Wells, Eiríksson and

---

15 Eoin Magennis, 'In search of the "moral economy": food scarcity in 1756–57 and the crowd' in idem and Peter Jupp (eds), *Crowds in Ireland, c.1720–1920* (Basingstoke, 2000), pp 189–211; Thomas Bartlett, 'The end to moral economy: the Irish militia disturbances of 1793', *Past and Present*, 99 (1983), 41–64; Martyn J. Powell, 'Ireland's urban houghers: moral economy and popular protest in the late eighteenth century' in Michael Brown and Sean Patrick Donlan (eds), *Law and other legalities of Ireland, 1689–1850* (Aldershot, 2010), pp 231–53; S.J. Connolly, 'The houghers: agrarian protest in early eighteenth-century Connacht' in C.H.E. Philpin (ed.), *Nationalism and popular protest in Ireland* (Cambridge, 1987), p. 159; Patrick McNally, 'Rural protest and "moral economy": the Rightboy disturbances and parliament' in Allan Blackstock and Eoin Magennis (eds), *Politics and political culture in Britain and Ireland, 1750–1850* (Belfast, 2007), pp 262–82; Roger Wells, 'The Irish famine of 1799–1801: market culture, moral economies and social protest' in Andrew Charlesworth and Adrian Randall (eds), *Markets, market culture and popular protest in eighteenth-century Britain and Ireland* (Liverpool, 1996), pp 163–93; Andriès Eiríksson, 'Food supply and food riots' in Cormac Ó Gráda, *Famine 150: commemorative lectures series* (Dublin, 1997), pp 67–94; Michael Huggins, *Social conflict in pre-Famine Ireland: the case of county Roscommon* (Dublin, 2007), pp 169–87; John Cunningham, *'A town tormented by the sea': Galway, 1790–1914* (Dublin, 2004), pp 73, 76, 78, 86–98; idem, 'Popular protest and a "moral economy" in provincial Ireland in the early nineteenth century' in Francis Devine, Fintan Lane and Niamh Puirséil (eds), *Essays in Irish labour history* (Dublin, 2008), pp 26–48; idem, '"Compelled to their bad acts by hunger": three Irish urban crowds, 1817–45', *Éire-Ireland*, 45 (2010), 128–51.   16 Magennis, 'In search of the "moral economy"', pp 190–1 and passim; Cunningham, 'Popular protest and a "moral economy"', p. 27; Mark Harrison, *Crowds and history: mass phenomena in English towns, 1790–1835* (Cambridge, 1988); for Thompson on Harrison see 'The moral economy reviewed', p. 260, note 1.   17 Bartlett, 'The end to moral economy', 42; Thompson, 'The moral economy reviewed', p. 344; E.P. Thompson, 'Patrician society, plebeian culture', *Journal of*

the eighteenth and early nineteenth-centuries. Extensive use has also been made of the 'outrage papers' – a remarkable assemblage of the intelligence received by the Irish administration at Dublin Castle – and the registers of correspondence (much of which has not survived) for information on the early nineteenth century, and for the 1840s in particular. It is possible as a result to construct an account on food protest that melds the episodic perspectives previously available for the eighteenth century and the fuller, but still incomplete, studies that exist for the early nineteenth century with the evidence gleaned from these sources to provide an account of the scale, distribution and character of food motivated protest spanning its duration.

The resulting reconstruction is inevitably less complete than is optimal. It is not possible in the Irish case to emulate either Thompson's 'thick description' of food rioting in eighteenth-century England, or Bohstedt's location of English food rioting within 'the dynamic of provision politics' over the longer period of three centuries, but it does permit the conclusion that Ireland sustained a continuous tradition of food rioting spanning a century and a half.[25] Based on a sample of more than 280 food riots (Tables 2.1 and 2.2) from the period 1709–1845, and a substantially greater number of 'plundering provisions' incidents in 1846–50 (Tables 3–5), this study traces the phenomenon from the early eighteenth century, when the first identifiable food riot took place, through the middle and later decades of the same century when it was a distinct presence on the Irish economic and social landscape. It would be misleading to describe the latter as a 'golden age' of food protest, as Bohstedt has denominated the period 1740–1801 in England, because the number of incidents in Ireland was palpably smaller, and because the pattern of activity that can be identified then was sustained through the early decades of the nineteenth century.[26] In any event, Tables 2.1 and 2.2 suggest the food protest may have contracted after 1817 as it established an increasingly firm rural foothold as the number of land poor rose. Societal attitudes were also changing, for though food protest continued to peak – in 1822, 1830–1, 1837, 1840 and 1842 – in the wake of bad harvests, it was pursued less intently during the 1820s and 1830s than previously. It could be contended, indeed, that it was already in decline (as it was in England), and that it would have continued to contract, had not the plight of the landless and land poor, which reached its grim nadir during the Great Famine, sustained a pattern of food protest in 1846–7 that was more intense than any previously witnessed in Ireland. This was a unique, and unusual, episode because it was fuelled by hunger in a way that was rarely the case previously, and because the assumption by the state of the primary burden of providing relief swept away what remained of the reciprocation that was a feature of earlier food rioting episodes. As a result, the late 1840s constituted the last notable phase of food protest. A number of incidents occurred thereafter, but they were largely isolated

25 Thompson, 'The moral economy', passim; Bohstedt, *The politics of provisions*, passim. 26 Bohstedt, *The politics of provisions*, p. 105; idem, 'Food riots and the politics of provisions', p. 105.

events and the absence of any protest in 1861, when parts of the country teetered on the brink of famine once again, indicate that – a century and a half after it had commenced – purposeful food protest was no more.

This study opens with an attempt to identify the temporal and geographical distribution of food rioting (Chapter 1). The location of the practice in time and space is a necessary prelude to the exploration of the motivation and purpose of those who engaged in the activity, and the attempts to identify the causes, motivation and varied forms that food protest assumed (Chapter 2). Because food protest was prompted primarily by the anxiety stirred by high prices rather than by hunger or even acute scarcity, rioters employed a variety of strategies. These are summarized by Walton and Seddon as:

(a) the *blockage* or *entrave* that prevented the export of grain from an area ...;
(b) the price riot or *taxation populaire* in which food was seized by protesters, a just price set, and the lot sold;
(c) the *agrarian demonstration* in which farmers destroyed their own produce as a dramatic protest; and
(d) the *market riot* in which the crowd took retributive action against commercial agents (e.g., bakers, millers) or local magistrates in the form of looting or 'tumultuous assembly to force dealers or local authorities to reduce prices'.[27]

In keeping with its urban focus, food protesters in Ireland in the eighteenth century pursued options (a), (b) and (d) by preference, for though food stocks were targeted for destruction (a variant on option (c)) on occasion, the object of Irish protesters was less to express disapproval of the engagement by farmers, millers or others in commercial practices than to enhance the early availability of foodstuffs. Moreover, it was seldom resorted to prior to the 1840s, and only occasionally then. By contrast, both urban and rural crowds sought frequently to blockade (*entrave*) the movement of foodstuffs (grain and potatoes especially) by incapacitating ships, by intercepting carts, and by targeting mills and food stores. The emblematic practice of selling appropriated foodstuffs at an affordable price – the *taxation populaire* – which was normative in France from the second quarter of the seventeenth century and has been identified in many contexts in which food rioting took place – was also pursued in Ireland in the eighteenth and early nineteenth centuries; it was complemented by a variety of related tactics – such as obliging merchants to sell grain at market, transferring appropriated grain to

27 Walton and Seddon, *Free markets and food riots*, pp 25–6, drawing on John Stevenson, 'Food riots in England, 1792–1818' in R. Quinault and John Stevenson (eds), *Popular protest and public order: six studies in British history, 1790–1920* (London, 1974), p. 3; see also Louise A. Tilly, 'Food entitlement, famine and conflict' in R.I. Rotberg and T.K. Rabb (eds), *Hunger and history: the impact of changing food production and consumption patterns on society* (Cambridge, 1985), pp 141–3.

the custody of a local magistrate and taking possession of the contents of food stores, attacking mills and compelling farmers, carriers and merchants to bring goods to market – that were variants on (d). But these were largely superseded by the appropriation of foodstuffs, which was, by some measure, the preferred *modus operandi* in the second quarter of the nineteenth century as economic conditions deteriorated and 'plundering provisions' displaced food rioting as the primary manifestation of food protest.

Food rioters did not always behave in a manner that was explicitly communitarian, of course. Their interventions could result in the destruction of property – buildings, machinery and foodstuffs – and displays of violence as a result of which people were killed and injured. This notwithstanding, food protest was largely pursued in a controlled fashion, which is consistent with the benign model of a 'moral economy' that is sometimes championed. But this is not invariably the case. Food protest did not conform to a distinct and distinguishable template, and protesters did not always conduct themselves in a disciplined manner; its inherently fluid boundaries embraced actions that many in society at large found disagreeable, and that sat uneasily with the mutuality that is integral to the ideal of the 'moral economy'. These behaviours ought not to be narrowly defined. As elsewhere, food protest in Ireland was not unchanging. Though it retained an urban presence, its virtually exclusive urban anchorage in the eighteenth century was diluted as commercialization penetrated the countryside, and while it embraced a greater diversity of forms there than it possessed earlier, the effects of economic and demographic expansion and the example of agrarian protest facilitated its adoption by the expanding ranks of the land poor in what were to become its rural heartlands.

Food rioting never emulated, still less displaced, the varieties of direct action that defined agrarian protest in the countryside.[28] But as it contracted in its traditional eastern and southern urban base, and its spatial footprint expanded to embrace the midlands in the late eighteenth century; western Connaught, north Munster and the western seaboard ports in the early nineteenth; and most of the country, but the midlands, south and west in particular, in the 1840s, the distinc-

28 Food rioting has been described as 'the most widespread form of social protest throughout major parts of western and central Europe since the early modern period' (Manfred Gailus, 'Food riots in Germany in the late 1840s', *Past and Present*, 145 (1994), 157); and as 'the most classic form of protest' in eighteenth-century France (C.A. Bouton, *The flour war: gender, class and community in late* ancien régime *French society* (Philadelphia, 1993), p. 6). According to Walton and Seddon, between the mid-sixteenth and mid-nineteenth centuries 'riot was the most common form of popular protest, and uprisings related to food ... the most common form of riot' (Walton and Seddon, *Free markets and food riots*, p. 25). In addition, commenting on eighteenth-century England, John Stevenson has observed that 'the most persistent and widespread riots were those associated with food, for it has been calculated that two out of every three disturbances ... were of this type' ('Food riots in England, 1792–1818', p. 33). In Germany in the period 1 Jan. 1847–30 June 1849, it accounted for 10 per cent of disturbances; according to John Bohstedt it may have constituted 40 per cent of all protests in England and Wales between 1790 and 1810: *Riot and community politics in England and Wales, 1790–1810* (Cambridge, MA, 1983), p. 14. This was not true of Ireland; agrarian protest was more commonplace.

tion, once clear cut, that one can draw between food rioting and agrarian protest, and food protest and crime, becomes increasingly blurred (Chapter 2). Indeed, it maybe that one consequence of its increasing embrace by the rural land poor is that the distinction that one can draw between food and other forms of protest in the eighteenth and early nineteenth centuries breaks down, and that, as the official attitude attests, it is best seen during the Great Famine as one of a range of behaviours that embraced classical food protest, food appropriation, the theft (of foodstuffs and livestock), brigandage (including piracy), and the full range of violent and intimidatory actions that were a feature of agrarian protest.

Having identified the changing manner in which food rioting was pursued in Ireland, the focus shifts to the features of food protest in order to establish the seasonal, organizational and other considerations that defined the phenomenon (Chapter 3). An attempt is also made to establish the number that engaged in food protest, the extent to which it was a gendered activity, and the degree to which the crowds ('mobs') that pursued food protest were reliant on violence to realize the 'moral expectations' that guided their actions. This evokes the 'legitimizing notion' that is integral to the Thompsonian model of a 'moral economy'.[29] Indeed, the moral authority that food protest possessed for most of its existence derived in large part from the acceptance that the populace possessed a *droit de subsistence*. This was not articulated in a sustained or coherent fashion in Ireland, but the implicit acknowledgement that the right to alimentation trumped other claims meant that food protesters were extended a measure of sympathy that was rarely offered to other 'mobs' even those that engaged in allied forms of collective expression. Yet, this too was neither constant nor unchanging, and the resort to intimidation, the appeal to violence, and the increased disposition to appropriate foodstuffs synergized with the changing official disposition to such forms of protest in the nineteenth century to cause the authorities to adopt an increasingly less sympathetic attitude. The response of the authorities and the attitude of the public provide the focus of Chapter 4.

From a purely statistical perspective, it can be shown that the civil and military authorities inflicted more casualties upon food protesters than food protesters did upon the producers and dealers in food that were their focus. The relationship of protesters and the authorities was not immutable, of course. It oscillated between confrontation and accommodation, which is nearly as revealing as the temporal pattern of the ebb and flow of protest as a measure of the strength of the phenomenon. It is critical, certainly, to any attempt to evaluate the applicability of E.P. Thompson's contention that the food riot was an exemplary manifestation of the 'moral economy' that ante dated the competitive 'political' economy fostered by the industrial revolution, since Thompson's influential concept presumes reciprocity. In other words, the occurrence of food rioting, and still less provisions plundering, is not of itself evidence of the existence of a 'moral economy'. It necessitated a reciprocal response on the part of those – mer-

29 Thompson, 'The moral economy', 78.

chants, magistrates, millers, shippers, farmers and others – who were engaged in the purchase, sale, shipping, retail and distribution of the foods and allied goods that rioters targeted over and above the ordinary rules and regulations that determined the quotidian operation of the market in such commodities.

In the near half century since E.P. Thompson presented his concept of a 'moral economy', and in the quarter century since he sallied forth with his comprehensive defence of the idea, the term as well as the concept has been extended by historians and anthropologists to a great variety of locations and contexts.[30] This attests to its versatility and attractiveness. It is not a testament to its applicability, for while Thompson's pugnacious *riposte* (1991) attests to his enduring belief in its ideological as well as historical value and the limits of the readings of his detractors, the case in favour of its modified application cannot easily be dismissed. John Bohstedt has marshalled a strong argument in support of his assessment that food rioting was a manifestation, less of the commitment of 'the men and women of the crowd' to defend 'traditional rights and customs' (as propounded by Thompson) than to what he terms 'an ethos of collective self-help'. Chapter 5 engages with the concept of a 'moral economy' from a number of vantage points to establish if food protest in Ireland possess distinct or unique characteristics, and more generally to connect it to the broader tradition of protest in other jurisdictions.

This study of Irish food protest was not undertaken with the object of testing the applicability of Thompson's influential thesis. Yet, it is not possible to pursue the subject without reference to his comments on that jurisdiction, and still less his contention that food rioting was emblematic of the pressures experienced as society transitioned from a 'customary moral economy' to a capitalist commercial and industrial world. Indeed, because the trajectory of Irish economic history differs from that of England, it may be that Bohstedt's conclusion that 'food riots were measures of emergency self-defense rather than eruptions of an alternative moral-economic order', and thus a manifestation of a 'pragmatic' rather than a 'moral economy', is more pertinent.[31] These are not, of course, the only relevant interpretative perspectives. Andy Wood's contention – based on his analysis of the 'politics of social conflict' in the Peak District over several centuries – that one cannot assume 'plebeian' antipathy to economic change is obviously pertinent, as is John Walter's and William Reddy's conception of food protest as a form of pre-modern political expression.[32] The latter contention

---

30 See Bohstedt, 'Food riots and the politics of provisions in world history', passim; Edelman, 'E.P. Thompson and moral economies', pp 49–66; Palomera and Vetta, 'Moral economy: rethinking a radical concept', 413–32; Bouton, *The flour war*, chapter 1; Randall and Charlesworth, 'The moral economy: riot, markets and social conflict', pp 1–32.   31 Thompson, 'Moral economy', 78–9; Bohstedt, 'The moral economy and the discipline of historical context', 268, 269, 270; idem, 'The pragmatic economy, the politics of provisions and the "invention" of the food riot tradition in 1740' in Randall and Charlesworth (eds), *Moral economy and popular protest*, pp 55–92.   32 Andy Wood, *The politics of social conflict: the Peak Country, 1520–1770* (Cambridge, 1999); below, pp 226–7.

might seem hardly pertinent in the Irish context given the prevailing inclination to perceive of popular protest as apolitical. It was, of course, if one adheres to a Marxist or a traditionally revisionist definition of the political, but there are other definitions. It may be, moreover, that the problem rests with where the comparisons are drawn, and that if a parallel is required it is sought elsewhere in Europe. In the event, it is salutary to observe, as we seek attempt to make sense of Irish food protest that late early modern Ireland was as much a part of the European *ancien régime* as it was a part of the British industrial and Atlantic commercial world with which most comparisons are drawn.[33]

33 This observation is informed both by the location of Irish society in the European *ancien régime* by S.J. Connolly and by the more recent suggestion that Ireland's constitutional relationship with Britain conforms to the European model of a composite monarchy: S.J. Connolly, *Religion, law and power: the making of Protestant Ireland, 1660–1760* (Oxford, 1992); D.W. Hayton, James Kelly and John Bergin (eds), *The eighteenth-century composite state: representative institutions in Ireland and Europe, 1689–1800* (Basingstoke, 2010), introduction.

The chronology and geography of Irish food protest, *c*.1700–*c*.1860

INTRODUCTION

In Ireland, as elsewhere, food rioting generally occurred when the populace perceived that their capacity as consumers to access foodstuffs at an affordable price was diminished or endangered. Triggered by economic conditions, and specifically by food price inflation, protesters identified the retention of food in a locality as a priority. To this end, they targeted ships and shippers engaged in the transport of foodstuffs, and intercepted wherries, barges and carts embarked on the same activity. They were no less disposed to target the warehouses and stores of merchants, the mills of mill owners, and, on occasion, the barns of farmers and others possessed of substantial quantities of food. And, having commandeered the food contained therein, they sought either to make it available directly at an affordable price, to compel owners to release it onto the local market, or to appropriate it to distribute in the manner they thought fit (in which case the owner might be at a total loss).

Consistent with the fact that the purpose of food rioting was to enhance the availability of foodstuffs, protesters used force in a controlled manner, though this did not preclude confrontation that resulted in physical injury and, on occasion, in fatalities. They were less restrained when it came to property, and ships, boats, carts and other modes of carriage used to ferry goods out of a port or region, were routinely immobilized and stores, bakeries and shops ransacked. Food rioting was not, in other words, a ritualized activity, though it possessed a rationale and a grammar of behaviour that distinguish it from other forms of protest and that are deserving of particular investigation because of what they reveal of social relations between the poor and those who were better off. It is still more revealing, however, of the response of the populace to the prospect of dearth and distress during an era when famine and subsistence crises were common place, and of the evolving response of the state and civil society to one of the most emblematical manifestations of poverty.

BACKGROUND AND BEGINNINGS, 1709–12

The first identifiable food riot in Ireland dates from the early eighteenth century. Ireland, therefore, does not mirror England where food rioting in the modern era

was pursued for 300 years spanning the mid-sixteenth to the mid-nineteenth centuries.[1] Though the land expropriation and plantation that was integral to the
New English conquest had still more profound economic impact on patterns of
land use in Ireland than the forces of 'commercialization' had on Tudor and
Stuart England, there are no Irish equivalents to the anti-enclosure and food riots
identified in England during this time and no transitional phase whereby, by the
end of the seventeenth century, 'grain riots ... [had] replaced ... enclosure riots
as the characteristic form of artisanal unrest'.[2] There was, as a result, nothing
comparable in Ireland to the food riots that took place in England in 1629–31
though the harvest failure and trade depression that blighted the economies of
both islands in the late 1620s resulted in serious food shortage in Ireland from
1627.[3] This was the case also in 1641–2 when there was further harvest failure;
during the early 1650s when the country experienced a major demographic crisis;
and in 1674 when harvest failure elicited a prohibition on the exportation of all
manner of foodstuffs out of the 'realm'. One may, as a result, conclude that (as
with duelling, recreational sport and organized sociability) food rioting emerged
later in Ireland than it did in England because the economic, commercial and
social conditions required to sustain such activities were still in the process of
taking root.[4] Furthermore, food rioting drew on established patterns of behaviour
– 'a repertoire of proven tactics' – which required a sufficient demographic concentration generally only to be found in an urban context, which was not in place
in Ireland until the beginning of the eighteenth century.[5]

It has been calculated that the population of Ireland doubled (from 1.4 to 2.8
million) between 1600 and 1712. The alteration of its composition was still more

---

1 Indeed, it may have lasted longer as Buchanan Sharp maintains it was pursued in the medieval era: 'The food riots of 1347 and the medieval moral economy' in Randall and Charlesworth (eds), *Moral economy and popular protest*, pp 33–54; Bohstedt, *The politics of provisions*, passim; Bohstedt, 'The pragmatic economy, the politics of provisions and the "invention" of the food riot tradition in 1740', pp 56–8; Andy Wood, *Riot, rebellion and popular politics in early modern England* (Basingstoke, 2002), pp 96–8.   2 Raymond Gillespie, *The transformation of the Irish economy, 1550–1700* (Dundalk, 1991); Bohstedt, *The politics of provisions*, pp 21–91, 98; Wood, *Riot, rebellion and popular politics*, pp 95–100; John Walter, 'Grain riots and popular attitudes to the law: Maldon and the crisis of 1629' in John Brewer and John Styles (eds), *An ungovernable people: the English and their law in the seventeenth and eighteenth centuries* (London, 1980), pp 48–81.   3 Raymond Gillespie, 'Harvest crises in early seventeenth-century Ireland', *Irish Economic and Social History*, 11 (1984), 10–13; Bohstedt, *The politics of provisions*, pp 32, 54; Bohstedt, 'The pragmatic economy, the politics of provisions and the "invention" of the food riot tradition in 1740', p. 57. I wish also to thank Raymond Gillespie for guidance on this point.   4 Patrick Fitzgerald, 'The great hunger? Irish famine: changing patterns of crisis' in E. Margaret Crawford (ed.), *The hungry steam: essays on emigration and famine* (Belfast, 1997), pp 115–16; James Kelly and Mary Ann Lyons (eds), *The proclamations of Ireland, 1660–1820* (5 vols, Dublin, 2014), i, 319–21; James Kelly, *'That damn'd thing called honour': duelling in Ireland, 1570–1860* (Cork, 1995), chapter 1; idem, *Sport in Ireland, 1600–1840* (Dublin, 2014), chapter 1; James Kelly and M.J. Powell, 'Introduction' in idem (eds), *Clubs and societies in eighteenth-century Ireland* (Dublin, 2010), pp 17–35.   5 Bohstedt, 'The moral economy and the discipline of historical context', 270.

significant, as its Anglophone component increased during the same period from *circa* one to *circa* twenty per cent as a consequence of the migration of settlers from England and Scotland.[6] It has been contended that the economic and cultural modernization that ensued was as marked in Munster as it was in Ulster in the early seventeenth century. This claim has not found favour, but its very suggestion points to the order of the demographic change taking place, even if the three major waves of primarily Scottish immigration (in the 1610s, 1650s and 1690s) ensured that Ulster was the most anglicized province by the end of the century.[7] As food rioting in Ireland was inaugurated in an anglicized environment, anglicization was a prerequisite. So too was urbanization.

Food protest in Ireland commenced and was long pursued in urban settings where access to meal and flour was vital to a 'labouring population' for whom, John Post has calculated, 'food and drink accounted for some 60–75 per cent of the household budget ... when cereal prices stood at normal levels'.[8] Estimating the populations of the main cities and towns in Ireland in the seventeenth and early eighteenth centuries is inherently hazardous, but the number and size of Ireland's urban spaces grew as a consequence of the central place urbanization was afforded in the plantation process, increased commercial activity, and the preference of certain settlers – artisans and operatives in particular – for an urban lifestyle.[9] The proportion of Ireland's population that were urban dwellers in the eighteenth century was 'significantly lower than in England or the Dutch Republic', and may not have exceeded 12.5 per cent. Ireland may also have fallen 'behind the general trend of accelerated urbanization' identifiable in Europe after 1750, but this does not mean that the country did not experience significant urbanization.[10] Dublin, for example, embarked on a period of rapid expansion

---

6 L.M. Cullen, 'Population trends in seventeenth-century Ireland', *Economic and Social Review*, 6 (1974–5), 149–65; Gillespie, *The transformation of the Irish economy, 1550–1700*, pp 12–19; James Kelly and Ciarán Mac Murchaidh (eds), *Irish and English: essays on the Irish linguistic and cultural frontier, 1600–1900* (Dublin, 2012), pp 20–5; Nicholas Canny, *Making Ireland British, 1580–1650* (Oxford, 2001). 7 Nicholas Canny, 'Migration and opportunity', *Irish Economic and Social History*, 12 (1985), 7–32; Raymond Gillespie, 'Migration and opportunity: a comment', *Irish Economic and Social History*, 13 (1986), 90–5; Nicholas Canny, 'A reply', ibid., 96–100; Robert Whan, *The Presbyterians of Ulster, 1680–1730* (Woodbridge, 2013); Michael Griffin, *The people with no name: Ireland's Ulster Scots, America's Scots Irish and the creation of the British Atlantic world, 1689–1764* (Princeton, 2001). 8 John D. Post, 'Nutritional status and mortality in eighteenth-century Europe' in L.F. Newman (ed.), *Hunger in history: food shortage, poverty and deprivation* (Oxford, 1990), 247; Steven Engler, J. Lutenbacher, F. Mauelshagen and J. Werner, 'The Irish famine of 1740–1741: causes and effects', *Climate of the Past*, 9 (2013), 1173 [available at: http://www.clim-past-discuss.net/9/1013/2013/cpd-9-1013-2013.pdf]. 9 Raymond Gillespie, 'Irish agriculture in the seventeenth century' in Margaret Murphy and Matthew Stout (eds), *Agriculture and settlement in Ireland* (Dublin, 2015), pp 127–8, 138; idem, 'The small towns of Ulster, 1600–1799', *Ulster Folklife*, 36 (1990), 23–30; idem, 'Dublin, 1600–1700: a city and its hinterlands' in Peter Clark and Bernard Lepetit (eds), *Capital cities and their hinterlands in early modern Europe* (Aldershot, 1996), pp 84–101; idem, 'Small towns in early modern Ireland' in Peter Clark (ed.), *Small towns in early modern Europe* (Cambridge, 1995), pp 148–65. 10 Engler et al., 'The Irish famine of 1740–1741', 1166.

Table 1: Select urban population estimates, 1650–1841

Dublin		Cork		Limerick		Bandon		Kinsale & Liberties	
1659	21,950(e)[11]	c.1659	12,065(e)	c.1659	3,105(e)	c.1659	2,692(e)	c.1659	5,492(e)
1685	45,000			c.1680	c.5,000	1685	c.2,250		
1706	62,000	1706	17,595	1706	11,868				
1725	92,000	1725	35,232						
1744	112,000	1744	37,570						
1760	140,000	1760	44,460	1766	13,675				
1778	154,000					1775	c.4,000		
1798	182,000	1796	57,033	1792	c.40,000	1798	c.4,610		
1821	224,000	1821	71,500	1821	59,045	1821	10,179	1821	7,068
1841	254,000	1841	80,720	1841	66,554	1841	9,049	1841	6,918

Youghal		Ennis		Carrick-on-Suir		Waterford		Dundalk	
c.1659	973	c.1659	667(e)			c.1659	4,117(e)	c.1659	1,577(e)
		1682	550					1670	2,000
1765	3,326								
				1799	10,863			1782	5,000
1821	8,969	1821	6,701	1821	7,466	1821	28,679	1821	9,256
1841	9,939	1841	9,318	1841	11,049	1841	23,216	1841	10,782

Drogheda		Kilkenny		Wexford		Armagh		Belfast	
c.1659	4,012(e)	c.1659	1,311	c.1659	2,255(e)	c.1659	409	c.1659	1,472(e)
		1702	c.5,000	1700	3,000 (e)	1670	1,000		
		1731	7,740					1757	8,549
						1770	1,948	1776	15,000
		1801	14,975					1802	19,000
1821	18,118	1821	23,230	1821	8,326	1821	8,135	1821	37,277
1841	17,300	1841	19,071	1841	11,252	1841	12,041	1841	63,730

Derry/ Londonderry		Longford		Athlone		Sligo		Galway	
c.1659	2,638(e)	c.1659	162(e)	c.1659	1,075	c.1659	1,220(e)	c.1650	c.6,000
1706	2,848					1732	1,797	1706	6,403
				1749	c.2,500	1749	2,468	1782	14,000
1788	10,262					1791	7,240	1787	17,000
		1813	3,062	1800	c.4,000			1813	24,684
		1831	4,516	1821	10,922	1821	9,283	1821	27,779
1821	16,971	1841	4,966	1841	6,393[12]	1841	14,318	1841	17,275[13]
1841	15,196								

Source: *Irish historic towns atlas* (3 vols, Dublin, 1996–2012) for Bandon, Athlone, Kilkenny, Derry/ Londonderry, Dundalk, Armagh, Limerick; Raymond Gillespie and Stephen Royle, *Irish historic towns atlas, no. 12: Belfast, part I* (Dublin, 2003); Brian Ó Dalaigh, *Irish historic towns atlas, no. 25: Ennis* (Dublin, 2012); Fiona Gallagher, *Irish historic towns atlas, no. 24: Sligo* (Dublin, 2012); Jacinta Prunty and Paul Walsh, *Irish historic towns atlas, no. 28: Galway* (Dublin, 2016); Seamus Pender (ed.), *A census of Ireland, circa 1659: with supplementary material from the poll money ordinances (1660–1661)* (Dublin, 1939); A.J. Fitzpatrick and W.E. Vaughan, *Irish historical statistics: population, 1821–1971* (Dublin, 1978); David Dickson, *Old world colony: Cork and south Munster, 1630–1830* (Cork, 2005), p. 662; Billy Colfer, *Wexford: a town and its landscape* (Cork, 2008); David Dickson, 'The demographic implications of the growth of Dublin 1650–1850' in R. Lawton and R. Lee (eds), *Urban population development in western Europe* ... (Liverpool, 1989), pp 178–89.

11 The 1659–60 poll tax counted adult males; a multiplier of 2.5 has been employed to establish a population estimate. 12 The area delimited as Athlone in 1821 had changed by 1841. 13 The area delimited as Galway in 1821 had changed by 1841.

fuelled by immigration, as a result of which its population doubled to perhaps 45,000 during the reign of Charles II, 1660–85, and it doubled again between then and the mid-1720s.[14] The order and rate of growth was less spectacular elsewhere. With an estimated population of 35,000 in 1725, Cork was by some margin the largest of a lattice of Munster ports – some such as Skibbereen and Dungarvan small in scale; others, Limerick, Kinsale, Youghal and Waterford, more imposing – and inland towns – Bandon, Mallow, Carrick-on-Suir and Clonmel – that possessed populations of sufficient mass by the second quarter of the eighteenth century to forge the communal identity necessary to sustain a 'mob', which was a prerequisite for food protest. This was true also of the main ports on the east coast – Dublin, Drogheda, Dundalk and Belfast most notably; of Galway and Sligo on the west coast, and Derry/Londonderry to the north, but as the country's economy expanded in the second half of the eighteenth century, and population growth accelerated, the number of urban centres with sufficient demographic mass to sustain a crowd appreciated accordingly (Table 1).

Though it would hardly have happened in its absence, a rising urban population on its own could not have sustained a pattern of food protest. It was also predicated on commercialization, which acutely shaped lives and lifestyles in urban settings and, by irrevocably altering the order and nature of economic activity, fostered the growth of what John Walter has called 'harvest-sensitive poverty'.[15] The most accessible index of commercialization in seventeenth-century Ireland is the increased trade in goods, the most measurable manifestation of which was the augmented volume of agricultural commodities exported, and consumer goods imported. Furthermore, it both assisted with the percolation and encouraged the use of money that was at its most advanced in urban areas, and in those (contiguous) rural areas with the most direct and developed links to the fast growing commercialized regions of the British Isles, western Europe and the Atlantic.[16] It was, for example, observed of county Cork in the 1720s that it 'sent forth large quantities of barley, as it abounded in tillage'.[17] Elsewhere in the

---

14 David Dickson, 'The demographic implications of the growth of Dublin, 1650–1850' in Richard Lawton and Robert Lee (eds), *Urban population development in western Europe from the late-eighteenth to the early-twentieth century* (Liverpool, 1989), pp 178–89; idem, *Dublin: the making of a capital city* (London, 2014), pp 92–4. A guide to the impact of immigration on the population may be secured from the 1659 'census' which indicates the ethnic (native/Irish and settler/English) composition of the adult male population: Seamus Pender (ed.), *A census of Ireland, circa 1659: with supplementary material from the poll money ordinances (1660–1661)* (Dublin, 1939).   **15** John Walter, 'The politics of protest in seventeenth-century England' in M.T. Davis (ed.), *Crowd actions in Britain and France from the middle ages to the modern world* (Basingstoke, 2015), p. 60.   **16** Donal Woodward, 'Irish trade and customs statistics, 1614–1641', *Irish Economic and Social History*, 26 (1999), 54–80; L.M. Cullen, *Anglo-Irish trade, 1660–1800* (Manchester, 1968), chapters 1 and 2; Gillespie, 'Irish agriculture in the seventeenth century', pp 122–9; Thomas M. Truxes, *Irish-American trade, 1660–1783* (Cambridge, 1988), chapter 1.   **17** [George Rye], *Considerations on agriculture treating of the several methods practised in different parts of the kingdom of Ireland, with remarks thereon* (Dublin, 1730), introduction; Dickson, *Old world colony,* chapters 4 and 5.

country, Dublin was already embarked by that date on the development of the
port facilities that was to make it the country's dominant trading centre, while
Drogheda was one of the country's 'main grain markets', and a particular focus
for northern and Scottish buyers.[18]

Given the pace with which trade grew and commercialization advanced in the
second half of the seventeenth century, and the fact that the 1640s was a 'watershed' in the history of 'the politics of provisions' in early modern England, the
absence of food rioting in Ireland during those occasions in the early 1650s, the
1670s and the late 1680s when conditions were difficult, is noteworthy. The
kingdom was not unique in this respect to be sure.[19] The Restoration era in
England produced 'little crisis mortality', and it may be that municipal authorities generally took appropriate precautionary actions in the manner of Waterford
Corporation, which in 1663 responded to a 'greate scarcity of corne' caused by
'abuses in the market as well as by scarcity' by fining and expelling a freeman
for engrossing 'a shipload of wheate'. It may be also that it was not necessary to
intervene routinely in this manner as food production exceeded demand for most
of the period, and since few Irish towns possessed either the critical demographic
mass, or the attendant dependence on purchased foodstuffs to sustain a purposeful food 'mob', that this was why they were not then a feature on the landscape.[20] If so, this remained the case through the 1690s when, in stark contrast
to France and Scotland, Ireland avoided the major famines, attributable to 'meteorological disasters', which cost tens of thousands of lives. As a result, there was
nothing in Ireland equivalent to the cluster of two dozen food riots precipitated
by bad harvests in England between 1693 and 1695.[21]

Ireland also evaded the worst consequences of the complex of environmental,
economic and military conditions that made the early years of the eighteenth century particularly difficult for the people of large parts of Europe. Yet the kingdom continued to be drawn ineluctably into existing European and emerging
Atlantic commercial systems. This necessarily resulted in the movement of large
amounts of grain and other agricultural products internally as well as abroad, as
Charles O'Hara (*c*.1705–76), a percipient analyst of the island's economic development, later recalled:

18 Dickson, *Dublin: the making of a capital city*, pp 122–8; L.M. Cullen, 'Eighteenth-century flour
milling in Ireland', *Irish Economic and Social History*, 4 (1977), 23.   19 Pádraig Lenihan, 'War and
population, 1649–42', *Irish Economic and Social History*, 24 (1997), 1–21.   20 Séamus Pender (ed.),
Corporation of Waterford council books, 1662–1700 (Dublin, 1964), pp 47–8. Bohstedt's 'census' lists
eight (possibly nine) incidents in England between 1662 and 1690: John Bohstedt, 'Census of riots
– second century (1650–1739)', available at web.utk.edu/~bohstedt/; Bohstedt, *The politics of provisions*, chapter 3.   21 John D. Post, 'Meteorological historiography', *Journal of Interdisciplinary
History*, 34 (1973), 728; Karen J. Cullen, *Famine in Scotland: the 'ill years' of the 1690s* (Edinburgh,
2010); Bohstedt, *The politics of provisions: food riots*, pp 98–100; Bohstedt, 'The pragmatic economy,
the politics of provisions and the "invention" of the food riot tradition in 1740', p. 58.

... As the colonies abroad began to encrease, and with them the British and French navigation demands for beef grew more frequent in the south of Ireland, and gradualy encrcasd: and in proportion as it did, the graziers of Munster turnd their grounds to feeding, and came towards the Conaught fairs for their store cattle.[22]

While the augmented economic activity identified by O'Hara was beneficial to the kingdom as a whole, and profitable for the producers, for the merchants who organized its conveyance to port and arranged its export, and shippers who carried it further, it was not without implication for the emerging class of labourers and artisans, in urban areas primarily, for whom availability and price were vital concerns. This was not a preoccupation when, following a bumper harvest, there was a ready supply of staple foodstuffs. When the harvest disappointed, however, the combination of reduced stocks and rising prices inevitably aroused anxiety among these price-sensitive elements of the community. It is a matter of little surprise, therefore, that the high points of food rioting in Ireland in the eighteenth and early nineteenth centuries chime with the high prices in staple foodstuffs – oats, wheat, flour, bread and potatoes – that were a feature of famine and subsistence crises.[23]

The first identified instances of food protest in Ireland date from the winter of 1709–10. They coincide with a threatened shortage in the kingdom, and one of the three 'significant clusters' of food riots in England between 1650 and 1740. Information is sketchy, but it is notable that the 'mob' which 'rose in a very tumultuous manner' in Cork on three occasions in January 1710 targeted the houses of merchants who were 'concerned in the business of corn' and that their victims included Theodore Vansevenhoven, then the most successful Dutch merchant at Cork, whose quayside house was one of those that was pulled down.[24] Food rioting and the destruction of property and goods were not unconnected activities, as we shall see. But because the destruction of the fabric of a building was more commonly associated with the 'mobs' that targeted brothels, it may be the case that this early eighteenth-century Cork 'mob' was not fully schooled in the conventions that guided food protest.[25] In any event, the 1709/10 attacks and the authorisation in 1714 of the payment to Vansevenhoven of compensation for 'corn lost in the riot', which suggests that he may have been targeted once more,

22 David Dickson and D.F. Fleming (eds), 'Charles O'Hara's observations on county Sligo, 1752–73 (NLI, O'Hara papers, MS 20397)', *Analecta Hibernica*, 46 (2015), 95. 23 For a guide to prices see Liam Kennedy and M.W. Dowling, 'Prices and wages in Ireland, 1700–1850', *Irish Economic and Social History*, 24 (1997), 62–104, especially figs. 6–10. 24 John Bohstedt, 'Census of riots – second century (1650–1739)', available at web.utk.edu/~bohstedt/ (accessed March 2015); Christopher Crofts, Cork to Sir John Perceval, 27 Jan. 1709/19 (BL, Egmont papers, Add. MS 46978, p. 297); Dickson, *Old world colony*, p. 379. 25 James Kelly, '"Ravaging houses of ill fame": popular riot and public sanction in eighteenth-century Ireland' in D.W. Hayton and A.R. Holmes (eds), *Ourselves alone?: Religion, society and politics in eighteenth- and nineteenth-century Ireland* (Dublin, 2016), pp 84–103.

possibly in 1712 when there were further economic difficulties, indicate that the food protesting impulse had taken hold in Ireland by that date. It is noteworthy certainly that the object on both occasions was to demonstrate to traders and officials that the populace would oppose the free and unhindered movement of grain if it threatened the local supply line or resulted in inflated prices. Signally, the authorities were not disposed to be unresponsive, and they used the powers available to them then, as they had done at prior moments of difficulty, to moderate the upwards pressure on food prices by prohibiting the export of grain. Thus in 1697, the Privy Council approved proclamations proscribing the export of grain from Ulster, Leinster and then the whole of the country when the commodity had 'become so dear as to make the subsistence of the poor very uneasy in some parts'.[26] And heartened by the resulting 'good effect', the Council had recourse in March and December 1709 to the same legal instrument to prohibit the exportation 'of all manner of corn, grain and meal' when called upon by the corporations of Cork and Kinsale to intervene to prevent 'the destruction of several poor families'.[27]

While the imposition of an embargo on the exportation of food in 1709 was consistent with the established pattern of behaviour when distress threatened, the presentation in January 1712 of 'a petition' (originating in New Ross, county Wexford) on behalf of 'the poore inhabitants of Ireland' calling for intervention suggests that this was the expectation. Persuaded that the merchants of New Ross, Waterford and other ports in the south-east had 'filled up their store houses with corn in order to transport the same' to the Crown's 'enemies', the petitioners identified a number by name and the volume of grain they were believed to have in their possession in support of their appeal to the lords justices 'to order a proclamation that noe transportation of corn be allowed' until further notice.[28] No such prohibition was implemented, because it was not warranted, but the fact that the petition was presented was perhaps as indicative as the more dramatic events in Cork in the winter of 1709–10 that the populace had concluded it was entitled to intervene when their access to foodstuffs was endangered by shortages or by price inflation. The implication – that the population believed that their needs took precedence over private property, the market place and the laws and regulations that scaffolded them – was one side of an equation, whose other side was the acknowledgement by the elite that it was incumbent on them to make use of the powers available to them to alleviate distress. The attack on the property of Theodore Vansevenhoven, the imposition of an embargo on

---

26 Kelly and Lyons (eds), *The proclamations of Ireland, 1660–1820*, ii, 370–2, 373; May to Matthew, 3/13 July 1697 in HMC, *Manuscripts of the marquess of Bath*, iii (London, 1908), p. 136. 27 Kelly and Lyons (eds), *The proclamations of Ireland, 1660–1820*, ii, 616–17, 623–4; Richard Caulfield (ed.), *The council book of the Corporation of the City of Cork* (Guilford, 1876), p. 338; Richard Caulfield (ed.), *The council book of the Corporation of Kinsale* (Guilford, 1879), pp lxix, 338. 28 Petition, 29 Jan. 1711/12 in P.H. Hore, *History of the town and county of Wexford* (6 vols, Dublin, 1900–11), i, 376–7.

food exports in 1709, and the presentation of a petition on behalf of 'poore inhabitants' to the lords justice in 1712 in support of a further embargo were manifestations of this equation in practice. Even combined, they cannot be said to comprise a moral economy as rounded as that identified and described for England at this time. But it was more than a weak silhouette of an emerging world view that was to evolve and to develop in the decades that followed.

CHRONOLOGY AND GEOGRAPHY, *c*.1720–*c*.1822

With these elements of a 'moral economy' in place, it was inevitable that there would be further instances of food protest when food price stability was threatened. As Jean Meuvret has observed of seventeenth-century France, 'the common people … were committed to stable prices'.[29] Since stable prices were more likely when the economy was performing well, the fact that there were no food protests during the remainder of the 1710s or early 1720s suggests that conditions were not sufficiently troubling at any point during these years (the 'low' of 1716–20 included) to precipitate protest.[30] This was certainly not the case during the more difficult years of the late 1720s when a sequence of poor harvests plunged the country into a crisis that was at its deepest in 1728–9.[31] Significantly, given the duration and nature of the difficulties encountered, there was no rioting during the early years of the crisis, which began with the first of a sequence of four poor harvests in 1725, as the main food-producing regions in the south of the country were not severely impacted either by shortages or by food price inflation. But as the economic environment deteriorated, and northern and eastern parts of the kingdom experienced famine in the wake of the poor harvest of 1728, the impact of the increased demand for foodstuffs on price and supply was greeted with alarm by the populations of the mainly coastal urban centres of Munster and Leinster. A number were sufficiently agitated to engage in food rioting to prevent the removal of food out of the region.

The signal for the most concentrated series of food riots yet to take place in Ireland was provided by the 'town people' of Cork city. Animated by the 'dearness of provisions … particularly oatmeal', in the spring of 1729, a 'mobb' several hundred strong equipped with 'clubs and other instruments of mischief' assembled in the city on 25 February and marched on and 'plundered' several 'granaries and store houses'.[32] Other urban crowds followed suit. The sequence

29 Jean Meuvret, *La problème des subsistences à l'époque de Louis XIV* (3 vols, Paris, 1977), i, 39, iii, 155, cited in Bouton, *The flour war*, pp 8–9.   30 L.M. Cullen, 'Problems in and sources for the study of economic fluctuations 1660–1800', *Irish Economic and Social History*, 41 (2014), 18.   31 Kelly, 'Harvests and hardship: famine and scarcity in Ireland in the late 1720s', pp 65–106.   32 *Dublin Intelligence*, 4 Mar. 1729; *An express from Cork, with an account of a bloody battle fought between the mob of that city and the standing army; in a letter from a person there to his friend here in Dublin* (Dublin, [1729]).

of events is sketchy, but reports of riotous interventions in Waterford, Limerick, Youghal, Clonmel and 'other places in the south' attest to the resolve of the populace of these Munster centres both to moderate food prices and to prevent the transportation of foodstuffs out of the region.[33] This was a matter of major consequence for the population of the 'north', where the impact of the poor harvest of 1728 was most keenly felt, and where there was no identifiable 'mob' activity. Indeed, outside of Munster the only locations to experience food rioting were Drogheda, where the crowd was prompted by an empty market to march to the town's quays on 5 March 1729 to interrupt the loading of thirty tons of oatmeal on a ship and to prevent another 'laden with barley, oats and oatmeal' from departing the port, and Dublin where, on Patrick's day, a mob boarded potato boats berthed at Aston Quay.[34]

This explosive, and short-lived, outburst of popular anger troubled the authorities, who apprehended that the primary consequence must be to deter those with 'provisions' for sale from bringing them to market. Their worst fears proved unfounded for though there were anxious reports from Waterford, Drogheda and Dublin in March that 'the mobb ... are resolved to rise againe', there were no further incidents in 1729.[35] It was almost a year before there was another case of food rioting; on this occasion an unspecified number of 'disorderly persons' in Clonmel 'prevented the carrying of corn and other goods' out of the town. There were no further incidents, as the good harvest of 1729 eased the apprehensions of the public, and with it this significant episode in the history of food rioting in Ireland drew to a close.[36]

Though precise information on each incident is elusive, the occurrence of eight food riots[37] in 1729–30 was not only unprecedented for Ireland (Table 2.1), but also proportionate to what happened in the late 1720s in England where 13 food riots took place in 1727, six in 1728 and three in 1729.[38] More significantly, perhaps, it defined the early eighteenth-century heartland of food rioting in Ireland as urban and concentrated in the southern and eastern coastal ports (Map

33 Ambrose Phillips (ed.), *Letters written by Hugh Boulter, lord primate of all Ireland* (2 vols, Dublin, 1770), i, 228, 230; Lords justices to British Privy Council, 26 Mar. 1729 (TNA, PC2/90 f. 458); Waterford City Archives, Corporation of Waterford council books, 7 Mar. 1728/9.   34 *Faulkner's Dublin Journal*, 8 Mar. 1729; Minutes of the Revenue Commissioners, 7 Mar. 1729 (TNA, CUST1/21 f. 82); *Dublin Intelligence*, 18 Mar. 1729.   35 Waterford City Archives, Corporation of Waterford council books, 7 Mar. 1728/9; *Dublin Gazette*, 29 Mar. 1729; *Dublin Weekly Journal*, 19 Apr. 1729.   36 Kelly and Lyons (eds), *The proclamations of Ireland*, iii, 202.   37 At Cork, Waterford, Clonmel, Youghal, Limerick, Drogheda and Dublin (1729), and Clonmel (1730). It is appropriate here to correct the record in one respect. In the account of food rioting in Cork in 1729 published in 1992, I concluded, based on a report sent from Cork dated 10 Mar. 1729, which referred to a food riot in Cork 'the day before yesterday' that there was a further food riot in the city on 8 March. This was an error; the account conveyed on 10 March describes the events of 27 February, albeit in a manner that could be misread: Cathaldus Giblin (ed.), 'Catalogue of Nunziatura di Fiandra, pt. 5', *Collectanea Hibernica*, 9 (1966), 13; Kelly, 'Harvests and hardship', 88; Magennis, 'Food scarcity in 1756–7', p. 196.   38 Bohstedt, 'Census of riots – second century (1650–1739)'.

1). This mirrored the main trading locations in foodstuffs, and the link is confirmed by the fact that Clonmel was the only inland urban centre to experience food rioting in both 1729 and 1730. Clonmel's susceptibility to food protest reflected its location in one of the main food-producing regions of the country, and its place at the heart of the country's grain and flour trade. These features also characterized the twin towns of Carrick, in south county Tipperary, and Carrickbeg, in county Waterford, which straddled the river Suir, which was the primary waterway supplying Waterford city. The 'mobb or common people' of the town in 1734 affirmed the primarily southern orientation of food rioting when their refusal to 'permitt or suffer any corn or cattle to be brought from the county of Tipperary' prompted the mayor, sheriff and citizens of the city of Waterford to appeal to the lord lieutenant, the duke of Dorset, for assistance.[39] The failure to respond positively to the request indicated that conditions were not sufficiently serious to warrant intervention. The authorities had little choice but to intervene seven years later, when the southern half of the country succumbed to the most grievous crisis of the century, and one of the three 'super crises' of the early modern era.

Table 2.1: Food riot sample, 1710–1845

Year	Number	Year	Number	Year	Number	Year	Number
1710	3	1764	1	1781	1	1816	2
1712	1?	1765	2	1783	7	1817	43
1729	7	1766	8	1784	6	1819	1
1730	1	1767	3	1789	1	1822	5
1734	1	1768	3	1790	2	1824	3
1740	9	1769	1	1791	2	1826	1
1741	3	1770	1	1792	4	1827	1
1745	1	1771	1	1793	10	1829	1
1746	1	1772	3	1794	2	1830	5
1748	1	1773	1	1795	5	1831	5
1753	2	1774	2	1796	1	1837	3
1756	4	1775	2	1800	11	1838	1
1757	7	1776	1	1801	7	1839	3
1758	2	1777	3	1808	5	1840	13
1759	3	1778	9	1812	17	1842	25
1760	1	1779	1?	1813	2	1845	2

39 Waterford City Archives, Corporation of Waterford council books, 29 Mar. 1734. This episode has been mis-ascribed to Waterford city in several histories: E. Downey, *The story of Waterford* (Waterford, 1914), p. 366; Joseph Hansard, *The history, topography and antiquities … of the county and city of Waterford* (Dungarvan, 1870, Lismore, 1977), p. 53.

The famine of 1740–1 reduced a large part of the population of the southern part of the country to desperate straits, as a result of which perhaps as much as 13 per cent of the population of the island may have perished.[40] It was, as this suggests, much more serious than the famine of 1728–9, and it not only resulted in more food riots – twelve – but also in their assuming a wider geographical footprint (Table 2.1). Indeed, all four provinces were affected, as the ports of Belfast, Galway and Sligo experienced food rioting for the first time.[41] These were not the only new locations, moreover, as there was rioting also at the southern ports of Dungarvan and Kinsale in addition to Drogheda, Cork, Dublin, Youghal and Carrick-on-Suir, which had previous experience of such events.[42] With rioting in three urban centres within its boundaries in 1740, it might be concluded that county Cork was the epicentre of the phenomenon, but this would be to oversimplify. Every sizeable southern port and inland centre that was a conduit of foodstuffs, whether destined for export or for consumption elsewhere in the country, possessed the requisite characteristics. One may instance Carrick-on-Suir, where a large crowd 'rose' on 25 April 1741 to prevent a boat with a cargo of oats embarking for Waterford, where it was required by the Corporation 'to feed the poor'.[43] In Drogheda, the local 'mob' responded to the presence of 'a number of north country people to buy oatmeal' by boarding and temporarily disabling a ship bound for Scotland with fifty tons of oatmeal on 14 April 1740, while similar actions were reported at Galway port later the same year and at Sligo port in April 1741.[44] In Dublin, meanwhile, the sale at a 'low price to the poor' on 31 May 1740 of loaves, oatmeal, bacon and butter seized from a number of bakers' shops and meal stores, and the targeting on Monday, 2 June, of mills located 'about' the city demonstrated that 'the imposition of popular price control by collective action' (*taxation populaire*), which had been resorted to in France since the mid-seventeenth century, and more selectively in England since the 1690s, was also a powerful motivation.[45] The variety of loca-

40 See Michael Drake, 'The Irish demographic crisis of 1740–41' in T.W. Moody (ed.), *Historical Studies VI* (London, 1968), pp 111–18; Dickson, *Arctic Ireland: the extraordinary story of the great frost and forgotten famine of 1740–41*, passim; David Dickson, 'The other great Irish famine' in Cathal Póirtéir (ed.), *The Great Irish Famine* (Cork, 1995), pp 50–9; David Dickson, '1740–41 famine' in John Crowley et al. (eds), *Atlas of the Great Irish Famine, 1845–52* (Cork, 2012), pp 23–7; L.M. Cullen, 'The Irish food crisis of the early 1740s: the economic conjuncture', *Irish Economic and Social History*, 37 (2010), 1–23; Cormac Ó Gráda and Diarmaid Ó Muirithe, 'The famine of 1740–41: representations in Gaelic poetry', *Éire-Ireland*, 45:3 and 4 (2010), 1–22; James Kelly, 'Coping with crisis: the response to the famine of 1740–1', *Eighteenth-Century Ireland*, 27 (2012), 99–122; Engler et al., 'The Irish famine of 1740–1741', 1161–79. Saliently, 13 per cent was one per cent more than succumbed during the Great Famine: Engler, op. cit., 1174. 41 *Dublin Newsletter*, 24 June, 26 Aug. 1740; *Pue's Occurrences*, 26 Aug. 1740, 25 Apr. 1741. 42 *Dublin Newsletter*, 6 Dec. 1740; Dickson, *Arctic Ireland*, pp 26–9, 34, 55. 43 *Dublin Gazette*, 25 Apr. 1741. 44 *Faulkner's Dublin Journal*, 22 Apr. 1740; *Pue's Occurrences*, 26 Aug. 1740, 25 Apr. 1741; Magennis, 'Food scarcity', p. 197. 45 Kingsbury to Price, 31 May (NLW, Puleston Papers, Add. MS 3548D); *Pue's Occurrences*, 3 June; *Dublin Gazette*, 3, 7 June; *Dublin Newsletter*, 3, 7, 21 June; *Dublin Daily Post*, 3 June; *Faulkner's Dublin Journal*, 3, 7 June 1740; John Swift, *History of*

tions in which food protest was reported in 1741 cautions against assuming an indivisible connection between food protest and major areas of food production, and reinforces, what has been established by Bouton and others with respect to the phenomenon elsewhere, that attempts to straitjacket food rioting into too narrow an interpretative framework invariably fail to acknowledge its particular, sometimes unique, regional and national qualities.[46]

If the augmented number and extended geographical footprint of food rioting in 1740–1 were harbingers of a more regular pattern of such protest in Ireland, it was to require another subsistence crisis in the mid-1750s before it acquired a distinctly regional pattern spanning the kingdom's main urban centres. In the meantime, the impact of 'a violent storm with rain' in the autumn of 1744 and of a 'violent fall of snow' in the early months of 1745, which so depleted food and fodder levels that 'cattle died, and the people starved for want of corn', prompted the populace of Waterford to riot once more in 1745.[47] The fact that this once-off event was replicated in subsequent years – in Drogheda (1746) and Limerick (1748)[48] – suggests that urban populations now believed they possessed the moral authority to intervene to ensure the availability of food at an acceptable price when conditions were sufficiently difficult, and the link between food protest and the economic cycle was affirmed when, beginning in 1753 with food rioting in Cork and Kilkenny, the 1750s witnessed the most sustained sequence of food riots to date.

The high point was the subsistence crisis of 1756–7. The proximate cause was 'the extreme wetness of the season by which such damage was done both to corn and hay and potatoes, that a scarcity of bread and loss of cattle was apprehended', and the population's fears were proved justified when 'a dreadful winter [in 1756–7] and severe spring [in 1757]' caused such 'distress for want of corn' that 'many families ... quit their habitations', housekeepers were reduced to begging, while others – 'the pale specters of town and country' – struggled with the inflated prices demanded for food.[49] It is a measure of how difficult conditions were that the number of incidents in 1756–7 was in excess of that reported in the more threatening environment of 1729–30 (Table 2.1), and extended over a wider geographical area than ever before since as well as Belfast, which negotiated the

the Dublin bakers and others ([Dublin], 1948), p. 117. For the French and English parallels see Bouton, *The flour war*, pp 6, 8; J.D. Post, *The last great subsistence crisis in the western world* (Baltimore, 1977), p. 69. **46** Post, *The last great subsistence crisis*, p. 69; Bouton, *The flour war*, chapter 1; Bohstedt, *The politics of provisions*, p. 100. **47** Dickson and Fleming (eds), 'Charles O'Hara's observations on county Sligo', 98; Spencer to Price, 5 Nov. 1744 (NLW, Puleston papers, Add. MS 3548D.27); Downey, *The story of Waterford*, pp 328–9; Waterford City Archives, Corporation of Waterford council books, 25 Sept. 1746. **48** *Dublin Courant*, 25 Mar. 1746; *Dublin Weekly Journal*, 5 June 1748. **49** Dickson and Fleming (eds), 'Charles O'Hara's observations on county Sligo', 106–7; Dickson, *Old world colony*, p. 309; Charles O'Conor, *The Protestant interest considered, relative to the operation of the popery acts in Ireland* (Dublin, 1757), p. 30; O'Conor to Curry, 21 May 1756 in R.E. Ward and C.C. Ward (eds), *The letters of Charles O'Conor* (2 vols, Ann Arbor, 1980), i, 13.

Map 1: The location of known food riots in Ireland, 1710–84

most intense food rioting in its history, and familiar locations in Munster and on the east coast, it embraced Wexford, which experienced three episodes of rioting in the spring of 1757.[50] It may be, the available figures suggest, that there were more riots during the severe famine of 1740–1 than there were during the 1756–7 subsistence crisis, but the difference was modest. Moreover, food rioting as a form of protest continued to appreciate. The clearest indication of this is provided by its expanding geographical footprint (Map 1) and the involvement of women, which was particularly remarked upon in accounts of what transpired in Wexford and Kilkenny.[51] Furthermore, these trends were sustained, as women were active participants in the riot aimed at preventing the exportation of potatoes from Youghal in April 1760, while the occurrence of food rioting in New Ross, county Wexford and Sligo in 1758 attested further to its attraction to the urban populace, which was now growing rapidly (Table 1).[52]

It is noteworthy also that food protesters now targeted a wider range of foodstuffs. The abolition in 1759 of the controversial prohibition on the export of live cattle to England introduced in 1667 aroused concerns in certain quarters that the price of meat must inevitably rise.[53] Anxious that this should not come to pass elements of the Dublin crowd not only targeted and killed cattle destined for live export in the summer of 1759, but also sought to immobilize the vessels upon which they were to be ferried.[54] Comparable protests at Cork and Wexford underlined the ease with which the crowd in different locations could be roused to protest against regulatory as well as commercial changes that threatened existing patterns of food supply, and as if to prove that they were not guided by irrational fear, the general improvement in economic fortunes that followed in the early 1760s resulted in the interruption of such activity, though food rioting as such did not cease (Table 2.1).[55] 'The people have so much a better bottom than they had formerly, ... the lowest families will keep together, and ... reap the benefit', Charles O'Hara observed pertinently in 1762. The problem, as Richard Woodward noted not long after he became Church of Ireland dean of Clogher in

50 Magennis, 'Food scarcity in 1756–7 and the crowd', pp 198–201; R.E. Burns, *Irish parliamentary politics in the eighteenth century, 1714–60* (2 vols, Washington, 1989–90), ii, 223; Hore, *History of Wexford*, v, 398–400; *Universal Advertiser*, 12 Feb. 1757; *London, Evening Post*, 29 Jan. 1757; T.M. Truxes, 'Introduction: a connected Irish world' in idem (ed.), *Ireland, France, and the Atlantic in a time of war: reflections on the Bordeaux–Dublin Letters, 1757* (London and New York, 2017), p. 4. 51 John Bohstedt, '1756–57 riots: third century (1740–1850)', available at web.utk.edu/~bohstedt/ (accessed March 2015); *Gentleman's Magazine*, 27 (May 1757), pp 234–5; *Pue's Occurrences*, 23 Apr. 1757. 52 *Public Gazetteer*, 5 Apr. 1760; Hore, *History of Wexford*, i, 394–5; *The journal of John Wesley* (4 vols, London, 1827), ii, 392; below, pp 136–7. 53 Cullen, *Anglo-Irish trade*, p. 4; John O'Donovan, *An economic history of livestock in Ireland* (Cork, 1940), p. 110. 54 Bedford to Stone, 22 May 1759 in Lord John Russell (ed.), *The correspondence of John, fourth, duke of Bedford* (3 vols, London, 1842–6), ii, 377; Desmond Clarke, *The unfortunate husbandman: to which is prefaced a short account of Charles Varley's life and times* (London, 1964), p. 15; NAI, Index of departmental letters and papers 1760–89, i, 296, 299. 55 Horace Walpole, *Memoirs of the reign of George II*, ed., John Brooke (3 vols, New Haven and London, 1985), iii, 88; *Public Gazetteer*, 1 Sept. 1759.

1764, was that the number of poor remained perturbingly high, and may even have grown. Further, because the fears that prompted the 'mob' to engage in food rioting were easily aroused, it only took a poor harvest to prompt the crowd into activity.[56] This is precisely what happened in the mid-1760s following the 'remarkably hot and dry' growing season of 1765, as a result of which 'the potatoes fail'd' and 'the price of corn' rose 'to a prodigious price all over Ireland' in 1766.[57] The responsiveness of municipal officials in Cork was sufficient to deflect the initial riotous impulse in that city in October 1765, but it was insufficient to allay the anxiety manifest there or elsewhere in the spring of 1766 with the result that another spike in food rioting, comparable to that previously experienced in 1729, 1740 and 1757, ensued (Table 2.1).[58] Interestingly, the food riots that took place, while not quite spanning the full range of behaviours associated with such activity, embraced the now familiar practice of distributing food at reduced prices (*taxation populaire*) in Kilkenny, the obstruction of grain shipments at Dungarvan and a shipment of potatoes at Kinsale, and resistance to the exportation of live cattle at Belfast, Newtownards and Drogheda. In addition, a revealing pointer to the future was provided by the action of a 'mob' at the inland town of Castledermot, county Kildare, which intercepted and destroyed flour *en route* to Dublin, and by the townsmen of the minor port of Wicklow who 'brought in flour and corn from an adjacent mill [and] sold [it] there at a moderate price'.[59]

Table 2.2: Food riot sample, 1710–1845 (5-year totals)

1706–10	1711–15	1716–25	1726–30	1731–5	1736–40	1741–5
3	1?	–	8	1	9	4
1746–50	1751–5	1756–60	1761–5	1766–70	1771–5	1776–80
2	2	17	3	16	9	14
1781–5	1786–90	1791–5	1796–1800	1801–5	1806–10	1811–15
14	3	23	12	7	5	19
1816–20	1821–5	1826–30	1831–5	1836–40	1841–5	Total sample
46	8	8	5	20	27	286

---

56 Dickson and Fleming (eds), 'Charles O'Hara's observations on county Sligo', 113; James Kelly, 'Defending the established order: Richard Woodward, bishop of Cloyne (1726–94)' in idem et al. (eds), *People, power and politics: essays on Irish history, 1660–1850* (Dublin, 2010), pp 148–54. 57 Dickson and Fleming (eds), 'Charles O'Hara's observations on county Sligo', 114.   58 C.B. Gibson, *The history of the county of the city of Cork* (2 vols, Cork, 1861), ii, 211; *Freeman's Journal*, 19 Oct. 1765.   59 Colles to Colles, 14 June 1766 (NAI, Prim Collection, no 87/92); Waterford City Archives, Corporation of Waterford council books, 30 June 1766; Caulfield (ed.), *Corporation book of Kinsale*, p. 280; *Public Gazetteer*, 21, 28 June, 5 July 1766; *Dublin Mercury*, 19 Aug. 1766; *London*

The appreciating popular belief in the legitimacy of food rioting was underlined by the fact that the practice was not discontinued, as had previously been the case, once the subsistence crisis of 1766–7 drew to a close. There was, as the order of identifiable incidents attests (Table 2.1), no year in the late 1760s and early 1770s in which a food riot did not take place in some location or another. More significantly, the number of identified food riots in the years 1767–70 equalled the number that took place when the 1766 crisis raged, and is exceeded by the number reported during the early 1770s (Tables 2.1 and 2.2). Since these were difficult years across much of Europe, and the linen industry in Ireland experienced particular challenges, this pattern does not resist explanation, but it is still noteworthy that food rioting was now a regular occurrence as opposed to the spasmodic event it had been for more than half a century.[60] Moreover, there would almost certainly have been a greater number of incidents had the acreage assigned to tillage not continued to increase. But the fact that crowds rose twice in Waterford in 1768 to oppose the exportation of hides, and that the tactics employed by rioters (including the resort to 'anonymous' letters, intimidation, and destroying sacks of flour) in the early 1770s bear comparison to those employed by agrarian protesters, who had emerged in the 1760s as a significant rural phenomenon, and urban journeymen opposed to the importation and consumption of foreign textiles, is further evidence of its normalization.[61] This is the implication also of the leadership provided the Kinsale 'mob' by local fishermen, who resisted the exportation of potatoes in 1766 and wheat in 1768; of the targeting of forestallers by the Dublin crowd in the early 1770s; of the more ready resort to the destruction of property by rioting crowds, and of the decision of parliament in 1772 to denominate 'anti-export disturbance' an offence.[62]

Given the augmented readiness of the populace to engage in food rioting in response to changes in the economic environment, it is a matter of little surprise that the outbreak of hostilities in Britain's North American colonies in 1775 prompted further food protests. Yet, it was less the interruption of the regular pattern of Atlantic trade than the increased demand for provisions by the Royal Navy and the effect it had on food prices which was the primary causative factor

Evening Post, 22 Aug. 1767. **60** Post, 'Nutritional status and mortality in eighteenth-century Europe', pp 249–57; Post, 'Meteorological historiography', 728; Conrad Gill, *The rise of the Irish linen industry* (Oxford, 1925, 1964), pp 123–37; W.H. Crawford, *Domestic industry in Ireland: the experience of the linen industry* (Dublin, 1972), p. 6. **61** Dickson and Fleming (eds), 'Charles O'Hara's observations on county Sligo', 116–17; Memorial of Thomas Grubb, merchant, 8 Feb. 1768 (NAI, Isabel Grubb's notes from petitions in PRO, 1915, pp 4, 5–6); James S. Donnelly, 'Irish agrarian rebellion: the Whiteboys of 1769–76', *RIA proc.*, 83C (1983), 296–8; Martyn J. Powell, *The politics of consumption in eighteenth-century Ireland* (Basingstoke, 2002), p. 176; *Freeman's Journal*, 19 Mar. 1772; *Finn's Leinster Journal*, 16 Nov. 1768, 28 Aug. 1773, 22 Oct. 1774. **62** Caulfield (ed.), *Corporation book of Kinsale*, p. 280; *Finn's Leinster Journal*, 30 Apr. 1768, 9 Jan. 1774; *Hibernian Journal*, 18 May 1772; *Freeman's Journal*, 24 Aug. 1773; Clements to Macartney, 24 Aug. 1773 in Thomas Bartlett (ed.), *Macartney in Ireland, 1768–72* (Belfast, [1979]), p. 243; Cunningham, 'Popular protest and a "moral economy"', p. 30; *Hibernian Chronicle*, 30 Aug. 1773; *Hoey's Publick Journal*, 25 Aug. 1773; 11 George III, chap. 7.

at the outset. The impact of this was felt particularly acutely in Munster, which accounts for the disproportionate presence of Cork and other southern towns (Skibbereen, Waterford, Ross and Bandon) on the list of locations where rioting was reported in the early years of the war.[63] However, because food protest shadowed the fortunes of the economy, the highpoint of wartime food rioting coincided with a serious credit crisis and 'a total stagnation in the different branches of the weaving business' in 1777–8.[64] This had the effect of reducing disposable income, prompting 'manufacturing tradesmen' in Drogheda and neighbouring towns to protest in 1778 in an attempt to influence the price of food (Table 2.1).[65] Elsewhere, rioting in Waterford in 1776, Cork, Bandon, Ballina and Kilkenny in 1778, and at Clarecastle, county Clare in 1781 aimed at resisting the movements of foodstuffs, particularly potatoes, reflected the mounting importance of this starchy tuber in the popular diet as well as the dependence of the increased numbers resident in the kingdom's expanding urban spaces on purchased food.[66]

It is noteworthy also, as the occurrence of protest in these locations attests, that the 1770s and early 1780s witnessed the incremental expansion of food rioting from the ports and larger urban centres, where it was concentrated for half a century, to smaller towns, and, after a modest fashion, to the countryside as 'harvest sensitive poverty' increased in tandem with the growth in the proportion of the population – the labouring poor – that was dependent on purchased foodstuffs. The fact that there are few reports of food rioting from such locations prior to this is consistent with the identifiably urban character of the phenomenon to this point, but the interception by the mob at Kilkenny in 1778 of 'carriages of oatmeal' *en route* to Dublin was illustrative of the intensifying unease among an expanding social group in the capital's hinterland at the implications of the accelerating commercialization of agriculture.[67] Another illustration is provided by the decision of the Catholic archbishop of Dublin, John Carpenter, to admonish those parishioners of Ballymore-Eustace and Eadestown[68] 'who destroyed some cars and corn belonging to a gentlemen in the neighbourhood'.[69] The expanding geographical footprint of food rioting to which this attests was

63 Theresa M. O'Connor, 'The embargo on the export of Irish provisions, 1776–1779', *IHS*, 2 (1940–1), 7–8; Aiken McClelland, 'Amyas Griffith', *Irish Booklore*, 2 (1972–6), 13–14.   64 *Dublin Evening Journal*, 30 Apr., 9 May, 18, 20 June 1778.   65 L.M. Cullen, *An economic history of Ireland since 1660* (London, 1972), chapter 4; idem, 'Problems in and sources for the study of economic fluctuations 1660–1800', 8, 18; *Dublin Evening Journal*, 16, 18 June 1778; *Finn's Leinster Journal*, 4 July 1778; Vincent Morley, *Irish opinion and the American Revolution, 1760–83* (Cambridge, 2002), p. 181.   66 *Finn's Leinster Journal*, 11 Sept. 1776, 21 Mar., 8 Apr. 1778, 31 May 1781; Dickson, *Old world colony*, p. 443; *Dublin Evening Journal*, 2 Apr. 1778; *Hibernian Chronicle*, 16 Mar. 1778; Morley, *Irish opinion and the American Revolution, 1760–83*, p. 181.   67 *Finn's Leinster Journal*, 23 May 1778.   68 Ballymore Eustace, county Kildare, was until 1836 in county Dublin. Eadestown is nearby in county Kildare.   69 M.J. Curran, 'Instructions, admonitions etc. of Archbishop Carpenter,' *Reportorium Novum*, 2:1 (1957–8), 156; Brian Mac Giolla Phádraig, 'Dr John Carpenter, archbishop of Dublin, 1760–86', *Dublin Historical Record*, 30 (1976–7), 16; *Finn's Leinster Journal*,

manifested further during the subsistence crisis of 1782–4 when the country experienced another peak in food rioting.[70]

Unlike previous crises, when food protest was concentrated in one moment, the thirteen incidents that took place in 1783–4 were nearly equally divided between the summer of 1783 (7) and the early months of 1784 (6). Most took place in the traditional Munster urban heartlands of food rioting (Cork, Clonakilty, Youghal, Kinsale, Waterford, Carrick-on-Suir, Clonmel), but a majority of those datable to the summer of 1783 occurred in unfamiliar small towns or in rural locations (Kilcock, county Kildare; Gorey, county Wexford; Mullingar, county Westmeath; Newtown Bellew, county Galway and Gorteen, county Mayo).[71] Furthermore, both the focus and the nature of food protest differed according to location. This is exemplified by the prioritization of 'searching for concealed provisions' in the countryside. Thus, at Kilcock, 'a riotous mob' about a hundred strong descended on local farmers in mid-June 1783 in search of foodstuffs; the object at Gorteen, county Mayo, was to 'rescue' potatoes from forestallers, while at Gorey, county Wexford, local farmers were compelled to bring grain to town.[72] At Clonakilty, meanwhile, the mob that assembled in May sought to prevent 'several sloops ... in that harbour ... freighted with potatoes' transporting them out of the area, to which end they 'tore away the rigging, demolished the mast yards etc., and cast the anchors overboard'.[73] This was in keeping with the anticipated pattern on such occasions in southern port towns. It was also resorted to at Passage, county Waterford, in January 1784 when a Portuguese ship was prevented from loading potatoes. Though the intervention was judged sufficiently serious to elicit a complaint from the Portuguese foreign minister, it was a less secure pointer to the strength of the food rioting impulse than the actions of substantial mobs at Clonmel and Kinsale, which forcibly entered and appropriated foodstuffs from mills, stores and warehouses in 1784.[74]

The public and political attention afforded the 'terrible tumults' that took place in the spring of 1784 reflected the seriousness with which such behaviour was increasingly perceived. Yet, in common with previous surges, it ceased as rapidly as it began, and while there was a further incident later in the year, which demonstrated that the reflexive disposition to riot survived the good harvest of 1784 and the broader improvement in the economic environment (Table 2.1), it was the last

---

24 Mar. 1787. Carpenter's intervention is undated; but it can safely be assigned to the 1770s.
70 James Kelly, 'Scarcity and poor relief', 38–62.   71 *Volunteer Journal* (Cork), 15 May, 30 June 1783; Captain G. Walpole to [ ], 5 July 1783 (NAI, Index to Departmental letters and papers, 1760–89, ii, 83); *Dublin Evening Post*, 17 June, 1, 12 July 1783; Patrick Bellew to Michael Bellew, 11 July 1783 (NLI, Bellew papers, MS 27126/1); Kelly, 'Scarcity and poor relief', 49–50   72 *Dublin Evening Post*, 17 June, 1, 12 July 1783; Kelly, 'Scarcity and poor relief', 49–50.   73 *Volunteer Journal* (Cork), 15 May 1783.   74 *The parliamentary register; or, History of the proceedings and debates of the House of Commons of Ireland* (17 vols, Dublin, 1782–1801), ii, 347; *Hibernian Journal*, 6 Feb. 1784; *Volunteer Journal* (Cork), 22 Mar. 1784; Hort to Carmarthen, 24 Feb. 1784 (TNA, FO/63/5); Jacobs to Greer, 12 Feb. 1784 (PRONI, Greer papers, D1044/686, 687A).

incident of note for five years. Indeed, though the economic problems experienced by the rural land poor during the mid- and late-1780s was sufficient to sustain a phase of serious agrarian unrest in north Munster and south Leinster, and conditions in Dublin were sufficiently challenging to witness the intensification of the phenomenon of 'stripping' children, food rioting all but ceased in the interval between the kingdom's emergence from the throes of the 1782–4 crisis and the difficult economic environment of the early 1790s (Table 2.1).[75]

Statistically, 1791–5 was the busiest quinquennium of food rioting in the eighteenth century in Ireland (Table 2.2). Yet, whereas previous peaks can be linked to a famine or subsistence crisis, this was not the case then. This fact notwithstanding, the resumption in food rioting after a hiatus spanning the second half of the 1780s was clearly economically motivated. Indeed, it may be said to have commenced with 'seven weeks incessant rain' in 1789 that gave rise to 'fears for our corn harvest'. The resulting loss of foodstuffs was not of sufficient magnitude to precipitate a crisis, but it did have an unsettling effect, as a result of which, the Irish merchant, Nathaniel Trumbull, informed one of his Scottish correspondents in August 'all our ports have been shut against the exportation of grain and flour'.[76] There were no identifiable major food riots in 1789, but the ensuing combination of lean years and high summer prices in 1790 and 1791 prompted *émeutes* at Clarecastle, Galway, Waterford and Carrick-on-Suir whose purpose was to deter the transportation of grain (oats mainly) and potatoes out of these locations.[77] This environment was sufficient to sustain food protest at the low-intensity level previously experienced in the 1760s and 1770s, but when the urban populations of Munster were troubled by a surge in food prices in November 1792, the outcome was altogether more dramatic; it precipitated serious food rioting in Waterford, Bandon, Clonakilty, Cork and Ennis. The depth of the populace's anxiety was demonstrated most vividly in Bandon and its environs, which experienced rioting over two days when the 'urban mob' not only 'broke open ... the mills and corn store' of 'a very respectable merchant in this town', but also 'destroyed all the machinery in the mill' there, and in other mills at Kilbrittan, which was six miles distant, and at Shannonvale (near Clonakilty), which was 14 miles from Bandon.[78]

75 Donnelly, 'The Rightboy movement 1785–8', 120–202; James Kelly, '"This iniquitous traffic"; the kidnapping of children for the American colonies in eighteenth-century Ireland', *Journal of the History of Childhood and Youth*, 9:2 (2016), 233–46. The fullest description of an incident from these years is provided by Edward Newenham, but he does not state where it took place: Newenham to Washington, 14–26 Aug. 1789 in W.W. Abbot (ed.), *The papers of George Washington: presidential series* (4 vols, Charlottesville, 1976–9), iii, 462–4.   76 Newenham to Franklin, 26–8 July 1787 (American Philosophical Society, Franklin papers, xxxvi/162); Trumbull to Alex and James Robertson, 19 Aug. 1789 (New York Public Library, Trumbull papers, Letterbook 1). Curiously, a formal embargo on exports by proclamation was not instituted until December: Kelly and Lyons (eds), *The proclamations of Ireland*, iv, 483.   77 P. Power (ed.), 'A Carrickman's diary 1787–1809', *Journal of the Waterford and South-East of Ireland Archaeological Society*, 15 (1912), 66; *Freeman's Journal*, 22 June 1790; *Ennis Chronicle*, 12 July 1790; *Dublin Morning Post*, 19 May 1791.   78 *Dublin Chronicle*, 8, 24, 27 Nov. 1792; Dickson,

Dublin negotiated these years relatively unscathed, due at least in part to the sophistication of the poor relief available to those in need in the capital.[79] But 'the monstrous price' to which provisions ascended in 1793 was more than 'the poor industrious manufacturers ... [and] the lower orders of the public in general' were willing to tolerate, and, beginning in May, the combination of high prices, and high unemployment in the increasingly hard-pressed textile sector, precipitated a more sustained sequence of food riots than previously witnessed at one location (Tables 2.1, 2.2), and the first food riot in the city since 1778.[80] Though the number of incidents in the city and suburbs (6 in 1793, 1 in 1794 and 5 in 1795, or 70 per cent of the total identified for these years) may not provide a full register of the scale of riotous intervention, it explains why some excitable contemporaries (influenced by current events in France) concluded nervously that the city was in the grips of 'insurrection and outrage'.[81] This was to misinterpret the aims of the protesters, though their unwillingness to provide any recompense to the owners of the food they seized may account for this characterization.

The pattern of food rioting continued to evolve as this indicates, since as well as the surge in incidents evident in the early 1790s, the increased involvement of women, and larger numbers of protesters, suggest that these were more inclusive gatherings than was generally the case previously. As a result, they were capable, as the Bandon crowd demonstrated in 1792, of pursuing more ambitious interventions. Furthermore, the manner in which the Dublin crowd, particularly that from the distressed Liberties quarter, targeted retailers (huxters and shop-owners) as well as merchants, forestallers and hoarders; the frequency with which carts conveying grain and other commodities to the capital were intercepted, and the expansion of the range of targeted foodstuffs to embrace butter, cheese, bacon, fowl and bread as well as the main staples – grain, flour and potatoes – indicated that it continued to appeal in its metropolitan heartland.[82] It certainly possessed a larger geographical footprint nationally than ever (see Map 2). The attention afforded boats on the still embryonic canal network, which facilitated the movement of goods to Dublin, was but the most striking manifestation of this.

Old world colony, p. 384; *Hibernian Journal*, 27 Nov. 1792; *Clonmel Gazette*, 24 Nov. 1792; Westmorland to [ ], 28 Nov. 1792 (NLI, Lord lieutenant's correspondence, MS 886 ff 17–9); *Ennis Chronicle*, 6 Dec. 1792. 79 James Kelly, 'Charitable societies: their genesis and development, 1720–1800' in idem and M.J. Powell (eds), *Clubs and societies in eighteenth-century Ireland* (Dublin, 2010), pp 89–108; Mel Cousins, 'The Irish parliament and the relief of the poor: the 1772 legislation establishing houses of industry', *Eighteenth-Century Ireland*, 28 (2013), 95–115. 80 *Freeman's Journal*, 16 May 1778, 25 May, 13 June 1793; *Ramsey's Waterford Chronicle*, 6 Oct. 1789; *Dublin Morning Post*, 3 Apr. 1794. 81 Francis Higgins to Edward Cooke, 24 Oct. 1796 in Thomas Bartlett (ed.), *Revolutionary Dublin, 1795–1801: the letters of Francis Higgins to Dublin Castle* (Dublin, 2004), p. 114. 82 Drennan to McTier, 8 May 1793 in Jean Agnew (ed.), *The Drennan–McTier letters* (3 vols, Dublin, 1998–9), i, 152; *Hibernian Journal*, 15, 22 May, 16 Dec. 1793, 11 Oct. 1794, 28 May 1795; *Freeman's Journal*, 21 May 1792, 6 June 1793, 31 May 1794, 23 May 1795; *Dublin Chronicle*, 23 May 1793; *Clonmel Gazette*, 25 May 1793, 9 Apr. 1794; *Dublin Morning Post*, 3 Apr. 1794.

Map 2: The location of known food riots in Ireland, 1789–1820

The identification of an active pattern of food protest in the 1790s sits uneasily with E.P. Thompson's contention that food protest atrophied in late eighteenth-century Ireland, and with Tom Bartlett's suggestion that the 'moral economy' died in the 1790s.[83] Yet the absence of food protest in the second half of the 1790s, when revolutionary insurgency and counter-revolutionary activity were endemic, suggests also that food rioting should not be viewed through lens that do not take account of the larger political context. The fact that the modest spike in food riots identifiable in Ireland in the mid-1790s virtually coincides with the substantially larger cluster of 'around 150' that occurred in England in 1795–6 points also to an international dimension that must also be borne in mind. The comparability of the economic misfortunes of both jurisdictions at this time is, though, in keeping with the broader interpretation that it was the desire to ensure access to foodstuffs that gives food rioting its particular character and dynamic.[84] It also helps to explain why in Ireland, as in England, the next significant cluster of food rioting coincides with the subsistence crisis of 1800–1.[85]

The statistical spike in the tabulation of the sample of food riots identifiable for 1800–1 (Table 2.1) is consistent with the rising trajectory of food rioting during the eighteenth century. The pattern of rioting during these years is also revealing of its expanding spatial footprint, since in contrast to the early and mid-1790s when conditions in industrial Dublin pushed the capital to the fore for the first time in a number of decades, the pendulum swung back in the direction of Munster, which, as the provincial location of nearly 60 per cent of the sample of identifiable incidents between 1710 and the end of 1801, remained the heartland of Irish food rioting. With riots in Limerick, Youghal, Clonakilty, Cork, Ennis and Drogheda in 1800–1, it might also be concluded that the familiar Munster pattern was strengthened by incidents in the still more compact urban communities of Mallow, Baltimore, Cashel and Killaloe.[86] This claim is vitiated, however, by the fact that food rioting was taking root in the countryside by this point, and incidents at Borrisoleigh and Drombane, both in county Tipperary, in 1800, and at Cahirconlish, county Limerick, in 1801, indicate that the trend, already visible in the last quarter of the eighteenth century, continued to strengthen.[87] While the fundamental underlying cause of this was the rise in the country's population from *c.*4.42 million in 1791 to *c.*7 million in 1821 and the absence of comparable growth in employment and income, the more pertinent demographic development was the increase in the size of its urban and rural labouring components and the 'dense concentrations of vulnerable land-poor or

83 Above, pp 14–16. 84 Bohstedt, 'The pragmatic economy', p. 59; Roger Wells, *Insurrection: the British experience, 1795–1803* (Stroud, 1985); David Dickson, 'Taxation and disaffection in late eighteenth-century Ireland' in Clark and Donnelly (eds), *Irish peasants: violence and political unrest, 1780–1914*, pp 37–63. 85 Wells, 'The Irish famine of 1799–1801', pp 163–93. 86 Wells, 'The Irish famine of 1799–1801', pp 181, 182, 183; *Cork Advertizer*, 7 June, 12 Aug. 1800, 26 Feb. 1801; Brian Ó Dalaigh (ed.), *Corporation book of Ennis* (Dublin, 1990), pp 36, 314–15; *Ennis Chronicle*, 26 Feb., 26 Mar. 1801. 87 *Ennis Chronicle*, 6 Nov. 1800; Thomas Power, *Law, politics and society in eighteenth-century Tipperary* (Oxford, 1993), p. 194; *Cork Advertizer*, 4 Apr. 1801.

landless populations' which were dependent on the foodstuffs (the potato primarily) they grew for subsistence; this resulted inevitably in their increased vulnerability to exogenous shock.[88]

The temporal distribution of known incidents during these years suggests that there was a reversion to the pattern of food rioting that was normative in the first half of the eighteenth century when food protest was largely confined to years of crisis. There was, as a result, less of what can be described as 'low intensity' food rioting in the intervening years. Despite this, the impulse remained strong.[89] Ireland contrasts with England in this respect, for though the number of food riots in Ireland in 1800–1 was dwarfed by the number of incidents in England, this was the last episode of major food rioting in the latter jurisdiction, whereas the trajectory was still upwards in Ireland.[90] Counting food riots is inherently hazardous,[91] but the pattern of identifiable incidents in Ireland (Tables 2.1 and 2.2) suggests that, in contrast to the period spanning the mid-1760s to the mid-1780s, it was confined once more to those years when the reality of high prices caused by poor weather conditions and bad harvests, and the fear of real dearth prompted the crowd's interventions. Thus in 1808, the effects of a severe frost and heavy snow, which destroyed a proportion of the potato crop in the ground late in 1807 and augmented 'the miseries which oppress all classes of the community', prompted a minor surge in food protest that was not confined to any one region, though the single-most adverted to incident occurred in Galway where 'the populace' prevented a ship laden with meal departing the port for Derry/Londonderry.[92]

Four years later, following a poor harvest in 1811, the country experienced a further spike in food rioting. Employing a mixture of traditional strategies, which are most readily identifiable in the reports of events at port towns (Galway, Drogheda,

---

88 Walter, 'The politics of protest', p. 70; David Dickson, Cormac Ó Gráda and Stuart Daultrey, 'Hearth tax, household size and Irish population change, 1672–1821', *RIA proc.*, 82C (1982), 155; Engler et al., 'The Irish famine of 1740–1741', 1167.   89 See especially John Cunningham, 'Popular protest and a "moral economy"', passim.   90 Bohstedt, 'The pragmatic economy', pp 59–60; Table 2.1; Bohstedt, 'Food riots and the politics of provisions', pp 105–6; John Stevenson, 'Bread or blood' in G.E. Mingay (ed.), *The unquiet countryside* (London, 1989), p. 31, maintains that the 'last major wave of food disturbances to affect England occurred in the years 1816–18' but he acknowledges it overlapped with Luddism.   91 The approach employed here is reliant on the press. Because food protest was newsworthy, it is unlikely that the press declined to report incidents on which they had information. Indeed, it was alleged in 1812 that some papers elevated a 'trifling commotion', which took place in Limerick on 13 April, 'into an insurrection' (*Freeman's Journal*, 27 Apr. 1812). While it is reasonable to assume that all incidents in towns with newspapers were reported, it cannot be assumed that this is complete. And if the response of the sovereign of Belfast to the publication of a 'ballad penn'd in favour of the mob' in 1756 is an accurate guide, it may be that local officials successfully discouraged reporting (Macartney to [ ], 31 July 1756, 11 Aug. 1756 in George Benn, *A history of the town of Belfast from the earliest times to the close of the eighteenth century* (Belfast, 1877), pp 595–6). This was alleged in 1812 (Cunningham, 'Popular protest and a "moral economy"', p. 37). It may be that rural food rioting was underreported, but the extensive coverage of agrarian protest cautions against assuming this to be the case in the eighteenth century, and improved communication between the country and Dublin Castle suggests that few incidents dating from the early nineteenth century passed unreported.

Belfast, Clonakilty, Skibbereen, Waterford and, possibly, Limerick), the most striking feature of the cluster of riots that took place in 1812 is that these locations were
exceeded by the number of inland settlements in which crowds assembled to prevent the movement of grain and other foodstuffs out of their communities.[93] Given
the dependence of Dublin on supplies from its provincial hinterland, urban locations
next to or near inland waterways that now conveyed grain to the capital were particularly susceptible, and rioting was reported from the mid-Leinster towns of
Edenderry, Philipstown (Daingean), Kildare, Tullamore, Rathangan and Carlow. In
Munster, meanwhile, the well-established tradition of food riot was pursued in a
more restrained fashion than previously at Carrick-on-Suir, county Tipperary, while
the influence of agrarian protest was in evidence in the food riots that took place in
the county Cork towns of Midleton and, possibly, Kilworth.[94]

The breach of the Royal Canal at Mullingar in 1813 to prevent the transportation of potatoes out of the area, and an incident at Bangor, county Down, directed
at cars also ferrying potatoes, demonstrates that food rioting in the early nineteenth
century was not invariably a response to price and availability because food supplies were normal that year.[95] But the closeness of the connection was underlined
in 1816–17 when Ireland, like most of the rest of Europe, experienced a severe
subsistence crisis, ultimately traceable, John Dexter Post has argued, to the ash and
dust spewed into the atmosphere by the volcanic eruption of Mount Tambora,
Indonesia, in 1815. One of the features of the crisis was an 'upsurge of pillage,
rioting, vagrancy and criminal violence' across the continent of Europe. Food rioting took place in France, Belgium and Great Britain in 1816,[96] and though Ireland
avoided this fate then economic conditions were challenging. Reduced demand
ensured a 'depressed marketplace', though the country remained well supplied with
food until the impact of a poor harvest in 1816 pushed up the price of bread and
potatoes, and reduced the amount available for sale as a result of which markets
were thin by May 1817. 'A fever of an infectious and alarming nature' made matters markedly worse.[97] Informed reports to the effect that 70,000 people in Dublin
and 7,000 in Waterford were in need of relief in the early months of 1817 provide
an indication of the scale of distress then, and conditions continued to dis-improve.
High food prices were a particular concern, and one of the key factors in precipi-
tating one of the most intense spate of food rioting in the island's history.[98]

92 Cunningham, 'Popular protest and a "moral economy"', pp 31–2; *Belfast News Letter*, 17 Jan.
1808; *Freeman's Journal*, 27 Apr. 1808.   93 Booker to Trumbull, 1 Apr. 1812 (NYPL, Trumbull
papers, Box 1); *Cork Advertiser*, 13 June 1812.   94 Cunningham, 'Popular protest and a "moral
economy"', pp 32–7; Cunningham, *Galway, 1790–1914*, p. 86; *Belfast News Letter*, 10 July 1812;
Cork Advertizer, 30 Apr., 5, 7 May 1812; *Freeman's Journal*, 27 Apr. 1812.   95 Cunningham,
'Popular protest and a "moral economy"', p. 37.   96 Riots in England were reported in Ireland:
Ennis Chronicle, 1, 8, June, 3 July, 14 Dec. 1816.   97 *Ennis Chronicle*, 1 June 1816, *Freeman's
Journal*, 14 Nov., 9, 21 Dec. 1816, 1, 17 May, 6, 11 June 1817. J.B. Trotter, *Walks through Ireland
in 1812, 1814 and 1817* (London, 1819), pp 272–3, 299, 303, 330, 342, 371–2.   98 Post, *The last
great subsistence crisis*, pp 52–3, 68–73; Cunningham, 'Popular protest and a "moral economy"', p.
37; *Freeman's Journal*, 9 Dec. 1816, 15, 16 Jan. 1817; Barker and Cheyne, *An account of the rise,*

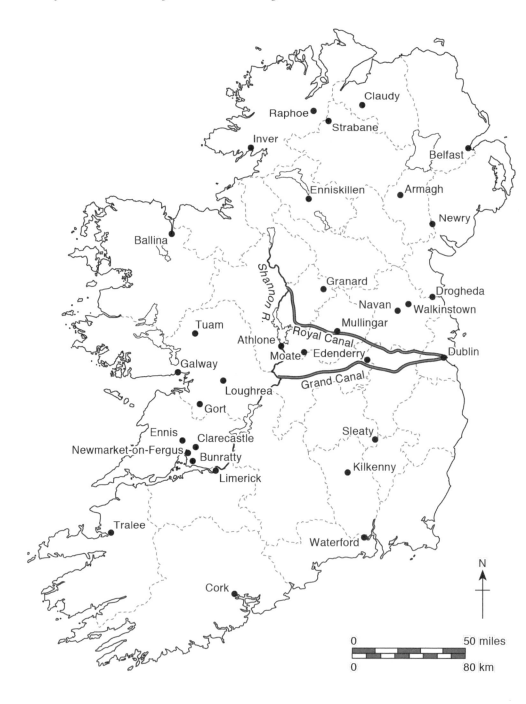

Map 3: Food protests in Ireland, 1817

The most compelling evidence for this is the record number of identifiable incidents – at least forty – in the space of little more than six months. Assigned to three 'phases' by John Cunningham, who has investigated the episode most closely, his otherwise admirable analysis does not afford full recognition to the fact that this was the first time that food rioting achieved a near island-wide geographical distribution (see Map 3). There was, as is to be expected given the pattern of events in 1812, a handful of incidents in towns and villages along the waterways and road routes linking the food-producing midlands with Dublin, but the expansion of the arc of protest beyond its previous heartland to embrace Granard, county Longford, and Moate and Athlone, in county Westmeath, is still significant. There were also incidents at ports such as Limerick, Cork, Waterford, Dublin, Drogheda, Belfast, Ballina and Galway, which had a tradition of food rioting, but disturbances at Blennerville (Tralee), county Kerry, Inver, county Donegal, and Strabane, county Tyrone are a further indication of the greater readiness of smaller communities to take direct action, and of the adoption by rural labourers and smallholders as well as urban artisans of food rioting as a form of protest. This was more obvious in the pattern of food rioting in counties Clare and Galway and, in a more dispersed fashion, in west and central Ulster, since it pointed towards what was to become still more apparent in the 1820s and 1830s – that as the numbers of landless and land poor rose food rioting became increasingly common in those regions experiencing the most rapid population growth.[99]

If the number of food riots reported in 1817 justifies its characterisation as 'possibly the worst' year 'for the Irish poor' between 'the great famines' of 1740–1 and 1845–9, it is ostensibly paradoxical, given the intensifying poverty that was a feature of Irish life in the quarter century before the Great Famine, that the phenomenon of food rioting seems to have weakened thereafter.[100] Since one of the foundations on which this claim is built is the contraction in the number of food riots reported in the press (Tables 2.1 and 2.2), it may be that closer inquiry will reveal more incidents (in the countryside particularly), which will modify this conclusion.[101] Whether this is the case or not, the diminished number of

progress and decline of the fever lately epidemical in Ireland, i, 3, 38.   **99** Post, *The last great subsistence crisis*, p. 73; Cunningham, 'Popular protest and a "moral economy"', pp 38–44; T.M. Abbot, 'The Downshire estates at Edenderry, 1800–1856' (MA, NUIM, 2004), pp 38–9; *Belfast News Letter*, 17 Jan., 13 June 1817; *Freeman's Journal*, 20 Dec. 1816, 15 Jan., 10, 11, 15 Feb., 29, 30 May, 6, 11, 12, 18, 19, 20 June, 2 July 1817; TNA, HO100/192, f. 164; Joseph Robbins, *The miasma: epidemic and panic in nineteenth-century Ireland* (Dublin, 1995), p. 39; Jordan, *Land and popular politics in Ireland: county Mayo*, pp 94–5; *Gentleman's Magazine*, 87 (1817), pp 619–20; Swift, *History of the Dublin bakers*, pp 203–5; Emmet O'Connor, *A labour history of Waterford* (Waterford, 1989), p. 18.   **100** Cunningham, 'Popular protest and a "moral economy"', p. 38; Joel Mokyr and Cormac Ó Gráda, 'Poor and getting poorer? Living standards in Ireland before the Famine', *Economic History Review*, 41:2 (1988), 209–35.   **101** The main source of the incidents that populate the tabulated sample (Tables 2.1 and 2.2) is the press, and food riots feature less frequently in the 1820s and 1830s. The obvious implication is that there were fewer incidents, but it may be that the press is not the best

mentions of food riots in the press dovetails with the increased disinclination of the respectable to tolerate food protest to suggest, that, as had happened in England some two decades earlier, the disposition to engage in such protest may have weakened during the 1820s and 1830s.[102] Reports received by the Chief Secretary's Office, which was the clearing house for intelligence from all parts of the island, and accounts in the press indicate that food protest continued to take place, and that it reflected economic conditions, but the clusters that synchronize with the regional famines and subsistence crises that occurred in 1822, 1830–1, 1837 and 1839 were not only modest in size by comparison with those of the 1810s, but also not of the same order as those identified at comparable moments in the eighteenth century (Tables 2.1 and 2.2). The changing geography of protest is also significant, as the dominance long exercised by urban centres in southern and eastern regions continued to weaken; a higher proportion of incidents now occurred in the countryside and along the western seaboard (Map 4).

The 1822 crisis was a turning point, for though 'an estimated one million people were obliged to seek aid' in ten counties extending from county Leitrim southwards to west county Cork, it is striking that claims to the effect 'that more than half the people of this county [Mayo] are unable to procure half enough to eat', and that the 'afflicted' were 'dying of hunger' in county Clare, did not precipitate proportionate surges in food rioting.[103] The population was not passive to be sure. There were disturbances in May in Ennis, Limerick and in county Mayo, and attacks on potato boats at Clarecastle and Killaloe, county Clare. It was also reported that 'the country people on the banks of the [Grand] Canal and River Shannon will not suffer any potatoes to leave their neighbourhood', but such protests were not common, and they were less revealing than the demonstrations of 'patience' referred to in the *Clare Journal* in quelling the instinct to protest.[104] This is unexpected, but it is suggestive of the beginnings of a change in public attitude that was not unconnected with the conditionality on which relief was promised: 'aid was refused to any parish where', in the words of the Clare County Relief Committee, 'tumult, plunder or illicit distillation prevailed'.[105] Moreover, the ability of the Ennis Relief Committee to relieve 8,000 in one month demonstrated that these were not idle pronouncements as bodies of this kind could provide subsidised and below cost foodstuffs in sufficient volume to make it clear that these agencies were a more reliable source of food than the time-honoured practice of food rioting, and the contrasting geographical footprint

register of food protest as it became increasingly rural based. The sample presented for these years is based on a survey of the Chief Secretary's Office Registered papers in the National Archives of Ireland for 1818–22, a word search of the press and an engagement with the secondary literature. **102** Below, pp 238–40. **103** *Freeman's Journal*, 6 May 1822; Timothy P. O'Neill, 'Clare and Irish poverty, 1815–1851', *Studia Hibernica*, 14 (1974), 8, 15–19; Thomas Reid, *Travels in Ireland in 1822* (London, 1823), pp 263–4, 276–82. The counties most acutely affected were Leitrim, Sligo, Mayo, Galway, Clare, Limerick, Kerry, Cork, and Roscommon and Tipperary. **104** *Freeman's Journal*, 8, 13, 15 May 1822; Knox to Goulburn, 20, 21 Dec. 1822 (NAI, RP/1822, 3206); O'Neill, 'Clare and Irish poverty, 1815–1851', 26. **105** O'Neill, 'Clare and Irish poverty, 1815–1851', 17.

of food protest in 1817 and 1822 would suggest that this lesson was not lost on sections of the populace.[106]

CHRONOLOGY AND GEOGRAPHY, *c*.1822–45

In any event, 1822 set a precedent that evolved into a trend. It did not mean that food protest was discontinued. There were two incidents in county Clare in 1824 when potato boats leaving the county were intercepted on the Shannon, which attest to continuing unease in food producing areas at the transportation of food-stuffs along waterways.[107] More famously, Dublin city experienced a serious out-break of bread rioting in the summer of 1826, attributable to high unemployment caused by the further contraction of the textile sector, which featured attacks on bakers' shops, and there were incidents in county Carlow in 1827 when what was described as 'mobs of a most alarming nature … threaten[ed] the peaceable inhabitants with destruction if they were not supplied with food'.[108] This did not escalate, as apprehended, into a fully-fledged riot, but mobs continued to inter-vene, as was the case with the 'large crowd' that had recourse to *taxation popu-laire* at Galway in August 1829, to enforce down potato prices.[109] While isolated incidents such as those identifiable in the 1820s are suggestive of an enduring popular belief in a *droit de subsistence manqué*, the continuing response of the crowd throughout the country to subsistence crises offers a more reliable guide to the strength of the food protest impulse (Map 4). There were three significant moments of this kind in the 1830s – 1830–1, 1837 and 1839–40.

The summer of 1829 was very wet, and the impact of the ensuing poor har-vest on food prices and food supply was felt particularly acutely in county Mayo from where it was reported in the summer of 1830 that

> distress continues unmitigated, and famine is advancing upon us with rapid strides. Cases of individual suffering are hourly accumulating – rob-beries are committed for the purpose of obtaining a comfortable meal, even with the concomitants of being branded as a felon. Store-houses are broken open and plundered – cattle slaughtered in the fields, and parts of their carcasses carried off to satisfy the cravings of hunger.[110]

In locations with little by way of a tradition of food protest and an *ad hoc* relief system (in Enniskillen, for example, it was observed that there was 'no scarcity

106 Flannan Enright, 'Terry Alts: the rise and fall of an agrarian society' in Matthew Lynch and Patrick Nugent (eds), *Clare: history and society* (Dublin, 2008), pp 226–7. 107 O'Neill, 'Clare and Irish poverty, 1815–1851', 26. 108 Swift, *History of the Dublin bakers*, pp 206–7; *Freeman's Journal*, 9 Aug. 1826; Alexander to Talbot, 15 Mar. 1827 (NAI, SOC 2831/1) quoted in Shay Kinsella, 'Milford Mills and the creation of a gentry powerbase: the Alexanders of county Carlow, 1790–1870' (PhD, DCU, 2015), p. 179. 109 Cunningham, *Galway, 1790–1914*, pp 89–90. 110 Report from the *Connaught Telegraph* carried in *Belfast News Letter*, 29 June 1830; see also Brendan Hoban,

of provision in this quarter, but the price is beyond the reach of poor persons'),
it was a relatively straightforward task to pre-empt food rioting by raising subscriptions 'for the purpose of devising the best means of alleviating the distress
that prevails among the labouring class, in consequence of scarcity of employment, and the high price of provisions'.[111] These conditions were tailor-made for
traditional-style food protest, however, and there was a major, and well publicized, episode in Limerick, and other incidents at Dunshaughlin, county Meath,
at a number of locations in county Clare and county Mayo, and on the canal
routes to Dublin in the summer of 1830. A march of 'some hundreds' behind a
'banner' to Foxford, and the dispersal of an assembly of men, women and children, estimated at 6,000, who gathered to protest at Buckfield outside Westport
in January 1831 illustrate further that the community had not forsaken the disciplined approach that is synonymous with classic food protest, but these incidents took place against a backdrop of more disorderly activity as reports in the
Connaught Telegraph of 'the increasing discontent of the lower classes of the
people of in this country' bear witness. Some were guided in their behaviour by
the admonition of the Archbishop Oliver Kelly of Tuam that the people should
eschew activities that were 'repugnant to the laws of God and man', but others
were less compliant, and the activities of the Steel Boys in county Mayo and the
Terry Alts in county Clare illustrate that, taken in the round, protest in these
counties conformed more closely to agrarian than to classic food protest.[112]

The pattern of events in 1837 was not altogether different. Once again the
poor and marginalized were reduced to extremis by the 'high price of potatoes'
in those parts of the country where the crisis was most acute. Conclusions
arrived at to the effect that, because 'the crop had not failed … there is ample
reason to believe that … the supply of potatoes is abundant' informed the relaxed
attitudes that obtained in certain quarters. But claims during the high summer
that the level of 'distress and destitution' experienced in the country demanded
'prompt' intervention acquired added authority when they were issued against a
backdrop of food riots in Limerick, Ennis and Castledawson (county
Derry/Londonderry); in these instances the protesters targeted the acquisition of
food for those in distress (Limerick), and the prevention of its movement out of
the region (Ennis and Castledawson).[113] The prioritization of access to potatoes
in the accounts of food protest across the country – Castledawson, Belfast and
Newtownards included – is noteworthy in this context. It suggests that though
the heartland of food protest may have shifted westwards, the dependence on the

---

Tracing the stem: Killala bishops (Dublin, 2015), pp 266–9.   **111** *Belfast News Letter*, 29 June 1830,
carrying reports from the *Enniskillen Chronicle*, *Kilkenny Journal* and *Derry Sentinel*.   **112** David
Lee, 'The food riots of 1830 and 1840' in idem and Debbie Jacobs (eds), *Made in Limerick* (2 vols,
Limerick, 2003), i, 56–60; *Belfast News Letter*, 29 June 1830; *Connaught Telegraph*, 19, 22 Jan., 2
Feb. 1831; Jordan, *Land and popular politics in Ireland*, pp 95–6; Enright, 'Terry Alts: the rise and
fall of an agrarian society', pp 226–7.   **113** *Tralee Mercury*, 17 May, 15 July 1837; *Freeman's Journal*,
12, 24 June 1837; *Belfast News Letter*, 1 Aug. 1837; *Tuam Herald*, 15 July 1837.

potato of 'the labouring and poorer classes' and 'distressed operatives', who provided the rank and file of urban mobs, meant that they were as determined as their rural equivalents to inhibit actions that would result in the contraction of the available supply. One may single out the 'mob' at Newtownards, which demonstrated its resolve to maintain traditional patterns of provisioning in January 1839 by intercepting and spilling potato carts as they proceeded through the town and by attacking the 'potato mill' for which they were destined.[114]

The critical importance of securing access to a supply of potatoes was underlined in the following years as distress prompted comparable interventions 'in the neighbourhood of Limerick' in 1839, in Killala (county Mayo), Pullaheeny (county Sligo), Scariff (county Clare), Portroe (county Tipperary) and Galway in 1840, and in Wexford, Mayo, Sligo and Cork in 1842.[115] Moreover, these incidents were but one feature of a larger response, particularly manifest in the west and mid-west in 1840 and 1842, that also involved the routine posting of notices setting potato prices, the convening of meetings for the same purpose and, in urban areas, increased monitoring as officials contrived (in vain) to anticipate shortages.[116] But as illustrative as these trends were of the vulnerability of the land poor, their dependence on the potato was not so complete that food protest focussed exclusively on restricting the movement of this commodity. The intervention in 1840 of local communities to prevent the conveyance of provisions along the river Shannon, attacks on provision stores in counties Cork, Limerick, Dublin and Down, and on mills and carts carrying flour in Clare and Tipperary indicated that the intensified preoccupation with the potato did not come at the expense of the other staples.[117] Furthermore, if the pattern of events observable in the 1820s and most of the 1830s points to the conclusion that food rioting wanted for some of its previous vitality as respectable opinion adopted an increasingly negative outlook, the rise in the number of recoverable incidents in 1840 and 1842 underlines the enduring capacity of the crowd to respond to the prospect of hunger by direct action (Table 2.1). This was certainly the case in the mid-west and west. Galway city, as John Cunningham has shown, sustained a strong tradition of food protest through the first half of the nineteenth century, but so too did Ennis and Limerick, which rivalled it as the island's primary food rioting urban redoubts at that point.[118] Indeed, the geographical origins of the

---

114 *Belfast News Letter*, 1 Aug. 1837, 27 Aug. 1838, 25 Jan. 1839. **115** *Connaught Telegraph*, 31 July, 1839; *Freeman's Journal*, 4, 12 July 1839, 18 June 1840, 31 May 1842; *Nenagh Guardian*, 11 June 1840; *Kerry Evening Post*, 8 June 1842; NAI, Registered papers, 1839, division 1, vol. 1, 5/10661, 27/10765, 26/11151, 7/14687, 14745, 15223, 15225. **116** NAI, Registered papers, 1840, division 1, 5/8811, 9247, 10661, 10727, 27/ 10765, 11/10709, 11015, 11167, 26/11151, 27/12717; Registered papers, 1842, division 1, 1/9377, 4/10425, 6/8335, 10211, 7/8709, 11/10325, 10659, 14/10907, 17/9087, 10277, 10709–11, 11035, 11037, 19/10411, 26/9257, 26/9399, 17/9549, 19/9619, 27/9669, 31/10203. **117** NAI, Registered papers, 1840, division 1, 5/10247, 10713, 27/10415, 11055, 11195, 8/11623, 16/11807, 6/12421, 17/12517. **118** Cunningham, *Galway, 1790–1914*, pp 86–98; *Freeman's Journal*, 12 June 1837, 4, 12 July 1839; Lee, 'The food riots of 1830 and 1840', pp 60–5.

reports – actual and apprehended – received at Dublin Castle in the summer of 1842 embraced 21 counties, and though eight (Antrim, Armagh, Dublin, Kilkenny, Meath, Queen's county, Westmeath and Wicklow) featured but once, the prominence of Limerick (7 mentions), Tipperary (6), Cork (6) Clare (3), Galway (4), Mayo (3) and Sligo (3) attests to the enduring conviction of the urban and rural populace that this was an appropriate response when access to affordable food was endangered.

Indicatively, following on the 'distress' experienced in parts of the country in the summer of 1839, there was something of a resurgence in food protest in north Connaught (following a lull lasting for most of the 1830s) in the early 1840s as the local population sought to frustrate merchants and shippers embarking cargoes of food. They certainly had cause in the summer of 1842. Animated by reports that 'potatoes and meal have risen to a price that puts anything like a sufficiency of food beyond the reach of numbers', the populace contrived to prevent the movement of oatmeal and potatoes out of Ballina and Sligo. Similar incidents in Athlone, county Westmeath and Ballymahon, county Longford indicated that, as was the case two years earlier, distress was not confined to a narrow region.[119] Comparable events at Cork and Wexford ports, threatened unrest at Carlow, and a surge in less well-reported incidents of 'plundering provisions' across the country during the summer months served to ensure not only that the number of food protests in that year exceeded the number identified for any year since 1817 but also to underline the increasingly disruptive effects of a reduced potato harvest. And, as the renewal of attacks on carts, barges and ships that carried food out of food-producing regions attests, these modes of transportation were now a prime target for local crowds conditioned to think in local terms. It captured the tendency – exemplified by the attempt by the populace of Sligo to prevent people from county Leitrim purchasing potatoes at market in their town – to engage in the long-standing instinctual impulse 'to other' those who were not part of the community and to look inwards for solutions, which was at increasing odds with the commercial world that presumed the unfettered movement of goods.[120]

The enduring character of the protest impulse to which these patterns attest was underlined by two incidents in June 1842. The first of these was the 'Clare massacre' which was the emotional label given to an episode at Clarecastle and Ennis on 4–6 June 1842 that resulted in five deaths. Precipitated by the attempt by the populace 'to prevent the removal of potatoes by "strangers"' and the unloading of flour and meal from vessels at Clarecastle quay as a result of which two persons – a woman and a policeman – lost their life, the confrontation

119 *Connaught Telegraph*, 8 June 1842; *Freeman's Journal*, 31 May, 9 June 1842; *Nenagh Guardian*, 11 June 1842; NAI, Registered papers, 1842, division 1, 26/9399, 31/10203, 5/10413, 27/10571, 13/10675, 10889, 10891, 10893, 24/11057, 6/11449, 11963, 21/13657. 120 *Kerry Evening Post*, 8 June 1842; *Nenagh Guardian*, 11 June 1842; *Belfast News Letter*, 24 June 1842; NAI, Registered papers, 1842, division 1, 26/9399.

between the crowd and the authorities reached its bloody climax when three people died as the crowd that attacked Bannatyne's grain stores on Mill Road, Ennis, was fired upon by the police on the third day of this prolonged protest.[121] The second incident, which took place in Galway on 13 June, was only slightly less dramatic, not because the magistrates, police and soldiers assembled in response manifested greater restraint, but because the 'mob' assumed effective control of the city for the day, and because the episode was taken up and reported in the *Illustrated London News* (Fig. 1).[122]

Though each event was remarkable in its own way, neither was unprecedented. Yet the fact that the Clare riot was discussed at a meeting of Daniel O'Connell's Loyal National Repeal Association in August 1842, and that Sir Francis Burdett (1770–1844), the political radical, gave notice in the House of Commons on 29 June of his intention to 'call the attention of government to the late provision riots in Galway' indicates that both incidents garnered attention well above the ordinary.[123] They have certainly contributed to the impression that the 'moral economy' in Ireland was as vigorous then as it had been at virtually any point in its history, when this was not the case since the government and the generality of the elite was disposed to be less accommodating than they had been in the past. Furthermore, it is apparent from the mapping of known incidents between 1820 and 1845 that food rioting was spatially concentrated in the counties in the western half of the country with the fastest growing populations, the largest percentage of poor and a strong tradition of agrarian protest (see Map 4).

This is not to imply that the pattern of food protest was now geographically rather than socially determined. Reports from county Mayo to the effect that 'large numbers of people' responded to the 'extreme distress resulting from a very poor potato harvest' in 1830–1 by swearing 'to prevent the export of oats' may, on first consideration, be seen to suggest that the popular commitment to the code that sustained food rioting was robust. But the fact that the oath was tendered at *night* by Steel Boys – a local body of agrarian protesters – and that they sought to compel the populace to adhere to their position on a variety of other issues – the distraint of cattle, tithe arrears, rent default etc. – identified with agrarian protest, indicates that in this area at least food protest functioned as a sub-set of agrarian protest rather than as a distinct and separate phenomenon, which may account for the absence of food rioting in this county during the 1830s.[124]

121 Ciarán Ó Murchadha, *Sable wings over the land: Ennis, county Clare, and its wider community during the Great Famine* (Ennis, 1998), pp 14–5; Joseph Power, *A history of Clarecastle and its environs* (Ennis, 2004), pp 414–18; *Nenagh Guardian*, 11 June 1842; *Cork Examiner*, 13 June 1842; Alf MacLochlainn, 'Social life in county Clare, 1800–1850', *Irish University Review*, 2:1 (1972), 59. 122 Cunningham, *Galway, 1790–1914*, pp 90–1; *Freeman's Journal*, 16 June 1842; *Cork Examiner*, 17 June 1842; *Illustrated London News*, 25 June 1842. 123 *Freeman's Journal*, 31 Aug. 1842; *Kerry Examiner*, 28 June 1842. 124 Jordan, *Land and popular politics in Ireland*, pp 95–6; Desmond McCabe, 'Social order and the ghost of a moral economy in pre-Famine Mayo' in Raymond Gillespie and Gerard Moran (eds), *'A various country': essays in Mayo history, 1500–1900* (Westport, 1987), pp 91–112; McCabe, 'Law, conflict and social order: county Mayo, 1820–1845', chapter 4.

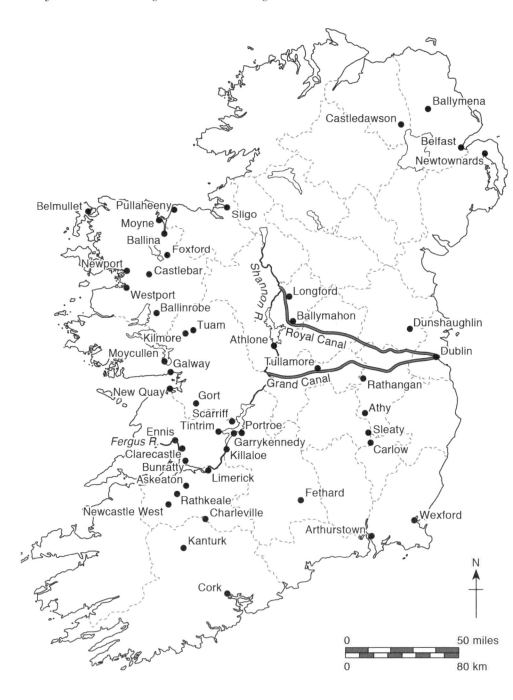

Map 4: The location of known food riots in Ireland, 1821–45

The situation was not always straightforward, however. Andries Eiríksson's investigation of 'the pattern of food riots and lower class protest in the Clare and Limerick region in the 1830s and 1840s' is particularly revealing since it suggests, contrary to the situation in county Mayo, that what he terms 'protest crime' was not only commonplace in the mid-west, but also a feature of a larger disturbed area embracing much of north Munster, and a ribbon of west midland counties.[125] It is less than clear what proportion of his category of 'protest crime' can be denominated 'food rioting', but it is observable that the latter peaked during the early summer months, and that it was most visible when prices were high in the years following a poor harvest (1830, 1837, 1839, and 1842) in keeping with the pattern traceable back to the 1720s. It differed from 'classic' food protest, however, in its increasingly rural and nocturnal character, its greater reliance on violence and intimidation, and (as exemplified by county Mayo in the early 1830s) the participation of bodies of men in uniform, which was emblematic of agrarian protest.

It is arguable, indeed, if it is possible to sustain a clear distinction between food and agrarian protest in this region at this point. Eiríksson maintains that food protesters in Clare and Limerick were less reliant on violence – less predisposed to issue death threats, to fire shots at houses and to engage in arson; less likely to administer beatings, to issue anonymous threatening and admonitory notices (in English), and more likely, in the manner of classic food rioters, to operate during daylight and to include female participants – but the distinction can be fine in practice.[126] The increased involvement of rural labourers in food protest, and the rising tension between farmer-producers, who pursued the best market price, and labourer-consumers, who were land and cash poor, certainly contributed to this pattern of behaviour.[127] But the fact that access to land was a more common cause of protest than access to food, and that the number of attacks on farmers was exceeded by those directed at millers and merchants, cautions against concluding that the perceptible narrowing of the gap between food protest and agrarian protest that had been underway for several decades had, or would ever arrive at a point where the two were indistinguishable. This was not how the Royal Irish Constabulary was disposed to perceive it, of course. But those persons, female and male, who engaged during daylight hours in food protest unrobed and with un-blackened faces, clearly perceived that there was a distinction, and they contrived by these means to appeal to the reservoir of public sympathy for this activity.[128] The fact that there were more than a dozen allied protests in county Clare in 1842, climaxing with the bloody three-day episode in Ennis in May, certainly counsels against suggesting that the trends identifiable in the 1820s and 1830s meant the days of food protest were drawing to a close. Yet the shrinking geographical space

125 Eiríksson, 'Food supply and food riots', p. 71; idem, 'Crime and popular protest in county Clare, 1815–1852', passim. 126 Eiríksson, 'Food supply and food riots', pp 72–5. 127 Enright, 'Terry alts: the rise and fall of an agrarian society', p. 226; *Freeman's Journal*, 12 July 1839. 128 Eiríksson, 'Crime and popular protest in county Clare, 1815–1852', passim.

that food protest then occupied, and the declining number of identifiable incidents, is consistent with a pattern of contraction that (in Ireland as in England) was seemingly headed in one direction.[129]

Why this should be the case, given the scale and depth of poverty in Ireland and the capacity displayed in 1842, and still more in 1846–7, to sustain an extensive pattern of food protest, is less easily explained, but, among a range of factors, it can be suggested that the moral suasion that was a defining feature of food protest at its peak in the eighteenth and early nineteenth century was in retreat. The commentator, who was prompted to observe of the population of county Clare in 1822 that 'the patience of this afflicted people is unequalled in the history of mankind, dying of hunger without committing any excess worthy of notice', accounted for their quiescence by reference to the fact that many were 'ashamed' to make their distress known. What he failed to note, though it lay at the root of the attitudinal change to which he alluded, was that the shame and embarrassment that caused families 'who never knew or felt want' to conceal their plight was a manifestation of the attraction of a culture of respectability that was to achieve ascendancy in the course of the nineteenth century.[130] The anger expressed by the sovereign of Belfast, George Macartney, in 1756 at what he perceived as the encouragement given to food rioters by a sympathetic press, was seldom in evidence in the half century that followed because the respectable were disposed to be empathetic.[131] It was not that empathy was no longer shown in the early nineteenth century (it can be identified in the initial response to food protests in 1846–7), but it exerted less ascendancy in the public sphere. This is the implication of the criticism voiced in 1812 which accused the press of elevating a 'trifling commotion' in the city of Limerick into a major episode and of encouraging food rioting by 'continually thundering denunciations of starvation into the [people's] ears'.[132] Another commentary from the same year, first published in the *Ennis Chronicle* but taken up by *The Freeman's Journal*, went further. It alleged that 'newspaper publications' actually encouraged riotousness by 'agita[ting] the public mind on the subject of provisions'.[133]

This commentary might be perceived as a classic instance of shooting the messenger, but it was a pointer to the shift in attitude that encouraged early nineteenth-century newspapers not only to portray food rioting as 'shameful' but also to downplay the seriousness of individual incidents. There were often particular reasons for this, but it is still noteworthy, because it echoes the embarrassment that influenced behaviour in county Clare in 1822; it was now claimed

129 Power, *A history of Clarecastle*, pp 414–18; Eiriksson, 'Crime and popular protest in county Clare, 1815–1852', passim.   **130** *Clare Journal* quoted in *Freeman's Journal*, 6 May 1822. **131** Macartney to [ ], 22, 31 July, 11 Aug. 1756 in Benn, *History of Belfast*, pp 594, 595, 596; Magennis, 'In search of the "moral economy"', p. 199.   **132** *Freeman's Journal*, 27 Apr. 1812, reprinting an article originally carried in the *Limerick Gazette*. The article was particularly critical of *The Patriot* newspaper which, it alleged with heavy irony, 'strained the tumult into an insurrection'.   **133** *Cork Advertiser*, 25 Apr. 1812.

by social leaders that food protest reflected badly on the community in which it took place. This sentiment was plainly in evidence at a meeting convened by the mayor of Galway in 1817 when criticism was openly directed at 'a clandestine memorial' 'forwarded by a few individuals' who, it was alleged, 'represent[ed] the population of the town of Galway as being actuated by a spirit of hostility to the laws of the land, and of riotous insubordination, subversive of the peace of the country' in order to secure the imposition of 'the rigorous and coercive operation of the Peace Preservation Act'.[134] It was also manifest in sharp exchanges between the *Limerick Chronicle* and the *Clare Journal* in 1842 when the Ennis paper challenged the claims of its rival that the root cause of popular opposition to the conveyance of grain from county Clare to Limerick was the disturbed state of the county town. And something similar was at play in Galway when the *Galway Vindicator* dismissed accounts published elsewhere of the food riot that took place in the city on 13–14 June 1842 as a 'tissue of gross misrepresentation'.[135] Local pride was obviously at stake on both occasions, as was the perception that such incidents reflected poorly on local administrators. But there was also a wider communal understanding, borne out of the appreciating identification by the respectable and the middling sort of food rioting with lawlessness and poverty; as far as they were concerned, intervention of this kind was antithetical to the values society ought to prioritize.

This attitudinal shift did not mean that the press, the middling sort and the elite, whose empathy was critical if food protest was to be tolerated, possessed a moral monopoly. The support expressed for those in extremis in 1822 was genuine, but the expectation increasingly was that they would demonstrate 'patience and resignation', which is what the *Kilkenny Moderator* called for in 1817, and the Catholic clergy increasingly counselled, and await the arrival of relief that the government and civil society chose to dispense.[136] It was a message many on the margins were reluctant to take on board, as the ongoing patterns of agrarian protest and food rioting attests. Yet the fact that the former was vigorous while the latter showed signs of weakening indicates that the chasm that once separated food rioting from agrarian protest in the countryside, and from workers' combinations in towns and cities, had narrowed. Food protest was not unique in this respect. The advancing culture of respectability, underway for several decades, also found good reason to object to demotic sports and the code of honour, which were also visibly in retreat by the 1820s.[137] Food rioting possessed more

<hr>

134 *Belfast News Letter*, 17 Jan. 1817, describing a riot in Galway opposing the transport of grain to Derry; Cunningham, *Galway, 1790–1914*, p. 87.   135 Power, *A history of Clarecastle*, pp 414–15; Cunningham, *Galway, 1790–1914*, p. 91.   136 Cunningham, 'Popular protest and "a moral economy"', p. 42; Timothy P. O'Neill, 'The Catholic Church and relief of the poor, 1815–45', *Archivium Hibernicum*, 31 (1973), 138–9; Donal Kerr, *The Catholic Church and the Famine* (Dublin, 1996), p. 20. Interestingly, the people would be congratulated in the Queen's speech in 1847 for their display of 'patience and resignation'; the irony was evidently lost on its authors: Thompson, 'Moral economy reviewed', p. 264; below, p. 65.   137 See James Kelly, 'The decline of duelling and the emergence of the middle class in Ireland' in Maria Luddy and Fintan Lane (eds), *Politics,*

social capital than sport because of the belief (enshrined in the concept of a *droit de subsistence*) that the entitlement to food took precedence over other rights, rules and regulations. This did not secure it against contraction. But it did mean the impulse endured and was available to be appealed to by the urban and land poor when circumstances warranted. This was the case in 1840 and 1842. It was still more spectacularly manifested during the Great Famine.

'PLUNDERING PROVISIONS', 1846–57

Responding to Famine, 1845–6

The Great Famine witnessed a dramatic surge in food protest. This peaked in 1846–7 (Tables 5.1, 5.2), and declined thereafter in keeping with the pattern described by Cormac Ó Gráda, who has observed of famines generally that 'protest and resistance … give way to apathy and hopelessness as … the crisis worsens'.[138] There are identifiable continuities between the patterns of food protest pursued before and during the Great Famine, of course. But because food rioting was now categorized as an 'outrage' by the police, and grouped with other food related offences in the category denominated 'plundering provisions', it is not possible to correlate the figures for food rioting assembled for the eighteenth and early nineteenth centuries (Tables 2.1–2.2) with the figures for the offence of 'plundering provisions' compiled by the Constabulary Office (Table 5.1) or even with the more selective statistics assembled from the incomplete returns for 1846 and those cases reported to the Chief Secretary's Office listed in the registers of incoming correspondence (Table 5.2). Moreover, though the offence of 'plundering provisions' was introduced in 1842,[139] the official 'return of outrages reported to the Constabulary Office' were formally assembled for the first time in 1848.[140] An incomplete set of monthly returns exists for 1846, and they can be combined with the registers of the papers received by the Chief Secretary's Office to provide a statistical perspective on food protest for the duration of the Famine. The resulting data, summarized in tables 3–5, echo and amplify the case made by Eiríksson, Kinealy and Cunningham that the long held view that the famine years were 'conspicuously for their tranquillity' is not simply misleading; it is wrong. Impelled by acute distress, the late 1840s sustained the most intense period of food protest in Irish history.[141]

society and the middle class in modern Ireland (Basingstoke, 2010), pp 89–106; idem, *Sport in Ireland, 1600–1840* (Dublin, 2014), pp 192–203, 214–18, 228–33.   **138** Cormac Ó Gráda, *Eating people is wrong, and other essays on Famine* (Princeton, 2015), p. 1.   **139** The term is encountered in returns for July and August 1842. It was not employed in 1839 and 1841 (NAI, Official papers, 1839/22, 1842/83).   **140** *Return of outrages reported to the Constabulary Office … 1848, 1849, 1850, 1851, 1852, 1853, 1854, 1855* (Dublin, 1849–56), NAI, CSO, ICR/1.   **141** The claim that the famine years were tranquil was advanced in the 1950s by K.B. Nowlan, 'The political background' in R.D. Edwards and T.D. Williams (eds), *The Great Famine: studies in Irish history, 1845–62* (Dublin, 1956), p. 138. This view was unchallenged until the 1990s, when it was overturned by Eiríksson

The statistics for 'plundering provisions' and the qualitative accounts in the outrage files and in the press indicate that the country negotiated the impact of the loss
of 40 per cent of the potato crop in 1845 without serious food rioting in the winter
of 1845–6. This was true even of those areas, Galway notably, where the army garrison was called out in November 1845 to resist those elements of the populace that
contemplated blocking the exportation of corn.[142] Comparable disquiet was manifest
at the same moment at Newport Pratt, county Mayo; and in December in county
Longford, arising out of which carts ferrying provisions between Longford town
and Rathowen (county Westmeath) travelled with an escort. But other than the
'plundering' of a store belonging to the Dublin Steam Packet Company at
Tullamore in December and the brig William IV on the Galway coast in January,
there were no identifiable cases of crowd intervention.[143] The populace remained
uneasy, however, and price inflation in the spring of 1846 heightened concern that
the 'store of food' was sufficiently precarious to justify intervention. Provision riots
at Kinvara and Gort in south county Galway in early March,[144] and an attempt 'to
prevent strangers buying potatoes' at Ballyvaughan, county Clare, a week later
attested to the restiveness of the population in one part of the country. And the
likelihood of imminent widespread protest was heightened by accounts in the same
month from county Roscommon of an attack by 'a party of persons ... [on] three
carmen who were conveying loading from Boyle to Longford for the canal boats';
by a 'riotous assembly' prompted by concerns about the availability of provisions at
Kilkenny; and by a flurry of calls for police and military reinforcements and for
escorts for carts and barges.[145] Reports in early April from Rutland, county Donegal,
that a smack, which had come to the port from Skerries to receive a cargo of potatoes, was immobilized by a small crowd; and from Tarbert, on the northern coast-

('Food supply and food riots', pp 67–94) and Kinealy, *The Great Famine*, pp 68–9, 89, 94, 144–7,
and most recently Cunningham, '"'Tis hard to argue starvation into quiet": protest and resistance,
1846–47', pp 10–33. For a review of the surge in publication on the Great Famine in the 1990s,
see Cormac Ó Gráda, 'Making Irish famine history in 1995', *History Workshop Journal*, 42 (1996),
87–104.   **142** NAI, Registered papers, 1845, division 1, vol. 1, 11/22865, 22921, 23323. According
to a report in *Nation*, 29 Nov. 1845, the riotous 'disposition' of the Galway fishermen 'to resist the
exportation of corn' was overcome by the intervention of the local clergy: Cunningham, *Galway,
1790–1914*, pp 126–7.   **143** NAI, Registered papers, 1845, division 1, vol. 1, 21/23769, 15/29283;
idem, 1846, 11/145, C/1035, 11/1479, 1933. Anonymous letters were circulated in Galway in
February calling on the Town Commissioners 'to provide food for the people, and to prevent the
exportation of corn, otherwise the people would themselves prevent the exportation': Kernan to
Pennefeather, 5 Feb. 1846 (NAI, OP: Galway, 1846/11/2541).   **144** NAI, Registered papers, 1846,
division 1, vol. 1, 5/5787. The situation in south county Galway and north county Clare was such,
Ulick, the first marquis of Clanricarde, observed that 'no speculator would dare risk a cargo of food
to be conveyed through the country in its present disordered and anarchical condition': Clanricarde
to Kennedy, 5 Feb. 1846 (NAI, Relief Commission papers, 3/1/491), quoted in John J. Conwell,
'Ulick John de Burgh, first marquis of Clanricarde ... and his county Galway estate during the
Great Famine' (MA, NUIM, 2002), p. 25.   **145** NAI, Registered papers, 1846, division 1, vol. 1,
5/6365, 7787, 7929, 14/7875, 19/5885, 17/7373, 8341 25/7795, 7799; Drinkwater (?) to Redington,
26 Mar. 1846 (NAI, OP: Roscommon, 1846/25/7709).

line of county Kerry, that 'a mob of country people' delayed the transportation of one hundred barrels of meal across the Shannon estuary (for the destitute at Ballybunion, who were in a 'worse condition') provided further evidence of escalating disquiet from many parts as the spring progressed.[146]

The discomposure to which these incidents attested was particularly acute in county Tipperary, where requests for military and police escorts for the flour carts that were a familiar presence on the roads of the south of the county were given added impetus by reports in late March from nearby Whitegate, county Clare, that a crowd of about 100 people prevented farmers with grain to sell accessing Williamstown Harbour from where it was scheduled to be transported down the Shannon.[147] There was, to outward appearances, no reason why the populace of county Tipperary should respond more assertively than the populace elsewhere, but urban dwellers, traditionally reliant on purchased food, and the rural land poor, obliged by the destruction of the potato to become food purchasers, looked on with mounting anger as attempts to access food at an affordable price collided with the aspiration of farmers, millers, merchants and sundry dealers to profit from the strong demand for their produce. They looked instinctively for relief to local and national government, and when they showed no signs of intervening, they vowed to help themselves. The *Tipperary Free Press* explained a few weeks later:

> The uncertainty of obtaining even one meal a day of bad lumpers[148] under which our unfortunate people have been for some time suffering, has been rendered unendurable by the want of sympathy on the part of government. At the meeting of the corporation [of Tipperary] held on the 25th [March] *ultimo*, the state of the poor was discussed, and Government called on to send a Commissary with a supply of Indian flour to this town, but no notice whatever was taken of the matter. At that meeting it was suggested that another meeting should be called, and a subscription entered into, but that was also unheeded. The people at length, stimulated by hunger, attacked the Cahir flour carts …[149]

Fired up by the 'extremity of distress' to which they were reduced, an attempt, commencing on 9 April, to commandeer provisions *en route* to or from Clonmel, Carrick-on-Suir, Cahir and Tipperary, inspired food protest on a scale more characteristic of France than Ireland. Indeed, it seemed as if the whole of the urban and land poor in the county mobilized during the week of 9–16 April as crowds ranging in size from 'several hundreds' to 'four or five thousand' (the latter the esti-

---

146 Holmes to Redington, 5 Apr., Drombain to Lincoln, and enclosures, 7 Apr. 1846 (NAI, OP: Donegal, 1846/7/8423, 8631); Mann to Drombain, 23 Apr. 1846 (NAI, OP: Kerry, 1846/12/10175). 147 Pennefeather to Shaw, 29 Mar., Report for inspector, 30 Mar., Bianconi to Pennefeather, 30 Mar. 1846 (NAI, OP: Tipperary, 1846/ 27/7897, 7939, 7889); NAI, Registered papers, 1846, division 1, vol. 1, 27/7749, 7897. 148 The *lumper* was a variety of potato, prolific and widely cultivated in Ireland: Cormac Ó Gráda, 'The lumper potato and the Famine', *History Ireland*, 1:1 (1993), 22–3. 149 The *Tipperary Free Press* quoted in *Kerry Examiner*, 21 Apr. 1846.

mated order of the 'mob' that descended on Clonmel on 13 April) targeted mills at or near Carrick-on-Suir, Clonmel, Fethard and Clogheen; cargo boats on the river Suir; convoys of carts on the main roadways; and meal stores and bakers' shops – indeed any place in the region embracing south county Tipperary and the adjoining parts of counties Waterford and Cork at which food might be secured.

Given their scale, it was inevitable that disturbances were not only widely reported in the press but also a subject of comment in parliament, while, behind the scenes, magistrates, landowners (nobility and gentry) and others bombarded Dublin Castle with appeals for military assistance.[150] Momentarily stunned by the loss of control and taken aback by the damage inflicted – Clonmel was described on 15 April as in 'a horrible state ...as if it had been sacked by an army of Sikks' – the priority was to restore order.[151] The reinforcement of the army, the recruitment of special constables, and the galvanizing of local elites meant the authorities had resumed control within a week, though incidents continued to occur sporadically.[152] The episode, which accounted for more than eighty per cent of the cases of plundering provisions in Munster in April 1846 (and two-thirds of the national total) also spurred local corporations to take immediate steps to ease the plight of the needy, and the combination of local subscriptions and employment was sufficiently ameliorative to ensure not only that there was no repetition of these events in county Tipperary during the summer months, but also that the number of incidents of food plundering nationally declined to one third its April level in May and June (Tables 3.1 and 3.2).

There were incidents of provisions plundering in seventeen counties during these three months, but none came close to the twenty reported in county Tipperary; indeed, the six incidents in counties Cork and Galway was double the number reported from county Meath and triple that in counties Waterford and Down (Tables 3.2–3.5). Most of the country resembled King's county where the realisation that 'the labouring classes are suffering' was accompanied by a relieved acknowledgement that they were 'suffering in silence; they are bearing up against hunger and sickness with almost incredible patience'.[153]

150 *Freeman's Journal*, 15 Apr., 23 July 1846; *Kerry Examiner*, 21 Apr. 1846; *Cork Examiner*, 20 Apr. 1846; *Belfast News Letter*, 17 Apr. 1846; County inspector's report, 13 Apr., [ ] to Pennefeather, 14 Apr., Glengall to [Redington], 13, 14 Apr., Riall to Redington, 14 Apr., Ryan to Redington, 13 Apr., Lismore to Bessborough, 15 Apr., Harvey to Bessborough, 16 Apr., Barton to Donoughmore, 17 Apr., Outrage report, 29 Apr., Memorial of Edward Brazill, 24 July, Glengall to Bessborough, 16 Apr. 1846 (NAI, OP: Tipperary, 1846/27/9025, 9055, 8929, 8989, 8931, 8947, 8993, 9091, 9641, 10585, 21335, 9327); Bowen to Redington, 14 Apr. 1846 (NAI, OP: Cork, 1846/6/9033); Christine Kinealy, *The Great Irish Famine: impact, ideology and rebellion* (Basingstoke, . 2002), pp 124–5. **151** *Kerry Examiner*, 21 Apr. 1846. **152** Resident magistrates to Redington, 16 Apr., Shaw to Redington, 17 Apr., Redmond to Pennefeather, 17 Apr., Redmond to Pennefeather, 19 Apr., Phipps to Redington, 18 Apr., Purdy to Pennefather, 24 Apr., Bagwell to [ ], 23 Apr., [RM] to Pennefeather, 24 Apr., James [ ] to [ ], 30 Apr. 1846 (NAI, OP: Tipperary, 1846/27/9113, 9325, 9349, 9413, 9425, 10171, 10185, 10203, 10735); *Cork Examiner*, 21 Apr. 1846. **153** Report from *Tipperary Vindicator* on conditions in Tullamore in *Freeman's Journal*, 30 Apr. 1846; also Blake to Redington, 9 Oct. 1846 (NAI, OP: Roscommon, 1846/25/27489).

Table 3.1: Plundering provisions, 1846: monthly totals by province
(official figures)

Province	Apr.	May	June	July	Sept.	Oct.*	Nov.	Dec.	Total
Munster	23	3	3	–	12	[32]	41	81	[195]
Leinster	4	2	2	–	9	[19]	28	61	[125]
Ulster	1	2	1	1	4	[8]	9	26	[52]
Connaught	1	3	4	–	2	[11]	10	13	[44]
Total	29	10	10	1	27	70	88	181	416

Source: National Archives of Ireland, CSO, OP, 1846/9; *Return of outrages reported to the Constabulary Office during the year 1850, with summaries for preceding years* [Dublin, 1851]), pp 14–15

Table 3.2: Plundering provisions, 1846: MUNSTER, county monthly totals
(official figures)

	Apr.	May	June	July	Aug.	Sept.	Oct.*	Nov.	Dec.	Total
Tipperary	19	–	1	–	–	1	[4]	15	48	[88]
Cork	2	3	1	–	–	3	[12]	20	27	[68]
Limerick	–	–	–	–	–	7	[5]	3	3	[18]
Kerry	–	–	–	–	–	–		1	2	[3]
Waterford	1	–	1	–	–	1	[2]	2	1	[8]
Clare	1	–	–	–	–	–	[9]	–	–	[10]
Total	23	3	3	0	0	12	[32]	41	81	195

Table 3.3: Plundering provisions, 1846: ULSTER, county monthly totals
(official figures)

	Apr.	May	June	July	Aug.	Sept.	Oct.*	Nov.	Dec.	Total
Donegal	–	–	–	–	–	1	–	5	8	[14]
Fermanagh	–	–	–	–	–	1	[3]	–	6	[10]
Cavan	–	–	–	–	–	2	[4]	–	4	[10]
Armagh	–	1	–	–	–	–		1	3	5
Tyrone	–	–	1	–	–	–	[1]	3	1	[6]
Monaghan	–	–	–	–	–	–	[1]	–	3	[4]
Down	–	1	–	1	–	–	–	–	1	3
L'derry	–	–	–	–	–	–	–	–	–	0
Antrim	–	–	–	–	–	–	–	–	–	0
Total	0	2	1	1	0	4	[9]	9	26	52

Table 3.4: Plundering provisions, 1846: LEINSTER, county monthly totals
(official statistics)

	April	May	June	July	Aug.	Sept.	Oct.*	Nov.	Dec.	Total
Queen's co.	1	–	–	–	–	–	[3]	9	12	[25]
King's co.	–	–	1	–	–	1	[6]	9	7	[24]
Kilkenny	–	–	–	–	–	2	[1]	1	11	[15]
Longford	–	–	–	–	–	3	[3]	3	5	[14]
Meath	–	2	1	–	–	1	–	3	4	11
W'meath	1	–	–	–	–	–	[3]	3	4	[11]
Wexford	1	–	–	–	–	–	[4]	–	5	[10]
Kildare	–	–	–	–	–	–	–	–	5	5
Louth	–	–	–	–	–	–	–	–	5	5
Wicklow	–	–	–	–	–	2	–	–	2	4
Carlow	–	–	–	–	–	–	–	–	1	1
Dublin	–	–	–	–	–	–	–	–	–	–
Total	3	2	2	0	0	9	[20]	28	61	125

Table 3.5: Plundering provisions, 1846: CONNAUGHT, county monthly totals
(official statistics)

	April	May	June	July	Aug.	Sept.	Oct.*	Nov.	Dec.	Total
Galway	1	2	3	–	–	1	[5]	5	5	[22]
Sligo	–	1	–	–	–	–	[3]	1	5	[10]
Roscommon	–	–	–	–	–	–	[1]	1	3	[5]
Leitrim	–	–	1	–	–	1	[1]	2	–	[5]
Mayo	–	–	–	–	–	–	[2]	–	–	[2]
Total	1	3	4	0	0	2	[12]	9	13	[44]

Source: National Archives of Ireland, CSO, OP, 1846/9
The individual provincial and county figures for October, which are not provided in the original return,
have been calculated with the assistance of the 'Return of the number of offences ... specially reported in
each county during each of the years from 1846 to 1850 inclusive' in *Return of outrages reported to the
Constabulary Office during the year 1850, with summaries for preceding years* [Dublin, 1851]), pp 14–15; see
Table 6.1

Poorly reported incidents at Milford Mills, county Carlow, on 13 May when 'a
vast concourse of men, women and children' congregated at John Alexander's
flour mills; at Killorglin, county Kerry, where a military escort was called for on
27 May to assist the police to overcome resistance to the transportation of meal
to Killarney; and in the seaside village of Narin, county Donegal, where the peasantry, who assembled in 'great numbers' in mid-May, 'proceeded to acts of vio-

lence towards the country people who were delivering potatoes' to four small vessels in the port, demonstrate that the crowd was not patient in all parts of the country, and not least in areas where little or no disorder was recorded by the Constabulary.[154] These were one-off incidents typically as the combination of imported food, state funded relief works and food aid ensured that the country was largely protest free during the traditional hungry months of summer. This did not mean that the inclination to appropriate foodstuffs, driven by fear or need, ceased. The seizure of Indian meal and wholemeal on carts originating in Galway, and of oatmeal *en route* from Frankford Mills, King's county, to Templemore, county Tipperary in June highlighted the unease of the populace.[155] The 'threaten[ed] turn out of a large portion of the labouring classes' at Tralee in July, which elicited a call for the army 'to protect the town from the possibility of plunder', was still more revealing of the appreciating alarm as it slowly dawned that the 1846 harvest would not bring relief. It was underlined by instances of dignified protest in county Mayo in August and September – the largest of which involved a crowd of 'poor persons' variously estimated at between 10,000 and 40,000 marching on Castlebar in August in an attempt to draw attention to the fact that 'there is not a stone of sound potatoes among the whole of us'. The crowd, estimated at 400–600, that descended on Belmullet was more assertive; the participants were only dissuaded from making good their threat 'to break open the stores' in the town 'upon the remonstrance of the Protestant clergyman, the parish priest and … the magistrate'. But they were not cowed; they vowed that there would be 'a great outbreak amongst them, and the consequences would be serious if some relief was not immediately given', and the reports of 'utter destitution' that emanated from these and other quarters indicated that they deserved to be taken seriously.[156]

Viewed in retrospect, it is clear that these incidents were a harbinger of the near island-wide surge in food protest that followed in the autumn and winter of 1846 (Tables 3.1–3.5; Map 5). The immediate cause was *phytophthora infestans* (the potato blight), which took a still-more severe toll on the potato harvest in 1846 than it had in 1845,[157] with the result that, having all but emulated the high level previously achieved in April by September, the number of reported incidents of plundering provisions climbed rapidly in the following months (Table 3.1). The first clear indication that the scale of food protest would scale new

---

154 Kinsella, 'Milford Mills', pp 327–8; Saunders to [Redington], 27 May 1846 (NAI, OP: Kerry, 1846/12/12033); Holmes to Redington, 20, 24 May 1846 (NAI, OP: Donegal, 1846/7/12225, 20031); also Wade to inspector general, 29 Apr. 1846 (NAI, OP: Cork, 1846/6/10739). 155 Kernan to Pennefeather, 25 June 1846 (NAI, OP: Galway, 1846/11/19291); Kelly to Pennefeather, 16 June 1846 (NAI, OP, King's county, 1846/15/18807). 156 Stokes to Redington, 13 July 1846 (NAI, OP: Kerry, 1846/12/20521); Dawson to Drombain, 18 Aug., Sligo to Bessborough, 24 Aug. 1846 (NAI, OP: Mayo, 1846/22681, 22895); Derenzi to [ ], 3 Sept. 1846 (NAI, OP: Roscommon, 1846/25/23401); Kerr, *The Catholic Church and the Famine*, p. 11. 157 *Freeman's Journal*, 10 Aug., 15 Sept. 1846; Peter Solar, 'The Great Famine was no ordinary subsistence crisis' in E.M. Crawford (ed.), *Famine: the Irish experience: subsistence crises and famines in Ireland* (Edinburgh, 1989), pp 112–33.

Figure 1: Food riot, Galway, June 1842 (*Illustrated London News*, 11 July 1842). This famous image provides a perspective on the involvement of women and children in food protest.

heights was provided in early August in county Cork; there the recognition that 'the potato crop is totally lost' (meaning 'the only resource left for feeding the population is ... manufactured corn') was a source of 'consternation' and 'despair'. A call aimed at 'assembling' the 'multitudes' in order to 'bring public opinion to bear against the landlords and to get down rents' was issued, only to be withdrawn when it was pointed out that it would excite 'alarms' that must have the effect of discouraging the government from 'devising means to alleviate our miseries and better our condition'. The confidence in our 'parental govern-ment' expressed in the printed announcement calling off the meeting (Fig. 2) was not shared by all, however, and within weeks there were reports of 'large bodies assembling in a disorderly and riotous manner, demanding peremptorily food or labour', and 'expressing a determination, in case of refusal, to help themselves whenever food is to be had'. Protest was initially concentrated in the south-west of the county, at Skibbereen and Ballinspittle most notably, but the fear that fuelled protest there was more broadly felt and, beginning in September, there were descents upon bread and bakers' shops in the eastern part of the county in Youghal, Cloyne, Killeagh and Castlemartyr, while there were also food related protests elsewhere in the county – in Macroom and Mitchelstown.[158]

158 Lucas to Little, 7 Aug., Pinch to Fleming, 31 July, Sheerin and Armstrong to [ ], 6 Aug.,

The interruption of the movement of grain by cart to Waterford; the interception by a crowd of 600–700 people of 'carts conveying oats for shipment at
Westport Quay', and a small surge in provisions plundering in county Limerick
in September demonstrated that the impulse to engage in food protest was not
confined to one area of the country. Indeed, a further large march in county
Mayo (on Ballina), and reports from the constabulary and resident magistrates in
Queen's county, King's county, Kilkenny and Kerry warning of the likelihood of
disturbance pointed to the expanded footprint of the evolving pattern of
protest.[159] The most celebrated incident took place at Dungarvan, county
Waterford, on 28 September. Several days of orchestrated protest culminated in
a confrontation, and a protester was fatally injured when the military fired on the
crowd that sought to rescue a number of men that had been taken into custody
for breaking into a corn store. This ensured the event was widely reported, but
the encounter was more notable for what it revealed of the determination of
divers urban, coastal and local communities of Munster, and elsewhere, to prevent the movement of grain; this was the implication of the interruption of the
shipping of grain out of Dungarvan and the suspension of 'the corn trade on the
river Blackwater between Lismore and Cappoquin and Youghal'.[160] Though on
first glance, a throwback to the form of food protest that was normative in
Munster in the eighteenth century, reports of seizures, clashes and confrontations
at various points along or close to the coastline – at Youghal, Ballynatray, Cloyne
and Killeagh (county Cork), Clashmore and Pilltown (county Waterford) for
example – in early October captured the anger of the coastal populace just as
fully as the plethora of disturbances that were more obviously famine related in
a variety of small and mid-size inland towns – Castlemartyr, Macroom,
Carrigtwohill, Midleton, Mallow, Castletownroche, Kilbrittain, Buttevant,

---

Knaresborough to Redington, 12 Aug., Burke to [ ], [Oct.?], Godby to Redington, 21 Sept.,
Rowland to Knaresborough, 23 Sept., Knaresborough to Redington, 22, 26 Sept., Bell to
Labouchere, 24 Sept., [ ] to [ ], 26 Sept., Gernon to [ ], 30 Sept. 1846 (NAI, OP: Cork,
1846/6/19081, 22023, 22025, 22047, 22265, 23595, 25895, 25897, 25979, 26195, 26591).   **159**
Howley to [Redington] (2), 18 Sept. 1846 (NAI, OP: Waterford, 1846/29/24081, 25035); High
sheriff to [ ], 10 Sept., Barron to Redington and enclosure, 22 Sept. 1846 (NAI, OP: Mayo,
1846/21/23951, 26829); Reports by sub-inspectors Aiken, 26 Sept., Pepper, 26 Sept., Warburton,
2 Oct., Memorial of four JPs to Lt. Col. Dunne, 2 Oct. 1846 (NAI, OP: Queen's county, 1846/24/
25921, 25923, 26411, 28115); Warburton to Labouchere, 8 Sept., Drought to Labouchere, 25 Sept.
1846 (NAI, OP: King's county, 1846/15/23459, 25913); Roberts to Labouchere, 24 Sept. 1846
(NAI, OP: Kilkenny, 1846/14/25789); McKeon to Redington, and enclosure, 25 Sept. 1846 (NAI,
OP: Kerry, 1846/12/26375).   **160** See Howley to [Redington], 14, 15, 18 Sept., Stuart de Decies,
22, 27 Sept. 1846 (NAI, OP: Waterford, 1846/29, 23895, 24069, 24081, 25731, 26193) for events
leading up to Dungarvan and William Fraher, 'The Dungarvan disturbances of 1846 and sequels'
in Des Cowman (ed.), *The Famine in Waterford* (Waterford, 1995), pp 137–52; *Freeman's Journal*,
28 Sept., 5 Oct. 1846; *Connaught Telegraph*, 7 Oct. 1846; *Nenagh Guardian*, 7 Oct. 1846; Howley
to Redington, 29 Sept., 3, 26 Oct., de Decies to Labouchere, 19 Sept., 2, 6, [7] Oct., Petition of
the merchants of Dungarvan, 1 Oct. 1846 (NAI, OP: Waterford, 1846/29/26315, 26913, 26755,
29359, 26395, 27153, 26961, 27299) for events in the town.

Glanworth – as 'workhouses and [the] meeting places of relief committees' became 'focal points for venting the anger and frustration provoked by rising unemployment and food prices'.[161]

By then, the country was in the throes of the most acute episode of food-related protest it had ever experienced (Map 5). Fuelled by desperation, given compelling voice by a member of the protesting crowd that assembled in Banagher, King's county, in September who pronounced that 'hunger will break through a stone wall', and by anger at the tardiness of both 'the government and the gentry ... in adopting measures to their relief,' the number of incidents of provisions 'plundering' surged. Having climbed to double and then to triple its previous maximum in October and November, it peaked at six times its April level in December (Table 3.1).[162] Moreover, it was possessed of a more extensive spatial footprint. A greater number of incidents (32) occurred in county Cork than county Tipperary (19) in October and November; King's and Queen's county, Galway and Limerick experienced ten or more incidents in the three months September to November, while the accelerating rate of protest meant that ten counties (Cork, Tipperary, Limerick, Donegal, Queen's county, King's county, Kilkenny, Longford, Westmeath and Galway) witnessed ten or more incidents in the three months October to December (Tables 3.1–3.4). Food protest was, as these figures attest, more acute in the south than elsewhere at this moment, but it is a measure of its prevalence that Queen's county, King's county, Kilkenny, Monaghan, and Sligo, which were largely undisturbed to this point, and Galway where the authorities had largely kept matters under control, all experienced multiple incidents in the later months of 1846. Similarly, attempts were made along the west coast – at Galway and Westport notably – to prevent exportation, and to inhibit the overland movement of foodstuffs in counties Waterford and Limerick. Only five counties (Antrim, Derry/Londonderry, Dublin, Clare and Mayo) reported no incidents of food protest in November and December, and only three counties (Antrim, Londonderry and Dublin) were protest free in 1846.[163]

---

161 *Freeman's Journal*, 28 Sept., 2, 5, 7, 8 Oct. 1846; *Nenagh Guardian*, 7 Oct. 1846; de Decies to [Labouchere], 6, [7] Oct. 1846 (NAI, OP: Waterford, 1846/29/26961, 27299); Donnelly, *The land and the people of nineteenth-century Cork*, pp 89–90; Ware to Redington, 20 Oct., Plunkett to Redington, 10 Nov., Lucas to Bernard, 9 Nov., Memorial of magistrates and inhabitants of Castletownroche, 17 Nov., Knaresborough to Redington, 18 Nov., Kingston to Percy, 20 Nov., 1846 (NAI, OP; Cork, 1846/6/28675, 31255, 31291, 32093, 32283, 32881); Joseph Hernon, 'A Victorian Cromwell: Sir Charles Trevelyan, the Famine and the age of improvement', *Eire-Ireland*, 22 (1987), 21. 162 Drought to Labouchere, 25 Sept. 1846 (NAI, OP: King's county, 1846/15/25913); [ ] to Redington, 30 Sept. 1846 (NAI, OP: Cork, 1846/6/26591). 163 *Nenagh Guardian*, 17 Oct. 1846; Report of Sub-inspector Pepper, 5 Oct., Cannon to Redington, 4 Nov., Report of Thomas Cannon RM, 10, 23 Nov., 10 Dec., Eager to de Vesci, 9 Dec. 1846 (NAI, OP: Queen's county, 1846/24/26935, 31207, 30573, 32619, 35379, 40867); Warburton to Labouchere, 8 Sept. 1846 (NAI, OP: King's county, 1846/15/23459); Ormond to Labouchere, 6 Dec., Innes to Labouchere, 7 Dec., Mosse to Labouchere, 11 Dec., Roberts to Labouchere, 24 Dec. 1846 (NAI, OP: Kilkenny, 1846/14/34107, 34227, 34973, 37173); Kirwan to Bessborough, 5 Oct. 1846, White to Drombain, 5 Oct. 1846 (NAI, OP, Galway: 1846/11, 26983, 27341); French to Redington, 7 Oct.

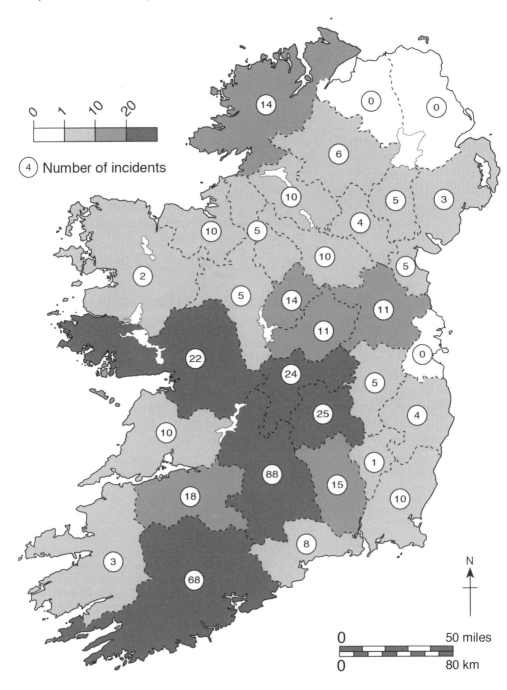

Map 5: Plundering provisions, 1846 (official statistics)

Table 4.1: Plundering provisions, 1847: monthly totals by province (CSO figures)

Province	Jan.	Feb.	Mar.	Apr.	May	June	July	Aug.	Sept.	Oct.	Nov.	Dec.	Total
Munster	55	13	4	13	66	24	13	6	6	19	9	9	237
Leinster	32	4		3	9	3	4	–	1	1	4	3	64
Ulster	29	1	2	2	7	4	2	1	–	–	–	–	48
Connaught	34	5	5	11	23	12	6	9	1	5	2	3	116
Total	150	23	11	29	105	43	25	16	8	25	15	15	465

Source: National Archives of Ireland, Registered papers, 1847: division 1, vols 1–2

Table 4.2: Plundering provisions, 1847: MUNSTER, county monthly totals
(CSO figures)

	Jan.	Feb.	Mar.	Apr.	May	June	July	Aug.	Sept.	Oct.	Nov.	Dec.	Total
Tipperary	25	–	–	–	16	–	1	–	–	1	1	2	46
Cork	12	11	1	3	14	10	4	2		5	1	2	65
Limerick	4	–	1	2	12	4	6		3	8	1	1	42
Kerry	7	1	2	2	11	5	1	1	3	5	5	2	45
Waterford	7	1	–	2	6	2	–	–	–	–	–	–	18
Clare	–	–	–	4	7	2	1	3	–	–	2	2	21
Total	55	13	4	13	66	23	13	6	6	19	10	9	237

Source: National Archives of Ireland, Registered papers, 1847: division 1, vols 1–2

In keeping with the rapidly changing pattern of food protest, Cork was surpassed as the most riot prone county by Tipperary in December 1846 when the two accounted for an imposing 92.6 per cent of the Munster total (and 41 per cent of the national total) of reported incidents of provisions plundering (Table 3.1, Map 5). The absence of monthly constabulary returns for 1847 complicates the task of tracking its evolving pattern, but the more select register of reports received at the Chief Secretary's Office confirms that food protest remained at a higher level in Munster than elsewhere, and indicates that the gap between Cork and Tipperary and other counties in the province had narrowed appreciably by January 1847 (Tables 4.1, 4.2).

It is not possible to establish the relative strength of the varieties of food protest embraced within 'provisions plundering' in the autumn and winter of

(NAI, OP: Monaghan, 1846/23/25157); O'Connor to Bessborough, 2 Oct. 1846 (NAI, OP: Sligo, 1846/26/26555); Cunningham, '"'Tis hard to argue starvation into quiet": protest and resistance, 1846–47', pp 16–17, 20.

Table 4.3: Plundering provisions, 1847: ULSTER, county monthly totals (CSO figures)

	Jan.	Feb.	Mar.	Apr.	May	June	July	Aug.	Sept.	Oct.	Nov.	Dec.	Total
Donegal	3	–	1	1	6	3	1	–	–	–	–	–	15
Fermanagh	4	–	1	–	–	–	–	–	–	–	–	–	5
Cavan	3	–	–	–	–	–	1	1	–	–	–	–	5
Armagh	4	1	–	1	–	–	–	–	–	–	–	–	6
Tyrone	5	–	–	–	–	1	–	–	–	–	–	–	6
Monaghan	5	–	–	–	1	–	–	–	–	–	–	–	6
Down	2	–	–	–	–	–	–	–	–	–	–	–	2
L'derry	–	–	–	–	–	–	–	–	–	–	–	–	0
Antrim	3	–	–	–	–	–	–	–	–	–	–	–	3
Total	29	1	2	2	7	4	2	1	0	0	0	0	48

Source: National Archives of Ireland, Registered papers, 1847: division 1, vols 1–2

Table 4.4: Plundering provisions, 1847: LEINSTER, county monthly totals (CSO figures)

	Jan.	Feb.	Mar.	Apr.	May	June	July	Aug.	Sept.	Oct.	Nov.	Dec.	Total
Queen's co.	4	–	–	–	–	–	–	–	–	–	–	1	5
King's co.	4	1	–	1	3	–	–	–	–	–	1	–	10
Kilkenny	6	1	–	–	–	–	1	–	–	–	1	–	9
Longford	3	–	–	–	–	–	–	–	1	–	–	–	4
Meath	2	–	–	–	–	1	–	–	–	–	1	1	5
W'meath	1	–	–	–	–	1	1	–	–	–	–	–	3
Wexford	–	1	–	2	4	1	2	–	–	–	1	–	11
Kildare	5	–	–	–	–	–	–	–	1	–	–	–	6
Louth	2	–	–	–	1	–	–	–	–	–	–	–	3
Wicklow	2	1	–	–	1	–	–	–	–	–	–	–	4
Carlow	–	–	–	–	–	–	–	–	–	–	–	–	0
Dublin	4	–	–	–	–	–	–	–	–	–	–	–	4
Total	33	4	0	3	9	3	4	0	1	1	4	2	64

Source: National Archives of Ireland, Registered papers, 1847: division 1, vols 1–2

1846–7, but it is demonstrable that conventional food rioting continued. An arresting instance occurred in Carrick-on-Suir, county Tipperary, on 30 September when 'a man … marched in front of a large concourse of the people with a large staff in his hand on the top of which was placed two loaves of bread'.[164] There were other incidents in the same county when grain, flour and other provisions were appropriated, but they were not on the same scale as the interventions that

164 Briscoe to Redington, 30 Sept. 1846 (NAI, OP: Tipperary, 1846/27/26371).

Table 4.5: Plundering provisions, 1847: CONNAUGHT, county monthly totals
(CSO figures)

	Jan.	Feb.	Mar.	Apr.	May	June	July	Aug.	Sept.	Oct.	Nov.	Dec.	Total
Galway	15	3	3	4	13	4	3	3	–	2	1	3	54
Sligo	2	–	–	–	3	4	1	–	–	–	–	–	10
Roscommon	4	–	–	–	–	1	–	–	–	–	1	–	6
Leitrim	2	–	–	1	–	1	–	–	–	–	–	–	4
Mayo	11	2	2	6	7	2	2	6	1	3	–	–	42
Total	34	5	5	11	23	12	6	9	1	5	2	3	116

Source: Source: National Archives of Ireland, Registered papers, 1847: division 1, vols 1–2

had taken place in mid-April.[165] Most were conducted by crowds that were small by comparison with those previously reported; a large proportion (including the practice of 'exacting contributions in wheat from farmers' in the barony of Lower Ormond) had more in common with agrarian protest than orthodox food protest; and some were evidently spur-of-the-moment interventions. Yet the sheer number of incidents (in November and December particularly) lends credence to the view advanced in county Tipperary that the populace was driven by the conviction that they must exert every sinew in order just to survive: 'the general belief that this country must depend entirely on its own resources till next January, ... create[d] a sense, and in some respect a well-founded alarm among the destitute class that the exportation of so considerable a portion of the only food they have here to depend on would leave them without any'.[166]

The mood was comparable in Leinster, or at least in those counties – Queen's and King's counties, Kilkenny, Longford and Meath – that accounted for more than two-thirds of the province's total of plundering provisions incidents in the winter of 1846–7 (Table 3.4). In King's county, for example, those identified as 'languishing poor and ... thoughtless labourers' embarked in October on a sequence of actions aimed at disrupting the movement of flour, and at preventing its transportation, via Shannon Harbour, out of the county.[167] Meanwhile, in nearby county Galway, which was increasingly disturbed (Table 3.5), a compa-

165 Stoney to [Redington], 5 Sept., Harvey to Redington, 19 Oct. 1846 (NAI, OP: Tipperary, 1846/27/23443, 28369).   166 Kelly to Redington, 16 Oct., William [ ], Nenagh, to Redington, 4 Nov., Worrall to Gallby, 16 Dec., Osborne to [Redington], 21 Dec., French to [ ], 18 Dec. 1846 (NAI, OP: Tipperary, 1846/27/28073, 30381, 36745, 37205, 35923). Comparable sentiment was ascribed to the large crowd that successfully resisted the movement of grain to Limerick: 'they would not suffer the corn to go to Limerick ... the potatoes were all gone, they had nothing to live on but grain, and while they were starving it was all sending from the country, and no food of any kind coming back in return': Hutcheson (?) to Redington, 1 Nov. 1846 (NAI, OP: Limerick, 1846/17/29875).   167 Neal Brown to [Redington], 18 Oct., 2 Nov., Rosse to [Redington], 21, 29

rable series of interventions was pursued in an attempt to inhibit the transport of 'meal ... out of the town' of Galway, its movement within the county, and between King's county and Galway city. As a result, not only were the roads in parts of the county deemed 'totally unsafe to convey provisions', 'cuts' rendered certain routes unpassable.[168]

Officials and landowners in the main food-producing counties protested in their communications with Dublin Castle, and in their responses to calls for protection from millers, merchants and dealers, that they did not have the resources to guarantee the safe storage and transport of foodstuffs. Yet, as evidenced by the pattern of events in county Tipperary, their determination that there would be no repeat of what had happened in April was as consequential as the deterioration in order in ensuring, as 1846 drew to a close and 1847 began, that a majority of the provisions plundering incidents in that county (and further afield) bore an increasingly closer resemblance to distress-induced crime and agrarian protest than traditional food protest. As a result, there was an increased disposition among the respectable to conclude that the country was descending into lawlessness.[169] 'The country', Edward Jones wrote the lord lieutenant from Clonmel on 3 January,

> is in as state of nearly perfect anarchy. ... the people ... appear to believe that the restraining power of the law is removed. The well-disposed and industrious feel uneasy for the safety of their properties. They know and hear of cattle and sheep being killed and carried away, of boats and carts being plundered, and of assaults and petty robberies being daily committed on almost every road, and at the same time they are not ignorant that scarcely the least exaction is being made to check such practices.[170]

The knight of Kerry was no less activated by the targeting of cattle in the southwest, while the third earl of Rosse, writing from Parsonstown, King's county, advised the chief secretary, Henry Labouchere, in December that the 'indiscriminate system of plunder' then obtaining could only be combated by 'a really efficient police system'. What all three failed to acknowledge was that the situa-

Oct., Drought to Redington, 24 Oct., Kelly to Redington, 25 Oct., 2, 26 Nov., 14 Dec., McMullen to Labouchere, 2 Nov. 1846 (NAI, OP: King's county, 1846/15/28373, 30075, 28819, 29753, 28893, 28931, 30145, 33027, 35275, 35271, 300087).   **168** Blake to Redington, 7 Oct., Kernan to Redington, 12, 13 Oct., Lawrence to Labouchere, 14, 18, 22, 27 Oct., Fitzgerald to Redington, 8 Nov. 1846 (NAI, OP: Galway, 1846/11/27843, 27635, 27731, 29767, 228027, 28513, 29131, 30877). Cuts were also made to roads in county Cork: Lees to Redington, 4 Dec. 1846 (NAI, OP: Cork, 1846/6/33959).   **169** For the attitudes of local magistrates and landowners, see Public notice by magistrates, 28 Sept. 1846, Merchants of Carrick-on-Suir, 29 Sept., Stoney to Redington, 12 Nov., Glengall to Labouchere, 25 Nov., Glengall to [ ], 4 Dec. 1846, Magistrates of Tipperary to Labouchere, 11 Jan. 1847, Ryan to Labouchere, 5 Jan. 1847, Copy report to Captain Ogle, 14 Jan., McEvoy to [Labouchere], 3 Feb. 1847 (NAI, OP: Tipperary, 1846/27/22907, 26547, 31477, 33123, 33961, 1847/27, 152, 192, 489); *Nenagh Guardian*, 17 Oct. 1846; *Freeman's Journal*, 12 Oct. 1846.   **170** Jones to Bessborough, 3 Jan. 1847 (NAI, OP: Tipperary, 1847/27/72).

tion was equally difficult in other parts as famine protest became progressively less structured as it approached its historic peak in the mid-winter of 1846–7.[171]

Though the transformation from orchestrated protest, which was in the ascendant in county Tipperary in April, to the less disciplined forms of protest that were increasingly prevalent in the winter of 1846–7, was stark, Tipperary was not unique in this respect. It can also be detected in county Galway.[172] The most notable index of the trend in Queen's county is provided by the numbers that were tried and imprisoned for 'larceny' at the spring and summer assizes in 1847, but the change is also identifiable elsewhere in the midlands and in the mid-west. [173] In county Clare, for example, protest commenced in mid-September with a march by 'a large body of persons, between two and three thousand', through the streets of Ennis, who did 'not evince the slightest disposition to commit a breach of the peace, but … to publicly exhibit their destitute condition'.[174] However, when it emerged in mid-October that relief was insufficient, elements of the population responded in a more assertive manner.[175] There were strikingly fewer incidents of food plunder in county Clare than in county Tipperary or Cork (Table 3.2), but this registered less strongly on the community as 'the appalling apprehension of famine' incited a spate of violent interventions – the shooting of horses notably – targeted at discouraging 'rich farmers from disposing of their corn'.[176] There was an increase also in allied forms of intimidation of the kind associated with agrarian protest, such as that perpetrated by a gang of about ten men, armed with guns, dressed in women's clothes and sporting 'blackened faces' who threatened Richard Floyd of Ballycar and beat his workmen while conveying a warning 'not to thresh or sell any more corn'.[177] This, and other like events, encouraged officials to redouble their appeals to Dublin Castle for support; at a meeting in Newmarket-on-Fergus in October magistrates called for additional troops 'to enforce submission to the laws and to put down that system of terrorism which', they maintained, 'is paralysing every relation of society in the country'.[178]

This was seriously to misinterpret events, even in county Clare where orthodox food rioting was conspicuously weak, as the discipline that had long defined

171 Rosse to Labouchere, 9 Dec. 1846 (NAI, OP: King's county, 1846/15/34773); Knight of Kerry to Redington, 28 Dec. 1846 (NAI, OP: Kerry, 1846/12/37931). 172 Robbie to [ ], 2 Nov. 1846 (NAI, OP: 1846/11/30057). 173 A list of cases and result of cases tried … at [Queen's] county assizes, spring, summer 1847 (NAI, OP: Queen's county, 1847/24/188, 262); Elliott to Redington, 12 June 1847 (NAI, OP: Queen's county, 1847/254). 174 Leyne to Redington, 15 Sept. 1846 (NAI, OP: Clare, 1846/5/23897). 175 Leyne to Redington, 16 Sept. 1846 (NAI, OP: Clare, 1846/5/23947); *Freeman's Journal*, 15 Oct. 1846. 176 Leyne to Redington, 20, 21, 22, 23, 28, 29 Sept., 12 Oct. 1846 (NAI, OP: Clare, 1846/5/25309, 25727, 25629, 25631, 26345, 266693, 27697); *Freeman's Journal*, 19 Oct., 4 Nov. 1846; Ciaran Ó Murchadha, 'The years of the Great Famine' in Matthew Lynch and Patrick Nugent (eds), *Clare: history and society* (Dublin, 2008), pp 248–50; Ó Murchadha, *Sable wings over the land*, pp 74–83. 177 Leyne to Redington, 21 Sept. 1846 (NAI, OP: Clare, 1846/5/25309); *Freeman's Journal*, 7 Oct. 1846. 178 Memorial of the magistrates of Newmarket-on-Fergus, 20 Oct. 1846 (NAI, SOC, OP: Clare, 1846/5/29333).

food protest was not entirely absent. The actions of 'an assembly of labourers to the number of from 400 to 500 at Clarecastle, who... prevented the shipment of some cargoes of oatmeal for Limerick'; of the crowd of one hundred men later the same month who compelled a miller at Scariff to sell meal at below cost and who broke into a corn store in nearby Tuamgraney; and of a still larger 'mob of about 2,000', which intercepted a boat bearing oatmeal and flour on the Shannon, attacked a mill at O'Brien's Bridge in the course of which they warned farmers not to sell their corn there, extracted a price of sale promise, and 'plundered a [baker's] shop in the village of all the bread it contained' demonstrate that crowds had not entirely forsaken traditional forms of food protest, such as *taxation populaire* that was now seldom resorted to.[179] This was the case also at Banagher, King's county, Castlecomer, county Kilkenny and Sligo town in September when 'large masses of men of the labouring class' protesting at the lack of employment and food were persuaded to disperse by the assurances of local officials that steps would be taken to alleviate their plight.[180] The recourse to the quintessential urban phenomenon of bread rioting provides a still more striking illustration of the persistence of traditional forms of protest though the greater propensity for violence is consistent with the conclusion that it too was in decline.

Following its re-commencement in October 1846, bread carts and bakers' shops were targeted in Monaghan, Limerick, Newry, Armagh, Mountmellick, Sligo, Birr, Banagher and Kilkenny.[181] Similar protests, albeit on a larger scale, were pursued in Belfast on 18 December 1846; in Dublin in January 1847, when 'a great number of bakeries in the neighbourhood of the Liberty as well as in the northern ends of the city' (King Street, Church Street and Pill Lane) were plundered; in Cork in February when an armed mob of labourers attacked bread shops in the city; in Youghal in April, involving a crowd of five hundred 'starving' people, and in Drogheda in May when several hundred 'famished-looking beings' robbed bakeries and provision stores.[182] Moreover, small towns and vil-

179 Hennessey to Revenue Commissioners, 7 Oct., Thomas Bailey to Redington, 31 Oct., John Ryan to [ ], 29 Oct., James Denniston to [ ], 29 Oct. 1846 (NAI, OP: Clare, 1846/5/27885, 29941, 29929, 29933). These were elements of a more sustained effort to prevent the movement of foodstuffs along the Shannon: see Eiríksson, 'Food supply and food riots', pp 77–85; Ciarán Ó Murchadha, 'The onset of famine: county Clare, 1845–1846', *The Other Clare*, 19 (1995), 29; Kerr, *The Catholic Church and the Famine*, p. 13.   **180** Drought to Labouchere, 25 Sept. 1846 (NAI, OP: King's county, 1846/15/25913); Roberts to Labouchere, 24 Sept. 1846 (NAI, OP: Kilkenny, 1846/14/25789); O'Connor to Bessborough, 2 Oct. 1846 (NAI, OP: Sligo, 1846/26/26555).   **181** French to Redington, 7 Oct. 1846 (NAI, OP: Monaghan, 1846/23/27157); Kidd et al. to [ ], 17 Dec. 1846 (NAI, OP: Armagh, 1846/2/37127); *Freeman's Journal*, 2, 5, 16, 19 Oct., 4 Nov. 1846; *Anglo-Celt*, 11 Dec. 1846; *Belfast News Letter*, 2 Feb. 1847; Ormond to Labouchere, 6 Dec. 1846 (NAI, OP: Kilkenny, 1846/14/34107).   **182** *Nation*, 26 Dec. 1846, 8, 13 Feb. 1847; *Belfast News Letter*, 11 Jan. 1847; Christine Kinealy, *This great calamity: the Irish Famine, 1845–52* (Dublin, 1994), p. 69; Christine Kinealy and Gerard MacAtasney, *The hidden famine: poverty, hunger and sectarianism in Belfast, 1840–50* (London, 2000), pp 62–3; *Freeman's Journal*, 11, 12 Jan. 1847; *Tralee Chronicle and Killarney Echo*, 16 Jan. 1847; *Cork Examiner*, 15 Jan., 5 Feb. 1847; Gearoid Ó Tuathaigh, 'An age of distress and reform: 1800 to 1860' in Art Cosgrave (ed.), *Dublin through the*

lages were not exempted, and meal stores and bakeries were targeted in the early months of 1847 in locations as far apart as Markethill (county Armagh) in January; Burtonport (county Donegal) in January and April; Tarbert (county Kerry) in February; Castlemartyr (county Cork) in March, Youghal (county Cork) in April, Knockraha and Midleton (county Cork) in June, and Athlone (county Westmeath) also in June.[183]

Yet as revealing as these incidents are of the communal solidarity that sustained food protest over a century and a half, they were exceeded by the number in which despair manifestly prevailed over community. The impact of the harsh economic environment, which drove food protest to record levels in the winter of 1846–7, was critical in this respect. It also prompted an increase in organized agrarian protest (by bodies such as the Terry Alts in the mid-west, and the Molly Maguires in the north midlands, south Ulster and the north-west); it encouraged employment protests and riots, attacks on those labouring for low wages on public works schemes, and overt acts of intimidation, such as the stipulation 'that no corn is permitted to go to market along the high roads', that were distant from the traditional style of food protest.[184] It was perhaps inevitable that this should happen as 'the bonds of society ... dissolved' under the weight of the Great Famine.[185] As a result, the politics of provisions became increasingly confrontational as landowners and officials prioritized the maintenance of law and order; farmers, millers, merchants and dealers continued to chase after the highest price; and the populace did what was necessary to secure access to food. Definably orthodox food protest could and did continue, as has been established, but it no longer functioned as a distinctive phenomenon but as a constituent of what officials tellingly denominated 'plundering provisions'.

ages (Dublin, 1988), p. 102; Graham Davis, 'Making history: John Mitchel and the Great Famine' in P. Hyland and Neil Sammels (eds), *Irish writing: exile and subversion* (London, 1991), p. 108; Cunningham, ""Tis hard to argue starvation into quiet"', p. 22; *Nation*, 22 May 1847. **183** NAI, Registered papers, 1847, Division 1, vol. 1 2/3 (Armagh); 7/126 (Donegal); 6/507, 6/567, 6/897 (Cork); 30/254 (Westmeath); Sandes to Redington, 13 Feb. 1847 (NAI, OP: Kerry, 1847/12/119); Testimony of attack on Youghal bakery, 19 Apr., Osborne to Redington, 3 June 1847 (NAI, OP: Cork, 1847/6/655, 902); Routh to Greaves, 5 Jan. 1847 (NAI, OP: Kerry, 1847/12/21). It may be observed of the latter document that it is misfiled with documents appertaining to county Kerry. **184** Cunningham, ""Tis hard to argue starvation into quiet": protest and resistance, 1846–47', pp 20–1; Breandán Mac Suibhne, '"Bastard Ribbonism": the Molly Maguires, the uneven failure of entitlement and the politics of post-Famine adjustment' in idem and Enda Delany (eds), *Ireland's great famine and popular politics* (London and New York, 2016), pp 192–7; Kenny to Redington, 21 Oct., Leyne to Redington, 11 Nov. 1846 (NAI, OP: Clare, 1846/5/28843, 31485); Hornby to Redington, 6 Nov. 1846 (NAI, OP: Galway, 1846/11/31653); Hornsby to Redington, 5, 12 Nov., Walker to Redington, 26 Nov. 1846 (NAI, OP: Limerick, 1846/17/30671, 31483, 33273; NAI, OP: Leitrim, 1846/16/5229, 27639; NAI, OP: Roscommon, 25/5913, 8253, 19971; NAI, OP: Cavan, 1846/4/19769; NAI, OP: Armagh, 1846/2/36775); Coulson to Labouchere, 25 Sept., 31 Dec. 1846 (NAI, OP: Tyrone, 1846/28/25925, 37917); de Decies to Redington, 28 Sept. 1846 (NAI, OP: Waterford, 1846/29/26341). **185** The phrase belongs to Revd James McHale, a parish priest in county Mayo, in a public letter to the editor of the *Freeman's Journal*, 12 Oct. 1846.

'*Black '47*'

The mid-winter peak in provisions plundering contracted dramatically, and in some counties, came to a complete cessation in February 1847. A tabulation of the incidents reported to the Chief Secretary's Office suggest that it fell back nationally in February–March to a level comparable to that registered in April–May 1846 (Tables 3.1, 4.1). What this meant in practice was that while food protesters remained active in parts of Munster and Connaught – counties Cork, Galway and Mayo notably – the availability of public works dissuaded potential protesters in most of Ulster and Leinster and large parts of Connaught and Munster. This proved short-lived, however, as the premature suspension (beginning in March) of the public works initiatives that had provided as many as 700,000 men with the wherewithal with which to purchase food in 1846–7 sparked a sharp rise in protest as those in need were left with no alternative, the resident magistrate at Ennis reported to Dublin Castle, but to 'help themselves'.[186] Identifiable in the slight bounce in the 'plundering provisions' statistics for April for Munster and Connaught, the ensuing surge peaked in May at a level not far in arrears of that previously experienced in the winter of 1846–7, before falling back in June and July as initial resistance to the provision of direct relief (soup kitchens) faded (Table 4.1).[187] Despite this, protest did not revert to the low level witnessed in the summer of 1846, though it was more provincially concentrated with Munster and Connaught accounting for some 80 per cent of the total in the months of July, August and September, and 85 per cent in the three months October–December (Tables 4.2–4.5). The picture was inevitably more variegated at county level in the provinces of Leinster and Ulster (Tables 4.3 and 4.4), but the dramatic fall off registered there was replicated in counties Roscommon (Connaught) and Tipperary (Munster) (Tables 4.2 and 4.5). One must, of course, allow for the possibility that the data extracted from the registers of the Chief Secretary's Office (Table 4.1–4.5, 5.1) for 1847 under-represent the level of protest. The summary returns assembled by the Constabulary Office for 1847 (Table 5.2) suggest that the number of food plundering incidents might have reached twice the level registered in 1846, but because a comparison of the Constabulary returns with those registered by the Chief Secretary's Office sug-

186 The reduction in employment on public works, which commenced 20 Mar., had arrived at a point by the end of June when all but 28,000 of the 700,000 once employed had been discharged: Peter Gray, *The Irish famine: new horizons* (London, 1995), p. 58; RM (Ennis) to Redington, 25 Mar., 7 May 1847 (NAI, OP: Clare, 1847/5/279, 523); for further illustration of the impact of the suspension of relief in county Clare see: NAI, OP: Clare, 1847/5/ 301, 312, 314, 345, 484, 490, 523; and in county Cork, see Donnelly, *Land and the people of nineteenth-century Cork*, pp 89–91.
187 See, for examples of resistance in county Clare, O'Brien to Redington, 12 May, RM (Ennistymon) to Redington, 31 May 1847 (NAI, OP: Clare, 1847/5/490279, 523); *Nation*, 15 May 1847; *Leinster Express*, 22 May 1847; *Freeman's Journal*, 29 May 1847; in Cork, Green to Redington, 7 May, Outrage report, 14 May, Grant to inspector general, 7 July 1847 (NAI, OP: Cork, 1747/6/745, 786, 1264); *Cork Examiner*, 21 June, 10 Sept. 1847, and in county Louth: NAI, Registered papers, 1847, division 1, vol. 1, 20/110, 112.

gests that the former includes the offence denominated 'provisions taken', which were not the result of crowd interventions, the smaller dataset is a more reliable guide to crowd protest. It is not possible even to speculate as to the number of incidents of 'provisions plundering' that might be categorized as 'food riots', but the number of incidents entered in the CSO registers suggest that the order of the food protest that took place in 1847 was comparable to that which took place in 1846.

Table 5.1: Plundering provisions, 1846–50: annual totals by county and province (CSO figures*)

	1846	*1847*	*1848*	*1849*	*1850*	*Total*
			MUNSTER			
Clare	10	21	5	4	3	43
Cork	68	65	7	3	–	143
Kerry	3	45	3	–	1	52
Limerick	18	42	3	8	3	74
Tipperary	88	46	13	6	6	159
Waterford	8	18	3	2	1	32
Total	195	237	34	23	14	503
			LEINSTER			
Carlow	1	4	–	–	–	5
Dublin	–	4	1	–	–	5
Kildare	5	6	–	–	–	11
Kilkenny	15	9	–	–	–	24
King's co.	24	10	1	–	–	35
Longford	14	4	1	–	–	19
Louth	5	3	1	–	–	9
Meath	11	5	2	–	–	18
Queen's co.	25	5	2	–	–	32
Westmeath	11	3	1	–	–	15
Wexford	10	11	1	–	–	22
Wicklow	4	4	–	–	–	8
Total	125	68	10	0	0	203
			CONNAUGHT			
Galway	22	55	13	5	–	95
Leitrim	5	4	–	–	–	9
Mayo	2	42	13	8	1	66
Roscommon	5	5	–	–	–	10
Sligo	10	10	4	–	–	24
Total	44	116	30	13	1	204

	1846	*1847*	*1848*	*1849*	*1850*	*Total*
			ULSTER			
Antrim	–	3	1	–	–	4
Armagh	5	6	–	–	–	11
Cavan	10	5	3	–	–	18
Donegal	14	15	2	–	–	31
Down	3	2	2	–	–	7
Fermanagh	10	5	–	–	–	15
L'Derry	–	–	–	–	–	0
Monaghan	4	6	–	–	–	10
Tyrone	6	6	–	–	–	12
Total	52	48	8	0	0	108
National total	416	469	82	36	15	1018

Source: This table combines the official returns for 1846 (NAI, CSO, OP, 1846/9), with the incidents reported to the Chief Secretary's Office (NAI, CSO Registered papers, 1847–50: division 1, vols 1–2)

Table 5.2: Plundering provisions: annual totals by county and province, 1846–50 (official figures)

	1846	*1847*	*1848*	*1849*	*1850*	*Total*
			MUNSTER			
Clare	10	44	17	3	2	76
Cork co.	67	141	23	5	–	236
Cork city	1	8	–	–	–	9
Kerry	3	57	5	3	–	68
Limerick co.	16	108	25	23	1	173
Limerick city	2	35	–	–	2	39
Tipperary	88	109	36	16	5	254
Waterford co.	8	48	9	3	–	68
Waterford city	–	–	1	–	–	1
Total	195	550	116	53	10	924
			LEINSTER			
Carlow	1	7	–	–	–	8
Dublin	–	30	4	1	–	35
Kildare	5	17	2	–	–	24
Kilkenny	15	30	2	–	–	47
King's co.	24	19	3	2	–	48
Longford	14	21	4	–	–	39
Louth	5	16	2	–	–	23
Meath	11	26	6	1	–	44
Queen's co	25	17	8	1	–	51

	1846	1847	1848	1849	1850	Total
Westmeath	11	15	2	–	–	28
Wexford	10	16	13	1	–	40
Wicklow	4	7	–	–	–	11
Total	125	221	46	6	0	398

CONNAUGHT

	1846	1847	1848	1849	1850	Total
Galway	22	102	34	10	–	168
Leitrim	5	30	1	–	–	36
Mayo	2	41	23	21	–	87
Roscommon	5	31	2	1	–	39
Sligo	10	18	3	–	–	31
Total	44	222	63	32	0	361

ULSTER

	1846	1847	1848	1849	1850	Total
Antrim	–	13	1	–	–	14
Armagh	5	32	1	–	–	38
Cavan	10	19	2	1	–	32
Donegal	14	27	2	–	–	43
Down	3	21	1	–	–	25
Fermanagh	10	17	1	–	–	28
L'Derry	–	16	–	1	–	17
Monaghan	4	18	1	–	–	23
Tyrone	6	35	–	1	–	42
Total	52	198	9	3	0	262
National total	416	1191	234	94	10	1945

Source: This table combines the returns for 1846 (Returns of outrages reported to the Constabulary Office during 1846 (NAI, OP, 1846/9) with the official returns assembled by the Constabulary Office (NAI, CSO/ICR/1, *Return of outrages reported to the Constabulary Office ... 1848, 1849, 1850* (Dublin, 1849–51)).

This is not to imply that the changes underway in the winter of 1846–7 did not intensify in the spring and summer of 1847 as the distinction that one could draw in the spring of 1846 between food protest and famine-induced crime narrowed still further. The most striking manifestation of this is the surge in sheep and cattle stealing, but the nature of what was taking place is depicted more precisely in the report from the spring assizes at Tralee, county Kerry, which adverted to the 'great and unusual number of petty thefts committed on all kinds and descriptions of property'.[188] Tralee was not exceptional in this respect, moreover. The 'report of criminal cases disposed at Parsonstown quarter sessions' in the summer of 1847 lists 91 cases of theft, while the 221 individuals charged with livestock theft (cows 92; sheep 110; horses 8, and pigs 11) at Kanturk, county

188 Drummond to Redington, 20 Jan. 1847 (NAI, OP: Kerry, 1847/12/62).

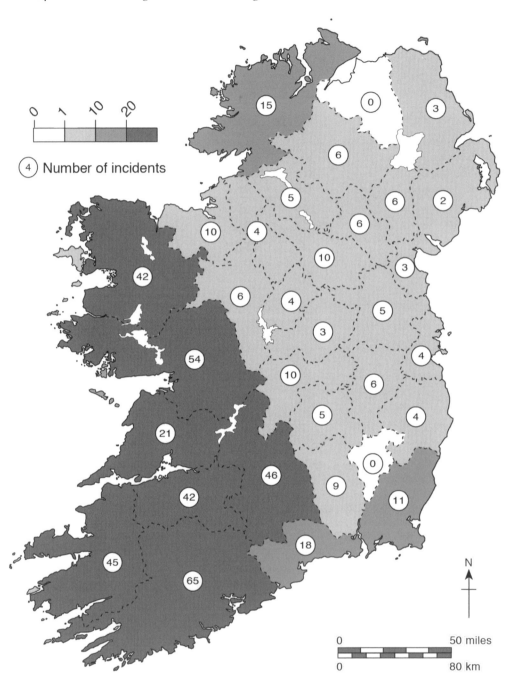

Map 6: Plundering provisions, 1847 (CSO figures)

Cork, in July exceeded those pursued for 'minor larceny' (191), 'assault' (166) and 'burglary' (39).[189]

While the willingness of the courts to hand down short sentences in all but the most aggravating cases indicate that the authorities were disposed to show these offenders some understanding (albeit not quite of the order once extended to food rioters), the courts went about their business against a backdrop of continuing food protest. The crowds that engaged in this pursuit attacked cars and carts ferrying meal, examples of which occurred in Munster (Clare, Cork, Kerry, Limerick, Tipperary and Waterford); in Connaught (Galway, Mayo, Roscommon and Sligo), and Leinster (Kildare, Louth and Queen's county).[190] The allied practice of targeting canal barges and boats on the inland canals and riverine waterways was also pursued when the opportunity presented, and there were reported incidents in counties Armagh and Fermanagh as well as Kildare, King's county, Queen's county, Clare, Limerick and Tipperary.[191] Bakeries and meal stores were another familiar target for the hungry,[192] as were mills, though the deployment of (armed) guards combined with other precautions to ensure there were fewer reports of mills being attacked and fewer importunate pleas from millers and merchants for military and police protection in 1847.[193]

By comparison, other examples of direct action may have increased in the heartlands of food protest. The practice of crowds descending on urban centres – previously prevalent in Munster in the autumn of 1846 – proved particularly alarming. The urgent call for military reinforcements to protect Tarbert and Ballylongford, county Kerry, in February was one manifestation of the fear this generated, but concerns were also expressed in respect of Killorglin, Cahirciveen and Listowel caused by 'large assemblages', dismayed at the suspension of public works, 'calling out for employment or blood'.[194] The crowds that engaged in

189 Report of criminal cases disposed at Parsonstown quarter sessions commencing 30 June 1847 (NAI, OP: King's county, 1847/15/455); Report of the Kanturk quarter sessions, 2 July 1847 (NAI, OP: Cork, 1847/6/1007); see also *Freeman's Journal*, 29 May 1847 for proceedings in county Clare. **190** NAI, Registered papers, 1847, division 1, vols 1–2, 6/199, 822, 1106, 1149 (Cork); 12/316, 318, 320 (Kerry); 17/506, 571, 615, 656, 782, 1059, 1075, 1078, 1921 (Limerick); 27/82, 2425 (Tipperary); 29/182 (Waterford); 13/1 (Kildare); 20/35 (Louth); 24/387, 392 (Queen's co.); 11/210, 322, 482, 522, 752, 848, 1181, 1197 (Galway); 21/245, 318, 403 (Mayo); 25/54, 766 (Roscommon); 26/199 (Sligo); Clanohy to Redington, 12 May, Outrage report, 12 July 1847 (NAI, OP: Cork, 1847/6/773, 1038); Police report, 14 Apr., 17 Oct. 1847 (OP: Clare, 1847/5/389, 1122); *Cork Examiner*, 21 June 1847; *Nation*, 15 May 1847. **191** NAI, Registered papers, 1847, division 1, vols 1–2, 2/53 (Armagh); 10/35, 85 (Fermanagh); 13/10, 15, 20, 24, 102, 105, 190, 195, 212, 220 (Kildare); 15/425 (Kilkenny); 24/387 (Queen's co.); 5/612 (Clare); 17/784 (Limerick); 27/1077 (Tipperary); Boyle to Redington, 23 Jan., 13, 20 Dec. 1847 (NAI, OP: Kildare, 1847/13/24, 213, 220). **192** Above, pp 78–9; *Leinster Express*, 22 May 1847. **193** NAI, Registered papers, 1847, division 1, vols 1–2, 1/15 (Antrim); 2/108, 147, 193 (Armagh); 7/136, 151 (Donegal); 5/367 (Clare); 6/13 (Cork); 13/64 (Kildare); 14/17, 32 (Kilkenny); 20/19 (Louth); 17/511 (Limerick); 29/70 (Waterford); 16/50 (Leitrim); 26/194 (Sligo); Bannatyne to Redington, 31 July 1847 (OP: Clare, 1847/5/1213); *Nation*, 15 May 1847. **194** Sandes to Redington, 13 Feb., Memorial of justices of the peace, 26 May, Cheevers to Redington, 22 Sept. 1847 (NAI, OP: Kerry, 1847/12/119, comparable protests in county Cork – at Charleville, Youghal, Castlemartyr, Mallow, Killeagh, Kanturk and elsewhere – and in counties Clare and Limerick, were regarded with only slightly less trepidation; but the most revealing illustration of the galvanizing impact that the cessation of public works had on protest occurred in county Wexford.[195] Hitherto, only moderately impacted by food protest, the suspension of public works in the spring of 1847 prompted 'provision riots' at Enniscorthy, Ferns, Oulart, Gorey, Taghmon and New Ross involving crowds ranging from two hundred to a thousand. At Enniscorthy, for example, on 24 May a crowd descended 'from the country demanding labour, or a sufficient quantity of food, and stating that if their demand was not immediately complied with, they would assemble in greater force, and help themselves'. Few of these incidents culminated in violent scenes as the protesters were amenable to persuasion that help would be forthcoming if they retired. This did not prevent disorder at New Ross in mid-May or deter other crowds, 'some amounting to 1000, demanding money, or taking what they think will suit them', but it demonstrated that the reciprocity that was integral to a functioning 'moral economy' survived as more than just a memory in county Wexford (Map 6).[196]

County Wexford was unusual though not unique in this respect. Yet the 'moral economy' that provided food protesters with agency and encouraged the authorities to assume responsibility was not strongly in evidence in 1847. It was certainly missing as the government pursued the suspension of public works, and the populace responded by plundering the stores of relief committees throughout the country. These were a tempting target for food protesters. But the fact that strikingly few facilities of this ilk were singled out prior to the suspension of public works is a testament to the populace's deference to the committee's that managed them, the volunteers and officials that ran them, and the state which funded them. When the state ceased to provide relief through the medium of public works, they not only signalled their prioritization of fiscal economy over what remained of the 'moral economy' but also deprived relief committees of the moral protection that had allowed them to function to this point largely unmolested. The number of incidents in 1847 varied regionally, but it mirrored the boarder pattern of distress and the footprint of food protest. Thus, though it is not difficult to identify relief committees that were 'plundered' in Leinster and Ulster, they were few in number when compared with those reported from the heartlands of food protest in Munster and Connaught. In Ulster, for example, relief committee stores were broken into in five counties – Armagh, Cavan,

331, 431); *Nation*, 15 May 1847.   **195** NAI, Registered papers, 1847, division 1, vol. 1, 6/38, 507, 567, 573, 596, 599, 668, 733, 744, 856, 735, 745, 796, 1252 (Cork); Bailey to Redington, 7 Oct., 8 Dec. 1847 (NAI, OP: Cork, 1847/6/1274, 1510); *Nation*, 15 May 1847; *Leinster Express*, 22 May 1847; *Freeman's Journal*, 29 May, 18 June, 12 Sept. 1847; *Tralee Chronicle*, 15 May 1847.   **196** NAI, Registered papers, 1847, division 1, vol. 2, 31/79, 93, 124, 129, 135, 139, 142, 146, 147, 156, 158, 163, 165, 191(Wexford); Mansfield to [ ], 30 Apr., Rathbone to [Redington], 26 May, 18 June, Pigot to Redington, 13 May 1847 (NAI, OP: Wexford, 1847/31/141, 188, 204).

Donegal, Tyrone and Monaghan – but only county Donegal (with 8) registered more than two incidents, while county Wexford, with four examples, was the sole county in Leinster to register more than two. (The others were Kilkenny (1), King's (2); Meath (1), and Wicklow (1).)[197] By contrast, in Connaught, there were fifteen incidents in country Galway alone (but only two in county Leitrim and one in county Roscommon), whereas in Munster, counties Cork (22) and Kerry (18) experienced as many or more than the provinces of Leinster, Ulster and Connaught, and numbers well in excess of the other counties in the province (Limerick 11, Waterford 9, Clare 6 and Tipperary 3).[198]

Comparable descents on workhouses, government meal depots, public meal stores and soup kitchens provide a further illustration of the manner in which the brutalizing impact of severe famine in 1847 hastened the social breakdown, which militated against structured food protest.[199] This can be demonstrated by the pattern of events in county Mayo, which, having eschewed food protest in 1846, embraced it in the more elemental form in which it was pursued in 1847. It is improbable (given the virtual absence of food rioting in the county in the 1830s) that this could have occurred in the absence of the Great Famine as it required a dis-improvement of this scale to bring about what a coastguard officer arrestingly described in July as 'the bonds of society fast rending asunder' to transform 'the whole community ... [into] a mass of lawless and uncontroulable plunderers'.[200] This was the view of Chief Officer Cary, who was stationed at Belmullet in the north-west of the county. It may be that he exaggerated, but the fact that the populace in that area concluded that the authorities chose to 'overlook their depredations' and believed that they were entitled to intercept ships *en route* to and from Galway and other western ports was as indicative as the actions of bands of armed rural dwellers who targeted wealthier farmers that the always fluid boundary between food protest and what contemporaries denominated 'outrage' no longer obtained in this region. Cary's preoccupation was with the fishermen on the county Mayo coast who had devised a means of boarding and plundering ships at sea. Ostensibly no more than the extension of the practice

197 NAI, Registered papers, 1847, division 1, vols 1 and 2, 2/213 (Armagh); 4/291, 317 (Cavan); 7/91, 131, 138, 159, 175, 177, 197, 201 (Donegal); 23/139 (Monaghan); 28/24, 195 (Tyrone); 14/215, 263 (Kilkenny); 15/359, 380 (King's co.); 22/250 (Meath); 31/45, 192, 217, 218 (Wexford); 32/145 (Wicklow). **198** NAI, Registered papers, 1847, division 1, vols 1 and 2, 11/13, 14, 368, 409, 465, 491,525, 578, 653, 667, 705, 711, 713, 750, 763, 981, 1008 (Galway); 16/356, 443 (Leitrim); 25/489 (Roscommon); 5/626, 872, 1268, 1354, 1433, 1436 (Clare); 6/14, 302, 584, 720, 724, 746, 783, 823, 785, 839, 889, 897, 901–2, 903, 939, 975, 985, 1025, 1029, 1106, 1252, 1254, 1301 (Cork); 12/179, 233, 274, 293, 296, 298, 336, 338, 349, 397, 401, 416, 435, 446, 503, 522, 526, 543 (Kerry); 29/137, 151, 178, 179, 181, 189, 199–200, 222, 230 (Waterford); 17/633, 645, 774, 781, 832, 884, 925, 1023, 1075, 1078, 1198 (Limerick); 27/28, 1189, 1617 (Tipperary). **199** NAI, Registered papers, 1847, division 1, vols 1 and 2, 7/9, 38 (Donegal); 5/1370 (Clare); 6/1037, 1041 (Cork); 12/348, 359, 422, 515, 530 (Kerry); 17/542, 1768 (Limerick); 20/110, 112 (Louth); 31/269 (Wexford); *Nation*, 15 May 1847; *Leinster Express*, 22 May 1847. **200** Cary to Neame, 6 July 1847 (NAI, OP, Mayo, 1847/21/430).

long pursued by those who interrupted the movement of grain along rivers and canals, the manner in which bodies of fishermen up to forty in number boarded ships hugging the Mayo coastline from their currachs, and once they were aboard and had taken temporary control, helped themselves to a portion of the cargo was something the authorities could not countenance. Quickly categorized as piracy, delays in assigning revenue cruisers permitted the fishermen to intercept and appropriate provisions in varying quantities from between ten and twenty ships in the summer of 1847.[201] One may speculate as to the extent to which the skill and bravery of the fishermen assisted the community of which they were a part to negotiate 'Black '47'. But it is more significant in the history of food protest that it was regarded by the authorities as an illustration of the fact that, as it was then pursued, food protest had crossed the vague and indistinct boundary that separated illegal behaviour that was tolerable from illegal behaviour that was impermissible.

It was a conclusion that many, who had little or no knowledge of these events, had arrived at independently, encouraged by the increased recourse to robbery, intimidation and reliance on weapons (guns mostly) that was now a feature of much food protest, and violence in rural society more generally.[202] The *Nenagh Guardian* reflected this concern vividly in the autumn of 1847:

> It is frightful to behold, and deplorable to contemplate the vast and increasing bands of armed men, who nocturnally prowl about the country in all directions, who ... seem by their atrocious conduct not to value either life or property. Intimidation is becoming every day greater, and resistance to the payment of rents, and defiance to all lawful authority, more manifest.[203]

The augmented resort to violence and lawlessness that this writer perceived, and the decline in confidence in the agencies of the state indicated by attacks on workhouses, soup kitchens and bodies such as the Mining Company of Ireland (county Waterford) anticipated but did not herald the immediate cessation of food protest/provisions plundering.[204] The reduced number of 'food riots' reported in the press[205] echo the decline identifiable in the CSO registers and Constabulary Office returns. The impulse was sufficiently firmly anchored, how-

201 NAI, Registered papers, 1847, division 1, vol. 1, 21/53, 58, 80, 120, 226, 240, 241, 251, 250, 265, 298, 306, 309, 310, 332, 338, 340, 367, 368, 372, 396, 399, 405, 406, 416, 435, 441, 438, 448, 473, 477, 482, 488); Pigot to Redington, 13 May 1847 (NAI, OP: Mayo, 1847/31/161, 190, 270, 288, 372, 397, 401, 430, 447, 1848/31/190). 202 See, for examples, Ryan to Redington, 5 Jan. 1847 (NAI, OP: Tipperary, 1847/27/152); Police report, 14 Apr., RM (Ennis) to Under Sec., 15 Apr., 17 Oct. 1847 (NAI, OP: Clare, 1846/5/29931, 1847/5/389, 352, 1122); *Cork Examiner*, 15 Oct. 1847; Leyne to Redington, 13 July 1848 (NAI, OP: Clare, 1848, 5/596). 203 Quoted in the *Cork Examiner*, 15 Oct. 1847. 204 NAI, Registered papers, 1847, division 1, vol. 2, 29/70, 182 (Waterford). 205 See, for example, *Cork Examiner*, 10 Sept., 8, 15 Oct., 1 Nov. 1847; *Tuam Herald*, 12 Oct. 1847.

ever, and the degree of need sufficiently strong in Munster and parts of Connaught (Tables 4.1. 4.2 and 4.5), to ensure it continued, albeit on a much reduced scale and increasingly indivisible from plundering provisions, for the duration of the Great Famine.

1848 and the end of food protest
'Black 1847' effectively signalled the end of food protest as a distinctive phenomenon. Though this is not a full endorsement of John Cunningham's observation, based on his investigation of the situation in Galway, that 'this form of protest all but disappeared during 1847, with subsequent disorder taking the form of robbery', the trend he has identified in his admirable history of that town echoed what was an intensifying national trend.[206]

The figures for 'plundering provisions' for 1848 assembled by the Constabulary Office in their annual 'return of outrages' indicate it was of the same order and geographical distribution as the offence identified as 'demand or robbery of arms' with half the reported 234 incidents in Munster, 27 per cent in Connaught, 20 per cent in Leinster and a mere 4 per cent in Ulster (Table 5.2). In keeping with the pattern identified for 1847, the smaller number of incidents registered by the Chief Secretary's Office echoed this regional distribution though a higher percentage were from Munster (41 per cent) and Connaught (37 per cent) combined; Leinster accounted for 12 per cent and Ulster for 10 per cent (Table 5.1). Be that as it may, the figures demonstrate that ongoing difficulties in securing access to affordable food combined with the tradition of direct action to sustain a rapidly contracting pattern of food protest. Indeed, six counties (Tipperary, Cork, Galway, Limerick, Clare and Mayo) accounted for two-thirds (Tables 5.1 and 5.2) of the total, and some two-thirds (22) of the island's 32 counties registered two or less incidents (Table 5.1). And in a further demonstration of the attenuation of food protest, an increased proportion of those interventions that did take place were targeted at relief stores, meal depots, soup kitchens and workhouses, and in a new development, at schools, commercial enterprises and a religious meeting house.[207] Mills, cars, carts, boats and barges ferrying foodstuffs, and relief officials were still regarded as eligible targets, but the fact that they were exceeded by locations (and in some counties these were the sole target) that were engaged in the provision of relief, or that had access to foodstuffs arising out of its institutional role, was of itself a demonstration of the populace's acceptance of its dependence on the state and of the limits of the combination of self-help, assertiveness and of local government and civil society that had sustained earlier food protest.[208]

206 Cunningham, *Galway, 1790–1914*, p. 96.   **207** NAI, Registered papers, 1848, division 1, vols 1–2, 4/177, 230 (Cavan); 5/538, 687, 771 (Clare); 6/197, 198, 276 (Cork); 7/190, 257 (Donegal); 8/1 (Down); 9/27, 182 (Dublin); 11/91, 376, 541, 654 (Galway); 12/59 (Kerry); 21/ 129, 140, 143, 148, 185, 270, 313 (Mayo); 22/98 (Meath); 26/22–6, 51, 52–3, 67 (Sligo); 30/205 (Westmeath). **208** NAI, Registered papers, 1848, division 1, vols 1–2, 7/1848 (Donegal); 5/596, 1027 (Clare);

Since this reflected deeper forces at work in Irish society, it will comes as no surprise that the pattern identifiable in 1848 intensified in 1849 and 1850. While the variation in the number of outrages reported by the Constabulary Office and the number of incidents entered onto the registers maintained in the Chief Secretary's Office (Tables 5.1 and 5.2) means these data are even less consistent than in preceding years, the spatial contraction of the identifiable pattern of protest to four counties[209] in two provinces (Munster and Connaught),[210] and to the first half of the year, is a secure illustration of the fact that plundering provisions is no longer commonplace. The thirty incidents reported to the Chief Secretary's Office for 1849 included attempts to plunder cars carrying provisions in counties Clare, Galway, Mayo, Tipperary, Limerick and Waterford, the targeting of boats (counties Clare, Galway), sea-going vessels (Mayo) and meal stores (Tipperary and Limerick), and a few examples of attacks on relief committees and poor law guardians (Monaghan, Mayo and Clare).[211] The pulse of protest beat sufficiently strongly to ensure it retained its place in both the Constabulary Office returns and on the register of the Chief Secretary's Office, but the fact that incidents were recorded by the Chief Secretary's Office from only seven counties in 1849 and from four by the Constabulary Office in 1850 indicated that the Great Famine surge in provisions protest was over.[212]

This did not mean that there were no further instances of food rioting. In February 1850, the mayor of Limerick requested military aid to assist with the containment of a 'large mob' that targeted the bakers' carts and bread shops in that city.[213] Further incidents of plundering provisions in King's county (1) in 1851, in Limerick (4) in 1853, in Galway (1) and Limerick (1) in 1855 attest to the fact that in Ireland, as in Cornwall and Devon in England, there were locations that acted as 'a sort of a retreat center for "traditional" disorders'. These locations survived in England into the 1860s.[214] It remains to be established for

---

6/279, 779 (Cork); 11/13, 19, 569 (Galway); 13/22 (Kildare); 15/303, 305 (King's co.); 19/75 (Longford); 17/1833 (Limerick); 21/158, 168, 237, 248, 273, 528 (Mayo); 24/49 (Queen's co.); 27/1015, 1134 (Tipperary); 29/492 (Waterford); Leyne to Redington, 13 July 1848 (NAI, OP: Clare, 1848, 5/596). **209** Limerick, Tipperary, Mayo and Galway account for three-quarters of all incidents (Tables 5.1, 5.2). **210** Munster and Connaught accounted for 90–100 per cent of the total returns (Table 5.1, 5.2). **211** NAI, Registered papers, 1849, division 1, vols 1–2, 5/213, 806, 808 (Clare); 11/209 (Galway); 17/86, 269, 383, 400 (Cork); 21/6, 30, 80, 119, 210, 234 (Mayo); 23/73 (Monaghan); 27/1214, 1913 (Tipperary); 29/278 (Waterford). **212** NAI, Registered papers, 1850, division 1, vols 1–2, 5/95, 97, 256 (Clare); 17/122, 129, 554 (Limerick); 27/27, 309, 515, 522, 526, 626, 683 (Tipperary). **213** NAI, Registered papers, 1850, division 1, vols 1–2, 17/122, 129, 554 (Limerick); Virginia Crossman, *Politics, law and order in nineteenth-century Ireland* (Dublin, 1996), p. 80. **214** CSO, ICR, *Return of outrages reported to the Constabulary Office, 1850–55* (Dublin, 1851–56); Bohstedt, *The politics of provisions*, pp 250–2. It may also be noted that claims, exemplified by the re-reading of the Captain Swing riots (1830), that belief in a moral economy in England survived the decline in food rioting and was sufficiently firmly rooted to assume a different form after its passing may be true also of Ireland: Peter Jones, 'Swing, Speenhamland and rural social relations: the "moral economy" of the English crowd in the nineteenth century', *Social History*, 32 (2007), 271–89.

certain when the last food riot occurred in Ireland. The intervention in April 1857 of the redoubtable Claddagh fishermen to prevent a ship departing Galway with potatoes is the last known.[215] Saliently, the fact that the authorities stopped publishing figures for plundering provisions a years earlier, in 1856, indicates that it had already ceased as far as they were concerned.

CONCLUSION

In the absence of a means of correlating food rioting as it was pursued in the eighteenth and early nineteenth centuries and 'plundering provisions' as it was enumerated by the authorities in the 1840s and 1850s, it is difficult to equate these two related phenomena. It is, as a consequence, difficult to put the extraordinary surge in food protest that took place in the 1840s in its historical perspective. What is clear is that the second half of the 1840s was a singular moment not only in Ireland but also throughout the continent as the devastation of the potato crop 'drove hunger protests across Europe' in 1847 – in England and Germany, France and Spain notably.[216] Press coverage of these events ensured that Irish opinion was well aware that food protest was a European-wide phenomenon,[217] and if they harboured any doubts as to its exceptional nature they had only to look about them at the fact that high-profile incidents in Cork, Dublin, Waterford and Belfast in the winter of 1846–7 were the first food protests in these major centres in two decades.[218]

Be that as it may, the paucity of food rioting thereafter indicates that, among its various casualties, the Great Famine dealt purposeful food protest a terminal blow. This outcome was a triumph for the nineteenth-century state, for the emerging new orthodoxy that prized respectability over custom, and for classical liberalism that expected those who sought relief to forsake direct action in return for its provision. The authorities were not bluffing when they signalled their readiness to suspend relief when they encountered food protest rather than accede to the pressure of the 'mob'. The 1840s was not the first time that this

---

215 Cunningham, *Galway, 1790–1914*, p. 97.   216 Bohstedt, *The politics of provisions*, p. 250; Ashley Rowe, 'The food riots of the forties in Cornwall', *Royal Cornwall Polytechnic Society*, 10 (1942), 51–67; Gailus, 'Food riots in Germany in the late 1840s', 162–93; Pedro Díaz Marín, 'Crisis de subsistencia y protesta popular: los matines de 1847', *Historia Agraria*, 30 (2003), 31–62; idem, 'Subsistence crisis and popular protest in Spain: the *motines* of 1847' in Cormac Ó Gráda et al. (eds), *When the potato failed: causes and effects of the last European subsistence crisis, 1845–1850* (Turnhout, 2007), pp 267–92.   217 Food rioting in England and on the Continent was reported in the Irish press: *Freeman's Journal*, 8, 12 Oct., 3, 5 Dec. 1846, 27 Jan., 3, 4, 24 Feb., 12, 19, 22, 26 May 1847; *Tralee Chronicle and Killarney Echo*, 4 Apr. 1846, 23, 30 Jan., 10, 13 Mar. 1847; *Cork Examiner*, 27 Jan., 30 Apr., 24 May 1847; *Belfast News Letter*, 5, 9 Feb. 1847; *Tuam Herald*, 13 Feb., 22 May 1847; *Tralee Chronicle*, 6 Mar. 1847; *Nation*, 27 Feb. 1847; *Leinster Express*, 22 May 1847; *Anglo-Celt*, 14, 21 May 1847; *Connaught Telegraph*, 26 May, 16 June 1847.   218 The last identified riots were Dublin in 1826, Waterford in 1819, Cork in 1817 and Belfast in 1812.

message was delivered to protesters, of course, but it was now articulated with particular clarity and effect (see Fig. 4). One may instance Martin French, a resident magistrate at Cashel, county Tipperary, who 'expostulated with' a body of 'five hundred persons of the labouring class' who descended on the town of Cashel on 2 May 1847 'on the folly of their attempting any violence, as such conduct would ... bring about the immediate suspension of ... all public employment ... and ... put a stop to the distribution of food by the [relief] committee'. The crowd contested French's argument, but they could not challenge the new reality he outlined that 'food should henceforth be distributed to the destitute' via 'the new system of relief [that] was now in operation'. Left with no option they had little choice but to 'quit the town and go home'.[219] The course of events in 1847 and afterwards indicates that some were still unwilling to acknowledge this reality, and by extension, the implication that food protest was increasingly futile.[220] It was not the first time that agents acting on behalf of the state signalled their intention to close the space that food rioting required to function, but this time the message and the policy were aligned. Deprived of the space it required to function, food rioting in Ireland was forced out of existence.

219 French to Redington, 3 May 1847 (NAI, OP: Tipperary, 1847/27/1086).   220 John Bohstedt argues differently: he contends dramatically that 'there was no food left for rioters to struggle over', but this sits uneasily with the harvest figures: Bohstedt, *The politics of provisions*, p. 272; Solar, 'The Great Famine was no ordinary subsistence crisis', pp 112–33.

2

Patterns of food protest

INTRODUCTION

As pointed out above, the chronology of food protest in Ireland mirrored disruptions to the food supply, which were most acute during famines and subsistence crises. This accounts for the clusters of food riots identified in 1729, 1740, 1756–7, 1766, 1783–4, 1800–1, 1812, 1817, 1822, 1830–1, 1840, 1842 and 1846–8. Sixty-three per cent of the sample of food riots tabulated for the period 1710–1845 date from such years (Tables 2.1 and 2.2), while the Great Famine accounts for a still larger percentage of the incidents of 'provisions plundering' recorded between 1845 and 1850 (Table 5.3). Yet, one cannot conclude that food rioting was prompted by hunger alone since, other than during the Great Famine, it seldom coincided with the moment when food was in shortest supply, was not confined to those moments in time when, and those places where the crisis was most acute. Food protest was a product of a conjuncture of factors that were most developed in the eighteenth century in urban centres, but which spread with commercialization and poverty to embrace the countryside in the early nineteenth. Towns and cities could not function in the absence of the movement of food from rural areas where it was produced to the urban spaces where it was purchased. This was an everyday activity when the economy functioned normally because the purchasing power of labourers and artisans and the price of food were in a state of stable or near stable equilibrium, but when times were difficult, and food was only available at a high price or a shortage was apprehended, those who depended on purchased food were incentivized to engage in food protest in anticipation that they might be enabled thereby to exert downwards pressure on prices or to improve supply. Indeed, as the concept of the 'moral economy' implies, they perceived that intervention was justified and anticipated an ameliorative response from those in authority. This explains why when it comes to identifying the factor or factors that triggered food rioting, high or rising prices is frequently more indicative than hunger, and why food protesters targeted those engaged in the production, processing, transport and marketing of food rather than local and state officials. It also explains why, because the object was to bring about an immediate (temporary) correction, food riots were not only short-lived, but also inherently conservative.

Table 5.3: Plundering provisions, 1846–50: annual provincial totals
(official figures)

	1846	*1847*	*1848*	*1849*	*1850*	*Total*
Munster	195	550	116	53	10	924
Connaught	44	222	63	32	–	361
Leinster	125	221	46	6	0	398
Ulster	52	198	9	3	–	262
Yearly total	416	1191	234	94	10	1945

THE EVOLVING NATURE OF FOOD PROTEST IN THE EIGHTEENTH CENTURY

The primary intention of food rioters during the formative phase of food protest in Ireland, which embraces the famine environments of the late 1720s and early 1740s, was to inhibit the movement of foodstuffs from the country's southern and eastern ports. To this end, crowds disabled ships to prevent the carriage of cargoes of grain out of port, or, when ships were still in port, discharged their cargoes on the quays; they intercepted cars and carts carrying grain; and, contrived, on occasion, to compel merchants to swear an oath that they would send grain and meal they purchased (for export or sale elsewhere) to local markets.[1] Statistically, assaults on ships and the interception of carts were the most common forms of interventions pursued by food protesters in Ireland during its 1729 and 1740–1 peaks, followed by attacks on grain stores and warehouses. Neither action was pursued in an unfocussed or destructive manner, moreover. The observation in the 'petition of the poore inhabitants of Ireland' to the lords justices in January 1712 that 'the merchants of Ross [county Wexford], Waterford, and all other merchants of sea ports' had 'fil[l]ed up their store houses with corn in order to transport ye same' indicates that the vulnerable monitored the activities of those who traded foodstuffs.[2] It was logical therefore that the mobs that rose in Cork in 1710 targeted quayside premises of 'the city's most successful Dutch merchant'.[3] Likewise, when 'the dearness of provisions' in Cork in the spring of 1729 prompted 'the common people' to gather 'in a tumultuous manner', they 'plundered several granaries and store houses'.[4] Drogheda and Limerick crowds did the same.[5]

Food riots could, as some of these incidents reveal, escalate to a point where anger trumped calculation and they became destructive. Following the example

---

1 The Cork crowd in March 1729, and the Limerick crowd in May 1748 tendered oaths to this effect: Giblin (ed.), 'Catalogue of Nunziatura di Fiandra, pt 5', 13; *Dublin Weekly Journal*, 4 June 1748. 2 Petition, 29 Jan. 1711/12 in Hore, *History of the town and county of Wexford*, i, 376. 3 Dickson, *Old world colony*, p. 379. 4 *Dublin Intelligence*, 4 Mar. 1729; Giblin (ed.), 'Catalogue of Nunziatura di Fiandra, pt 5', 13. 5 *Faulkner's Dublin Journal*, 8 Mar.; *Dublin Weekly Journal*, 8 Mar. 1729; Boulter to Newcastle, 13 Mar. 1729 in *Boutler letters*, i, 230.

set in Cork in the winter of 1709–10, mobs were with difficulty prevented from pulling down the houses of merchants in Youghal in December 1740 and in Sligo in April 1741, while it required the intervention of the lord mayor, sheriff and a party of soldiers to safeguard bakers' shops in Dublin in March 1741.[6] The most prolonged, and purposeful, instance of food rioting in Ireland during the 1740–1 famine took place in Dublin in the summer of 1740. Alarmed by the price of foodstuffs, which doubled between January and August;[7] perturbed by the reluctance of bakers to make cheap (and less profitable) 'household bread', and suspecting a 'combination' among 'bakers, mealmen and hucksters' not 'to sell bread unless it was at their price', the metropolitan crowd intervened. Protest commenced on Saturday, 31 May, with the seizure of loaves, oatmeal, bacon and butter from a number of bakers' shops and meal stores and their sale at a 'low price to the poor'. On the following day, Sunday, 1 June, the 'mob' targeted a ship moored on Aston Quay, and they were in the process of selling the bread and beef acquired thereby when they were interrupted by the arrival of the lord mayor and a party of soldiers. Undeterred by this and the arrest of some of their number, the crowd shifted their focus on Monday, 2 June, to the mills located 'about' the city; once again they seized food which they sold at below market prices.[8]

The decision of this Dublin crowd to sell appropriated food at less than the current market price was a feature of classic food protest. The Drogheda mob, which brought '30 tons of oatmeal' (some intercepted while being put on board a ship and more seized from the 'store houses in the town') to the 'town crane' on 5 March 1729, was animated by a comparable intention; they also delivered the key to the stores in which they deposited wheat to the lord mayor in order that both commodities could be 'brought to market' and sold at a fair price.[9] A few days later in Dublin, an 'unruly mob' that ventured 'among the potatoe boats' on Aston Quay 'sold the roots there for 3*d*. a peck, which was half [the market] price'.[10] There are no comparable examples to suggest that *taxation pop-*

---

6 Crofts to Perceval, 27 Jan. 1709/19 (BL, Egmont papers, Add. MS 46978 p. 297); *Dublin Newsletter*, 6 Dec. 1740; *Faulkner's Dublin Journal*, 10 Mar. 1741; *Pue's Occurrences*, 25 Apr. 1741; D.A. Fleming, 'The government and politics of provincial Ireland' (D.Phil., Oxford University, 2005), pp 21, 38–9.   7 Prices fell in April on the anticipation of grain imports; but a sharp upwards movement followed and continued until August when prices were double their January level: *Dublin Newsletter*, 13 May; *Dublin Daily Post*, 28 Apr., 3, 7 May; *Dublin Gazette*, 29 Apr.; *Faulkner's Dublin Journal*, 6, 24 May 1740; Drake, 'The Irish demographic crisis of 1740–41', pp 112–13.   8 Kingsbury to Price, 31 May (NLW, Puleston papers, MS 3548D); Richard Mathew to Lord Fitzwilliam, 14 June 1740 (NAI, Pembroke estate papers, 97/46/1/2/4/16); *Pue's Occurrences*, 3 June; *Dublin Gazette*, 3, 7 June; *Dublin Newsletter*, 3, 7 June; *Dublin Daily Post*, 3 June; *Faulkner's Dublin Journal*, 3 June 1740; Gilbert (ed.), *Calendar of ancient records of Dublin*, viii, 374–5; Dickson, *Artic Ireland*, pp 27–8; Swift, *History of the Dublin bakers*, p. 117; John O'Rourke, *The history of the Great Irish Famine of 1847* (Dublin, 1875), p. 18.   9 *Faulkner's Dublin Journal*, 8 Mar. 1729, 10 Mar. 1741; *Dublin Weekly Journal*, 8 Mar. 1729.   10 *Dublin Intelligence*, 18 Mar. 1729; *Dublin Gazette or Weekly Courant*, 18 Mar. 1729. A peck was the equivalent of two gallons and a quarter bushel.

ulaire was applied in the same manner in Munster at this time, though it was attempted, albeit not always successfully, during the far more severe crisis of 1740–1. It was first tried in May 1740 when the populace was so 'greatly enraged' at the bakers of Cork for making an insufficient amount of household bread that 'they broke open their shops', following which some of the rioters 'sold the ... bread, and g[a]ve them [the bakers] the money; others [simply] took it away'. Six months later at Kinsale an attempt by the populace to compel the captain of a ship carrying grain, which took shelter *en route* to Cork, to sell the cargo at '7 shillings per barrel less' than the market price at Cork was frustrated by the intervention of a customs officer. The Youghal crowd, which was particularly active in the winter of 1740–1, was more successful; it contrived to persuade those in the port's hinterland with barley reserves to sell them at the reduced price of 6s. 6d. a barrel.[11]

There may be other instances yet to be identified, but it is noteworthy, as the seizure in January 1741 of a boat laden with corn bound for Cork and other incidents attest,[12] that *taxation populaire* was not an invariable feature of the most common form of food rioting in early eighteenth-century Ireland – the intervention of the crowd to inhibit the movement of food. Furthermore, as was the case in Cork in 1712, and Drogheda in 1729, it was evidently far from the minds of those crowds whose interventions led to the destruction of foodstuffs. There is insufficient information on the 'riot' at Theodore Vansevenhoven's premises that resulted in the payment of £3 4s. compensation in 1714 for 'corn lost' to comment on what transpired on this occasion; the fact that the rioters at Drogheda 'cut the sacks that were carrying corn on board the ships at the key' in 1729 is more revealing.[13] Moreover, the Drogheda 'mobb' had reason to feel content at the outcome since, as well as preventing the movement of the sacks they targeted, their decision to 'cut the riggings' not only prevented 'two ships laden with barley, oats and oatmeal' from leaving port, but also convinced the merchant responsible, James Scholes, to 're-land the cargoes', which he agreed to do provided the Revenue Commissioners reimbursed him the duty he had already paid.[14] Heartened by such results, the 'mobb or comon people in and about the town of Carrick [-on-Suir] in the county of Tipperary and Carrick Beg in the county of Waterford' was emboldened in 1734 to prevent corn and cattle passing through *en route* to Waterford.[15] Since this intervention did not take place against the backdrop of a major crisis, it was an isolated episode. Yet its occurrence is indicative of the appreciating conviction of the populace that it was

---

11 Dickson, *Arctic Ireland*, pp 27, 34; *Dublin Newsletter*, 2, 6, 16 Dec. 1740; Kelly, 'Coping with crisis; the response to the famine of 1740–1', 114; *Pue's Occurrences*, 6 Dec. 1740. 12 Minutes of the Revenue Commissioners, 16 Jan. 1741 (TNA, CUST/1/31 f. 212). 13 Caulfield, *Corporation book of Cork*, p. 374; *Faulkner's Dublin Journal*, 8 Mar. 1729. 14 *Faulkner's Dublin Journal*, 8 Mar. 1729; Minutes of the Revenue Commissioners, 7 Mar. 1729 (TNA, CUST1/21 f. 82). 15 Memorial of the mayor, sheriffs and citizens of Waterford to the duke of Dorset, 29 Mar. 1734 (Waterford Archives, Corporation of Waterford council book).

entitled to intervene to prevent the movement of foodstuffs when it endangered their access to alimentation.

This was certainly the case in 1740 and 1741 when seven towns (Drogheda, Dublin, Galway, Dungarvan, Kinsale, Sligo and Carrick-on-Suir) experienced food rioting. The first to do so was Drogheda where the town 'rabble' was so perturbed by the presence of 'a number of north country people' who had come 'to buy oatmeal' that on 19 April 1740 they boarded 'a ship in the harbour bound for Scotland with 50 tons of oatmeal' and immobilized it by taking away 'the rudder and sails'. The restoration of the ships' tackle meant the vessel was soon seaworthy, but since this was accompanied by 'a resolution' (which was acceptable to the town magistrates) 'not to allow any more food to be exported', this was a positive outcome from the perspective of those who staged the intervention.[16] Few riots proceeded to such an agreeable resolution, however. The crowd that appropriated bread and beef from on board a ship at Dublin port on 1 June to sell at an affordable price encountered armed resistance, which had the effect of causing it to behave more violently in turn.[17] The 'mob' at Dungarvan responded in November to an attempt to send barley to Waterford with a threat to 'set fire to the ship' if it set sail. The 'mob' at Youghal was no less forceful, and it served to convince a local merchant 'to promise ... he would not ship' wheat he had acquired for exportation. Other owners were more defiant; a vessel from New York that took shelter in Kinsale harbour had its sails cut in an (unsuccessful) attempt to secure access to the cargo of food it had on board.[18] The resolve manifested in these instances was not particular to the crowd in south-coast ports, moreover. The Galway ship that docked at Sligo port 'to take away grain from that place' in April 1741 also had its sails cut, while in the inland port of Carrick-on-Suir, the populace 'stopt a boat loaded with oates going to Waterford' during the same month.[19]

The appreciating belief in the merits of direct action, implicit in the augmented number of locations that experienced food rioting in 1740–1, and in the forms that these interventions assumed, was extended and consolidated over the course of the ensuing four decades. The most striking testament to this is the greater readiness of urban crowds to resist the shipping of food in response to rising prices, the increase in the number of locations that experienced such interventions, and the number of food products that were targeted. This was particularly manifest during the 1750s, but even before then the economic difficulties experienced in the mid-1740s prompted another intervention by the lively Drogheda 'mob', which 'rose and unrigged three ... vessels laden with corn and meal for Scotland' in March 1746.[20] Economic conditions were better two years later, but 'a sudden rise of their market' prompted the Limerick 'mob' to assem-

16 Magennis. 'Food scarcity in 1756–7', pp 196–7; *Faulkner's Dublin Journal*, 22 Apr. 1740. 17 *Pue's Occurrences*, 3 June; *Dublin Gazette*, 3 June 1740. 18 *Dublin Newsletter*, 6 Dec. 1740; Dickson, *Arctic Ireland*, p. 34. 19 *Pue's Occurrences*, 25 Apr. 1741; *Dublin Gazette*, 25 Apr. 1741; Kelly and Lyons (eds), *Proclamations of Ireland*, iii, 291–2. 20 *Dublin Courant*, 25 Mar. 1746.

ble on 24 May 1748, and to proceed not only to 'cut away the rigging and anchors of a ship that was laden with oatmeal and ready to sail' but also to target the house of Joseph Sexton, the merchant, who had 'been buying up oatmeal for exportation'.[21] More indicatively, perhaps, five years later the 'populace' of the major inland town of Kilkenny was so alarmed by a 'late wet [spring] season' that it intervened in April 1753 'to prevent the sending away of oatmeal, or any other provisions from their market', while in the same month in the city of Cork the mere 'apprehension' that meal and potatoes were being 'bought up in great quantities for exportation' prompted the local 'mob' to force 'open some cellars'.[22]

The disposition of urban crowds to engage in food protest was still more evident in 1756–7, when 'mobs' in Dublin, Waterford, Drogheda, Wexford, New Ross and Sligo attacked ships, stores, granaries, mills and houses to prevent the transportation of grain out of these ports. A comparable intervention took place in Clonmel 'under pretence of stopping corn from being taken out of town'.[23] These actions may be characterized as pre-emptive, since they were precipitated by the apprehension of scarcity rather than by actual distress. As such, they conform to the fugitive model of food rioting that was dominant in Ireland to this point. There was a more extended variant that, based on those instances that have been identified, resulted in more sustained displays of rioting. Dublin city experienced one such outburst of popular anger in 1741;[24] it was also displayed in Belfast in 1756 and in Kilkenny ten years later.

The food riots that occurred in Belfast in the summer of 1756 are one of the best-known episodes of their kind.[25] They took place against the familiar backdrop of a poor harvest and unseasonable weather conditions, but the identifiable cause was a surge in the price of basic foodstuffs. Oatmeal prices on Belfast market almost doubled from 7s. 6d. a hundred weight in January to 14s. 8d. in July, while wheat peaked at 12s. in early August (up from 5s. 6d. a cwt in early January).[26] To compound matters, (contested) suggestions that merchants were profiteering exacerbated the populace's unease, but it was the 'exorbitant price' at which meal retailed in mid-July that spurred the crowd into action. Spearheaded by 'several weavers and other tradesmen [who] gathered together', the ensuing 'mob' 'prevented … any meal from being carried to the country; opened the meal cellars, and sold the same to the necessitous at a more moderate price'.[27] In most circumstances, food protest crowds dissolved at this point, but not this Belfast 'mob'. These initial disturbances were the signal for a

21 *Dublin Weekly Journal*, 4 June 1748; Fleming, 'Provincial Ireland', p. 113.   22 *Universal Advertiser*, 10 Apr., 1 May 1753.   23 *Pue's Occurrences*, 20 Nov. 1756, 19 Apr. 1757; *Belfast News Letter*, 30 Nov. 1756; *London Evening Post*, 29 Jan. 1757; Hore, *History of Wexford*, v, 398–400; *Universal Advertiser*, 12 Feb. 1757; William P. Burke, *History of Clonmel* (reprint, Kilkenny, 1983), p. 126.   24 Above, pp 36–7.   25 D.J. Owen, *History of Belfast* (Belfast, 1921), pp 94–5; Jonathan Bardon, *Belfast: an illustrated history* (Belfast, 1982), p. 33; Benn, *History of Belfast*, pp 593–6; Magennis, 'Food scarcity in 1756–7', pp 198–9.   26 Above, p. 40; Magennis, 'Food scarcity in 1756–7', pp 198–9; *Belfast News Letter*, January–July 1756.   27 *Belfast News Letter*, 21 May, 18 June, 20 July 1756.

sequence of incidents, mostly hazily reported, which included an attack on the house and cellars of several merchants and the theft of property (grain) to the value of £120, that so disturbed George Macartney, the acting town sovereign, he reported to Dublin Castle that 'all government and order are now at an end'. Macartney exaggerated, but his assessment was informed by a disturbing experience in a 'meal cellar' on 21 July when he was personally threatened, and by his conclusion that it was unreasonable to expect merchants to sell at below cost. This is seemingly what ensued, for though some merchants sought to pre-empt trouble by promising to sell at a fair price the oat meal they had 'laid in' in anticipation of a shortage, the fact that the price they quoted was at or above market price meant it had little impact. Indeed, such was the authority of 'the mobb' during the remainder of July that local officials declined to intervene. 'No justice of the peace dare issue a warrant', George Macartney reported on 31 July, adding that 'if he did it would be to no purpose, as his house would be pulled down, and himself be demolished with it'.[28] As a result, the cycle of disturbance persisted. The fact that the price of wheat continued to rise, though oatmeal moderated slightly – it stood at 13s. a cwt through August and most of September – certainly provided little grounds for optimism that the protest would soon cease. Indeed, it seemed that matters were destined to get worse when, in early August, 'a fresh mob' was 'got up' that not only 'carried off sacks of meal' from their female owner but also 'drag'd [her] out of her house [and] put [her] on a carr in order to duck her in the mill dam'. This was not the case, however. The atmosphere in the town remained tense for as long as food prices were high, which was for several months, but the combined efforts of 'an association for suppressing riots', of merchants to improve the food supply, and of various charitable initiatives meant there was no further disorder.[29]

If the combination of alleviatory and security measures ensured there was no repetition in Belfast in the early winter of 1756–7 of the food rioting of the preceding summer, events in that town confirmed the increasing ambition of those who engaged in food protest. This was the case also in Kilkenny where on 18 April 1757 'a great number of cars leaving the city with oatmeal were turned back'. This was not unprecedented, but the organization and fixity of purpose on display was unusual as the oatmeal was not just brought to the market house where it was offered for sale at 2d. per pottle;[30] it was replenished by the addition of 'large quantities of meal' taken from warehouses in the city, where it had been stored in order (it was alleged) 'to keep prices high' and made available to 'all as would buy'.[31] In Waterford, meanwhile, the mere 'appearance of the populace' in November 1756 prompted a number of merchants to direct that oatmeal

28 Macartney to [Waite], 22, 31 July 1756 in Benn, *History of Belfast*, pp 593–5. 29 *Belfast News Letter*, July–Dec. 1756; 3, 27 Aug., 7 Sept., 26, 30 Nov., 3 Dec. 1756; Macartney to [Waite], 11 Aug. 1756 in Benn, *History of Belfast*, p. 596; *Public Gazetteer*, 8 Sept. 1759. 30 A 'pottle' was normally a liquid measure equal to half a gallon or two quarts (*OED*). 31 *Pue's Occurrences*, 23 Apr. 1757.

that had been put 'on board several vessels' should be unloaded and 'kept for the use of the city', while in April 1757 the 'mob' demonstrated its reach and its commitment to *taxation populaire*, by appropriating 'a large quantity of oatmeal' from a mill three miles from the city, and transporting it 'to the town in five gabbards,[32] where it was sold at 3 half pence (1½d.) per pottle'.[33]

The augmented confidence of the crowd, to which these incidents bear wetness, was increasingly less hidebound by the economic cycle as John Wesley's account of a 'minor grain riot' in the port town of Sligo in May 1758 attests. In this instance, when a local mob unloaded a Dutch ship that had taken on a cargo of 'corn', they did so in order to sell it 'for the owners at the common price'.[34] Wesley's sympathetic reference to the 'calmness and composure' of the Sligo crowd echoes the wider impression that food rioting was a largely structured activity at this point. Its extension in the late 1750s to embrace opposition to the exportation of live cattle from Dublin port in 1759, following the relaxation of the long standing prohibition on the movement of livestock, and from Cork, Waterford, Belfast and Newtownards though the mid-1760s, is consistent with this.[35] So too is the widely reported case of the interception of bacon and ham on a vessel in Dublin port in 1767, and at Waterford in 1775, and the orderly, if occasional, enforcement of *taxation populaire* (for example, at Kilkenny and Wicklow) in 1766. Yet one must not highlight this rational aspect of the practice, or the belief in the concept of a just price, at the expense of its irrational, economically reactionary, dimension.[36] The latter was in evidence at Wexford in the winter of 1757–8 when a local merchant, Joseph Atwood, 'was most furiously opposed by a very numerous, furious and outrageous mob' when he sought to ship 'a considerable parcel of oates and wheat' he had purchased from the 'vast redundancy of grain' in the county that was the product of the abundant 1757 harvest.[37] It was in evidence again in May 1759 when 'a great number of riotous persons', who assembled at Dublin port, 'killed and maimed several parcels of live swine' lodged in yards about George's Quay, rather than allow them be exported to England; and in Youghal in 1760 when an attempt was made to disable a ship carrying potatoes.[38]

---

32 A sailing vessel for inland navigation (*OED*).   33 *Belfast News Letter*, 30 Nov. 1756; *Pue's Occurrences*, 19 Apr. 1757. One may also cite a similar episode in Drogheda in 1757 when the crowd that seized oatmeal from on board a ship sold the oatmeal for 'a penny a pound': *London Evening Post*, 29 Jan. 1757.   34 J.G. Simms, 'Connacht in the eighteenth century', *IHS*, 11 (1958–9), 311; *Journal of John Wesley*, ii, 392; Thompson, 'Moral economy reviewed', p. 295. John Cunningham's location of the riot at Jamestown, county Leitrim, is based on a misreading of Wesley's journal: Cunningham, *Galway, 1790–1914*, p. 90.   35 Above, p. 39; Clarke, *The unfortunate husbandman: to which is prefaced a short account of Charles Varley's life and times*, p. 15; NAI, Index of departmental letters and papers, 1760–89, i, 296, 299; *Public Gazetteer*, 1 Sept. 1759.   36 William to Barry Colles, 14 June 1766 (NAI, Prim Collection, no. 87/92); *Freeman's Journal*, 14 Mar. 1767; *Public Gazetteer*, 5 July 1766, 17 Mar. 1767; *Pue's Occurrences*, 17 Mar. 1767; Kelly and Lyons (eds), *Proclamations of Ireland*, iv, 97.   37 Hore, *History of Wexford*, i, 394–5.   38 *Pue's Occurrences*, 5 May 1759; *Public Gazetteer*, 5 Apr. 1760.

Though it might seem inappropriate to equate the interventions that took place on these occasions with the action of the 'riotous mob' that 'assembled at the different avenues leading from Patrick Street market', Dublin, on 1 September 1764 in order to 'force the provisions from those that were coming from said market, which they shamefully mangled and threw away', the fact that the action took place when market conditions were normal is obviously pertinent.[39] The problem is that the available information is rarely sufficiently rich to permit firm conclusions to be drawn as to the motivation of the riotous or the reasoning that guided their actions. And E.P. Thompson's confident pronouncements to the contrary notwithstanding, even when prices were high and the economic environment was unusually difficult, as in 1766, the reality of food rioting in Ireland was often more ambiguous than the emphasis on the popular perception of a just price, and adherence to customary market norms inherent in the ideal of the 'moral economy'.

1766 was unquestionably a difficult year, as the spike in the table of identifiable food riots suggests. Indicatively, the MP Agmondisham Vesey secured a loan of £500 from the lord lieutenant 'to purchase provisions, to be sold out to the poor inhabitants' of Kinsale such was the 'great scarcity ... in this town';[40] while 'a subscription was set on foot' in Kilkenny to supply the poor in that town with oatmeal at 25 per cent below the market price. However, as problems of supply, attributable to rising prices, frustrated the relief effort, the town 'mob' chose 'to break open the houses of the mealmen and farmers both by day and night', and to 'take away all the oatmeal they could find'; they brought the oatmeal to 'the stores of the poor, where it was received and paid for (to them who would receive payment) at the rate of 12s. per hundred [cwt.]'. To all intents and purposes this was a classic food riot, and the fact that the appropriated grain was escorted by the crowd 'with pipers before them' to the stores from where it was sold suggested that the Kilkenny crowd followed a clear line of action. Moreover, it was sufficiently disciplined to sustain the protest over several days, as an unusually detailed report of the episode to Barry Colles, who was mayor of the town in 1765, makes clear. 'Oatmeal taking became a great entertainment and employment of the mob, and they summoned their nightly meetings for this purpose by winding an horn in the streets and lanes of the citty, and then went on their severall excursions in search of oatmeal in the severall parts of the citty and libertys and even into the country'. This resulted inevitably in some damage to property (houses and chests were 'broke open'), some intimidation, and some expressions of 'rage and resentment against ... oaten mealmakers who had not put in what they [the crowd] deemed their quota of meal to the stores'. But it was kept within tolerable bounds until Monday 9 June when the 'mob' assumed a more destructive aspect. It is not clear why this was so but it seems as if the decision to parade and hang an effigy of one of the town's mealmen 'before his door' caused a larger than usual 'mob of many hundred people to assemble', and

39 *Freeman's Journal*, 8 Sept. 1764.   **40** Caulfield (ed.), *Corporation book of Kinsale*, p. 279.

that they 'immediately agreed' when it was suggested that 'they should fall on and demolish the starch yards', because their raw material was wheat. This 'was forthwith done, with all the circumstances of waste, mischief, malice and popular fury imaginable to the ut[t]er ruin of many families and the great terror and damage of many more'. Moreover, having accomplished this goal, the 'mob' reassembled on Tuesday, 10 June, when they identified the flour mills as their next target, and they were only prevented embarking on this, the third phase of their riotous enterprise, by the intervention of the mayor, Haydocke Evans Morres (1743–76), who was prevailed upon by the millers to call out the military garrison; a guard was set, and order was restored.[41]

Despite its extended and destructive course, the preparedness of the Kilkenny crowd to cease 'rioting' when the civil authorities summoned military support indicates that the rioters recognized that the tolerance they were sometimes afforded (as in this instance) had its limits. Equivalent incidents at this time are not readily identifiable, though the preparedness of bodies such as Dublin Corporation, which paid Patrick Callan £21 in July 1766 'as a compensation for the loss he had sustained by a riotous mob breaking into his house and taking fourteen casks of flour', can be characterized as another manifestation of the permissiveness that not only contributed to the increase in the frequency and to the expanded spatial footprint of food protest, but also to the greater intensity on display.[42] This was not true of all instances of food protest, of course. Familiar modes of activity, aimed at preventing grain being transported out of an area, whether on board ship or in carts, continued, and, occasionally, as in Cork in April 1770, the grain that was appropriated was promptly made available for general sale.[43] Descents on mills, grains stores and cellars occurred in Cork in 1767 and 1770, in Kinsale in 1768, in Limerick in 1772; on carts bearing provisions *en route* to Dublin in 1773 and 1774, and on a ship with 'some beef in her bulk' at Drogheda in 1775.[44] There was even a small spike in incidents in 1772 precipitated by the fear of 'an artificial scarcity' attributed to the presence at Dundalk of Scottish shippers, which resulted in a classic instance of *taxation populaire*, and an attack on a mill in Limerick.[45] But these must be set side by side with the 200 live cattle destined for exportation from Donaghadee to Scotland that were 'cut and maimed' in 1766; the green salt hides that were seized on the ship *Mary* out of Waterford in 1768 and cut to pieces; the barrels of beef, destined for exportation, that were 'cut open and destroyed by a mob assembled for that purpose' at the same port in 1768; the destruction of flour and bacon *en route* to Dublin in 1773 and 1774 and Cork in

41 William Colles to Barry Colles, 14 June 1766 (NAI, Prim Collection, 89/92); *Public Gazetteer*, 24 June 1766.   42 Gilbert (ed.), *Calendar of ancient records of Dublin*, xi, 340.   43 *Finn's Leinster Journal*, 18 Apr. 1770, 20 Jan., 24 Aug. 1773.   44 *Finn's Leinster Journal*, 4 July 1767, 30 Apr. 1768, 28 Apr. 1770; *Freeman's Journal*, 19 May 1772; *Hoey's Publick Journal*, 20 May 1772; *Limerick Chronicle*, 14 May 1772; *Hibernian Journal*, 8 Dec. 1775.   45 Donnelly, 'Irish agrarian rebellion: the Whiteboys of 1769–76', 296; *Hibernian Chronicle*, 12 Mar. 1772; *Hibernian Journal*, 18 Mar. 1772.

1774; and the attempt by journeymen coopers to do likewise to 'a parcel of bacon' on Waterford quay in 1775.[46] The rationale for the destruction of flour *en route* to Dublin and Cork was to compel carriers of flour to sell it in the public market because private sales conducted between mill owners and merchants served to raise 'the price of bread'. There was an ostensible logic to the crowd's action in this instance, as well as in the attempt to oblige carriers of potatoes and butter in 1774 to bring their goods to the New Market, Dublin, because the general economic environment was difficult. However, it registered negatively with officials at national as well as municipal level.[47] Moreover, it was soon overtaken by events, and was in a minor key when compared to the challenges posed successively by the disruption caused to trade by the outbreak of war in North America in 1776, and a further subsistence crisis in 1783–4.

The late 1770s and early 1780s witnessed an intensification of the trend, underway for several decades at this point, to target a wider variety of foodstuffs as the potato assumed a larger place in the popular diet and patterns of trade expanded. The more frequent targeting of potatoes from the mid-1770s was another manifestation of the greater trade in foodstuffs that resulted from the combination of improved roads and the construction of canals,[48] though these factors were arguably less consequential than the incentivization of milling and the communication of flour to Dublin and to external markets (particularly Britain).[49] In addition, the impact of demographic growth, as a result of which the population rose from *c*.2.2 million in 1750 to *c*.4.42 million in 1791, was a source not only of increased social tension – one pertinent manifestation of which was the emergence in the 1760s of organized agrarian protest – but also of the gradual extension to the countryside of the imperatives (moral as well as commercial) that fuelled food rioting.[50] The combined effect of these trends is to be found in the frequency with which crowds in rural towns objected to the movements of potatoes in the late 1770s and early 1780s. One may instance the 'great mob' that

46 *Public Gazetteer*, 21 June 1766, 1 Mar. 1768; Memorial of Thomas Grubb, merchant, 8 Feb. 1768 (NAI, Isabel Grubb's notes, 1915, p. 4); *Hibernian Chronicle*, 30 Aug. 1773; *Hibernian Journal*, 27 Aug. 1773, 6 Feb. 1775; *Finn's Leinster Journal*, 8 Jan. 1774, 1 Feb. 1775.   47 Clements to Macartney, 24 Aug. 1773 in Bartlett (ed.), *Macartney in Ireland*, p. 243; *Freeman's Journal*, 15 Oct. 1774; Donnelly, 'Irish agrarian rebellion: the Whiteboys of 1769–76', 296–8; *Dublin Mercury*, 7 Jan. 1775; *Dublin Gazette*, 25 Jan. 1775.   48 See the comments of 'Benevolus' on the distress of the poor in *Finn's Leinster Journal*, 23 May 1778, and additional observation on the canal trade in grain: *Finn's Leinster Journal*, 24 Mar. 1787.   49 Cullen, 'Eighteenth-century flour milling', 9–15.   50 Dickson, Ó Gráda and Daultrey, 'Hearth tax, household size and Irish population change, 1672–1821', 156; Liam Kennedy and L.A. Clarkson, 'Birth, death and exile: Irish population history, 1700–1921' in B.J. Graham and L.J. Proudfoot (eds), *An historical geography of Ireland* (London, 1993), pp 158–84; T.M. Devine, 'Unrest and stability in rural Ireland and Scotland 1760–1840' in Peter Roebuck and Rosalind Mitchison (eds), *Economy and society in Scotland and Ireland, 1500–1939* (Edinburgh, [1988]), pp 126–39; Donnelly, 'The Whiteboys, 1760–5', 20–55; idem, 'The Rightboy movement, 1785–8', 120–202; idem, 'Hearts of Oak: Hearts of Steel', 7–73; idem, 'Irish agrarian rebellion: the Whiteboys of 1769–76', 293–331.

'boarded' a vessel in Ballina port in March 1778 'and took out [a] whole cargo' of potatoes, or the 'trades people of Ennis to the number of 300 and upwards' who travelled on 20 May 1781 to the nearby port of Clarecastle 'in order to detain a boat which they understood had been loaded with potatoes ... intended for Limerick market'.[51] Rural food protesting crowds were less commonplace, though examples have been identified at Eadestown and Ballymore Eustace, county Kildare c.1779, which 'destroyed some cars and corn belonging to a gentleman in the neighbourhood', and in Gorteen, county Mayo, and Newtown Bellew, county Galway, in 1783.[52] And even if the rural populace felt it had less incentive, because it was less vulnerable to the surge in foods prices that was so crucial in generating food 'mobs', to engage in food rioting than its urban equivalent, food protest was no longer confined to ports and urban centres, as farmers 'close' to Mullingar could testify; they had 'upwards of 40 cars laden with oatmeal' taken from their stores during the 1783 phase of the 1782–4 subsistence crisis.[53]

Yet if the pattern of protest in evidence in the 1780s sustains the conclusion that by then the forces that drove food rioting embraced small as well as large trading towns, and increasingly those parts of the countryside engaged in the trade in foodstuffs, the statistical reality was that most food protest continued to take place in urban centres with populations large enough (see Table 1) and traditions of protest deep enough to permit the ready generation of a crowd. As a result, food rioters were more likely to target ships that sought to transport provisions out of an area, and merchants' stores than to intercept carts carrying grain between towns or to compel farmers to bring goods to market. This certainly was the predominant response of crowds in the southern sea ports of Waterford, Skibbereen, Cork and Ross to the impact of the augmented demand for foodstuffs for the navy and military during the early years of the American War of Independence, and more broadly – in Bandon, Cork, Kilkenny, Drogheda, Dublin – to the decline in commercial activity as the economic dislocation attributable to the war registered more negatively from 1778. The impact of the latter was vividly demonstrated by the 'great mob' that rose in Drogheda to oppose the transport of 'a great quantity of oatmeal' to Newry in the summer of 1778; 'the mob seized the whole when going out of town and sold it at 1*d*. per pound'.[54] Subsequently, 'the spirit of riot' was displayed in the nearby towns of Dunleer, Dundalk and Ardee, but the crowds in evidence there did not equate with that at Drogheda, which attacked the town jail and, having succeeded in rescuing a number of their 'companions' who had been detained, proceeded to

51 *Dublin Evening Journal*, 2 Apr. 1778; *Finn's Leinster Journal*, 8 Apr. 1778; *Hibernian Journal*, 30 May 1781.   52 Above, pp 42–3; *Dublin Evening Post*, 1 July 1783; Patrick Bellew to Michael Bellew, 11 July 1783 (NLI, Bellew papers, MS 27126/1).   53 *Dublin Evening Post*, 12 July 1783. 54 *Finn's Leinster Journal*, 4 July 1778; *Dublin Evening Journal*, 16 June 1778. This equated to 9*s*. 3*d*. per cwt. The Newry merchants has purportedly paid 16*s*. 8*d*. per cwt.   55 *Dublin Evening Journal*, 18 June 1778.

seize oaten meal.[55] It was in evidence also in 1783, and in 1784, as the 1782–4 subsistence crisis presented a familiar scenario of rising prices to which the populations of Clonakilty, Youghal, Kinsale, Waterford, Clonmel, Carrick-on-Suir and Drogheda responded in time-honoured fashion by disabling or unloading ships taking provisions – potatoes as well as grain – on board, by attacking and emptying grain mills and storehouses; and occasionally, as at Clonmel where a 'mob', two hundred strong, broke into the mill of the Jacob family, by invoking the principle of *taxation populaire*. In this instance the contents of the mill were sold 'for what they [the 'mob'] thought proper in the middle of the town'.[56]

These variants on the standard food rioting formula were sufficiently firmly rooted by then to ensure that they continued to be resorted to in its southern bastions during the 1790s and beyond, and also that they were adopted by crowds in western coastal ports in the early nineteenth century. The essential continuity of the tradition, manifested in the actions of 'the great mob', which travelled from Ennis to nearby Clarecastle in June 1790 'to dismantle a vessel' that, it was believed, 'was carrying away a cargo of oats and potatoes', was also evident at Cheekpoint, county Waterford, some two years later. Then a crowd from Waterford city repaired to this location 'to stop outward-bound vessels'. It was also in evidence in Waterford in April 1794 when the town 'mob' responded to the 'high price of provisions' by boarding 'outward bound vessels, laden with grain, which they stripped of their sails'.[57] The attempted occupation of potato boats on the Dublin quays in 1796; at Baltimore in 1800; at Galway on 21 April 1808; spectacularly at Cork in 1817 when a 'half dozen vessels' were compelled to unload cargoes of grain in order that it might be sold at a reduced price at market; at New Quay, in north county Clare, in 1827 and 1830; at Belmullet, county Mayo, also in 1830, Belfast in 1838, Killala, county Mayo and Pullaheeny, county Sligo, in 1840, and Wexford and Ennis in 1842 demonstrate that the tradition continued to be appealed to for the duration of the tradition of food protest.[58] But the increasing lengths of time between incidents suggest that though food rioters at Galway in 1790 and at Carrick-on-Suir and Waterford in 1791 recognized that the exportation of oatmeal and potatoes might be successfully disrupted by targeting warehouses, stores, cellars and shops,[59] the emphasis

56 *Volunteer Journal* (Cork), 15 May, 30 June 1783; *Freeman's Journal*, 5 Feb. 1784; *Volunteer Journal* (Dublin), 6 Feb., 22 Mar. 1784; *Parl. Reg. (Ire.)*, ii, 347; Hort to Carmarthen, 24 Feb. 1784 (TNA, FO/63/5); *Freeman's Journal*, 14 Feb., 22 Apr. 1784; Jacob to Greer, 12 Feb. 1784 (PRONI, Greer papers, D1044/686, 687A); Northington to Sydney, 26 Jan. 1784 (Yale University, Beinecke Library, Osborn Collection, Northington letterbook, ff 104–5). 57 *Freeman's Journal*, 22 June 1790; Jack Burtchaell, 'The *Waterford Herald* for 1792–3', *Decies*, 47 (1993), 12; *Clonmel Gazette*, 9 Apr. 1794; *Hibernian Journal*, 11 April 1794. 58 *Dublin Evening Post*, 12 Jan. 1796; Wells, 'The Irish famine of 1799–1801', p. 182; *Freeman's Journal*, 27 Apr. 1808, 12 June 1817, 18 June 1840; *Belfast News Letter*, 13 June 1817, 27 Aug. 1838; Cunningham, 'Popular protest and a "moral economy"', pp 32, 44; Cunningham, 'Three Irish urban crowds', pp 146–7; Jordan, *Land and popular politics*, p. 96; Enright, 'Terry Alts: the rise and fall of an agrarian society', p. 226; *Nenagh Guardian*, 11 June 1842. 59 *Ennis Chronicle*, 12 July 1790; Power, 'A Carrickman's diary,

had shifted from preventing the movement of food out of the country to retaining it in the locality and making it available.

This ought to, one might assume, have facilitated recourse to *taxation populaire*. It was certainly resorted to at Waterford in May 1791 when the mob that targeted stores in nearby Ferrybank sold the potatoes they appropriated 'at a low rate to those desirous of becoming purchasers', and at Cork in the summer of 1817.[60] But the strategy employed by 'the Dunlavin mob' was a more accurate harbinger of the future; its stipulation in June 1793 that it 'would not suffer potatoes to exceed 3*d*. per stone, or oatmeal 13*s*. per cwt' pointed to a day when food rioters operated at a greater remove than the pursuit of the *taxation populaire* demanded.[61] The continued trust placed in officials to apply market house regulations in those instances in which crowds 'lodged ... meal in the market', as at Cork in June 1817, was in keeping with this. But significant as it was, it took place in a context in which there was greater resort to intimidation and reliance on fear.[62] The most striking attestation to this was the increased seizure and destruction of foodstuffs. Food seizure was not unprecedented, of course, but it became more commonplace in the early 1790s and was more frequently accompanied by excess violence, against property primarily. It was exemplified by the action of the Bandon mob, which in November 1792 not only appropriated the corn, flour and meal it located in three mills and stores within an eight mile radius, but also destroyed the mills that were their focus.[63] Few food riots were pursued with quite this intensity, though the concerns that animated the Bandon crowd were also in evidence a few days later in Cork city where a large 'mob ... attacked stores and mills'. This crowd was interrupted when they 'were proceeding to carry away the corn and meal',[64] but the enhanced readiness to seize foodstuffs for distribution (free of charge) and to expand the point of attack, exemplified by the Ennis mob which protested at 'the present high price of turf', and burned churns and other milk related paraphernalia opposite the town courthouse in 1792,[65] was in keeping with the more assertive crowds that are detectible from the early 1790s.

The appropriation and distribution of food was the preferred *modus operandi* of the hard pressed population of Dublin in the mid-1790s. They responded to 'the monstrous high price of provisions' and to the resulting privation by forming 'mobs' that were perceived in certain respectable circles to take to the streets with impunity. This was not the case, but the frequency with which 'mobs' of

1787–1809', p. 66; *Dublin Morning Post*, 19 May 1791; Patrick Power, 'A bundle of Waterford papers being news items from Ramsey's *Waterford Chronicle* for 1791', *Journal of the Waterford and South-East of Ireland Archaeological Society*, 10 (1907), 160. **60** *Dublin Morning Post*, 19 May 1791; Cunningham, 'Popular protest and a "moral economy"', p. 44. **61** *Dublin Morning Post*, 15 June 1793. **62** *Gentleman's Magazine*, 87 (1817), 619–20; *Freeman's Journal*, 11 June 1817. **63** Dickson, *Old world colony*, p. 384; *Dublin Chronicle*, 24 Nov. 1792; *Clonmel Gazette*, 24 Nov. 1792. **64** *Dublin Chronicle*, 27 Nov. 1792. **65** *Ennis Chronicle*, 6 Dec. 1792; *Clonmel Gazette*, 15 Dec. 1792. In 1793, in and near Limerick city a 'number' of small assemblies of people targeted and, in a number of cases, 'cut down some improvements': *Clonmel Gazette*, 23 Feb. 1793.

'manufacturers' in distress 'were to be found on the streets of Dublin ... at midday carrying off flour and bread, and entering huxter and baker shops which they plundered' encouraged such conclusions.[66] It resulted in a sequence of comparable incidents that included a body of 'unemployed manufacturers ... plunder[ing] several cars with bacon and butter at Dolphin's Barn' *en route* to the city markets on 21 May 1793; a mob 'carr[ying] off thirty eight flitches of bacon, nine casks of butter and six sacks of meal and flour' on Kevin Street, also in May 1793; a 'party of manufacturers' from the earl of Meath's Liberty 'plunder[ing] several shops of bacon, butter, bread and cheese' in March 1794; a 'riotous mob' assembling on Thomas Street 'and seiz[ing] some cars laden with flour, bacon and other articles of provisions' that 'they possessed themselves of' in May 1795; and another 'riotous mob' robbing 'two cars laden with butter and bacon' near 'Marylebone lane' in May 1793.[67] It is a measure of the plight of the 'inhabitants of the Liberty' who were responsible for a majority of these seizures, and of the moral conviction that impelled them that, on 27 May 1795:

> a very numerous assemblage ... went in procession through divers parts of the metropolis, preceded by a loaf, hung round with crape and other sable[68] appendages on the point of a pole considerably elevated. Immediately after these symbols, which they intended should typify the distress of the times, followed another symbol of misery, personified by a lean wretched horse, on whom was mounted a person in the character of a Chief Mourner, who, ever and anon, looked upward to the loaf, and then with no ill-acted shew of sorrow, applied his handkerchief to his face, in token of grief for its diminutive appearance.[69]

A still more urgent, if less theatrically rich, demonstration of distress was displayed in January 1796, when 'a large number of working manufacturers and tradespeople', who had assembled at the quays 'adjoining the station of [the] potatoe boats' to protest at the price and the availability of this staple punctured the atmosphere with the refrain 'Bread or potatoes, we are starving'.[70] In point of fact, the crisis conditions that impelled food protest in Dublin in the mid-1790s had eased by this point. But the events of these years had accented the tendency of crowds, agitated by distress, or its prospect, to push the boundaries of what they were prepared to undertake in pursuit of affordably priced food.

---

66 *Freeman's Journal*, 25 May 1793, 23 May 1795; *Dublin Morning Post*, 3 Apr. 1794; Higgins to Cooke, 24 Oct. 1796 in Bartlett (ed.), *Revolutionary Dublin*, p. 114; C.J. Woods (ed.), *The journals of Thomas Russell* (Dublin, 1991), p. 75; *Clonmel Gazette*, 25 May 1793. 67 *Dublin Chronicle*, 23 May 1793; *Freeman's Journal*, 21 May 1793; *Dublin Morning Post*, 3 Apr. 1794; *Hibernian Journal*, 15 May, 26 May 1795. One might add another incident caused by 'a numerous mob' that 'plundered' huxter's shops on Francis Street, High Street and other locations in May 1795: *Freeman's Journal*, 23 May 1795. 68 Meaning dark or black. 69 *Hibernian Journal*, 28 May 1795. 70 *Dublin Evening Post*, 12 Jan. 1796; *Walker's Hibernian Magazine*, Jan. 1786, p. 93.

PATTERNS OF PROTEST IN THE EARLY NINETEENTH CENTURY

Dublin in the 1790s demonstrated that the combination of unemployment and a difficult trading environment could sustain a distinct and active pattern of food rioting. The character of food protest more generally was primarily determined by the price and availability of food, which is why the subsistence crisis of 1799–1800 provides a more reliable guide to protest at the end of the eighteenth century. It certainly confirms the trend, perceptible in 1783–4, of the diminishing riotousness of urban locations in the east and south, and anticipates the expanding impact of agrarian protest, and of the rural environment in general, on the manner in which it was pursued in the nineteenth century. This is not to imply that food protest then no longer took place in the urban spaces that had provided its primary bastions since its inauguration. There were food riots in Dublin in 1800, 1817, 1826, 1840 and 1847; in Belfast in 1808, 1812, 1817, 1838 and 1846; in Cork in 1801, 1817 and 1842; in Drogheda in 1801, 1812, 1817 and 1847; in Waterford in 1812, 1817, 1819 and 1846 and in Youghal in 1800, 1801 and 1846; in Clonakilty (1801, 1812), Dundalk (1800), Baltimore (1800), Carrick-on-Suir (1812, 1846), Skibbereen (1812), and Kilkenny (1817). But more incidents took place in Limerick (1800, 1817, 1830, 1837, 1839 and 1840), Galway (1808, 1812, 1817, 1824, 1827, 1829, 1831, 1840 (2), 1841, 1842, 1845), and Ennis (January and February 1801, 1817, 1822, 1830, May and June 1842 and 1846), which were its main urban bastions in the nineteenth century. Moreover, there were still more episodes in a variety of mainly rural inland urban locations in Munster, Leinster and Connaught with little or no previous history of food rioting; these include Mallow (1800), Cashel (1800), Killaloe (1800), Kilrush (1808), Edenderry (1812, 1817), Tullamore (1812, 1817), Rathangan (1812, 1817), Moate (1817), Athlone (1817 and 1842), Granard (1817), Mullingar (1813, 1817), Tuam (1817), Gort (1817, 1847), Loughrea (1817, 1842), Castlebar (1830), Sligo (1840 and 1842), Ballina (1817, 1830, 1842), and Westport (1831) (see Maps 2, 3 and 4).

This lengthy locational listing has been provided, not to reinforce the point that the geographical centre of food protest shifted inwards and westwards in the early nineteenth century, but to emphasize the fact that the manner in which it was conducted also changed. This is not to deny the many elements of continuity. The Skibbereen crowd that unloaded potatoes from a sloop destined for Dublin in April 1812 and deposited the cargo in the town's market house, from where it was sold at a reduced rate, demonstrates that *taxation populaire* had not been forsaken in the maelstrom of insurgency and confrontation that defined the second half of the 1790s, and that continued at a lower intensity in the early nineteenth century. It was in evidence again later the same month in Carrick-on-Suir where the crowd oversaw that meal appropriated from corn stores in that town was deposited in temporary storage pending its sale 'at a moderate price to be fixed'. And it was attempted in Belfast and Athlone in February 1817 when magistrates frustrated efforts in the former to 'affix a limited price on the pota-

toes offered for sale', and in the latter to sell 'at their own price' meal and potatoes that had been taken by 'a mob of several hundred'.[71] It was also the case that
attempts by a crowd to resort to *taxation populaire* could be frustrated by the
unwillingness, or the inability, of more aggressive elements to adhere to this
tradition. When in February 1801 'a large concourse of people' lodged a 'quantity
of oatmeal' in Ennis market house that they had 'brought off' from a corn store
at Drumbiggle, county Clare, they did so in the expectation that it would be
offered for sale at a reduced price, but their intentions were frustrated when the
grain was 'plundered, and carted away at night, by an hungry multitude of men,
women and children'.[72]

The readiness of the authors of the commentary describing this episode to
avow that 'hunger' was an issue in this instance is significant, but it could also
be invoked to legitimize actions that did not chime with the communitarian prin-
ciples of food protest. This was manifest in the report from Drogheda, also
dating from 1801, of a 'numerous body of men and some women' 'forcibly'
appropriating 'oatmeal and potatoes from persons who had purchased' the same
for resale elsewhere, and engaging in 'breaking open the store and houses of several inhabitants, and distributing the provisions contained therein amongst themselves'.[73] It may also point to an unacknowledged legacy of the political
radicalization of the 1790s since the preferred *modus operandi* of the crowds that
sought to set the price at which food was sold in the early nineteenth century
was not to vend the food directly but to 'swear' merchants, retailers, and,
increasingly, farmers not to sell at above a specified price – in historical terms
the *taxation populaire* they favoured bore closer comparison to that applied at
Dunlavin in 1793 than at Waterford in 1791.[74] It was demonstrated by the crowd
that mobilized at Killaloe, county Clare, in the spring of 1800 in order 'to swear'
the population 'not to sell their potatoes out of the parish or for a larger price
than half a guinea for eight bushels'; it was also resorted to in county Tipperary
in May 1800 when the Long family of Drombane were 'sworn to sell as much of
their potatoes as possible to the people of the area at 4s. 4d. per barrel and only
to feed their pigs once with them'; at Armagh in 1817 when 'unlawful oaths'
were tendered to farmers to deter them from 'asking higher prices for provisions
than the [crowd] was prepared to countenance'; and, in a variation on this theme,
it was reported from Kilworth, county Cork, in 1812 that farmers were sworn
not to take their potatoes to market.[75]

In practice, however, as was the case in Dublin in 1793 and 1795, a majority
of the 'mobs' that appropriated flour, grain and potatoes in the early nineteenth

71 Cunningham, 'Popular protest and a "moral economy"', pp 33–4, 35, 40; *Freeman's Journal*, 11
Feb. 1817; Report of Major General Mahon, Feb. 1817 (TNA, HO/100/192 f. 164). 72 *Ennis
Chronicle*, 26 Feb. 1801. 73 *Ennis Chronicle*, 26 Mar. 1801; Wells, 'The Irish famine of 1799–1801',
p. 181. 74 Above, p. 106; Cunningham, 'Popular protest and a "moral economy"', p. 42. 75
Power, *Law, politics and society in eighteenth-century Tipperary*, p. 194; Wells, 'The Irish famine of
1799–1801', p. 182; Cunningham, 'Popular protest and a "moral economy"', pp 35, 42.

century made no identifiable effort to sell the commodity they commandeered at a fair price.[76] John Cunningham has wisely cautioned 'that the sources' may 'not tell the full story', and observed, *à propos* of county Clare, that 'later disturbances drew on a repertoire of protest which was consistent with a developed moral economy'.[77] This is contestable, and it is in any event less tenable if food rioting is conceived of as a changeable and changing tradition that embraced more forms of protest than can be accommodated within the concept of a 'moral economy' as it is commonly understood. There are issues, certainly, with not distinguishing between the practices of appropriating provisions, even when it was unambiguously for communal rather than personal benefit, and taking temporary possession of foodstuffs so they could be sold at a reduced rate in a market or at a market house, and the money given to their owner, particularly when the pattern of incidents suggests that the former exceeded the latter.

What is certain is that after 1799–1801, provisions were *appropriated* with greater frequency from mills, warehouses, stores, ships and canal barges as the increased use made of the Grand and Royal canals to transport foodstuffs to the capital provided the rationale for food rioting in a variety of small country towns in the midland counties of Longford, Westmeath, Offaly, and Kildare (see Map 2). In general terms the *modus operandi* echoed that of previous decades. For example, the way that 'the considerable number of people, who declared their determination not to allow the food of the country to be taken away at this season of distress and scarcity', boarded three vessels laden with grain and butter at Dungarvan bears comparison with similar interventions conducted over many decades; the crowd in this instance 'proceeded to dismantle the vessels, and … succeeded in taking away their sails'.[78] Further instances of attacks on vessels at Cork, Belfast, Galway and Waterford in 1816–7, at Limerick and Belmullet in 1830, at Killala, county Mayo, and Sligo in 1840, and at Clarecastle, county Clare, in 1842, when 'a large concourse of people' deprived a ship in port of at least ten tons of flour and meal destined for those still worse off in the western part of that county, were pursued in a largely like fashion.[79] There were also cases of this kind during the early years of the Great Famine,[80] but one of the consequences of the surge in the number of incidents then and of the greater desperation that activated crowds was that this form of food protest accounted for a declining proportion of the total. This was part of a longer trend, attributable to the greater resolution of the authorities to ensure the unhindered move-

76 Wells, 'The Irish famine of 1799–1800', p. 181; Ó Dalaigh (ed.), *Corporation book of Ennis*, pp 314–15.   77 Cunningham, 'Popular protest and a "moral economy"', p. 44.   78 *Freeman's Journal*, 21 Dec. 1816.   79 Above, p. 105; *Freeman's Journal*, 11 Feb., 11 June 1817; *Gentleman's Magazine*, 87 (1817), 619–20; Cunningham, *Galway, 1790–1914*, p. 88; Cunningham, 'Popular protest and a "moral economy"', p. 44; O'Connor, *A labour history of Waterford*, p. 18; Lee, 'The food riots of 1830 and 1840', p. 56; Jordan, *Local and popular politics in Ireland*, p. 95; Power, *A history of Clarecastle*, p. 415.   80 Kinealy, *This great calamity*, p. 145; Fraher, 'The Dungarvan disturbances', p. 140; *Freeman's Journal*, 18 June 1840, 28 Sept., 7 Oct. 1846; *Nenagh Guardian*, 7 Oct. 1846.

ment of goods by sea; it was, for example, in evidence at Cork in 1816 when an attempt to 'dismantle' a ship laden with potatoes for a foreign market was frustrated by the mayor and sheriff.[81] But it is more notable, and in keeping with the transition of food rioting from a primarily maritime to a primarily inland phenomenon in the early nineteenth century, that the number of canal barges and river vessels that were intercepted exceeded sea-going vessels, and that they were exceeded in turn by attacks on cars and carts ferrying provisions from producers to millers and merchants, and from millers and merchants to urban consumers.[82]

This trend was not unanticipated. The proximity of food rioting to navigable waterways, long a feature of the geography of food rioting in England, was really only visible in Ireland in the eighteenth century in the Suir river valley.[83] The construction of the Grand and Royal Canals, and their completion to Shannon Harbour and to Termonbarry in 1804 and 1817 respectively, opened up the midlands to a much expanded commercial traffic in provisions. This created opportunities of which producers and wholesalers were eager to avail; it also generated fears in the local populace that resulted in a spate of food riots in or near to the urban centres along both routes, and direct attacks on the canals themselves (Map 2). Beginning in 1812 with riots at Edenderry, county Offaly, aimed at preventing the movement of provisions along the Grand Canal, and the communication of an anonymous letter to boatmen at Mullingar in 1813 warning against transporting potatoes to Dublin via the Royal Canal, a sequence of incidents occurred along both waterways and the Barrow extension (which brought the Grand Canal south to Carlow town) at Tullamore, Kildare, Rathangan, Carlow, Robertstown, Lanesborough, Granard, Moate and Mullingar during the decade that followed. They were comparable in the main to the attacks mounted on ships and carts carrying provisions, except that these protesters could interrupt trade for longer periods by emptying the canals of water. This did not require a major mobilization, but the participation of hundreds of men in breaching the Grand Canal between Philipstown (Daingean) and Edenderry in 1817, which disrupted the movement of food for a fortnight, and the breach reported from Mullingar, which resulted in the loss of water along a five-mile stretch of the Royal Canal outside the town, demonstrated what could be achieved with relatively little effort.[84] It was a more potent tactic certainly than that available to those seeking to inhibit sea-going vessels, though in most other respects the obstacles placed by food rioters in the way of those engaged in transporting food were akin to those traditionally deployed, and were resorted to increasingly in the nineteenth century in respect of vessels plying the river Shannon, the Shannon estuary and Galway Bay. This can

81 *Freeman's Journal*, 20 June 1816. 82 See, for examples of the interception of carts, O'Neill, 'The Catholic Church and relief', 138; Jordan, *Land and popular politics*, p. 96; *Belfast News Letter*, 1 Aug. 1837, 25 Jan. 1839; Lee, 'The food riots of 1830 and 1840', p. 61. 83 Bohstedt, *The politics of provisions*, pp 96, 133, 175, 207. 84 Cunningham, 'Popular protest and a "moral economy"', pp 32–3, 37, 41–2; *Freeman's Journal*, 10 Feb. 1817; Abbot, 'The Downshire estates at Edenderry, 1800–1856', pp 38–9; Post, *The last great subsistence crisis*, p. 73

be seen in action in 1822 when much of the west was gripped by famine, and again
in 1846–7, when conditions were still worse.

In May 1822, when conditions in county Clare were particularly difficult, a
boat, 'laden with flour', was 'attacked by the populace' on the river Fergus at
Clarecastle and 'ninety bags of flour were carried away'.[85] In addition, following
the example set by 'the country people on the banks of the canal', those residing
on the banks of the river Shannon would not 'suffer any potatoes to leave their
neighbourhood'.[86] Nearly a quarter of a century later, when east county Clare was
again wrestling with the threat of famine, similar tactics were employed once
more. They were resorted to at Clarecastle early in October 1846 when 'an
assembly of labourers, to the number of from 400 to 500 … proceeded to the
wharf at that place and prevented the shipment of some cargoes of oats' to
Limerick. And later in the month the owner of a mill at O'Brien's Bridge on the
Shannon river reported that he was frustrated in an attempt to send a 'boat to
Limerick with oatmeal and flour' as the vessel 'was intercepted at the first lock
on the [Limerick–Killaloe] canal' and obliged to turn back.[87]

The adoption by the rural population of the midlands, and of those parts of
counties Clare and Tipperary neighbouring the river Shannon, of tactics long
associated with urban food protest was an inevitable outcome of the acceleration
in the early nineteenth century of the ongoing movement of food protest from its
traditional southern and eastern urban bastions to the midlands and mid-western
counties. This did not hasten the cessation of food rioting in its traditional urban
bastions, as already mentioned, though the interval between incidents tended to
be longer, to be largely confined to the most challenging crises, and to possess
distinct, and distinguishing, characteristics. This is most striking in the case of
Dublin where bread riots occurred in 1817, 1826, 1840 and 1847. Commencing
on 19 June 1817 with attacks on 'baker's men … carrying baskets of bread' on
Thomas Street, this ostensibly spontaneous irruption escalated into a general
assault on bakers' shops and provisions stores, beginning on the south side of the
river Liffey, and extending across the river to Ormond market, which lasted, in
defiance of a curfew, for two days.[88] The cause on this occasion was the 'very
high price' of bread and oatmeal – which were 'the chief food of the lower orders
of the people'.[89] Nine years later, in August 1826, there was a repeat, on a
smaller scale, of these events as unemployment and falling wages (exacerbated by
the alignment of the Irish and English currencies) prompted 'a riotous mob of
several hundred persons' to descend on bakers, huxters and other shops at a
number of points in the city.[90]

85 *Freeman's Journal*, 8, 13 May 1822.   86 *Freeman's Journal*, 15 May 1822.   87 Revenue
Commissioners to Dublin Castle, 7 Oct. 1846, James Denniston to [ ] (NAI, OP: Clare,
1846/5/27885, 29933). Similar 'obstruction' was reported from Birdhill, county Tipperary, on the
other side of the river: Tracy to Redington, 5 Nov. 1846 (NAI, OP: Clare, 1846/5/30567).
88 *Saunders' News-Letter*, 20 June 1817 quoted in Swift, *History of the Dublin bakers*, pp 203–5.
89 *Freeman's Journal*, 9, 12 June 1826.   90 Swift, *History of the Dublin bakers*, pp 206–7; *Freeman's*

Further bread riots, and attacks on bread carts, were reported in January 1847 as food price inflation took hold; by then the proliferation of bread shops ensured such retail outlets were a favoured target in urban locations. Attacks were made also in the winter of 1846–7 on bread shops in Cork and Belfast. In the latter case, the descent on bakers' shops by a body of 200 men, until recently employed in the construction of the Belfast to Ballymena railway, echoed the pattern identifiable in other large towns. One may instance Waterford, where the forced entry of White's bakery in 1819, and Limerick where the focus on retail outlets in 1830 and 1837 was a further indication of the adaptation of food protest to the increasingly commercialized manner in which bread was traded. It also reflected the fact that baker's bread was an increasingly significant source of carbohydrate in urban areas.[91] It is thus not surprising that amid the plethora of incidents in the autumn of 1846, bread and bakers' shops featured prominently. Following on the pattern established in county Cork in the autumn and winter of 1846–7 when bread and bakers' shops were raided in Mitchelstown, Youghal, Cloyne, Killeagh, Mallow and Castlemartyr, those shops were among the most common targets in towns across the country.[92] Elsewhere, mills, meal and grain stores, potato stores and carts carrying grain and potatoes were the priority whereas the practice, pursued actively for a time in the eighteenth century, of intercepting bacon, butter, cheese and other provisions was distinguished by its rarity.[93]

SOUNDS AND SIGNS

Another, and perhaps still more indicative, manifestation of the mutability of food rioting is provided by the reporting of the cries uttered, and banners or other emblems borne by protesters. It may be that these were a feature of food riots in Ireland from the outset, since it is unlikely that those who engaged in food protest in Cork in 1729 or Dublin in 1740 did so silently, but there are no reports indicating that they either marched behind a banner or engaged in identifiable and resonant cries prior to the 1790s. Saliently, the cries and calls that are reported then and later echo those uttered in England, which suggests not only that the Irish public was more aware then of the manner in which food rioting was conducted in England than the intermittent reportage of such events in the Irish press implies, but also that they were disposed to borrow and emulate based on what they gleaned.[94] In any

Journal, 9 Aug. 1826.   **91** Ó Tuathaigh, 'An age of distress and reform: 1800–60', p. 102; Donnelly, *Land and people of nineteenth-century Cork*, p. 90; Christine Kinealy and Gerard MacAtasney, *The hidden famine: poverty, hunger and sectarianism in Belfast, 1840–50* (London, 2000), pp 62–3; Kinealy, *The great Irish Famine*, pp 127–9; O'Connor, *A labour history of Waterford*, p. 19; Lee, 'The food riots of 1830 and 1840', p. 57; *Freeman's Journal*, 12 June 1837.   **92** Burke to [ ], [Oct.], Godby to Redington, 21 Sept., Rowland to Knaresborough, 23 Sept., Knaresborough to Redington, 22 Sept., Bell to Labouchere, 24 Sept., [ ] to [ ], 26 Sept., Ware to Redington, 20 Oct. 1846 (NAI, OP: Cork, 1846/6/19081, 23595, 25895, 25897, 25979, 28675); above, pp 78–9.   **93** Above, pp 45, 103, 107; notable exceptions were Carrigaholt, county Clare in 1817, and Limerick in 1830: see below, pp 119, 171.

event, it is clear from the cries issuing from 'the large number of working manufacturers and tradespeople' that gathered at Dublin port on Sunday, 10 January 1796
calling out 'Bread or potatoes, we are starving' that protesters sought by that date
not only to communicate their concerns but also to introduce them into the public
sphere.[95] Other occasions followed, usually but not invariably in cases in which the
assembled throng had reached a significant numerical threshold. One of the better-
documented examples, from the port of Waterford in 1819, featured men, women
and 'ragged boys' marching behind a banner bearing the slogan 'Bread or work'.[96]
Seven years later, in the course of the less obviously orchestrated bread riots in
Dublin, Edward Walsh, a labourer, was heard pronounce that he would 'have bread
or blood', which anticipated the sentiment that was more routinely expressed by
protesting crowds in the mid-nineteenth century. It was, for example, appealed to
by members of the large crowd who responded to the summons conveyed by a 'bellman' at Ennis in 1842 following several deaths in the course of an attack on
Bannatyne's grain stores; some at least of this crowd 'openly declared that nothing
will gratify them but blood' on the grounds, one of their number explained, that 'we
must have blood for blood'. Yet the voices that directed the cry 'kill them, kill them
– they are only a handful' at the soldiers lined up in Dungarvan in September 1846
still better demonstrated the ease with which, in certain circumstances, food protest
could become violent.[97] These were not sentiments normally expressed, but they
reflected the genuine popular outrage that fuelled much protest of this nature at this
time. Interestingly, it was not the only sloganizing to which recourse was had at
Ennis in May 1842. Earlier in the incident, the crowd was heard to pronounce 'We
would rather die than starve'; this echoed the 'threatening exclamations' invoked by
the large crowd that targeted Campbell's 'potato manufactory' at Newtownards in
1839 which pronounced 'that the people might as well suffer themselves to be shot
as starved to death'. It also mirrored a popular proverb recorded by James Hall in
1813: 'better steal and be hung than die for want'.[98]

Comparable sentiments were expressed more frequently, and with more reason,
in 1846–7 because the crowd that assembled in April 1846 at Fethard, county
Tipperary, pronounced: 'we are in a state of actual starvation'. The crowd at
Killeagh, county Cork, protested in May that they would rather 'be shot than …
die of starvation', while that at Galway observed variously that 'it is better to die

94 Post, *The last great subsistence crisis*, p. 70; for examples of the reporting of food rioting in
England and Scotland see: *Hibernian Journal*, 12 Aug. 1795; *Ennis Chronicle*, 20 Aug. 1795, 25 Sept.
1800, 1, 8, June, 3 July, 14 Dec. 1816; *Freeman's Journal*, 27 Apr. 1812, 23 Aug. 1826.   95 *Dublin
Evening Post*, 12 Jan. 1796.   96 O'Connor, *A labour history of Waterford*, p. 19.   97 *Freeman's
Journal*, 9 Aug. 1826, 5 Oct. 1846; *Nenagh Guardian*, 11 June 1842; Power, *A history of Clarecastle*,
p. 416; Fraher, 'Dungarvan disturbances', p. 141 It is noteworthy in this context that a notice
posted on the Tholsel gate in Galway in 1817 was entitled 'Bread or blood': Cunningham, *Galway
1790–1914*, p. 88; see below, p. 122; and that the 'mob of country people' that attacked 'an escort
of cars loaded with provisions' on 6 July 1847 was warned 'they would have the provisions or our
lives': Report, 12 July 1847 (NAI, OP: Cork, 1847/6/1038).   98 *Belfast News Letter*, 25 Jan. 1839;
James Hall, *Tour through Ireland* (2 vols, London, 1813), i, 60.

by the sword than to die of starvation', that 'it is better to die trying to keep the food at home than to die later of starvation' and still more defiantly 'that they will not starve any longer'.[99] There were those, of course, who claimed that such pronouncements were fantastical. Colonel William Phipps of Oaklands, Clonmel, opined at the outset of the 1846–7 episode 'that the cry of starvation is in most instances a crafty pretext' for 'the worst of purposes', but this was unwarranted.[100] The plight of the population was genuine, and the increased recourse to such cries was an accurate barometer of desperation. Arrestingly put by 'a Tipperary peasant' who accounted for his presence among a protesting crowd in October 1846 by claiming that it was preferable 'we should be shot in the ditches than die of hunger', and by a large crowd estimated at five or six thousand which marched through Listowel, county Kerry, shouting 'Bread or Blood', recourse was also had to equivalently pithy but more moving sloganizing – most notably 'work or food' as the populace became more dependent on public works.[101]

As the awareness that relief, from whatever quarter it came, was crucial to their survival took commanding hold, the reported instances of crowds pronouncing in favour of work increased. This realization was sufficiently firmly rooted in advance of the Great Famine to cause the labourers and others who comprised the 'mob' that rose up in Limerick in June 1840 in protest at the price of provisions to demand employment, but it was articulated most insistently and frequently in 1846–7 when access to public works was a matter of life or death.[102] Calls for employment were, for example, voiced by gatherings at Banagher, King's county, Blessington, county Wicklow and Sligo in September 1846, in county Kerry in October, and in counties Kilkenny, Kerry and Donegal in December.[103] They were uttered still-more insistently in a larger number of locations in April and May 1847 in response to the premature suspension of public works upon which the needy, the necessitous, and, still more, the hungry had become dependent. This was the priority of the crowd, estimated at one hundred, which 'assembled' in the hamlet of Kilmurry Ibrickane, county Clare, 'and in a riotous manner demanded work' in April; of gatherings in the same county at Drumline, near Newmarket-on-Fergus, Ennis, Meelick and Ennistymon; at Ballingarry in county Limerick, and Ballinrobe,

99 County inspector's report, 13 Apr. 1846 (NAI, OP: Tipperary, 1846/27/9025); Donnelly, *The land and the people of nineteenth-century Cork*, p. 91; *Freeman's Journal*, 6 Oct. 1846; Cunningham, ""Tis hard to argue starvation into quiet"", p. 15.   100 Phipps to Redington, 18 Apr. 1846 (NAI, OP: Tipperary, 1846/27/9425).   101 *Freeman's Journal*, 3, 5 Oct. 1846; *Tuam Herald*, 3 Oct. 1846; Leyne to Redington, 15, 16 Sept. 1846 (NAI, OP: Clare, 1846/5/23897, 23947); Kerr, *The Catholic Church and the famine*, p. 13; Conwell, 'Clanricarde and his county Galway estates', p. 24.   102 Lee, 'The food riots of 1830 and 1840', p. 61.   103 Drought to Labouchere, 25 Sept. 1846 (NAI, OP: King's county, 1846/15/25913); Warburton to Labouchere, 23 Sept. 1846 (NAI, OP: Wicklow, 1846/32/25813); O'Connor to Bessborough, 2 Oct. 1846 (NAI, OP, Sligo, 26/1846/26555); Ormond to Labouchere, 6 Dec. 1846 (NAI, OP: Kilkenny, 1846/14/34107); Hewson to Bessborough, 29 Oct., Cheevers to Redington, 29 Oct., Dillon to Redington, 8 Dec., Dillon to Redington, 8 Dec., de Moylens to Redington, 29 Dec. 1846 (NAI, OP: Kerry, 1846/30085, 30149, 34967, 37913); Bulfin to Labouchere, 10 Dec. 1846 (NAI, OP: Donegal, 1846/7/36537).

county Mayo.[104] Similarly, a banner bearing the legend 'We are starving: bread or employment' unfurled in Galway in May of the same year echoed the sentiment 'we would rather die than starve' uttered at Clarecastle in 1842 and anticipated comparable protests in 1846 and 1847 in Ballingarry, county Limerick, Killorglin, county Kerry, Kilmurry and Ennistymon, county Clare, Oranmore, county Galway, Shannon Harbour, King's county, and Killarney, county Kerry where in October 1846 'a bellman was sent out, preceding a person carrying a flag, on which was an inscription indicating the distress of the population'.[105] Such displays provide a compelling illustration of the appreciating recognition by 'the labouring classes' of their dependence on public works and, in 1847 in particular, of the alarm they experienced following on from the fateful abandonment of the schemes of public works in the spring and summer of that year.

While a case can be made, based on these displays, that food rioters then were not only acutely conscious of their plight, but also making a political statement, the reality was that growing malnourishment and the increased inability of those in need to 'earn ... the means of existence' was sufficient to drive protest.[106] It was certainly sufficient in Dublin in the 1790s and 1826; and in Cork in June 1842 when 'the want of any employment, commensurate with the numbers who depend on it', prompted an 'assemblage of about 1,000 poor starving people, impelled by hunger, and the enormous price which potatoes have been selling for ... during the last few months' to break into the city potato market.[107] Appreciating poverty was also identified as the source of the 'great distress' reported at Clones, county Monaghan, and throughout Connaught in 1842. The difficulties experienced by the poor at Clones did not precipitate food protest, but the increased challenges experienced by 'the townspeople and poor tradesmen' elsewhere and 'by the labouring classes' in the countryside lay at the root of 'potato riots' in towns like Ballina, Athlone and Sligo in 1842.[108]

As the increased recourse to sloganizing attests, it is doubtful if food protest would have evolved in the manner in which it did in the early nineteenth century in the absence of the rise in literacy or the popular politicization that was one of the legacies of the French Revolution. It is pertinent in this context to highlight the practice in counties Clare and Tipperary in 1846 of posting notices

---

104 Information of W. McMahoney, 12 Apr. 1847 (NAI, OP: Clare/1847/5/345); RM (Ennis) to Redington, 25 Mar., 7 May 1847 (NAI, OP: Clare, 1847/5/279, 523); *Nation*, 15 May 1847; *Leinster Express*, 22 May 1847; *Freeman's Journal*, 29 May 1847; *Tralee Chronicle*, 15 May 1847; *Connaught Telegraph*, 12 May 1847.   105 Cunningham, *Galway, 1790–1914*, p. 142; Power, *A history of Clarecastle*, p. 415; *Freeman's Journal*, 5, 7 Oct. 1846; Lynch to [ ], 8 Jan. 1847 (NAI, Registered papers, 1847, division 1, vol. 1, 1847/11); *Tralee Chronicle and Killarney Echo*, 15 May 1847; *Nation*, 15 May 1847; *Leinster Express*, 22 May 1847; Information of John Lupton, 27 Nov. 1847 (NAI, OP: King's county, 1847/15/612).   106 Mokyr and Ó Gráda, 'Poor and getting poorer? Living standards in Ireland before the Famine', 209–35; *Nenagh Guardian*, 11 June 1842. 107 *Kerry Evening Post*, 8 June; *Nenagh Guardian*, 11 June 1842. 108 *Belfast News Letter*, 21 June 1842; *Connaught Telegraph*, 8 June 1842; *Freeman's Journal*, 31 May, 9 June 1842; *Nenagh Guardian*, 11 June 1842.

and plackards 'calling on the people to assemble' for various purposes that included preventing 'the sale of ... wheat', demanding work, and, more generally, 'of forcing the consideration of government, and of the landlords to their destitute condition'.[109] Though more work needs to be undertaken to locate such notices in their proper social and political context, they stand out because food protesters traditionally prioritized deeds rather than words. This makes the resort to verbal slogans, when it can be identified, and the use of 'notices' all the more interesting. Yet, it maybe that they are less revealing than the usage of effigies and emblems by a minority of crowds.

The potency of a well-chosen symbol was demonstrated to particular effect by the people of Kilkenny in 1766 when they paraded behind an effigy of a 'meal man'. Six years later, the 'distressed inhabitants of Limerick' had recourse to a similar tactic; they 'proceeded through the streets with the mayor's effigy (having a cap on, and a speech in one hand, and a rod in the other, with a rope about his neck, held by a chimneysweep as hangman)' in protest at the sanguinary consequences of their descent on the Lock Mills in that city in May 1772.[110] Almost half a century later, in January 1817, the decision of the manufacturers of Drogheda to parade the streets of that town 'with emblems of distress' set the tone for a more symbolically richer period, echoing that identifiable in contemporary England. The most powerful manifestation of this was provided by processions behind a loaf of bread attached to a pole (Fig. 3). An adaptation of the 'mourning loaf', draped in black crêpe (or smeared with blood), utilized in England, and resorted to in Dublin in 1795, a majority of the examples located in Ireland date from the 1840s.[111] It was, for example, resorted to in Limerick in 1840 when an element of a local crowd 'marched into town, bearing a loaf on the top of a pole', but it was more commonly encountered during the Great Famine. It was invoked in Portumna, Ballinsaloe and Tuam in county Galway; in Parsonstown, King's county, Ballinalee, county Longford; Ballyconnell and Virginia in county Cavan; Croom, county Limerick; Dungarvan, county Waterford, and in Cork city. It was in addition resorted to in Carrick-on-Suir in September 1846 when 'a large concourse of people' was preceded by a man bear-

109 See Whelan, *The tree of liberty*, pp 84–5; David Dickson, 'Paine and Ireland' in David Dickson et al. (eds), *The United Irishmen: republicanism, radicalism and rebellion* (Dublin, 1993), pp 135–50; James Kelly, 'Political publishing, 1700–1800' in Raymond Gillespie and Andrew Hadfield (eds), *The Oxford history of the Irish book, 1550–1800* (Oxford, 2005), pp 215–33; Kelly to [ ], 3 Sept. 1846, Public notice of the Magistrates of Carrick-on-Suir, 28 Sept. 1846 (NAI, OP: Tipperary/1846/27/23229, 22907); Leyne to Redington, 16 Sept. 1846, Memorial of magistrates of Newmarket on Fergus, 20 Oct. 1846 (NAI, OP: Clare/1846/5/23947, 29333); [Leyne] to Redington, 11 May 1847 (NAI, OP: Clare/1847/5/484). **110** William Colles to Barry Colles, 14 June 1766 (NAI, Prim Collection, 89/92); *Limerick Chronicle*, 14 May 1772; *Freeman's Journal*, 19 May 1772; below, pp 167–8. **111** John Stevenson, *Popular disturbances in England, 1700–1870* (London, 1979), pp 129–30; John Bohstedt, *Riots and community politics in England and Wales, 1790–1810* (Cambridge, MA, 1983), p. 7; Cunningham, 'Popular protest and a "moral economy"', p. 38; above, p. 107.

THE INTENDED
MEETING
AT THE
Cork Mountain
ADJOURNED FOR A MONTH.

Fellow Labourers and Sufferers,

As our ' NOTICE' has gone before the World, and its object is now pretty well understood, and as more serious and grave attention is likely to be arrested and bestowed on the causes which suggested our adopting such a course, and as the assembling of multitudes is calculated to excite alarm in many, and as others would fouly and falsely insinuate, that under an open and specious pretext, latent and ulterior objects were designed, we hereby NOTICE that no such Meeting will be held at the Cork Mountain or elsewhere, by us, on Saturday next. By thus giving it up, we defy our enemies, disappoint our slanderers, we gratify our Friends, the friends of humanity, and we will refrain from embarrassing a PARENTAL GOVERNMENT who are engaged in devising means to alleviate our miseries and better our condition.

Moreover, what was the true and only real object of our Meeting? Was it not to give evidence of the appalling calamity and of our consequent distressed state? to excite speedy attention to our craving wants? to bespake the generous forbearance as well as the just consideration of Landlords? and to call aloud by the voices of congregated thousands, on the Government to hasten to our rescue from Starvation, by devising prompt and efficient means of Relief? Well then let us have the furtherance of these our objects to the Press, where Public attention will be claimed and secured to them more effectually than amid the confusion and tumult of a Mighty Gathering.

This course will be less offensive, more prudent, and consistent with personal safety and public tranquillity, and let us request of the Editor of the SOUTHERN REPORTER (the uniform advocate of the duties of humanity, and of the rights of the people),to give insertion on next Saturday's paper to the observations that were intended to be made, on our part, at the Meeting, whereby we hope to appear more deserving of commisseration than unfeeling censure. Let us also request of our beloved Clergy, (our Guardians and comforters in peril and adversity) to repair to their Chapels on next Saturday morning, one hour before their usual time, so as to direct the early circulation of this NOTICE amongst their congration, and inform them that the reported Meeting will not BE HELD   And may we likewise most respectfully beg leave to request that they will publish that the Pastor of each Parish will appoint an early day, and will select Six or more intelligent and conscientious Farmers, and as many labourers (to represent their class,) that will preside over this Convention (after having invited any respectable gentleman or Magistrate resident in the District, to associate with them in the Work of Charity,) to confer together, in order to make an equitablearrangement, in the existing differences between the Farmers and Labourers, arising from the common calamity that has befallen all, by the failure of the Potato Crop, as this is at present a vexatious question, and the prolific source of much trouble, discontent and disunion.

Given and Dated this 13th Day of August, 1846, by your Fellow-Sufferers.

THE DISTRESSED FARMERS AND LABOURERS.

Figure 2: Poster cancelling meeting at Cork Mountain, 13 July 1846 (National Archives of Ireland, OP: Cork, 1846/6/22439). The proposal to convene a meeting attests to the organisational, strategic and political awareness of the peasantry of Cork, while the poster announcing its cancellation is revealing of the manner in which they had come to use print as a medium of communication.

ing a staff 'on the top of which were placed two loaves of bread', and in 1847 when crowds displayed their need for assistance in various parts of the country by 'carrying poles adorned with loaves of bread'. And, in a variation on the theme, 'a large body of people bearing a black flag' was observed 'going through the town' of Dingle, county Kerry, in September 1846.[112]

THE CHANGING CHARACTER OF FOOD PROTEST IN THE NINETEENTH CENTURY

These attempts to give verbal and visual expression to the concerns of those who engaged in food rioting are useful for what they reveal of the mindset of the populace, though such displays were dwarfed numerically by riots involving food appropriation and increasing conflict. This was true, particularly, of high-profile incidents that received extensive coverage, by reason of their size and location. The food riot that took place in Limerick in 1830 is a case in point. Precipitated by a rise in the price of oatmeal and by a scarcity of potatoes, the poorer parts of the population succumbed to 'panic'. The depth of their anxiety was made apparent on the morning of 25 June when five carts carrying oatmeal were stripped of their contents on Castle Street *en route* to George's Quay. It was the prelude to a hectic sequence of events as over the ensuing two days diverse elements of the city population seized oatmeal on board a ship moored at Arthur's Quay, raided the premises of ten merchants, grocers and other retailers, commandeered 200 bags of flour from Hogan's mill in the city, seized 60 bags of flour from a sail boat on the Long Dock, intercepted further bread carts, and targeted farmers in rural Annacotty. In the course of the 36 hours that they were active, as well as flour, oatmeal and bread, they appropriated, cheese, bacon, ham, lard and, not least, whiskey. Food rioters rarely targeted this range of commodities, but, as the presence of whiskey on the list attests, this was an instance when what commenced as an orthodox food riot assumed some at least of the features of looting as shop owners, merchants, millers and others wilted in the face of the fury of the mob.[113] As such it bears comparison with other, less dramatic, incidents in the Irish food rioting tradition in which protesters indulged their destructive capacities. Indicatively, no attempt was made in this instance to main-

---

112 Lee, 'The food riots of 1830 and 1840', p. 61; Cunningham, '"'Tis hard to argue starvation into quiet'", pp 24–5; Martin to Pennefeather, 14 May 1846 (NAI, OP: Cavan, 1846/4/11659); Briscoe to Redington, 30 Sept. 1846 (NAI, OP: Tipperary, 1846/27/26371); Warburton to Labouchere, 8 Sept. 1846 (NAI, OP, King's county, 1846/15/23459); Kinealy, *This great calamity*, p. 89; *Freeman's Journal*, 5 Oct. 1846; Information of Joseph Hayes, 25 Sept. 1846 (NAI, OP: Kerry, 1846/12/26375). 113 For a fuller account, from which this summary derives, see Lee, 'The food riots of 1830 and 1840', pp 56–9; Liam Hogan, 'The Limerick food riot of 1830' at https://medium.com/@Limerick1914/objects-of-a-deeper-interest-part-2 (accessed July 2016).

tain discipline, or in the comparable incident that occurred in the same city in June 1840, when meal and flour stores, bakeries, and cars carrying flour were compelled to respond by offering food for sale at a price the populace were prepared to pay.[114] Other interventions at this time were pursued in comparable fashion. Many, whether well documented as is the case of the episode at Clarecastle in 1842, or poorly chronicled, which is the case with proceedings at Doone, county Mayo, in 1831, simply do not conform to the classic image of the disciplined riot because the crowd prioritized the seizure of goods.

This point about food seizures must be considered in context, however, as Bohstedt's analysis of food rioting in England between 1790 and 1810 suggests that 54 per cent of cases resulted in the seizure of goods.[115] There is insufficient information with which to engage in a detailed comparison of the situation in Ireland at this time and later, but if the sample of instances of *taxation populaire* is adopted as a guide, it was not only never so firmly rooted in Ireland as it was in France, but also in decline in the early nineteenth century. If, as this implies, the orderly precepts of a 'moral economy' possessed diminishing purchase with the populace by then, it is consistent with the fact that food-motivated disturbances took place increasingly in or near to towns and villages in those parts of the mid-west and west where the population increase was highest and the pre-Famine economic crisis was concentrated. But because it was not exclusive to these regions, it is more reasonable and more accurate to describe and identify it as a feature of the culture of those on the economic margins whether they lived on the periphery in Ulster and north Leinster, where proto-industry was in economic free fall; in Connaught where the cultivation of marginal lands had increased rather than eased dependence on the potato; or in south Leinster and Munster where there was an expanding economic gap between farmers and cottiers and labourers.[116]

It was an outcome, of course, of the fact that as a result of uneven growth the land poor and labouring cohort of the population increased sharply between 1821 and 1841 in those parts of the south and west where demographic growth was highest. And it was accentuated by the effects of increased commercialization, which exacerbated the vulnerability of the cottiers and labourers who rented small plots of land from farmers, and who were the rural equivalent of labourers and marginalized artisans in towns.[117] In the absence of secure access to food-

114 Lee, 'The food riots of 1830 and 1840', pp 60–2.   115 John Bohstedt, 'Gender, household and community politics: women in English riots, 1790–1810', *Past and Present*, 120 (1988), 105; idem, *Riots and community politics in England and Wales, 1790–1810* (Cambridge, MA, 1983).   116 Liam Kennedy, 'The rural economy, 1820–1914' in Liam Kennedy and Philip Ollerenshaw, *An economic history of Ulster, 1820–1939* (Manchester, 1985), pp 1–61; Brenda Collins, 'Proto-industrialization and pre-Famine emigration', *Social History*, 7 (1982), 127–46; Eric Almquist, 'Labour specialization and the Irish economy in 1841: an aggregate occupational analysis', *Economic History Review*, 2nd series, 36 (1983), 506–17.   117 L. Kennedy and L.A. Clarkson, 'Birth, death and exile: Irish population history, 1700–1921' in Brian Graham and Lyndsey Proudfoot (eds), *An historical geography of Ireland* (London, [1993]), pp 158–84; Enright, 'Terry Alts: the rise and fall of an agrarian

stuffs, the poor were, as the augmenting pattern of rural and food protest attests, increasingly prone to take matters into their own hands climaxing in 1846–7 when the reality of famine resulted in a surge of disorder. Consistent with the country's primarily rural character, it was there that the impulse to engage in food rioting was now strongest.

One consequence of the increase in food rioting in towns and villages in the nineteenth century was a convergence in the manner in which food riots and agrarian protest were conducted. A word of caution is warranted. Food rioting and agrarian protest were, and remained, distinguishable phenomena, but the preparedness of labourers in rural Ulster in 1800 to incinerate barns in the expectation that it would convince farmers to lower food prices was a pointer to the future.[118] Indicatively, the practice of swearing individuals, reported in 1800 from Killaloe, county Clare, Drombane, county Tipperary, and from Kilworth, county Cork, and in 1812 from Carrick-on-Suir, to compel producers to sell food at a fixed price was in keeping with the *modus operandi* of rural protesters, while in another manifestation of shared concerns it is notable that the Caravats assembled in 1815 with the specific purpose 'of reducing the price of potatoes'.[119] Recourse to acts of condign and intimidating violence, administered in the name of Captain Slasher on the carriers of potatoes at Bottle Hill, Mallow in June 1800; 'threats and menaces' issued by the Steel Boys in 1830 to inhibit the movement of food in county Mayo in 1830; by the Terry Alts in county Clare in 1831–2 and by their successors in the same county in 1846–7, were more obviously in keeping with the tradition of agrarian protest. Furthermore, they demanded to be taken more seriously than the menaces and threats of 'severe treatment' cast in the direction of 'the owners of ... potatoe wherries' by the Dublin 'mobs' in 1795.[120]

Food rioting and agrarian protest are not always readily disentangled, but the action of the 'gang' that 'broke open the house of James McGrath of Borrisoleigh', county Tipperary, in May 1800, 'dragged him from his bed, beat him cruelly with a pitchfork, and forced him to swear to sell his potatoes at a certain price' points to the overlap, and the impact of agrarian disorder on the traditionally more restrained practice of food protest.[121] It is further highlighted

society', p. 225; Ignatius Murphy, *Before the famine struck – life in west Clare, 1834–45* (Dublin, 1996), pp 22–30; Mokyr and Ó Gráda, 'Poor and getting poorer? Living standards in Ireland before the Famine', 209–35.   118 P.A. Worthington, 'Dearth, death and disease: an analysis of mortality crises in five Lagan valley parishes 1700–1850' (MA, Queen's University Belfast, 1991), p. 248. 119 Wells, 'The Irish famine of 1799–1801', p. 182; Power, *Law, politics and society in eighteenth-century Tipperary*, p. 194; Cunningham, 'Popular protest and a "moral economy"', p. 35.   120 *Cork Advertizer*, 7 June 1800 ('severe flogging'); Jordan, *Land and popular politics in Ireland: county Mayo*, p. 95; Enright, 'Terry Alts: the rise and fall of an agrarian society', pp 226–7. It was also not a one way influence; the suggestion by Desmond Mooney that the grievances and concerns of labourers and smallholders in county Meath were 'taken under the wing of Ribbonism' in 1817 is noteworthy: Mooney, 'The origins of agrarian violence in Meath, 1790–1828', *Ríocht na Midhe*, 8:1 (1987), 58.   121 *Ennis Chronicle*, 6 Nov. 1800.

by the resort to anonymous and explicitly threatening letters in the tradition of those composed and issued by agrarian movements. Examples of this tactic have been identified at Bagenalstown, county Carlow, in 1808, Carlow quay in 1812, Mullingar, county Westmeath, in 1813; at Borrisokane, county Tipperary, in 1846, when the populace was called upon 'to assemble' for the specific purpose of preventing 'the sale of some wheat', at various locations in south-eastern county Clare, 'calling on the people of the surrounding parishes to' meet at an appointed time and place, while price setting notices were posted at Kilrush, county Clare, in 1808, and in 1846–7.[122] The appeal to anonymity should not be perceived of as an exclusively rural phenomenon, however, because of its more frequent deployment by those engaged in agrarian protest. The posting of threating notices headed 'Bread or Blood' in Galway (in this instance encompassing a threat upon the life of a local figure) and in Donegal town in 1817 may have many rural precedents but they were not without urban parallels.[123] The conveying of a threatening letter to Waterford Chamber of Commerce in 1819 indicates that there was an urban tradition of epistolary threats, which was particularly firmly rooted in that port town. It was previously manifest in 1768 when an 'extraordinary anonymous paper, threatening to burn any ship, or vessel' that carried oatmeal, hides or tallow was 'posted up against the exchange wall', and in 1784 when four mercantile firms of 'repute' were threatened with 'blood and destruction' if they exported the bacon that was then 'making up in Waterford'. Moreover, Waterford was not unique. In March 1772, 'all dealers of corn and meal' in Drogheda were threatened 'with assassination' if they 'exported any more of those necessaries of life'. This threat was not made good, but the matter was regarded with sufficient seriousness to elicit state and municipal proclamations offering a reward for the apprehension of those responsible.[124]

Anonymous threatening letters were commonplace from the autumn of 1846 when food protest effectively synergized with the stronger and more pervasive phenomenon of agrarian protest. This was an inevitable consequence of the fact that food protest then was driven disproportionately by cottiers and labourers who were impelled by hunger or by its imminent prospect. In keeping with the severity of the crisis, food protesters in south county Tipperary in April 1846 manifested more anger than was usually displayed on such occasions. Reporting on events in Clonmel on 13 April, the earl of Glengall noted that 'the populace

---

122 Cunningham, 'Popular protest and a "moral economy"', pp 31–2, 33, 37; Kelly to [Redington], 3 Sept. 1846 (NAI, OP: Tipperary, 1846/27/23299); Leyne to Redington enclosing threatening notices, 16 Sept. 1846, Memorial of magistrates of Newmarket on Fergus, 20 Oct. 1846 [ ], Ennis to Redington, 11 May 1847 (NAI, OP: Clare, 1846/5/23947, 29333, 1847/5/484). For an extensive sample of threatening letters, notices etc., see Stephen Randolph Gibbons (ed.), *Captain rock, knight errant: the threatening letters of pre-Famine Ireland, 1801–1845* (Dublin, 2004). 123 Cunningham, *Galway, 1790–1914*, pp 88–9; Cunningham, 'Popular protest and a "'moral economy'"', p. 38. 124 O'Connor, *A labour history of Waterford*, p. 19; *Dublin Mercury*, 1 Dec. 1768; Kelly and Lyons (eds), *The proclamations of Ireland*, iv, 117, 407–8; *Volunteer Evening Post*, 30 Dec. 1784; *Freeman's Journal*, 19 Mar. 1772.

behaved shamefully ... on the arrival of the flour carts, abusing and spitting etc. at the military and authorities', while William Ryan, a justice of the peace, observed of the large escorted convoy of 82 cars of flour that it was subjected to 'every description of abuse from the crowds of men, women and boys along the road'.[125] The vocal aggression manifested on this occasion was not sustained, but the impulse endured, and it threatened to escalate into murderous violence in county Waterford in September 1846 when, first, a mob levelled 'menaces, threats and opprobrious epithets' at Lord Stuart de Decies at Clashmore, and, second, another mob that sought to rescue 'gaoled' colleagues responded to calls raised in the Irish language to 'kill them, kill them – they are only a handful' when they were opposed by a detachment of dragoons at Dungarvan.[126] This was not inconsistent with the threat to 'murder' directed at the members of the Bridewell Guard that resisted the mob that attacked the North Main Street potato market in Cork in June 1842 or the desire to avenge the 'base and bloody murder' voiced by the crowd at Ennis also in June, but the plundering of provisions resorted to in 1846–7 brought matters to another level.[127]

This is implicit in the sheer concentration of incidents in south county Tipperary in April 1846, which threatened for a time, and in a manner not previously encountered, to take hold of the whole region. In point of fact, this episode was not especially longer than previous major episodes of food rioting, and it was brought to a conclusion as much because it was normative for such *émeutes* to cease of their own accord as because of the intervention of the authorities. It did not cause protest to cease, but the contraction in the number of incidents in the early summer of 1846 (Table 3.1) attested to the effectiveness of the relief that was dispensed in response, as well as the inherently seasonal character of food protest to this point. Moreover, in keeping with the severity of the crisis, when it resumed protest was more pervasive and pursued on a larger scale. The targeting of the movement of flour through King's county to Shannon Harbour in order that it might be transported along the Grand Canal to Dublin in the autumn of 1846 was one manifestation of this. The occurrence of bread riots in the main cities in the winter of 1846–7 attests to the fact that the crisis that commenced in the countryside did not leave the country's urban spaces untouched, while the targeting of carts carrying grain, meal and flour, and grain stores and other features of the organizational relief infra-structure bears witness to the adaptability of food protest. The crisis was most severe in the countryside, however, which explains why food protest not only overlapped with agrarian protest, which was commonplace prior to the Great Famine, but also assumed a pattern that bore increasing similarity. The two forms of protest may never have mirrored each other, but the embrace of theft, brigandage, 'intimidation' and vio-

125 Glengall to Redington, 13 Apr., Ryan to Redington, 13 Apr. 1846 (NAI, OP: Tipperary, 1846/27/ 8989, 8947). 126 Fraher, 'Dungarvan disturbances', p. 141; *Freeman's Journal*, 28 Sept., 5 Oct. 1846. De Decies, previously Henry Villiers-Stuart (1803–74), was ennobled in 1839. 127 *Kerry Evening Post*, 8 June 1842; *Nenagh Guardian*, 11 June 1842.

lence in the pursuit of food relief in the late 1840s not only complicates identifying orthodox food protest amid the multifarious incidents that were categorized as 'plundering provisions' but also attests to its decline as a distinctive phenomenon.[128]

CONCLUSION

The pattern of food protest that was pursued in Ireland for a century and a half went through a sequence of phases reflecting its changing history. Originating in the port and market towns of Munster and Leinster, it was assisted to take firm root along the southern and eastern littoral during the difficult second quarter of the eighteenth century when the populace wrestled with the reality of famine, first, in the late 1720s and, second, in the early 1740s. Of the two episodes, the latter was plainly the more consequential, not because it provided the context for more examples of direct action but because they embraced a larger number of locations. It also paved the way, following what one may designate its emerging phase, 1710–40, for a longer consolidating phase, spanning four decades, 1745–84, when the greater readiness of urban crowds to engage in food protest meant that it was not only not confined to those moments when distress was acute, but also adopted as a tactic by a diverse range of plebeian interests in an attempt to discourage economic practices, such as the exportation of live cattle, that seemed to threaten their well-being. Though the employment by niche interests of the strategies and techniques more usually identified with stereotypical food crowds could be conceived of as evidence of the weakening of this form of protest, the opposite is true. Food protest put down firm roots in advance of agrarian protest, which did not become a feature of the landscape until the 1760s, and though the latter sustained longer and more intense phases of activity during the ensuing nine decades, it was even more emphatically regional than food protest during the second half of the eighteenth century. Be that as it may, food protest, like agrarian protest, had arrived at a point by the 1780s when it seemed firmly anchored in the landscape for though still primarily urban in focus, it clearly possessed an appeal for certain rural dwellers. It did, to be sure, possess a restricted rural geographical footprint at that point, yet the disciplined manner in which it was pursued in its urban bastions, when set beside the responsiveness of the civil and political elites, means that one can characterize the patterns of food protest pursued during the final decades of the eighteenth century and first decades of the nineteenth, the years 1785–1822, as the mature phase of Irish food rioting. This left a visible legacy, primarily manifest in the organized manner in which food rioting was often conducted in towns and cities thereafter, though the com-

128 *Leinster Express*, 12 Dec. 1846; *Freeman's Journal*, 6 Jan. 1847; *Tralee Chronicle and Killarney Echo*, 16 Jan. 1847; *Cork Examiner*, 1, 15 Oct. 1847; *Tuam Herald*, 18 Mar. 1848 (NAI, OP: Kings county, 1846).

bined impact of the shift in its regional focus westwards, and its augmented embrace by rural dwellers, who were increasingly buffeted by the forces of commercialization, did not protect it from the contraction that defines the two decades, 1822–42, following the watershed famine of 1822. It resulted also in an intensification of an evolving relationship with agrarian protest that matured slowly and irrevocably during this time. The closeness of the relationship can be obscured by the fact that agrarian protest in the nineteenth century was hardly less episodic than it had been in the eighteenth century, and by the fact that food protest sustained its own obvious distinctive character, but this should not obscure the cross fertilization, the borrowings or the increasingly close geographical footprint they shared as food protest acquired identifiably rural features. As a result, when, in the late 1840s, the country, but the countryside particularly, was plunged into a crisis of acute severity, it sparked an explosion of hunger-fuelled protest that was unique in the history of food protest in Ireland. Viewed from a statistical perspective, it could be argued that this episode of 'plundering provisions' dwarfed everything that had preceded, when the reality is that the official figures conflate food rioting, agrarian protest, acts of group and individual desperation, and some (but not all) famine-induced crime. It was exceptional, in other words, and because of this, the pattern of protest pursued then must be conceived as different and distinct from earlier phases of food rioting. The identification of a number of food protests dating from the 1850s that echoed the food riots of the mature phase of food protest spanning the eighteenth and early nineteenth centuries might seem to suggest that traditional food protest survived the Great Famine, but it was not the case. Food protest was never just a matter of protesting; it was about surviving, and the world of political economy that then obtained not only provided new and better options in this regard but also expressly disapproved of such forms of behaviour. Traditional food protest was unsuited to the demographic, economic and social world that defined late nineteenth-century Ireland.

3

The structure of food protest

INTRODUCTION

INTRODUCTION

Though their course and outcome could be unpredictable, the manner in which most food riots were conducted indicates that food protest was a purposeful and (generally) organized activity. Food riot crowds required mobilizing, leadership, plans of actions and direction if they were to realise their object. It is possible to infer from some reports, and to deduce from others aspects of each or all of these, but it is not always possible to extract pertinent details from a majority of the brief, and often antipathetic, newspaper reports that are the primary repository of information on food protest in the eighteenth century. The documentation collected by the expanding state and the increased number of newspapers can permit a fuller reconstruction of certain incidents in the nineteenth century, but it is necessary to proceed warily; the intelligence and occasional reports conveyed from the localities can be more partisan than the accounts conveyed via the public sphere. Be that as it may, there is sufficient description, ancillary fact and serendipitous detail on the manner in which food protest was pursued to permit some conclusions. This chapter is more thematically diverse than its predecessors; it seeks to establish when food rioting took place, who participated, and the scale, organization and resort to violence by the crowds that engaged in this activity.

TIMING

A striking feature of the timing of food protest as it was played out on the Irish landscape is that it followed a temporal rhythm that was not solely determined by the price of food or its actual or perceived availability. These were key determinants, of course, for though a tabulation of the timing of food riots demonstrates that there was no month of the year in which a food protest did not take place, it was not evenly distributed. This is as anticipated. The availability of food adhered to a seasonal cycle, the inescapable implication of which was that food protest was most likely to occur during the spring and summer months when supplies were low and prices high. Based upon those incidents spanning the years 1710 to 1845 that can be securely dated, Irish food protest was concentrated in the first half of the year; January to June account for an imposing 78 per cent of the total, and July to December for the remaining 22 per cent (Table 6.1). Closer scrutiny reveals that the annual rhythm of food rioting began

Table 6.1: Food riots, 1710–1845: timing (by month): sample: 281

					1710–84							
Month	Jan.	Feb.	Mar.	Apr.	May	June	July	Aug.	Sept.	Oct.	Nov.	Dec.
Number	7	10	13	11	11	14	4	7	3	6	5	–

					1789–1845							
Month	Jan.	Feb.	Mar.	Apr.	May	June	July	Aug.	Sept.	Oct.	Nov.	Dec.
Number	16	14	18	13	31	60	20	7	–	2	4	5
Total	23	24	31	24	42	74	24	14	3	8	9	5
(percentage)	(8.2)	(8.5)	(11)	(8.5)	(15)	(26.3)	(8.5)	(5)	(1.1)	(2.9)	(3.2)	(1.8)

Table 6.2: Food riots, 1710–1845: timing (by season): sample (percentage)

Season	1710–84		1789–1845		1710–1845	
Spring (Mar.–May)	35	(38.4)	62	(33.9)	97	(34.5)
Summer (June–Aug.)	25	(27.5)	87	(43.7)	112	(39.9)
Autumn (Sept.–Nov.)	14	(15.4)	6	(3.3)	20	(7.1)
Winter (Dec.–Feb.)	17	(18.7)	35	(19.1)	52	(18.5)
Totals	91	(100)	190	(100)	281	(100)

in January, and that it was pursued at a medium level until May when there was a surge in activity that lasted three months.

Sixty-one per cent of food protest occurred during the four months March to June, and an imposing 26 per cent in June. The (by comparison) modest number of incidents in July (8.5 per cent) and August (5 per cent), which embraced the 'eight weeks of want', popularly denominated the 'hungry months', that spanned the interval between the depletion of the previous harvest and 'the new potatoes come in for general consumption', requires explanation. These could be difficult months, and were properly identified as such in the countryside in the decades before the Great Famine. This was not necessarily the case, however, in the urban centres that were long the primary heartland of food protest.[1] Moreover,

1 See Austin Bourke, *The visitation of God: the potato and the Great Irish Famine* ed. Jacqueline Hill and Cormac Ó Gráda (Dublin, 1993), pp 15–16, 29, 46–7 for a discussion of the timing of the potato harvest. There is surprisingly little agreement on what constituted the 'hungry months': Power, *A history of Clarecastle*, p. 417, maintains doubtfully that the 'hungry months' extended from March to July; Conor McNamara, 'This wretched people: the famine of 1822 in the west of Ireland' in Carla King and Conor McNamara (eds), *The west of Ireland: new perspectives on the nine-teenth century* (Dublin, 2011), p. 14, maintains they embraced June, July and August; and Andriès Eiríksson, 'Food supply and food riots', pp 73, 75, that they spanned June and July. The quotes, which were prompted by conditions in 1800, are from Altamont to Lucan, 31 May 1800 in Brigid

the combination of the availability of imported foodstuffs, the provision of organized relief, and the hope generated by the early harvest returns often served to ease the anxiety that fuelled protest in advance of the arrival of the harvest. Furthermore, though food prices may have peaked during the high summer, the primary trigger of food protest prior to the Great Famine was the earlier sharp upwards rise, rather than the stable high prices of summer. In other words, the public's mood tended to be more volatile when prices were rising, which generally preceded the so-called 'hungry months'; in 1817, for example, rioting peaked in April, May and, most of all, in June.[2] Given this pattern it is a matter of little surprise that – the exceptional environment of the Great Famine apart – the month with fewest riots was September (1.1 per cent of the sample) since, as in 1817, it usually featured a marked price adjustment in response to the improved availability of food staples, which explains why autumn was the season least prone to food rioting (Table 6.2). Tabulated according to the meteorological seasonal calendar, 35 per cent of food riots took place in the spring (March–May), 40 per cent in the summer (June–August), 7 per cent in the autumn, and 18 per cent in the winter, with January and February accounting for an overwhelming 90 per cent of the winter total (Table 6.2).

While there is an identifiable rationale to this seasonal pattern, a comparable analysis of the situation in France during the seventeenth and eighteenth centuries, and the more particular context of the Great Famine in Ireland indicate that environments and eras produced variations on this pattern. Saliently, the points of comparison between France and Ireland exceed the points of contrast, as food rioting was temporally concentrated in both jurisdictions, and 'the period between Easter and Michaelmas (March to September) [which] offered conditions most conducive to subsistence disturbances' in France overlapped with that in Ireland. Furthermore, the French had their equivalent to 'the hungry months' – the *soudure* spanning August and September – which equated with one of the two periods that 'generated the largest numbers of riots' (the other spanned the months of April and May).[3]

The pattern identifiable from the tables of incidents of provisions plundering generated from the data assembled by the constabulary and the reports registered by the Chief Secretary's Office demonstrate that behaviour was not only less obviously seasonal during the Great Famine, but also that the most food protest then occurred during the winter. This was the pattern certainly in 1846–7, but the different pattern registered in the winter of 1847–8, and still more so in 1848–9 and 1849–50 emphasizes the exceptional character of these years, and the

Clesham (ed.), 'Lord Altamont's letters to Lord Lucan about the Act of Union', *Journal of the Galway Archaeological and Historical Society*, 54 (2002), 31.   2 In 1817, prices at Waterford embarked on a sharp upwards curve in January, and another in April. Interestingly, prices fluctuated marginally through April to August, when the price of oatmeal moderated by 39 per cent: see Barker and Cheyne, *An account of the rise, progress and decline of fever lately epidemical in Ireland*, i, 38.   3 Bouton, *The flour war*, p. 7; Olwen Hufton, 'Social conflict and the grain supply in eighteenth-century France', *Journal of Interdisciplinary History*, 15:2 (1983), 320–4.

Table 6.3: Plundering provisions, 1846–50: timing (by month): sample 1226

	Jan.	Feb.	Mar.	Apr.	May	June	July	Aug.	Sept.	Oct.	Nov.	Dec.
46	n/a	n/a	n/a	29	10	10	1	–	27	70	87	181
47*	149	23	8	29	105	43	27	16	8	25	15	15
48	49	49	24	18	18	14	10	3	2	3	24	20
49	21	19	10	15	22	10	5	1	–	1	–	–
50	1	3	1	1	3	–	1	–	–	–	–	–
tal	220	94	43	92	158	77	44	20	37	99	126	216
rcentage	(17.9)	(7.7)	(3.5)	(7.5)	(12.9)	(6.3)	(3.6)	(1.6)	(3)	(8.1)	(10.3)	(17.6)

ırce: National Archives of Ireland, CSO, OP, 1846/9 (Returns of outrages reported to the Constabulary ice during 1846 (incomplete); CSO, Registered papers, 1847: division 1, vols 1–2; CSO/ICR/1: *Return of ʀages reported to the Constabulary Office during the year 1848, 1849, 1850* (Dublin, 1849–51).

impact of hunger on provisions plundering in the winter of 1846–7. This was the situation also in May 1847, but otherwise the most striking feature of the calendar of protest during the Great Famine (1846, 1847 and 1848) is the increase in activity in the autumn and early winter as, in stark contrast to what was normative when food protest can be equated with food rioting, the potato harvest served not to ease but to elevate popular fears (Table 6.3). The seasonal patterns registered during these years also attest to the importance of government relief and to the declining recourse to traditional forms of food protest as the crisis extended beyond 1847. In any event, the fact that the high points of food protest in Ireland do not equate with those identified in France, and that the patterns of protest identifiable in Ireland before and during the Great Famine vary indicates that the timing of food protest was shaped by and responded to its context. They also support the conclusion that food riots were not reflexive flare-ups fuelled by panic (though this emotion ought not to be discounted and was seldom entirely absent), but calculated interventions by social interests seeking either to anticipate or to respond to crisis, and to exert a measure of control over a situation in which they are often (wrongly) conceived of as powerless or demoralised.

COMPOSITION

The most compelling and demonstrable factor in prompting the assembly of a food protest crowd was the rise in the price of foodstuffs to a point where those dependent on purchased provisions perceived that it approached or was at a level that limited their capacity to access alimentation. There were other (related) factors, of course, such as profiteering by producers (farmers), merchants, shippers, bakers and retailers, and the allied practices of regrating and forestalling, which impacted people differently depending on their employment, location and the precise economic context; but they shared a common goal – all sought access to foodstuffs at an affordable price. Since those who purchased foodstuffs, or who required access to foodstuffs that were traded, did not constitute the poorest in society, food rioting was seldom – the Great Famine is the primary compelling exception – precipitated by immediate and pressing hunger. As a result, most food riot crowds comprised what contemporary commentators described as 'the common people'.[4] Who this meant in practice could vary depending on location and the attitude of those doing the describing, but it largely coincided with what the respectable – and particularly newspaper owners, editors and authors who determined the language that was used – in the eighteenth century denominated the 'mob' or, on occasion, the 'insolent mob', 'riotous mob' or 'unruly mob'.[5] Though less overtly pejorative than 'rabble', and less judgemental than 'plunderers' which were also employed intermittently, the term 'mob' was inherently more condescending than its less popular alternatives – terms such as 'the populace', a 'parcel of people', 'a number of persons', 'a number of fellows', 'a number of idle fellows', 'numbers of idle and disorderly persons', 'inconsiderate people', 'rioters' or 'riotous persons' – which were also employed.[6] It is also unhelpfully imprecise since there was, and is, no agreed definition on what defined the 'mob'. Yet because it was primarily invoked *in the eighteenth century* to describe riotous urban crowds, and it was used in the same context as 'townspeople' and 'band of citizens', albeit more commonly, it is clear that it embraced 'tradesmen, workmen and other labourers' who were, by reason of their income, and marginal social position, not only susceptible to economic shock, but also vulnerable to the impact of the shortages, high prices and distress that ensued when they occurred. Comparison may usefully be drawn with eighteenth-century France, where, according to Cynthia Bouton,

> food rioters came neither from the uprooted dregs of French society – the vagabonds and criminals – nor from the ranks of clients of the various

4 *Dublin Intelligence*, 4 Mar. 1729; Giblin (ed.), 'Catalogue of Nunziatura di Fiandra, pt 5', 13.   5 For examples of contemporary use of the term 'mob' or 'mobb' see Nicholas Hussey's *Dublin Post Boy*, 4 Mar. 1729; *Dublin Weekly Journal*, 5 Apr. 1729; Taylor to Percival, 30 Mar. 1729 (BL, Egmont papers, Add. MS 46994 f. 88); Kingsbury to Price, 3 May 1740 (NLW, Puleston papers, Add. MS 3548D); Minutes of the Revenue Commissioners, 1761–4 (TNA, CUST1/64–75 passim); *Dublin Courant*, 25 Mar. 1746; *Universal Advertiser*, 10 Apr. 1753; Hore, *History of Wexford*, i, 394, v, 398; Benn, *History of Belfast*, pp 594, 596; *Public Gazetteer*, 1 Sept. 1759, 24 June 1766, 1 Mar. 1768; *Freeman's Journal*, 8 Sept. 1764, 24 Aug. 1773; *Cork Remembrancer*, p. 143; Colles to Colles, 14 June 1766 (NAI, Prim Collection, no. 87/92); Feargus Ó Fearghail (ed.), 'Episcopal edicts of the diocese of Ossory', *Ossory, Laois and Leinster*, 2 (2006), 83; Gilbert (ed.), *Calendar of ancient records of Dublin*, xi, 340; *Finn's Leinster Journal*, 4 July 1767; *Hibernian Journal*, 18 Mar. 1772.   6 *Dublin Gazette or Weekly Courant*, 18 Mar. 1729; *Dublin Daily Post*, 3, 8 June 1740; *Pue's Occurrences*, 3 June 1740, 25 Apr. 1741, 20 Nov. 1756, 5 May 1759; *Dublin Newsletter*, 7, 24 June, 26 Aug. 1740; *Faulkner's Dublin Journal*, 8 Mar. 1729, 7 June 1740; *Universal Advertiser*, 1, 5 May 1753; *Belfast News Letter*, 30 Nov. 1756; *Public Gazetteer*, 21, 28 June 1766, 17 Mar. 1767; *Finn's Leinster Journal*, 25 Apr. 1770; *Hibernian Journal*, 18 May 1772.

machinating court factions ... They came overwhelmingly from the *menu peuple* – the common people – which included the families of artisans, journeymen, shopkeepers, day-laborers, small peasants and vine-growers.[7]

Bouton's reading echoes that of Eric Hobsbawm, who famously equated the mob with the *menu peuple* (in Italian the *populo* or *popolino*), and, using a description of the Napolitan *lazzari* (or *lazarroni*) from 1799 as his foundation, equated the 'mob' with those whom Karl Marx denominated lumpenproletarians:

> It was a combination of wage-earners, small property owners and the unclassifiable urban poor ... porters, a riot leading class ..., dockers ... and the apprentices and journeymen of the lower trades and crafts, such as rope-makers, smiths, ... tanners, tailors and shoemakers, ... the mass of hawkers and unclassifiable small dealers and people making ends meet, which filled preindustrial cities.[8]

As in France, the 'mobs' that gathered in Ireland in the course of the eighteenth century to assert their entitlement to access food at an affordable price comprised a broad swathe of those who engaged in manual labour, either on a causal or sustained basis. They did so because life for the 'common people' was inherently precarious. Bouton's summary of the situation in France echoes the situation in Ireland:

> Securing regular sustenance constituted a preoccupation among most of the common people. During normal years, these families managed, sometimes only through complex strategies in which all members played an integral part, to stay on the 'right side of the line between poverty and indigence'. During crisis years, however, disjunctures among prices, wages, and other expenses could threaten the very survival of the family unit. Then, these ordinary people turned in defense of their families to an 'economy of expedients' or 'makeshifts' that included rioting.[9]

Specific information is available in only a proportion of instances, but accounts of the involvement of weavers in a major food riot in Carrick-on-Suir in April 1741; of fishermen at Kinsale in 1766, 1768 and 1784; of 'journeymen coopers' at Waterford in 1769 and 1775, and Drogheda in 1775; tradesmen and labourers at Waterford in 1791, and 'starving manufacturers' and 'poor industrious

---

7 Bouton, *The flour war*, p. 3. 8 Eric Hobsbawm, *Primitive rebels* (Manchester, 1959), p. 113; also quoted in Cunningham, *Galway, 1790–1914*, p. 94. 9 Bouton, *The flour war*, p. 4, citing Michel Morineau, 'Budget populaires en France aux dix-huitième siècle', *Revue d'histoire économique et sociale*, 50 (1972), 203–36, 449–81; Olwen Hufton, 'Women in revolution, 1789–1796', *Past and Present*, 53 (Nov. 1791), 94; eadem, *The poor in eighteenth-century France, 1750–1789* (Oxford, 1974), p. 24.

manufacturers' in Dublin's Liberties in 1773 and in 1793 serve as a useful guide to the social class of those who comprised the 'mob' in urban Ireland in the eighteenth century.[10] Moreover, it did not change fundamentally subsequently for though its specific constituents altered with the geography of protest, it was still comprised overwhelmingly in the early nineteenth century of the *menu peuple* in those urban spaces in which it occurred. In Galway, for example, the Claddagh fishermen sustained a reputation comparable to that of the Cornish tin miners and the Kingswood (Somerset) colliers for rising to the defence of their community up to and beyond the Great Famine.[11] Reference to the fact that nineteenth-century urban food protest crowds were drawn from, or comprised, 'the labouring and poorer classes', 'journeymen tradesmen', 'unemployed tradesmen', 'the lower orders', 'the lower classes', and 'the manufacturing classes' indicates that this was the case also in other larger country towns and cities.[12] Precise information is again elusive, but the listing of those taken up and prosecuted in the wake of the bread riots in Dublin in August 1826 offers a useful corroborating perspective; it comprised 11 weavers, 5 labourers, 3 cotton printers, 3 glassblowers, 2 wool spinners, 3 bricklayers, a cotton dyer, a shipwright, a carter, a hatter, a carpenter, and a servant.[13] It may not mirror exactly the occupational membership of Dublin Ribbonism, in that it embraced few from the ranks of the 'petty bourgeoisie', but both drew strongly from the ranks of the 'wage earning proletariat'.[14]

The composition of the rural crowds was less diverse in keeping with the narrower occupational range in the countryside. Described, in the words of one commentator in 1846 as comprised of 'tradespeople, conacre tenants, small holders and cottiers', the addition of labourers to this listing provides a good guide to their membership, and a pointer to the fact that it overlapped with, when it did not equate with, that of the more representative agrarian movements. The major difference between them was scale and intensity. By comparison with food protest,

10 Dickson, *Arctic Ireland*, p. 55; Caulfield (ed.), *Corporation book of Kinsale*, p. 280; *Finn's Leinster Journal*, 30 Apr. 1768, 1 Feb. 1775; *Pue's Occurrences*, 16 Sept. 1769; *Hibernian Journal*, 8 Feb. 1775; *Volunteer Journal* (Dublin), 22 Mar. 1784; *Dublin Morning Post*, 19 May 1791; *Freeman's Journal*, 24 Aug. 1773, 13 June 1793. 11 *Illustrated London News*, 25 June 1842; *Nation*, 29 Nov. 1845; Cunningham, *Galway, 1790–1914*, pp 90–1, 95–6; Eoin Bourke (ed.), 'Poor green Erin': *German travel writers' narratives on Ireland from before the 1798 Rising to after the Great Famine* (Frankfurt, 2013), pp 296–8; John Cunningham, 'The mayor/admiral of Claddagh and Galway's moral economy' in Emmet O'Connor and John Cunningham (eds), *Lives on the left: studies in Irish radical leadership* (Manchester, 2016), pp 22–34; Bohstedt, *The politics of provisions*, pp 110–21, 134–7, 151–2, 177–80, 182–3, 186–7, 209–11; Robert Malcolmson, 'A set of ungovernable people: the Kingswood colliers in the eighteenth century' in Brewer and Styles (eds), *An ungovernable people: the English and their law in the seventeenth and eighteenth centuries*, pp 89, 93, 116–18. 12 *Freeman's Journal*, 15 Jan., 11, 12 June 1817, 15 May 1822; Cunningham, 'Popular protest and "a moral economy"', p. 38; Lee, 'The food riots of 1830 and 1840', p. 61. 13 Swift, *History of the Dublin bakers*, p. 207. 14 Michael Beames, 'The Ribbon societies: lower-class nationalism in pre-Famine Ireland', *Past and Present*, 97 (1982), 130–1; Tom Garvin, 'Defenders, Ribbonmen and others: underground political networks in pre-Famine Ireland', *Past and Present*, 96 (1982), 151.

agrarian protest was more overtly masculine, more aggressive and para-militaristic, and possessed of greater mobilizing capacities.[15] These distinctions were elided as the impact of pervasive destitution during the Great Famine reduced the narrowing gap that divided food and agrarian protest. This was manifest in various ways, but references to assemblies of 'countrymen' in 'the south and west', or more specifically to 'thousands of ... country people' tramping 'down the hills' and converging on towns and ports in search of food, assailing flour mills and intercepting carts, boats and ships offer a useful guide. They also provide a context in which to locate references to the involvement then of the land poor – those who contemporaries writing in 1846 identified as the 'lowest classes', which comprised farm servants, 'destitute labourers', 'unemployed labourers', the 'wretched people who have held small patches ... and have lost their entire supply of food', and those of 'the very lowest classes' (residing on holdings of less than 'eight acres of land') who had 'disposed' of their potatoes 'fearing they would rot'.[16] Though sometimes perturbingly subjective, these descriptions are still more useful as a pointer to the composition of protesting crowds than easily misread references by disscomforted town-dwellers and elements of the anxious landed gentry to 'a tumultuous body of people', a crowd of 'peasants', 'country people', 'countrymen', a 'crowd from the country', 'a large assemblage of country people' and a 'large crowd', and to pejorative references to 'marauders' or 'persons of bad character' which were also commonly invoked to describe these bodies.[17]

Moreover, contrary to the impression provided by generic descriptions of this kind, the crowds that engaged in food protest in the nineteenth century, and in the mid-nineteenth century especially, reflected the social divisions that were a feature of the urban and rural communities in which they were based, in particular, those between farmers and cottiers/labourers, and, less obviously, those between town dwellers and country people. Taking the former first, it is identifiable in county Clare in the autumn of 1846 when small farmers and labourers entered into a 'combination to intimidate ... rich farmers from disposing of their corn'.[18] Other than during 1846–7, food protest was seldom pursued in such a structured fashion, but the increased reference from the 1830s to examples of farmer producers demanding the highest market price for potatoes, refusing 'to sell in small quantities, even a stone, to accommodate the necessitous', of hoarding, and of profiteering heightened existing suspicions and exacerbated commu-

---

15 *Freeman's Journal*, 6 Oct. 1846; O'Neill, 'The Catholic Church and relief', 139; Abbott, 'The Downshire estates', p. 38; Jordan, *Land and popular politics in Ireland*, p. 96. **16** Glengall to Redington, 13 Apr. 1846, Memorial of Edward Brazill, 24 July 1846 (NAI, OP: Tipperary, 46/27/8989, 21335); *Nenagh Guardian*, 17 Oct. 1846; *Freeman's Journal*, 28 Sept., 6, 7 Oct. 1846; *Leinster Express*, 12 Dec. 1846; *Tralee Chronicle*, 15 May 1847. **17** Lismore to Bessborough, 15 Apr. 1846 (NAI, OP: county Tipperary, 1846/27/8993); *Tralee Chronicle*, 16 Jan. 1847; *Leinster Express*, 12 Dec. 1846; *Freeman's Journal*, 5, 7, 8, 30 Oct. 1846, 11, 12 Jan. 1847; Fraher, 'Dungarvan disturbances', p. 139. **18** Leyne to Redington, 20, 22, 23 Sept. 1846 (NAI, OP: Clare, 1846/5/25727, 25629, 25631). **19** Enright, 'Terry Alts', p. 226; *Tuam Herald*, 15 July 1837; *Freeman's Journal*, 4, 12 July 1839; Cunningham, *Galway, 1790–1914*, p. 91.

nity tensions.[19] It was not exclusive to farmers, of course. Town dwellers manifested little obvious sympathy with the plight of the rural labourers, and as exemplified by the 'fury' directed the way of 'several country persons who purchased potatoes' at Ballina in June 1842, and by the refusal to 'permit potatoes or meal' to be taken out of Sligo, Athlone, Ennis and Ballina in 1842 and Galway and elsewhere in 1846, the reality of high prices and shortage exposed tensions within as well as between the social groups out of which food protest emanated.[20]

SIZE

The size of the crowds that engaged in food protest varied considerably. Many accounts make no reference to the number of participants beyond referring imprecisely to the fact that an identifiable episode involved 'a number of idle fellows', a 'number of people', 'a small body of people', 'a parcel of people', 'a considerable number of people', 'a considerable mob', 'a great number of people', a 'numerous mob', a 'very numerous mob', a 'great mob', an 'immense crowd', 'large parties', 'a large body' or a 'large concourse'.[21] Some are more specific, however, and the variation in the numbers cited indicate that food crowds could vary dramatically. Reported numbers range from 40 participants in an attack on a ship in Dublin harbour in 1767 to 10,000 in a number of protests in the mid-nineteenth century. We have accounts of 100 at Kilcock in 1783, Whitegate, county Clare, in March 1846, and Balbriggan, county Dublin in 1847; 200 at Kinsale in November 1740, Twomilebridge, county Waterford in 1784, and Galmoy, county Kilkenny, in May 1847; 2–300 at Clonmel in May 1756; 'some hundreds' at Drogheda in 1778; several hundred at Athlone and Rathangan in 1817, Dublin in August 1826, and Clonmel on 14 April 1847; 'nearly three hundred' labourers at Galmoy, county Kilkenny in May 1847; 300 in an attack on an escorted potato boat on the Grand Canal in county Kildare in 1817; 300 plus at Clarecastle in 1781; 500 in Ballina, and on the Navan–Nobber road in 1817; 5–600 at Wexford in February 1757; 600 tradesmen in Tralee in 1817; 800 at Belmullet in January 1831; 1,000 at Carrick-on-Suir in April 1741 and Clarecastle in 1842; 1,500 at Fethard, county Tipperary, in April 1846; 2,000 in major riots in Limerick in May 1772, Cork in 1792, Limerick in 1840, and O'Brien's Bridge, county Clare, in 1846; 2–3,000 on Dublin quays in January 1796, Limerick in June 1840 and Ennis in September 1846; 3,000 at Drogheda in May 1812, at Ballingarry, county Limerick in May 1847 and

20 *Connaught Telegraph*, 8 June 1842; *Nenagh Guardian*, 11 June 1842; *Freeman's Journal*, 31 May 1842, 5 Oct. 1846.   **21** See, for example, *Dublin Gazette or Weekly Courant*, 18 Mar. 1729; *Dublin Newsletter*, 6 Dec. 1740; *Pue's Occurrences*, 5 May 1759; *Public Gazetteer*, 1 Sept. 1759; *Finn's Leinster Journal*, 28 Apr. 1770, 8 Apr., 4 July 1778; *Dublin Evening Journal*, 18 June 1778; *Freeman's Journal*, 15 Oct. 1774, 21 Dec. 1816, 5 Oct. 1846; *Nenagh Guardian*, 11 June 1842; Resident magistrate, Ennis, to Redington, 7, 11 May 1847 (NAI, OP: Clare, 1846/5/523, 484); Cunningham, 'Popular protest and "a moral economy"', p. 38; Abbott, 'The Downshire estates', p. 38.

Waterford in September 1846; 3–4,000 at Youghal in September 1846; 4,000 at
Ennis in 1842; 4–5,000 at Clonmel on 13 April 1846; 4–6,000 at Dungarvan in
September 1846; 5,000 in Belfast in 1812 and Cork in October 1846, and 5–6,000
at Listowel in December 1846. In addition, crowds, purportedly 10,000 strong,
marched into Castlebar in August 1846 to protest at the unavailability of food, and
through the town of Killorglin, county Kerry, in May 1847 'calling out for
employment'.[22]

Protesting crowds could, as this suggests, vary dramatically; gatherings of
more than 1,000 people were exceptional but the fact that even a small proportion involved this number of participants placed Irish riots on a scale equivalent
to those in England in 1816.[23] Moreover, numbers could oscillate quite sharply
in the course of a riotous episode. This was, understandably, more likely in incidents of longer than average duration. One may instance the crowd that objected
in 1839 to the operation of Campbell's potato mill in Newtownards, county
Down, whose assemblies ranged from 'several hundreds' to between two and
three thousand; the bloody encounter at Ennis, county Clare, three years later
when crowds ranged from one to four thousand; the various sized gatherings
ranging from hundreds to between four and five thousand that spearheaded
protest in south Tipperary in April 1846; the 600 to 1,000 at Scariff, county
Clare in October 1846, the 300 to 1,000 that gathered in county Limerick in May
1847 to enter mills, drive cattle and plunder provisions, and the 800 to 1,000 that
assembled to attack Cork Workhouse in February 1847.[24] Moreover, there is no
determinable correlation between the size of the crowds and the severity of the
crisis. There are, to be sure, numerous incidents dating from 1846–7 when gatherings of 'countrymen', sometimes several thousand strong, descended from the
rural hinterland on towns and cities (Clonmel, Carrick-on-Suir, Dungarvan,
Ennis), but a majority of the mobs that targeted mills, that sought to intercept

22 *Pue's Occurrences*, 6 June 1741, 17 Mar. 1767; *Finn's Leinster Journal*, 4 July 1767; Hore, *History
of Wexford*, v, 398; Burke, *History of Clonmel*, p. 126; *Dublin Evening Journal*, 16 June 1778;
Hibernian Journal, 30 May 1781; *Dublin Evening Post*, 17 June 1783; Roberts to Redington, 18 May
1847 (NAI, OP: Kilkenny, 1847/14/215); *Freeman's Journal*, 23 May 1772, 9 Aug. 1826, 15 Apr.,
28 Sept., 5, 6 Oct. 1846, 13 Jan. 1847; *Dublin Chronicle*, 27 Nov. 1792; *Dublin Evening Post*, 12 Jan.
1796; Leyne to Redington, 15 Sept. 1846, Ryan to [ ], 29 Oct. 1846 (NAI, OP: Clare,
1846/5/23897, 29929); Outrage report, 29 Apr. 1846 (NAI, OP: Tipperary, 1846/27/10585);
Knaresborough to Redington, 22 Sept. 1846 (NAI, OP: Cork, 1846/6/25641); *Leinster Express*, 22
May 1847; Cunningham, 'Popular protest and "a moral economy"', pp 40–2; Robbins, *Miasma*, p.
39; Lee, 'The food riots of 1830 and 1840', p. 61; Conwell, 'Clanricarde and his county Galway
estates', p. 24; *Tralee Chronicle*, 15 May 1847; *Nation*, 15 May 1847, Ó Murchadha, *Sable wings over
the land: Ennis, county Clare and its wider community during the Great Famine*, p. 15; *Kerry Examiner*,
21 Apr. 1846; Fraher, 'The Dungarvan disturbances', pp 138, 143; Jordan, *Land and popular politics in Ireland*, pp 94, 96; *Nation*, 15 May 1847. 23 Post, *The last great subsistence crisis*, p. 70. 24
Belfast News Letter, 25 Jan. 1839; Ó Murchadha, *Sable wings over the land: Ennis, county Clare and
its wider community during the Great Famine*, p. 15; *Freeman's Journal*, 15 Apr. 1846; *Kerry
Examiner*, 21 Apr. 1846; Moloney to Redington, 30 Oct., Bailey to Redington, 31 Oct. 1846 (NAI,
OP: Clare, 1846/5/29831, 29941); *Nation*, 15 May 1847; *Cork Examiner*, 5 Feb. 1847.

carts, to turn back ships and boats, or to seize foodstuffs from barns, market houses or the like were smaller. There was no normative, or ideal, size, but the plenitude of estimations that put assemblies at 100 (Kilmurray Ibrickane, county Clare, and Balbriggan, county Dublin in 1846–7), 200 (Belfast in December 1846, Scariff and Ennistymon, county Clare in 1847), 300 (Derry in 1835, Clare in 1846, Kilkenny in May 1847), 400 (Monaghan in January 1847, Drogheda in May 1847 and Cork in February 1847), 4–500 (Clarecastle in October 1846), 500 (Limerick in October 1846, Cashel in May 1847, and Youghal and Ballincollig, county Cork in April and July 1847), 600 (Ennis/Clarecastle, July 1842), 700 (Ennistymon, May 1847) and 1000 (Ballinasloe, March 1847) demonstrate that it was not only relatively easy to assemble a substantial crowd, but also that this was the case throughout 1846 and much of 1847.[25] Yet it is noticeable – as incidents of plundering provisions approached their numerical peak in the winter of 1846–7 – that the number of crowds of modest size increased. The interception *en route* from Tralee to Dingle of 'a quantity of flour' by 3 men was unusual, and perhaps the minimum necessary to stage a successful food heist, but it was not dramatically smaller than the gangs of 'ten or twelve men' that boarded and plundered a 'small sloop' at Ennis in April, or the groups of fishermen, also ten to twenty in number, that contrived to board vessels on the county Mayo coast in the summer of 1847.[26] The proliferation of incidents involving smaller crowds served to diminish the distinctive character of food protest and to close the gap that had long distinguished it from agrarian protest and, indeed, crime. The closure of this gap illustrates that mass participation was not simply a matter of numbers but a statement of community engagement. The greater involvement of women in crowds reinforced this as well as highlighting that food protest crowds were not composed exclusively of men.

GENDER: THE PARTICIPATION OF WOMEN

The involvement of women in food protest has been a subject of a lively debate between those who have argued, on the basis of what John Bohstedt has provoca-

25 Report of Captain Ogle, 14 Jan. 1847, Martin French, Cashel, to [Redington], 3 May 1847 (NAI, OP: Tipperary, 1847/27/192, 1086); *Belfast News Letter*, 1 Aug. 1837, 2 Feb. 1847; Power, *A history of Clarecastle*, p. 416; Revenue Commissioners to Dublin Castle, 7 Oct. 1846, Bailey to Redington, 31 Oct. 1846, Police report, 14 Apr. 1847, RM (Ennis) to Redington, 15 Apr., Plunkett to Redington, 28 Apr. 1847 (NAI, OP: Clare, 1846/5/27855, 29941, /1847/5/352, 389, 398); Testimony, 19 Apr., Grant to inspector, 7 July 1847 (NAI, OP: Clare, 1847/6/655, 1264); *Freeman's Journal*, 5, 7 Oct. 1846, 29 May 1847; Kinealy and McAtasney, *The hidden famine*, p. 62; *Nation*, 22 May 1847; *Leinster Express*, 22 May 1847; Bell to [Redington], 14 Mar. 1847 (NAI, OP: Clare, 1847/11/291).   26 Stokes to Redington, 23 Jan. 1847 (NAI, OP: Kerry, 1841/12/55); RM (Ennis) to Redington, 15 Apr. 1847 (NAI, OP: Clare, 1847/5/352); Pigot to Redington, 13 May 1847 (NAI, OP: Wexford, 1847, 31/161); Pigot to Redington, 1 May, Beach to [ ], 8 July 1847 (NAI, OP: Mayo, 1847/21/270, 401).

tively labelled the 'myth of the feminine food riot', not only that women were more riotous than men but also that their participation reinforces its almost unique image among riotous protest as a justifiable form of intervention.[27] There is little enough evidence available in the accounts of food rioting in Ireland to test these contrasting positions, which is a matter of some concern since Bohstedt's statistical method may undercount female involvement in food protest in England, as E.P. Thompson pointed out. The nub of the matter is how one assigns gender to crowds that are described in a manner that is 'sexually inde-terminate'. This is no less of a problem in Ireland, since based on the reports in which their presence is *explicitly* acknowledged there is little by way of justifica-tion for disagreeing with the conclusion, ventured by Bohstedt, that 'women did not dominate food riots' and that 'food riots were not a distinctly feminine province'.[28] This is not to suggest that women did not participate in food rioting in Ireland prior to the first incident, which dates from the spring of 1757,[29] when their involvement is referred to, or to deny that they were active participants in many of the later crowds that make no reference to the gender of their partici-pants. Indeed, the explicit participation of women in food protest in Ireland is referred to in less than twenty instances (7 per cent of the total) in the period 1710–1845, which is not only well below Bohstedt's 25 per cent for his sample for the years 1790–1810 but also below his estimation of the involvement of women in non-food riots (8 per cent) in England.[30] Why women in Ireland might be less predisposed to participate in food protest remains to be teased out, but it is certainly necessary to look for a reason different than that ventured by Bohstedt, who has argued of England that female engagement in food rioting was

---

27 This debate was inaugurated in 1971 with the contention that the 'initiators of the riots were, very often, the women': Thompson, 'The English crowd in the eighteenth century', 115–18. This elicited a detailed critique from Bohstedt: 'Women in English riots, 1790–1810', 88–93; idem, 'The myth of the feminine food riot: women as proto citizens in English community politics, 1790–1810' in D.G. Levy and H.G. Applewhite (eds), *Women and politics in the age of the democratic revolution* (Ann Arbor, 1990), pp 21–60, and idem, *The politics of provisions*, p. 183. Thompson's compelling reply, which challenges both Bohstedt's conclusions, and his methodology, can be found in 'The moral economy reviewed', pp 305–36. For more detached perspectives: Adrian Randall and Andrew Charlesworth, 'The moral economy: riot, markets and social conflict', p. 5; Bouton, *The flour war*, pp 17–19. 28 Bohstedt, 'Women in English riots', 89. 29 The first secure report of women par-ticipating in food rioting is from Kilkenny, 18 April 1757 (*Pue's Occurrences*, 23 Apr. 1757). According to a report in an English paper, another incident in Wexford a week later involved 5–600 women assembling to the beat of a corn-fan, armed with mops etc. This is mentioned in pass-ing in the *Gentleman's Magazine*, 27 (1757), p. 235, but corroboration has yet to be secured from an Irish source: see Bohstedt, '1756–57 riots: third century (1740–1850)'. 30 Bohstedt, 'Women in English riots', 92, 113. The identifiable percentage for Ireland for the eighteenth century is 3.7 per cent, and 7.8 for the period 1801–45. It is notable also that this level of engagement is markedly in arrears of the participation of women in the food and price riots that took place in Britain's North American colonies between 1776 and 1779. Indeed, Clark Smith maintains that 'women con-ducted nearly one-third' of these riots: Barbara Clark Smith, 'Food rioters and the American Revolution' in Daniel Pope (ed.), *American radicalism* (Oxford, 2001), pp 19, 35.

predicated on traditional household and community forms, which were more firmly rooted in 'unmanageable manufacturing districts' that were slower to move 'from communal to associational forms of solidarity for collective action'.[31] This trajectory is unsustainable in Ireland, given its pre-eminently agricultural economic base and its vibrant tradition of rural protest. Yet if there is no good reason to believe Irish women were any less vital in 'winning the family subsistence' than their counterparts in England this does not mean that there was less social space and fewer opportunities for women to engage in food rioting, and that Ireland bears closer comparison to France than to England in that respect.[32] It is notable in this context that women ceded leadership to men in two food protest incidents dating from the eighteenth century in which they were the progenitors. In the earliest of these, which took place at Kilkenny in April 1757, the local women who sparked a protest by turning back 'a great number of cars' leaving the jurisdiction laden with oatmeal found that the men who 'came to support them' not only assumed control but also directed that 'the meal was brought back to the market house' and made available at an affordable price. The situation was still more clear-cut in Dublin in May 1795 as the 'group of women' that stopped 'several cars loaded with flour ... were instantly seconded by a number of the other sex' in what was described as a 'previously concerted' move.[33]

It was unnecessary to engage in forward planning in this detail in those instances in which women were simply present as members of the crowd. One may instance the incident at Waterford on 14 May 1791 when 'a number of tradesmen, labourers etc., accompanied by a due proportion of women' attempted to exert downwards pressure on provision prices.[34] Their actions were not without impact, which is more than can be said of those incidents at Cork in June 1767 when 'several hundred men and women' responded to a false report that 'a large quantity of meal' had been secreted in cellars in the city, and at Galway on 8 July 1790 when a 'tumultuous mob of men and women' engaged in a similar action though there was 'not the smallest scarcity of provisions in this town or county'.[35] The suggestion, implicit in these accounts, that women were more likely to engage in food rioting when food was urgently needed is supported by the participation of men, women and children in an attack on warehouses and mills in Ennis in 1801, in the Dublin bread riots of 1817, in a descent on a bakery in Waterford in 1819, in an attack on a convoy of relief provisions bound for Moycullen, county Galway in 1824, which has encouraged John Cunningham to conclude that 'women and children ... were active participants in Galway food rioting', and in the highly publicized incidents at Ennis in June 1842, in which a woman (Catherine Fallon who was shot in the head) was one of the casualties, and at Galway a week later.[36] This conclusion is supported by the reports of the

31 Bohstedt, 'Women in English riots', 108–9, 113.   32 Bouton, *The flour war*, p. 19.   33 Bohstedt, 'Women in English riots', 94; *Pue's Occurrences*, 23 Apr. 1757; *Hibernian Journal*, 1 June 1795; *Walker's Hibernian Magazine*, June 1795, p. 570.   34 *Dublin Morning Post*, 19 May 1791.   35 *Finn's Leinster Journal*, 4 July 1767; *Ennis Chronicle*, 12 July 1790.   36 Wells, 'The Irish famine of

Figure 3: Food riot, Dungarvan, 1846 (*Pictorial Times*, 10 Oct. 1846). This image offers
a rare, albeit stereotypical vista on an Irish food riot. Uniquely, it demonstrates the
manner in which the Irish protesting crowd, comprising women and children as
well as men, may have borne a loaf as a symbol of their plight.

major riot that took place in Limerick in June 1830 when five cars were 'surrounded by a furious mob of men, women, and children', and robbed of the oatmeal they were carrying, though the incident is still more significant for the fact
that the women of Limerick took the lead on the second day when the mob targeted Hogan's mill.

Ten years later, the same female cohort displayed comparable resolve when
they comprised an estimated two-thirds of the 'several thousand' persons who
were provoked by rising prices and the activities of forestallers to protest in

1799–1801', p. 181; Swift, *History of the Dublin bakers*, p. 204; O'Connor, *Labour history of
Waterford*, p. 19; Cunningham, *Galway, 1790–1914*, pp 94–5; *Nenagh Guardian*, 11 June 1842;
Freeman's Journal, 16 June 1842; *Cork Examiner*, 17 June 1842.

Limerick once more, and were 'goaded' into violence by the aggression of the employees of 'a meal and flour office' they targeted. Be that as it may, the aspersive depiction of the women who protested in 1830 as behaving 'rather [as] a horde of wild Indians than a number of civilized beings' because of the manner in which they took possession of the flourmill, summed up the negative impression these episodes made on respectable opinion in the nineteenth century.[37] Comparable reports of women filling aprons, quilts and petticoats at Clarecastle, county Clare, combined with the visual depiction of their involvement in 'the Galway starvation riots' in the June 1842 edition of the *Illustrated London News* (Fig. 1) to affirm the less than flattering impression of women's engagement in the food rioting that was dominant on the eve of the Great Famine and to inform the stereotype, given expression by the *Nenagh Guardian*, that 'as was customary on such occasions, ... women were most violent in their demeanour, and evidently encouraging the men, by voice and action, in their riotous intention'.[38]

If this description of female engagement is correct the increased involvement of Irish women (and children) in food protest in 1846–7 was consistent with an evolving pattern though the number of reports referring to their participation remains modest. Be that as it may, the observation in the county inspector's report that 'a large number of persons, principally women and children' were responsible for attacking 'carts laden with flour' about a mile-and-a-half from Clonmel on 9 April 1846, and that they succeeded in appropriating eleven bags of flour set a precedent for assemblies of 'men, women and boys', and for the 'mob made up, for the most part, of women and children, accompanied by a gang of men' that was responsible for plundering 'all the bakers' shops' in Clonmel on 14 April.[39] The presence of women and children among the 'vast concourse of people' that journeyed in search of food from the hills of Old Leighlin and Clogenane to Milford Mills in county Carlow, and among those who targeted the purchasers of potatoes at Aughnacloy, county Tyrone, in May, supports the conclusion that women assumed a more active part in seeking out food as famine took hold in 1846.[40] Yet the virtual absence of food protest during the summer months and the acknowledgement that 'government stores' were more dependable sources for those in genuine search of nutrition cautions against concluding that they had a transformative impact or that their increased engagement meant that food protest was more persistent than previously. This period of relative quietude did not last, however, and the sharp acceleration in protest that followed the poor potato harvest in 1846 featured more interventions by

37 Lee, 'The food riots of 1830 and 1840', pp 56–7, 62.   38 Power, *A history of Clarecastle*, p. 416; *Illustrated London News*, 25 June 1842; *Nenagh Guardian*, 11 June 1842.   39 County inspector's report, 13 Apr., Ryan to Redington, 13 Apr. 1846 (NAI, OP: Tipperary, 1846/27/9025, 8947); *Kerry Examiner*, 21 Apr. 1846.   40 Kinsella, 'Milford Mills', p. 328; Coulson to Pennefeather, 15 May 1846 (NAI, OP: Tyrone, 1846/28/11819); *Freeman's Journal*, 15 Sept. 1846, referring to the behaviour of women in county Mayo.

women. They were responsible, for example, for preventing a ship carrying wheat from disembarking from Dungarvan at the height of the 'disturbances' that gripped that port in late September, and were active participants in a number of seizures of small amounts of flour *en route* to Clonmel and Tipperary in that county thereafter. They were also involved in crowds in Birdhill (county Tipperary), Ballinasloe and Galway in which the increasing desperation of the populace was registered in the deportment of the women present, and by their preparedness to risk their lives such was their need.[41] Impelled, as one sympathetic observer put it, by 'hunger and the cries of their famishing children', the participation of women in food protest was sustained into 1847, though the number of reports in which their presence is specifically cited comprise only a fraction of the total. Many of the incidents were little more than 'slight affair[s]', which was how the press characterized events at Dungarvan in September 1846, but this must not be interpreted as evidence of disinclination, and still less disinterest. The participation of 'some women and boys' among the crowd, 'supposed about 200', that targeted 'a cart load of flour' at Ennistymon in April 1847 was only one of a number of incidents in which women supported men 'clamouring for employment and food' as a consequence of the suspension of public works. Comparable episodes during the summer in which women and men overwhelmed the armed escorts attending convoys of flour and other provisions in counties Cork and Limerick reinforce the conclusion that women's greater engagement in food protest then was a manifestation of the heightened fear that seized the population in the more protest prone parts of the country at that moment. Be that as it may, it did not set a new norm.[42] Food protests remained a feature of the Irish landscape thereafter but the paucity of references to female participation suggests that they remained a minority presence.

This impression is consistent with the pattern of engagement conveyed during the many decades when conditions were not so difficult, and it sustains the conclusion that, by comparison with the contested assessment of the situation in England, food rioting was not an activity in which Irish women participated especially actively (certainly not as actively as men) and still less provided leadership and direction on a regular basis. This was particularly the case during the eighteenth century, for though their involvement rose during the early nineteenth century, and, as evidenced by the 'mob headed by a woman' that led the assault on 13 drays carrying potatoes to Dublin that was intercepted at Dunshaughlin, county Meath, in June 1830, women did on occasion take a more prominent part,

41 *Freeman's Journal*, 5 Oct. 1846; Hutcheson(?) to Redington, 1 Nov. 1846 (NAI, OP: Limerick, 1846/17/29875); Harvey to Redington, 19 Oct., Worrall to Gallby, 16 Dec. 1846 (NAI, OP: Tipperary, 1846/27/28369–71, 36745); *Freeman's Journal*, 15, 19 Oct. 1846. 42 Police report, 14 Apr. 1847 (NAI, OP: Clare, 1847/5/389); Report, 12 July 1847 (NAI, OP: Cork, 1847/61038); *Freeman's Journal*, 5 Oct. 1846; *Leinster Express*, 22 May 1847; *Cork Examiner*, 21 June 1847; *Nation*, 15 May 1847. The report in the latter refers to 'a mob of near 500 men and women' attacking a convoy of seven carts bearing flour to Ballingarry, county Limerick.

it was hardly of an order that would justify suggesting, in the Irish instance at least, that 'food riots were ... a distinctly feminine province'.[43]

ORGANIZATION

Regardless of the gender of their participants, most food rioters pursued a course of action that was structured as well as purposeful. The most compelling manifestation of discipline was the ability, on occasion, to enforce *taxation populaire*, or any of the variants thereon that optimally resulted in making staple foodstuffs available at an affordable price. These include conveying appropriated grain and other foodstuffs to market houses in order that they could be publicly sold or delivering the keys of a food store to a local official, since it required organizational method and discipline to pursue these tactics in an environment where food prices were rising sharply, and hunger was a possibility. These attributes were demonstrated by the Waterford city crowd in 1794; faced with a party of militia, which was 'sent to disperse them', the mob 'requested the keys of the stores [they had previously 'forcibly' entered] should be delivered to the mayor, and their demand being complied with, they dispersed without doing the smallest injury'.[44] They were manifest also at Carrick-on-Suir in May 1812 when the 'populace [which] had assembled in considerable numbers and proceeded to the actual perpetration of some very serious and alarming outrages' 'dispersed quietly' pursuant to the reading of the Riot Act; at Athlone in February 1817 when 'a mob of several hundred paraded the whole of the town' prior to breaking open 'all the stores that had either potatoes or meal stored in them' and selling the goods 'in the market place'; and at Ennis, county Clare, in September 1846 when 'a large body of ... between two and three thousand paraded through the streets of this town proclaiming that they and their families were in the utmost distress caused by the want of employment and, consequently, of food. They did not evince the slightest disposition to commit a breach of the peace but had evidently thus assembled to publicly exhibit their destitute condition'.[45] It required organizational discipline also to effect 'the concerted attack' on grain stores in the city and on ships berthed on the quays at Galway in March 1812; to sustain a protest march such as was undertaken by the 'mobs' at Kilkenny in 1766, Dublin in 1795 and 1796, and Limerick in 1830;[46] and, though it may be less obvious, to unload or incapacitate a ship, to breach a canal, and to intercept carts carrying provisions.

Little can be gleaned of the manner in which crowds were assembled, lead and directed when they undertook these and allied actions. It is reasonable to

43 *Belfast News Letter*, 29 June 1830; Bohstedt, 'Women in English riots', 89.   44 Above, p. 105; *Clonmel Gazette*, 9 Apr. 1794.   45 *Cork Advertiser*, 5 May 1812; Cunningham, 'Popular protest and a "moral economy"', p. 40; Leyne to Redington, 15 Sept. 1846 (NAI, OP: Clare, 1846/5/23897). 46 Above, pp 101–2; *Hibernian Journal*, 28 May 1795; *Dublin Evening Post*, 12 Jan. 1796; Cunningham, *Galway, 1790–1914*, p. 86.

assume, however, that the dynamic varied according to the location and size of the crowd, and that whereas an individual or a number of individuals – the 'directing intelligence' to employ John Bohstedt's term – might suffice to provide direction to a small to medium crowd, a large congregation would have been more challenging though evidently not beyond the capacity of the leaders of the communities from which they emerged. Moreover, one must not exaggerate the degree of orchestration required. Food protesters were guided by a combination of tradition, instinct and the overwhelming impulse to do something to alleviate their plight be that real or apprehended. Crowds that assembled with this purpose in mind could, as in the instances in which looting resulted and property was wantonly damaged, degenerate into a rabble hardly if at all distinguishable from other street 'mobs'. But they could also manifest a measure of discipline comparable to that presented by the military cadres called upon to bring them to heel. This was easier, it may be assumed, when a crowd was dominated by a body with an established group identity. The fishermen of Kinsale and the Claddagh, and the journeymen coopers of Waterford, which pursued crowd actions in the mid-eighteenth and early nineteenth centuries, meet this definition. The 'hardworking' fishing community of the 'Galway suburb called the Claddagh', for example, existed as a largely independent entity, which conceived of itself as 'the guardians of Galway Bay'. Describing the location in 1839, when it may have had 'up to 6,000 inhabitants', the German travel writer Knut Jongbohm Clement wrote: 'they have their own laws ... They do not have much to do with the city-dwellers and do not want to marry outside of their own village'.[47] One may also evoke the population of the Liberties quarter of Dublin, which sustained a tradition of factional as well as political association long before they embarked on an intermittent, but identifiable pattern of bread rioting in the 1790s.[48]

It was possible also for populations to concert to determine on a path of action when circumstances demanded. Take for example the case of 'the working people of the city [of Waterford, who] assembled in consequence of the high price of potatoes, meal etc. [in November 1792] and proceeded to the office of the chief magistrate [mayor] with whom they remonstrated on the subject'.[49] Their action was not unprecedented, moreover; in August 1773 a deputation of six people representing the 'starving manufacturers' of the city of Dublin waited with the same purpose in mind on the lord mayor, who promised to pursue their concerns.[50] And though food protest was virtually at an end by that point, the posting in October 1847 of a 'notice' in the neighbourhood of Bodyke, a small settlement near Scariff in eastern county Clare, calling on the local population to assemble demonstrated the organizational impact that the tradition of agrarian protest may have made. The 'notice' ran as follows:

47 Bourke (ed.), *German travel writers' narratives*, pp 296–8; Reid, *Travels in Ireland in 1822*, p. 309; Cunningham, 'The mayor/admiral of Claddagh and Galway's moral economy', pp 22–34. 48 James Kelly, *The Ormond and liberty boys: factional riot in eighteenth-century Dublin* (Dublin, 2006); Cunningham, *Galway, 1790–1914*, pp 93–5. 49 *Dublin Chronicle*, 8 Nov. 1792. 50 *Hibernian*

All persons in this parish are required and requested to collect and meet in the neighbourhood of Ballinahinch on Tuesday the 19th instant, without any disappointment at a hill commonly called Bohera in order that they shall consult with each other their distress. Let no person fail at their peril, and let no person have the assurance of pulling this down for eight and forty hours.[51]

Such notices notwithstanding, the influence and impact of existing traditions of collective action on food protest are not always unambiguous. The adoption in the nineteenth century of techniques more readily identified with agrarian protest offers a good indicator of the impact of this tradition. The practice of attacking, and wrecking, the residences and stores of merchants and others, which some food rioters engaged in, may also have been borrowed since it too was employed by other, predominantly urban, interests – brothel rioters notably. Both demonstrate that food rioting was a manifestation of an evolving spectrum of collective protest activity. In the eighteenth century, this embraced agrarian protest, houghing, combinations, campaigns opposing new fabrics and new modes of production, brothel riots, resistance to revenue officials, rescues, faction fighting and so on; and in the early nineteenth century, as the Special Commission in Queen's county was informed, 'preventing [the] exportation of provisions' occupied a space alongside 'regulating the price of land, attacking houses, administering oaths, delivering threatening notices, taking arms, taking away girls, murders of proctors and gaugers, ... digging up land, destroying fences, houghing cattle, [and] resisting the payment of tithes'.[52]

One can conclude from this that for some contemporaries at least food protest belonged on a spectrum that embraced 'agrarian conspiracy' and its extensive 'black catalogue of crimes' for though these were unrelated to 'the deficiency of food or want of employment' that fuelled protest in south Tipperary in the mid-1840s they were perceived to be connected and depicted by their critics then as 'against life, liberty and property'.[53] The populace not only thought differently, but also knew this was not the case, given the readiness with which they assembled when called upon. Indeed, it was frequently sufficient to sound a horn, bugle or bell for a crowd to gather at a designated location be it urban or rural. Yet one cannot conclude that the participation of the populace could be assumed; the intelligence received at Dublin Castle in September 1800 that the 'tradespeople'

Journal, 30 Aug. 1773.   **51** Plunkett to Redington, 21 Oct. 1847 (NAI, OP: Clare, 1847/5/1150) enclosing notice.   **52** See, inter alia, Tim Watt, 'The corruption of the law and popular violence: the crisis of order in Dublin, 1729', *IHS*, 39:153 (May 2014), 1–23; idem, 'Taxation riots and the culture of popular protest in Ireland, 1714–1740', *EHR*, 130 (2015), 1418–38; Powell, 'Moral economy and popular protest in the late eighteenth century', pp 238–51; Powell, *The politics of consumption in eighteenth-century Ireland*, pp 173–6; Kelly, '"Ravaging houses of ill fame"', pp 84–103; Gerard Curtin, *West Limerick: crime, popular protest and society, 1820–1845* (Ballynahill, county Limerick, 2008); Charles Townshend, *Political violence in Ireland: government and resistance since 1848* (Oxford, 1983), p. 21; and notes.   **53** *Nenagh Guardian*, 17 Oct. 1846.

in the city 'have had private meetings, but not appeared anywhere in bodies' suggests that there was prior planning, which has left little or no evidential traces, prior to purposeful protest. It does not mean, moreover, that there were no spontaneous irruptions, but the fact that the 'appearance ... of a disposition ... to riot on account of the dearness of bread' was not realized in Dublin in the autumn of 1800 is consistent with the conclusion that food protest crowds possessed a 'directing intelligence' and that certain individuals or interests exercised decisive authority at given moments.[54] Whatever form this took, the efficient, effective, and increased use of the horn to convene a crowd at locations as far removed from each other as Cork, Carrick-on-Suir, Newry, Belfast and Belmullet (county Mayo) in the three decades 1801–30 indicates that it functioned equally well in rural as in urban environments. And it was not an innovation particular to the nineteenth century.[55] Documented references to the use of drums, horns and bells to assemble crowds have been identified at Youghal in 1740, Kilkenny in 1766, Drogheda in 1778, and Clonmel in 1784, and their utility was such that they continued to be employed thereafter. They were resorted to at Ennis in 1842, and at Killarney, and Croom and Ballingarry (county Limerick) in 1846 and 1847. They were also integral to the large scale mobilization that occurred in county Waterford in September 1846 when for three nights in a row 'signal fires were ... lighted throughout this part of the country, and horns were heard blowing in different directions'. Horns, in short, were only one of a variety of props that assisted with the organization of crowds; the preparedness of the Kilkenny crowd to assemble (and march) behind a piper in 1766, and of others crowds to do likewise behind a bellman, or at Killarney behind 'a bellman ... preceding a person carrying a flag' is a further manifestation of discipline that is coeval with the phenomenon even if it was not resorted to on every occasion.[56]

VIOLENCE AND DAMAGE TO PROPERTY

The organized character of food rioting was seldom acknowledged by contemporary commentators, opinion formers or politicians. There were obvious reasons for this. Food protest embraced intimidation, breaking and entry, and the appropriation, theft and damage of goods and property, which predisposed commentators to conceive of it as intrinsically lawless even violent. They were encouraged in this view by the number of cases in which individuals were injured though a majority

54 Marsden to King, 27 Sept., cited in Wells, 'The Irish famine of 1799–1801', p. 180; *Freeman's Journal*, 22 June 1790. **55** Wells, 'The Irish famine of 1799–1801', p. 181; Cunningham, 'Popular protest and a "moral economy"', pp 33, 40; *Freeman's Journal*, 11 Feb. 1817; Jordan, *Land and popular politics in Ireland*, p. 96. **56** Bohstedt, 'Riot census III, 1740–41'; William Colles to Barry Colles, 14 June 1766 (NAI, Prim Collection, 89/92); *Dublin Evening Journal*, 18 June 1778; *Parl. Reg. (Ire.)*, ii, 347; *Freeman's Journal*, 5 Feb. 1784, 5, 6 Oct. 1846; Howley to [Redington], 18 Sept. 1846 (NAI, OP: Waterford, 1846/29/24081); Fraher, 'The Dungarvan disturbances', p. 139; *Nenagh Guardian*, 11 June 1842; *Tralee Chronicle and Killarney Echo*, 15 May 1847.

of those who were on the receiving end of mob anger were interested parties – farmers, millers, merchants, retailers and others engaged in the production, processing and sale of foodstuffs, and ships' captains, barge operatives, car drivers, and officials of state, municipality and county, who were engaged in or who facilitated its movement. It can be countered (with equal justification), since ebullitions were usually purposeful and rarely directed at injuring or killing people, that food rioting was neither inherently violent nor destructive. Most food crowds possessed clearly defined aims that were bound up with improving the availability of foodstuffs at an affordable price and, because there was no recognizable means of legally realizing this aim, they had no alternative but to appeal to force to compel those possessed of a surplus to share it with those in need, which necessarily involved breaking the law in respect of property ownership and the transportation of foodstuffs. As a consequence, food rioters employed a variety of strategies within a definable palate of objectives – one of the most important of which centred on the forcible prevention of the movement of food.

The prevention of the movement of food assumed different forms, but since the sea was the primary means of transporting goods, ships featured prominently on the short inventory of vessels that food rioters in port towns and cities aspired to intercept and or immobilize. Their priority in those cases in which it was not sufficient to 'threaten … destruction to the Capt[ain] and his vessel', which was the strategy of the Ballina mob in 1778,[57] was to render them (temporarily) unseaworthy. There were a number of ways by which this might be accomplished. The preferred, and easiest, way was to deprive a ship of its sails, or to render its sails inoperative (by vandalizing or other means) but, rudders were also seized, riggings cut, masts damaged, and cables, tackle and anchors taken away. The restoration of these parts, undamaged, indicated that some at least of those who targeted ships did so in a controlled and thoughtful fashion, but, as there was no manual as to what was proper behaviour, others chose to slash rather than to remove sails, to take away riggings and, on occasion, to saw down masts and to interfere with a ships' deck. The example of the crowd at Clonakilty in May 1783 provides an illustration of what might take place:

> A few days ago the inhabitants of Cloghnakilty, having had intelligence that several sloops then in that harbour, were freighted with potatoes, at a time when a most dreadful dearth of that useful necessary prevailed, assembled in large bodies, and in the first transports of their resentment, tore away the rigging, demolished the masts, yards etc., and cast their anchors overboard. They afterwards unloaded several vessels, and obliged such masters as informed them of their destination for Cork market, solemnly to swear, that they would dispose of their cargo there, and no where else.[58]

57 *Dublin Evening Journal*, 2 Apr. 1778. 58 *Volunteer Journal* (Cork), 15 May 1783.

The damage inflicted in instances such as this were often 'considerable' as the report of the attack on a sloop in Wexford harbour in 1757 indicated.[59] Each case was unique, but the cost involved in setting matters right could be significant; the damage to the mast and rigging could range from £50, which was the cost of replacing these features on a sloop at Cork in 1778, to £200, which was the estimate of the damage incurred by a ship whose mast was 'almost cut thro'' at Waterford in 1759.[60]

The losses incurred when houses, mills, barns, warehouses, grain stores and grain shops were targeted ranged comparably, but mobs, such as that which targeted bakeries, shops, 'a ship in the river', and 'several mills' in Dublin in the summer of 1740, caused 'great damage'.[61] The cost of repairing the destruction to property in those instances in which mills and stores were targeted simply to access foodstuffs may well have been less than the loss incurred when foodstuffs were appropriated, even if the owner was the recipient of the revenue accrued when they were sold at the price specified by a mob, but as the market in grain and flour expanded, the preparedness of food rioters to escalate the level of destruction up to and including the demolition of mills in the mistaken belief that this would interrupt, perhaps even halt, the movement of food and grain out of an area, inevitably increased the order of the losses incurred. Few contemporary estimates have been located upon which a reliable set of figures might be constructed. One can, however, offer some indication of the order of the damage by reference to the destruction inflicted by the Kilkenny mob upon millers and starch makers in that town in 1766; by invoking the Bandon mob, which devastated mills and emptied grain stores in three locations in southern county Cork in November 1792; and, on a more modest scale, by citing the action of the Carrick-on-Suir mob which stripped the roof of a number of meal stores in the town in 1812.[62] The latter cost less to put right than the estimated £2,000 compensation due to property owners in the town and vicinity of Clonmel in April 1846 and the £315 the bakers in the town sought to recover from churchwardens as a result of the 'late provisions riots'.[63] These were towards the upper end of the sums involved to be sure. But as with the damage done to foodstuffs, which could range from the £21 paid Patrick Callan by Dublin Corporation in 1766 as 'compensation for losses he sustained by a riotous mob' to the £376 7s. 11½d. paid Charles Varley in 1761 as 'recompense [for] the loss of his cattle destroyed by the mob of Dublin' two years earlier, food protest by its very nature involved the loss of somebody's property.[64]

In so far as it is possible to establish, a majority of the food riots initiated in Ireland in the eighteenth century were conducted within the reasonably generous

59 *Universal Advertiser*, 12 Feb. 1757. 60 *Public Gazetteer*, 1 Sept. 1759; Kelly and Lyons (eds), *Proclamations of Ireland*, iv, 258–60. 61 *Pue's Occurrences*, 3 June 1740; *Faulkner's Dublin Journal*, 3 June 1740. 62 Above, pp 101–2; *Dublin Chronicle*, 24 Nov. 1792; Dickson, *Old world colony*, p. 384; *Cork Advertiser*, 5 May 1812. 63 *Kerry Examiner*, 8 May 1846; *Cork Examiner*, 8 July 1846. 64 Gilbert (ed.), *Calendar of ancient records of Dublin*, xi, 340; Payments made by Treasury on account of King's letter, *Journal of the House of Commons of the kingdom of Ireland* (21 vols, Dublin, 1796–1803), xiii, 63.

behavioural parameters that the phenomenon accommodated. What this means in practice was that there were occasions, uncommon admittedly, when, having failed to locate the 'large quantity of meal' it believed lay 'secreted in some cellars ... in order for exportation', a crowd dispersed 'without doing any damage'.[65] There were occasions also when crowds responded to the appeal of trusted local officials who promised to address their concerns; in county Clare in 1790, a 'great mob' was dissuaded from 'dismantling' a vessel at Ennis 'by the timely interposition' of Sir Lucius O'Brien when he made it known that they were acting under the mistaken impression that it was 'carrying away a cargo of oats and potatoes'; in Belfast, in May 1808, a magistrate, with the assistance of a number of 'respectable gentlemen', convinced the crowd that had assembled to protest at high provision prices to disperse; while in Newpark, county Tipperary in October 1846 an angry crowd that surrounded carts ferrying oatmeal, 'declaring they would allow no food to leave the country whilst they were starving', was persuaded by the intervention of a 'popular magistrate ... and some others of the town' to allow the carts 'to proceed to their destination'.[66] But there was also occasions when crowds took a distinctly permissive attitude to the behavioural boundaries that defined the practice.

One notable boundary that it was permissible to cross was the destruction of food. This was not commonplace, and when resorted to its primary purpose was not to secure access to scarce foodstuffs or to bring about a reduction in prices but to disrupt the development of new and emerging patterns of food movement to which the populace objected. It was resorted to, for example, to dissuade merchants and others availing of bounties, such as those instituted in 1758, to encourage the movement of grain to Dublin. It was also the case that local interests sought to express disgruntlement at the actions of millers, particularly those located proximate to urban markets, who bought up grain in a locality in order to grind it into flour for sale outside the community. This was evidently a consideration with the Bandon mob that went on the rampage in November 1792; it made doubly sure that 'a very respectable merchant in the town' would not soon resume trading by 'wantonly throw[ing] all the corn, flour and meal [they encountered in his stores] into the river and destroy[ing] all the machinery in the mill'.[67] Some two decades earlier in August 1773, 'a great mob' 'cut and destroyed several sacks of flour' at the Coombe in Dublin, in what seems like an imitation of the pattern of slashing foreign fabrics then being pursued by artisans in Dublin and other urban centres.[68] The removal of barriers in the way of the exportation of live cattle, and the provision of incentives to encourage the exportation of hides and other commodities, which were also regarded negatively, also contributed to, and were at the root of, a variety of crowd driven interventions during the late 1750s, the 1760s and early 1770s, which resulted in the destruc-

65 *Freeman's Journal*, 7 July 1767. 66 *Freeman's Journal*, 22 June 1790, 8 Oct. 1846; Cunningham, 'Popular protest and a "moral economy"', p. 31. 67 *Dublin Chronicle*, 24 Nov. 1792; Dickson, *Old world colony*, p. 384. 68 *Hibernian Chronicle*, 30 Aug. 1773; Powell, *The politics of consumption*, p. 176.

tion of a variety of produce, including flour and potatoes, that were being read-ied for transportation.[69] Such actions rarely occurred at moments of acute dis-tress, and they were usually impelled by factors over and above that fuelling orthodox food protest. One may instance the disturbances orchestrated by the Terry Alts in county Clare in 1830 when the refusal of labourers to pay the full market price demanded by farmers for potatoes led to the destruction of a boat and three boatloads of potatoes at New Quay, and the spilling of the contents of sacks destined for Campbell's potato 'manufactory' at Newtownards in 1839.[70]

A more personalized course was pursued when crowds targeted the residences of merchants and officials. This was not clear cut in those instances in which pri-vate residences doubled up with or were part of the same complex of buildings in which a business was located, but the identification of six incidents of this kind between the attack on the house of Theodore Vansevenhausen in Cork in 1709–10 and the pulling down of several houses in Cork in 1777 indicates that it was conceived of as a legitimate crowd action. It may be that rioters were encour-aged to engage in this practice by its very effectiveness since in two instances – in Youghal in 1740 and Sligo in 1741 – it was sufficient to issue the threat that this would be done to bring merchants to heel.[71] Others were subjected to more measured sanctions. Joseph Sexton, a Limerick merchant who was blamed for a sudden spike in the price of oatmeal in that city in 1748, had his windows and furniture broken by a vengeful 'mob'.[72]

Sexton might have fared worse. Almost twenty years previously, the house of the then mayor of Cork, Hugh Millard, was 'torn down in pieces by the mobb' and the mayor 'assaulted' during the major food riot that gripped that city in 1729.[73] Millard's experience was unusual; municipal officials were not a prime target; forestallers and regraters were a different matter. The attacks on fore-stallers who sought to inhibit the movement of foodstuffs into Dublin in the early 1770s indicates that food rioters were not opposed in principle to meting out physical abuse to those that deviated from the code of behaviour they deemed appropriate, but forestalling was acknowledged in law as an offence, and it was a prominent target of many officials.[74] The fact that the only notable phys-ical assaults perpetrated in the three decades following the clash between mobs in Dublin in 1741 that resulted in two dead was a fatality at Waterford in July 1746, an assault on a female hoarder in Belfast in 1756, and an attempt at Youghal in 1760 to throw a man overboard from a vessel carrying potatoes is telling.[75] It indicated that in so far as those who engaged, and still more those

69 Above, p. 39; *Freeman's Journal*, 8 Sept. 1764; Gibson, *History of Cork*, ii, 211; *Public Gazetteer*, 1 Mar. 1768; *Finn's Leinster Journal*, 20 Jan. 1773, 11 Sept. 1773.   70 Enright, 'Terry Alts: the rise and fall of an agrarian society', pp 226–7; *Belfast News Letter*, 25 Jan. 1839.   71 *Dublin Newsletter*, 6 Dec. 1740; *Pue's Occurrences*, 25 Apr. 1741; McClelland, 'Amyas Griffith', p. 14.   72 *Dublin Weekly Journal*, 4 June 1748.   73 Caulfield, *Council book of the Corporation of Cork*, p. 482; *An express from Cork with an account of a bloody battle*, broadsheet.   74 Below, pp 194–5.   75 Waterford Archives, Corporation of Waterford council books, 25 Sept. 1746; Benn, *History of*

who provided direction were concerned, eighteenth-century food protest pursued a culture of controlled violence. This was not always easily sustained, not least since it was not always reciprocated by the authorities tasked with maintaining law and order.[76] Moreover, the evolving pattern of protest, and of rural protest in particular, countenanced greater aggression, and there are sufficient examples to suggest that food protest was not immune to this trend. Incidents in Waterford in 1768 and in Dublin in 1774 in which food protesters were observed bearing arms, and in Dublin in 1773 when they 'fire[d] on the soldiers' that pursued them having refused to heed the exhortation of the lord mayor 'to disperse', are certainly suggestive, and there were others.[77] The death, by 'a blow of an adze,' of one of the hands on 'a Scotch sloop' boarded by a number of coopers at Drogheda in December 1775 fits this pattern. It was followed three years later by the death of two men in Cork in 1778 when 'a mob' 'searching for provisions ... intended for exportation to the north of Ireland ... destroyed a great deal of property, breaking down the doors and windows of several ... merchants' warehouses, and cutting down the masts and destroying the rigging of ships'. It was in evidence once more in 1783–4 when two men died during an affray at Gorteen, county Mayo, in July 1783 precipitated by an attempt to 'rescue' potatoes from forestallers. In addition, the 'violent assault' (and robbery) of William Clark, a merchant at Cork, in 1778, and of the sovereign of the town of Kinsale when he intervened in a vain attempt to keep the peace in the face of riotous fishermen in March 1784, can be seen to fit this pattern, though they might equally plausibly be identified as run-of-the-mill assaults.[78] The fact that there were no more incidents of this kind in 1783 of 1784, or that the greater assertiveness manifest in Dublin in the challenging environment of 1792–3 and 1795 did not result in a surge of violent confrontations supports the latter conclusion. Indeed, while one might point to incidents such as that which took place in Carrick-on-Suir in 1791 when the 'mob' 'violently forced into the stocks three persons who ... were creating a corner' in oats and potatoes, there was little to distinguish this, or other instances in which forestallers were targeted in Ennis and Dublin, from what had happened in the 1770s.[79] Similarly, the fact that the 'Bandon mob', which left a trail of destruction in its wake in 1792, was armed was of largely symbolic import since there is no suggestion that weapons were used, though it is to be presumed that they, no more than the Dublin crowds that paraded the streets in the 1790s bearing pistols and hangers, were as aware as those who reported the incident of the additional threat they presented.[80] One

Belfast, p. 596; *Public Gazetteer*, 10 Apr. 1753; *Freeman's Journal*, 24 Aug. 1773, 15 Oct. 1774; *Hibernian Journal*, 27 Aug. 1773; *Dublin Mercury*, 7 Jan. 1775. **76** See below, pp 163–70. **77** NAI, Notes by Isabel Grubb from papers in PROI, 1915, p. 7; *Freeman's Journal*, 15 Oct. 1774; *Hibernian Chronicle*, 30 Aug. 1773. **78** *Hibernian Journal*, 8 Dec. 1775; *Cork Remembrancer*, pp 176–7; *Hibernian Chronicle* (Cork), 16 Mar. 1778; *Dublin Evening Journal*, 18 June 1778; *Dublin Evening Post*, 1 July 1783; Kelly and Lyons (eds), *The proclamations of Ireland*, iv, 258–60; *Hibernian Journal*, 22 Mar. 1784. **79** Power, 'A Carrickman's diary', p. 66; *Ennis Chronicle*, 6 Dec. 1792; *Freeman's Journal*, 30 May 1795. **80** *Hibernian Journal*, 27 Nov. 1792.

might even normalize the assault upon one of the principals of the firm of Cherry and Sykes of Waterford who was 'repeatedly struck' when their merchants' store in Waterford was invaded by a mob seeking oatmeal in April 1794.[81] However, this would be to disregard the underlying trend, which countenanced greater assertiveness on the part of those who engaged in food protest.

The most palpable manifestation of this was the more violent character of a proportion of the food riots that populated the 1808, 1812, 1817, 1842 and 1846–7 riot spikes, and the general disposition of crowds in the nineteenth century to behave more assertively. This did not result in injuries and fatalities in either 1808 or 1812, though the crowd activity at Kilrush, county Clare, and [Pallas]kenry, county Limerick, bore closer resemblance to that of agrarian protest, which was more disposed towards violence than orthodox food rioting.[82] This was still more strikingly a feature of protest in 1817, as evidenced by the nightly activities of armed bands in county Limerick,[83] and by other anonymous behaviours (threatening letters etc.) generally associated with agrarian movements pursued by rioters in counties Donegal, Galway and elsewhere.[84] The most compelling index of the greater propensity of food protesters to appeal to violence is provided by the greater daring of crowds. Three incidents from 1817 may be invoked. The preparedness of three hundred protesters in February 1817 to attack an escorted potato boat on the Grand Canal between Ticknevin and Robertstown, county Kildare, and of 'a furious multitude of about five hundred persons' to attack a convoy of sixteen cars bearing meal between Navan and Nobber, in county Meath, as a result of which two protesters were killed and several others wounded on each occasion, was emulated by a similar confrontation, also in June, in Limerick in which 'two lives [also] fell victims to this act of lawless turbulence'.[85] Since these were not the first occasions when two protesters died, nor the only incidents of this kind to occur in 1817, there is a danger of reading too much into them. They did not pass un-noted at the time, however, though it may be that it took until the 1830s, and further aggressive examples of food protest for it to become apparent that protesting crowds were more disposed to confrontation. This was the case, certainly, at Doone, Castlebar, county Mayo, in 1831 when the refusal of a crowd to be cowed by a warning volley of shots 'fired over their heads' was decisive in enabling them to seize a number of cartloads of meal.[86] The refusal of urban crowds at Londonderry in 1837, and at Sligo, Ballina and Athlone in 1842 to countenance the removal of

81 *Clonmel Gazette*, 9 Apr. 1794; *Hibernian Journal*, 11 Apr. 1794. 82 Cunningham, 'Popular protest and a "moral economy"', pp 31–2. 83 Traditional food rioters protested openly during the daytime; night protest defined agrarian protest, which made less claim to operate within a moral or common law. 84 *Gentleman's Magazine*, 87 (1817), p. 620; Post, *The last great subsistence crisis*, p. 73; Cunningham, 'Popular protest and a "moral economy"', pp 38–9; Cunningham, *Galway, 1790–1914*, pp 88–9. 85 Abbott, 'The Downshire estates', pp 38–9; Mooney, 'The origins of agrarian violence in Meath', 58; *Freeman's Journal*, 11, 12 June 1817. 86 O'Neill, 'The Catholic Church and relief of the poor', 139.

purchased potatoes by 'county people' was another manifestation of the same tendency, necessitating the provision of 'an escort of police to escape the fury' at Ballina.[87] It could also result in physical assaults on owners and shippers, as occurred at Pullaheeny, county Sligo, in June 1840 when 'the owner of the potatoes' and 'the crew of the vessel' in which they were being shipped were beaten 'very severely' by 'a mob of fellows'.[88]

But the most animatedly debated incident took place on Mill Road, Ennis in June 1842, when, on the third day of an eventful few days in that town and its environs, which had already claimed one casualty, armed police fired upon an angry crowd, as a result of which three people died and seventeen were wounded. The death subsequently of a policeman as a result of injuries incurred during the course of the riot, which brought the total death toll to five, attested to the violent nature of the episode, and this impression was reinforced by claims that 'every one of the police was struck before a shot was fired'. Yet there was a contrary perspective that registered more strongly with the public, which was that the police had not been authorized to open fire by the magistrates who were present and that they had done so when 'the people were in the act of retiring'. This was not the finding of the inquest that was convened within days of the incident, but by then calls for 'justice upon the blood spillers' were commonplace, and the 'Clare massacre', as the episode was labelled in certain quarters, was being linked to 'other [more famous] massacres' at Peterloo and Gurtroe.[89] The public mood was certainly agitated by incendiary claims by Charles O'Connell, the MP for county Kerry who participated in the coroner's inquest, that the combination of 'Orange squireens' and the 'paid and pampered ruffians' that constituted the police believed they could behave with impunity. Calls upon the authorities to ensure that the 'guilty party in the present case should not go unpunished' echoed the public's demand that 'the savagery of discharging loaded fire-arms among that defenceless and afflicted mass of Irish peasantry' was not permitted to pass unsanctioned, but they acquired little traction from either the inquest or the court of assize. While acknowledging that the police had fired on a retreating crowd the inquest judged that they had done so on instruction and after a warning was issued. In an ironic twist, three people were found guilty at the Clare assizes in July of attacking a boat and 'help[ing] themselves to a por-

87 *Belfast News Letter*, 1 Aug. 1837; *Freeman's Journal*, 31 May 1842; *Connaught Telegraph*, 8 June 1842; *Nenagh Guardian*, 11 June 1842. 88 *Freeman's Journal*, 18 June 1840. 89 The Peterloo 'massacre' took place in Manchester on 6 August 1819 when a peaceful meeting in favour of parliamentary reform was charged by the Manchester Yeomanry, a local force of volunteer soldiers, as a result of which between 10 and 20 people were killed and hundreds more injured: Robert Walmsley, *Peterloo: the case re-opened* (Manchester, 1969). The Rathcormac or Gortroe 'massacre' took place on 18 December 1834 in the civil parish of Gortroe near the village of Rathcormac, county Cork. Between twelve and twenty protesting locals were killed by soldiers enforcing the collection of tithes: Noreen Higgins-McHugh, 'The 1830s tithe riots' in William Sheehan and Maura Cronin (eds), *Riotous assemblies: rebels, riots and revolts in Ireland* (Cork, 2011), pp 80–95.

tion of the property of Messrs Bannatyne', but the refusal of the Crown 'to call for punishment upon these poor people' was properly applauded as an act of 'humanity'. It was politic in the circumstances and in the wake of an episode which demonstrated that the public continued to believe the authorities should act with restraint in cases of food protest.[90]

While the nature of the protest pursued in county Clare in June 1842, and the assertive way in which the Galway crowd behaved a week later – 'stones were thrown' at the police and military, obliging them 'to retreat to their respective barracks'; soldiers were 'assaulted'; the high sheriff was 'insulted', and the windows of un-lit houses were broken – is consistent with the conclusion that food rioting was pursued with greater aggression as the pre-Famine economic crisis intensified, food protests of this nature were unusual.[91] There was, moreover, another, more measured side to crowd activity at this time, which attests to the fact that the discipline that distinguished food protest from other forms of riotous activity endured. It was in evidence at Carlow in the summer of 1842:

> A few days ago, a number of poor men assembled in Carlow, and proceeded to the house of T. Haughton, esq., JP. They requested to see Mr H[aughton], and when that worthy magistrate appeared, he was addressed by the leader of the party to the following effect: 'Sir, we, and our wives, and our children, are starving; we cannot see them die of want; we are willing to work for food for our families; we cannot hold out another day: get us something to eat against to-morrow or we must take it by force'. Mr Haughton told them by no means to break the peace, as heavy punishment would follow, but he promised to bring their condition before the respectable inhabitants of the town. They were satisfied with this promise, and quietly took their departure.[92]

The inauguration of a subscription, which raised £300, and the provision of 'employment on the roads to the poor men' that assembled in Carlow demonstrated that controlled and purposeful protest could pay dividends, and it is not surprising therefore that there were comparable incidents during the Great Famine. One may instance the episode 'a little outside the town of Galway' in October 1845 when the 'large crowd' that assembled to intercept 'twenty-five cars, laden with meal' acceded to the remonstrations of a local resident magistrate; this not only prevented serious bloodshed but also prompted a relief initiative retailing Indian meal at '3s. per ton under cost price'. Several months later, when the spring protest was at its peak in county Tipperary, the crowd that gathered at Clonmel courthouse on Tuesday 14 April 1846 agreed 'to suspend further demonstrations' when they were assured that a local relief commit-

90 *Nenagh Guardian*, 11 June 1842; *Cork Examiner*, 13 June, 6 July 1842; *Freeman's Journal*, 16, 18 June, 9 July 1842; *Leinster Express*, 18 June 1842.   91 *Cork Examiner*, 17 June 1842; *Freeman's Journal*, 16 June 1842.   92 *Belfast News Letter*, 24 June 1842.

tee, which had just been established, would address their concerns.[93] And in November 1847 when Hamilton Lyster, a flour miller from Derrinsalla, county Tipperary, was 'intercepted by a crowd ... consisting of upwards of thirty persons' about a mile from Shannon Harbour, the attackers took only six sacks of flour from the nine carts that comprised the convoy.[94]

The endurance of this impulse notwithstanding, the disposition to engage in outrage was more in evidence during the Great Famine than earlier. It is notable, for example, that a potentially serious riot involving 'a hungry mob ... composed principally of women' was only averted at Ballinasloe in October 1846 'with the greatest difficulty' by the intervention of a local priest.[95] More pertinently, perhaps, there is evidence to suggest that the disposition of the 'labouring classes' to 'suffer in silence', identified at Tullamore in April, weakened subsequently as the populace perceived that promises made earlier in the year that relief would be forthcoming had not been honoured.[96] This was the import of the notice addressed 'to the gentlemen that rule the parish' of Bunratty, county Clare, in September:

> We the parishioners of Bunratty and Drumline deem it our duty before we take any other steps to tell you that we will not, nor can not by any possible means bear starvation and hunger any longer. We have no occasion to tell you our present situation. You know it, but you ought to thank God for not to be acquainted with it ... for we want nothing but work and fair wages, but mind one day or one hour is too long; therefore we will not be dealt with as we were last spring waiting by fair promises.[97]

A comparably 'formal notice' was served some weeks later on the magistracy by 'a large concourse of people' at Oranmore, county Galway, and the number of incidents of violent protest increased thereafter.[98] The administration of a severe beating to John Shepherd, who was left 'dangerously ill' at Newpark, county Tipperary, in December because he was suspected of selling two bags of wheat (he had brought to be ground) was an illustration of 'the alarming state' to which 'this vicinity' was reduced, and of the acknowledged 'insufficiency of the police force' in that locality as the year ended.[99]

Yet the violence associated with food protest was kept within bounds during the Great Famine. There were a number of notable incidents, but there was no equivalent to the violent confrontations that distinguished the 'Clare massacre' of 1842 or earlier incidents resulting in multiple fatalities. The most widely publi-

93 *Freeman's Journal*, 6, 9 Oct. 1846; *Nation*, 10 Oct. 1846; *Cork Examiner*, 20 Apr. 1846.
94 Information from John Lupton, 27 Nov. 1847 (NAI, OP, King's county, 1847/15/612).
95 *Freeman's Journal*, 19 Oct. 1846. 96 *Freeman's Journal*, 30 Apr. 1846. 97 Enclosure with Leyne to Redington, 16 Sept. 1846 (NAI, OP: Tipperary, 1846/27/23947). 98 *Freeman's Journal*, 5 Oct. 1846. 99 French (Cashel) to Redington, 18 Dec., Osborne to [Redington], 21 Dec. 1846 (NAI, OP: Tipperary, 1846/27/35923, 37205).

cized famine *contretemps* took place at Dungarvan in late September 1846 when one man died as a result of complications caused by 'a gunshot wound in the thigh' incurred when an angry crowd confronted the military company defending the town jail. He was one of 'two persons' who were 'dangerously wounded' on this occasion when the army fired 26 shots. Fifteen others 'received slight flesh wounds' and a number of soldiers were also 'very much injured' by the volleys of stones thrown by the 'mob'. There was a comparable outcome at Dunfanaghy, county Donegal in the summer of 1847 when two protesters were 'mortally wounded and others ... severely wounded' when another 'large concourse of people' overwhelmed a 'party of police' tasked with defending 'a store and a mill at Irishtown'.[100] There would surely have been more incidents of this kind, and more casualties had the 'forbearance' that defined the official response to the surge in protest in county Tipperary in the spring of 1846 not set the tone for what was to follow.[101] It is notable, for instance, that the encounter involving a 'large crowd' and three companies of soldiers 'outside the town of Galway' in early October resulted in nothing more serious than 'a few ... slight bayonet wounds'.[102] Indeed, it seems as if fatal injuries were as likely to occur accidentally as by design; indicatively a woman died from the injuries she received when she was run over by the cart she had mounted when a 'large mob' sought also in October 1846 to intercept a convoy of provisions *en route* from Galway to county Roscommon.[103]

The modest number of casualties attributable to food rioting during the Great Famine was due in large part to the control that was most in evidence during the early phases of the crisis. The tone was set in county Tipperary in April and May 1846, when the sundry assemblies of men, women and children that rose in protest directed their attention at bakers' shops, meal and flour stores, mills, and carts and boats carrying foodstuffs rather than people. The sheer concentration of such incidents distinguished this episode from others of its kind, but it was defined still more by the disciplined resolution on display, which meant no mill escaped a visit. This did not mean that the protesters eschewed property destruction. When a second descent was made on James Ryan's mill at Toberaheena (near Clonmel) it was undertaken with 'the intention of demolishing it'. This intention was frustrated, but the resolve was equally manifest in the targeting of the distillery of Messrs Stein and Co. at Marlfield because it utilized grain.[104] It was further in evidence in the targeting of 'shops generally' in Carrick-on-Suir, in the refusal to be awed by the armed escorts accompanying the convoys of carts that snaked through the countryside,[105] and in the willingness to do what was

100 Fraher, 'Dungarvan disturbances', p. 143; *Freeman's Journal*, 5 Oct. 1846, 5 June 1847; *Nenagh Guardian*, 7 Oct. 1846. 101 Below, pp 177–8. 102 *Freeman's Journal*, 6 Oct. 1846. 103 Kernan to Redington, 12, 13 Oct. 1846 (NAI, OP: Galway, 1846/11/27635, 277731). 104 *Cork Examiner*, 20 Apr. 1846; Bagwell to [ ], 23 Apr., Information of William Lynch of Tulaheena, 23 Apr. 1846 (NAI, OP: Tipperary, 1846/27/10185, 10725). 105 *Kerry Examiner*, 20 Apr. 1846; Pennefeather to Shaw, 29 Mar., County inspector's report, 13 Apr., Ryan to Redington, 13 Apr., Riall to Redington, 14 Apr., Lismore to Bessborough, 15 Apr., Purdy to Pennefather, 24 Apr. 1846 (NAI,

necessary, within limits, to achieve their aim. This was the case, for example, when boats were intercepted on the river Suir:

> The attack, which was apprehended yesterday, commenced this day [16 April]. The countrymen on both sides of the Suir having coalesced, proceeded in a body to a bridge which crosses the Suir at Kilshulan [*recte* Kilsheelan], a village ... on the road to Carrick-on-Suir, where they loosened a part of the parapet of the bridge with the intention of throwing it down, and stopping the navigation of the river; they likewise seized two boats which were on the river at the time – one laden with Indian corn, the other with wheat, which they immediately commenced to pillage.[106]

Though incidents on this scale are not difficult to locate, few serious injuries resulted. A policeman was 'gravely injured' in the course of 'attacks on the police conveying flour from a mill into Clonmel' on 14 April, and injuries may also have ensued at Kilsheelan when a mob 'attacked the military with stones' two days later. The presence of armed men among an assembly, several hundred strong, that gathered on the racecourse in the neighbourhood of Slievenamon, and that reputedly harboured plans 'to storm the town during the night' was potentially more serious, but this did not come to pass, and it was, in any event, more redolent of agrarian than food protest.[107] Be that as it may, it did nothing to allay public unease at the activities of food protesters. The observation of Robert Harvey of Abbey Mills on 16 April that 'the peaceable inhabitants have been put into alarm and anxiety with regard to their property by the appearance of an ungovernable mob' was put in its proper perspective by the second earl of Glengall who reported to Dublin Castle that the owners and operatives of Castlegrace and Flemingstown mills were 'more frightened than hurt' by the appearance of mobs. This came closer than any other comment offered at that moment to the reality of the situation then for a majority of the respectable population.[108]

It also meant, once the concerns that fuelled disorder were rekindled after the relative calm of the summer months, the 'fear' was easily re-animated.[109] The extensive coverage afforded events in Dungarvan in September was important in this respect, but it did not establish a pattern. There were many locations – Ennis, county Clare, Ballinsaloe and Galway, county Galway, and Banagher, county Offaly – where protesting crowds continued to behave in a disciplined manner, though the heightened distress fostered a greater propensity towards violent outrage that did not leave food protest untouched.[110] It was certainly in evi-

OP: Tipperary, 1846/27/7939, 9025, 8931, 8993, 10171). **106** *Cork Examiner*, 20 Apr. 1846; Glengall to Bessborough, [15] Apr. 1846 (NAI, OP: Tipperary, 1846/27/9237). **107** Riall to Redington, 14 Apr. 1846, Report of resident magistrate, Newtown Anner, 16 Apr. 1846 (NAI, OP: Tipperary, 1846/27/8931, 9113); *Cork Examiner*, 20 Apr. 1846. **108** Harvey to Bessborough, 16 Apr. 1846, Glengall to Bessborough, [15] Apr. 1846 (NAI, OP: Tipperary, 1846/27/9091, 9237). **109** Glengall to Labouchere, 25 Nov. 1846 (NAI, OP: Tipperary, 1846/27/33123). **110** Leyne to

dence in county Waterford in September and October following on a 'murder-ous attack' by a stone-throwing mob, possibly numbering 'three thousand per-sons', on Lord Stuart de Decies, the lord lieutenant of the county. De Decies escaped unhurt, albeit with 'some difficulty', but the event struck a chord that was played out during the more famous Dungarvan food riot when soldiers were assailed by volleys of stones, and by mobs, armed with sticks, spades and ham-mers.[111] Though the appearance then, and later, of mobs bearing shovels and spades offered a vivid and visible illustration of the dependence of the distressed on public works, and later of the alarm that seized large numbers of poor as the government cut back on these for fiscal reasons, their display in the autumn of 1846 mirrored popular disquiet as the impact of a second poor harvest struck home.[112] The most obvious manifestation of this was the surge in the volume of 'murderous and violent assaults upon the person in dwelling-houses and on the high roads, burglary, robbery, plunder of fire-arms, threatening notices' and 'thieving on a monstrous scale' – which some among the respectable refused to accept were 'the result of deficiency of food or want of employment'.[113]

The increased recourse to violence certainly left a visible mark on the pattern of food protest. It can be identified, for example, in the number of incidents in which in the winter of 1846–7 horses were shot to prevent the movement of grain and other foodstuffs; in the increased resort to the intimidation of farmers, shopkeepers and store owners; in levying contributions in wheat; in the burning of haggards, and in allied actions by agrarian protesters in pursuit of improved access to food.[114] But its impact was registered more starkly, and in a manner that attested to the increased disposition to engage in violence against the person, by the increased number of assaults on carmen, dealers in provisions and others encountered ferrying grain or intercepted with provisions in their possession; in the increased administration of beatings during food protests; in the stoning of the police when they intervened, and in high profile assaults such as that on Hugh Palliser Hickman of Fenloe, county Clare, a magistrate, who was 'brutally attacked in his own house' in October 1846 because, it was rumoured, of his lack of sympathy with calls for higher pay for those on public works.[115] In another

Redington, 15 Sept. 1846 (NAI, OP: Clare, 1846/5/23897); *Freeman's Journal*, 5 Oct. 1846. 111 *Freeman's Journal*, 28 Sept., 5 Oct. 1846; *Nenagh Guardian*, 7 Oct. 1846. 112 For examples of mobs bearing 'shovels and spades' in county Clare see Information of William Mahoney, 12 Apr. 1847 (NAI, OP: Clare, 1847/5/345); in Cork and Armagh where similar mobs sought to 'pillage the bread shops': *Freeman's Journal*, 26 June 1847; Pinchin to Fleming, 31 July, Godby to Redington, 21 Sept., Annesley to Labouchere, 3 Nov., Knaresborough to Redington, 18 Nov. 1846 (NAI, OP: Cork, 1846/6/22047, 23595, 30457, 32283); Kidd to [Redington], 17 Dec. 1846 (NAI, OP: Armagh, 1846/2/27127). 113 *Nenagh Guardian*, 17 Oct. 1846; *Tralee Chronicle and Killarney Echo*, 16 Jan. 1847; Osborne to [ ], 21 Dec. 1846, Hagarty to [ ], 16 Dec. 1846 (NAI, OP: Tipperary, 1846/27/36247, 36453); above, pp 76–9. 114 *Freeman's Journal*, 28 Sept., 16, 19 Oct., 4 Nov. 1846, 6 Jan. 1847 (NAI, OP: Tipperary, 1846/27/28073, 27263, 28833, 29631, 29821, 29899, 33999, 34239, 31721; /1847/192); Leyne to Redington, 20, 22, 23, 28, 29 Sept., 12 Oct. 1846 (NAI, OP: Tipperary, 1846/27/25727, 25629, 25631, 25345, 26693, 27697). 115 *Freeman's*

incident, when the crowd of 'country people' that 'poured into Dublin' in January 1847 'came into collision with the constabulary', two constables 'were beaten, one ... very severely'.[116]

One of the inevitable consequences of the surge in outrage was the reanimation of the disquiet that was previously in evidence during the spring of 1846. It proved more enduring on this occasion because it dovetailed with the alarm precipitated by the dramatic reduction in March and April 1847 of the number of people engaged in public works, which contributed to the 'alarm and apprehension' reported from county Clare in the summer of 1847.[117] Given this backdrop, it is unsurprising that the summer of 1847 witnessed a surge in protest with the explicit object of securing employment or food, and to more confrontation between protesters and police.[118] Significantly, it did not emulate the level it had reached in the winter of 1846–7, as the populace were faced with the reality of the fact that their dependence on organized relief diminished the efficacy of traditional food protest. This was made crystal clear to the crowd that gathered at Cashel, county Tipperary, in early May 1847, as the resident magistrate, Martin French reported:

> About five hundred persons of the labouring class came from different sides of the town, and almost half that number collected in one body opposite the house of Mr Cooper, the engineer under the Board of Works. I immediately got amongst them and expostulated with them on the folly of their attempting any violence as such conduct would surely bring about the immediate suspension of all public employment in the neighbourhood, and perhaps put a stop to the distribution of food by the [Relief] Committee. I also told them that the new system of relief was now in operation ... and that food should henceforth be distributed to the destitute ... I then expostulated further with them, and at length obtained from them a promise to immediately quit the town and go home. That promise they fulfilled. And in about a couple of hours afterwards, the town was very little more crowded than on ordinary days[119]

The implications of this new dispensation were made still more explicit by the communication of the Athboy Relief Committee to the people of the barony of Lune, county Meath, in December 1846 (Fig. 4), and at Kilconry, county Clare,

Journal, 30 Oct. 1846; *Leinster Express*, 16 Jan. 1847; French to [ ], 18 Dec. 1846, McEvoy to [ ], 3 Feb. 1847 (NAI, OP: Tipperary, 1846/27/35923, 1847/27/489); Kenny to Redington, 21 Oct., Memorial of magistrates, 20 Oct., Ryan to [ ], 29 Oct. 1846, Outrage report, 22 Dec. 1846 (NAI, OP: Tipperary, 1846/27/28843, 29333, 29929, 36605). **116** *Tralee Chronicle and Killarney Echo*, 16 Jan. 1847. **117** Report of RM (Ennis) to Redington, 11 May 1847 (NAI, OP: Clare, 1847/5/484). For public works see, Kinealy, *This great calamity*, p. 144; above, p. 80. **118** NAI, OP: Clare, 1847/5/257, 314, 345, 467, 491, 521, 576, 629, 625, 630, 660; Kinealy, *This great calamity*, pp 144–5; Cunningham, ""Tis hard to argue starvation into quiet"", pp 25–7; *Leinster Express*, 22 May 1847. **119** French to under-secretary, 3 May 1847 (NAI, OP: Tipperary, 1847/27/1086).

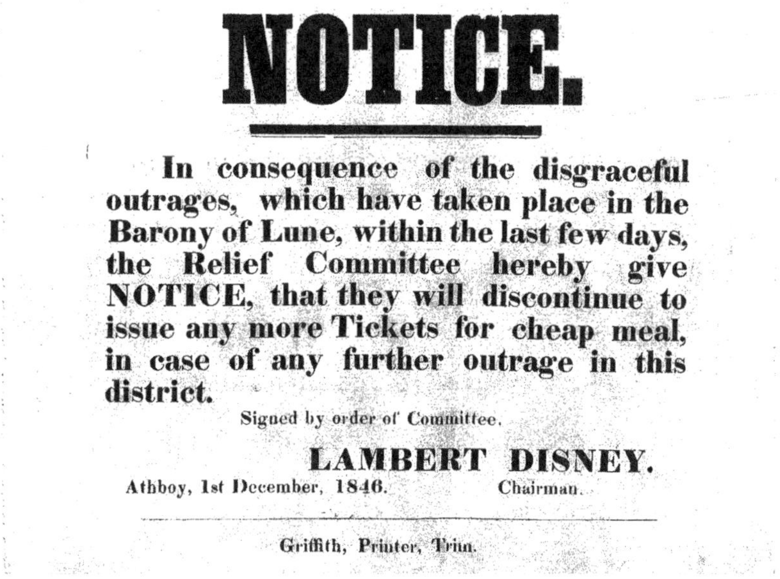

NOTICE.

In consequence of the disgraceful
outrages, which have taken place in the
Barony of Lune, within the last few days,
the Relief Committee hereby give
NOTICE, that they will discontinue to
issue any more Tickets for cheap meal,
in case of any further outrage in this
district.

Signed by order of Committee.

LAMBERT DISNEY.

Athboy, 1st December, 1846.   Chairman.

Griffith, Printer, Trim.

Figure 4: Athboy Relief Committee notice, 1 Dec. 1846 (National Archives of Ireland,
OP: county Meath, 1846/22/33703). The preparedness of relief committees to
'discontinue' issuing food were those in need engaged in riotous actions had
a dampening impact on food protest.

in July when 'rations were stopped' in response to the destruction of property by
those who objected to food handouts. A minority sought to sustain opposition
but the fact that the majority 'received steeped food quietly' when they 'saw we
were determined' taught the protesters a lesson they were not slow to learn.[120]

Food protest did not simply cease, of course, and neither, inevitably, did confrontation.[121] The latter impulse was exemplified by the recourse by a minority
of crowds to the forcible appropriation of foodstuffs, by the carrying of arms, and
by their willingness to set the authorities at defiance. Attested to, for example,
by the 'large body of people' that succeeded, despite the exertions of the police,
in appropriating five sacks of meal from Corban's mills near Kilworth, county
Cork, in June, and by the defiance shown by the 'wretched and famished inhabitants of the neighbouring parishes' that targeted the workhouses at Bantry and
Kanturk in September and October, these incidents all concluded without major

---

120 Abstract of police report, 10 July 1847 (NAI, OP: county Clare, 1847/5/1050); Athboy Relief
Committee notice, 1 Dec. 1846 (NAI, OP: Meath, 1846/22/33703). 121 Above, pp 80–90, 120–4;
Leinster Express, 22 May 1847; *Freeman's Journal*, 18, 26 June 1847. 122 Outrage report, 12 July,
Bailey to Redington, 7, 8 Oct. 1847 (NAI, OP: Cork, 1847/6/1038, 1274, 1275); *Cork Examiner*, 21
June, 10 Sept. 1847; M.E. MhicGiobúin, 'Edward Tierney and the development of Kanturk, 1823–
56' (MA, NUIM, 2002), p. 79.

injury.[122] It was not always the case. Some of the police that were 'pelted ... with stones' by an 'immense mob' of men and women at Ballingarry, county Limerick, in May were 'badly injured', as a result of which the crowd successfully made away with seven cartloads of flour and four cartloads of Indian meal. The Ennistymon, county Clare, crowd likewise demonstrated its preparedness to use violence when in May a 'shower of stones' issued in support of their demand for 'employment and food' prompted the police to return fire wounding three.[123] Other crowds continued to pursue aggressive protest through 1847, but it was an increasing gamble in the face of a determined state and the reduced prospect of success.[124] The combination of the strength of the state apparatus, its command of relief, and the severity of the distress that the population faced had by the middle of 1847 cowed a populace whose commitment to provide for itself was long exemplified by its appeal to the controlled application of force, to assert its *droit de subsistence*.

123 *Nation*, 15 May 1847; *Leinster Express*, 22 May 1847.   124 *Freeman's Journal*, 18 June 1847; *Tuam Herald*, 9 Oct. 1847; Bourke (ed.), *German travel writers' narratives*, p. 510; Bailey to Redington, 8 Dec. 1847 (NAI, OP: 1847/6/1510).

4

The response of the authorities and public
to food protest

INTRODUCTION

As the bodies tasked with the administration of the kingdom, both state and local authorities were mandated to combat riotousness, and a significant proportion of the incidents of food rioting were brought to a close by the intervention of officials (mayors, sheriffs and, later, resident magistrates) either on their own or assisted by troops or by the police. However, whereas there was little ambiguity about the appropriate response when a riot was political, agrarian or when it was directed towards frustrating the revenue raising arms of the state (the Revenue Commissioners most notably), food rioting animated ambivalent emotions, which is why some of the protests that do not include any reference to the involvement of local law officials or of the army or police were allowed to run their course. Officials were encouraged to adopt a permissive attitude during the eighteenth and early nineteenth centuries by the realization – arrived at over time – that most food riots were once-off, short-lived eruptions that posed no threat to the security of the state. This was the view, significantly, of the assistant secretary to the Treasury, Sir Charles Trevelyan, who observed calmly in October 1846, when Great Famine-induced protest was embarked on its dramatic second phase, that 'food riots are quite different from organized rebellion and are not likely to be of long duration'.[1]

So while commentators, politicians, officials and the generality of both the Protestant and Catholic elites were instinctively disposed to regard all forms of rioting uneasily because they constituted a breach of law and order, and to censure food protest because it disrupted the free and fluid exchange of goods (which was identified as an unambiguous public good), they were also inclined to treat food protesters with a measure of indulgence. This disposition did not extend so far as to acknowledge a *droit de subsistence* or to countenance *taxation populaire*; officials were also disposed to prosecute for assaults on the person and damage to property when rioters were responsible. It was not deemed inappropriate, however, in the eighteenth and early decades of the nineteenth centuries

---

1 Trevelyan to Auckland, 1 Oct. 1846, quoted in Cecil Woodham-Smith, *The great hunger: Ireland 1845–9* (London, 1962), p. 126 and Hernon, 'A Victorian Cromwell: Sir Charles Trevelyan', 21. For a broader commentary on the 'modest' aims of food riots across time see Walton and Seddon, *Free markets and food riots*, pp 29–30.

to permit protesters to express their anxieties, to bring pressure to bear on ships' captains, merchants and retailers to release stocks and to moderate prices; to overlook certain appropriations; and for magistrates to decline or to delay exercising the authority vested in them of calling out the nearest military garrison. Officials also colluded on occasion in ensuring that the full sanctions of the law were not applied. More controversially, they acceded in the sale and distribution of grain at reduced price through market houses, inaugurated relief initiatives, raised subscriptions and provided subsidised food and other reliefs. In so doing, they demonstrated that they understood if they did not fully empathize with those who engaged in food protest. This disposition was never complete and still less unconditional. It was palpably less developed, moreover, than the 'nourish the people' imperative that guided generations of Chinese emperors because of the enduring belief of the Chinese people that 'famines were not caused by nature but by the negligence of ... rulers'. It was also less refined than the 'social contract on subsistence' that shaped attitudes in France; but Irish officials were less repressive than their francophone *ancien regime* equivalents.[2]

A more useful comparison may be pursued with England, though historical as well as historiographical differences must be taken into account in any attempt to establish if food protest in Ireland manifested the reciprocation that is emblematical of the English 'moral economy'; or if the Irish economic system combined paternalism and commercialization, and compensated for the fundamental inequality that drove food protest by treating food rioting differently to other riotous behaviours, without ever ceding it legitimacy. The fact that food protest evolved alongside civil society – one manifestation of which was the expanding capacity of charitable relief – is also pertinent for if the enhanced capacity to respond to distress in the second half of the eighteenth century echoed the greater responsiveness to food rioting it has obviously implications for how food protest is viewed.[3] Furthermore, associationalism was not the only new tendency. The emergence, beginning in the late eighteenth and accelerating in the early decades of the nineteenth century, of a world view that trumpeted respectability and orderliness was at least as significant. And the increased emphasis on the protection of life, liberty and property encouraged by classical liberals and *laissez-faire* economists from the 1820s further diminished the permissiveness with which food rioting was regarded. These changes were not sufficient to interrupt food protest, but they served, parallel with the growth in state

---

2 Bohstedt, 'Food riots and the politics of provisions in world history', pp 10–11, 12–14; idem, *The politics of provisions*, p. 3; Cynthia Bouton, 'Provisioning, power and popular protest from the seventeenth century to the French Revolution and beyond' in M.T. Davis (ed.), *Crowd actions in Britain and France from the middle ages to the modern world* (Basingstoke, 2015), pp 81, 85–7, 95.   3 See Kelly, 'Charitable societies: their genesis and development, 1720–1800' in Kelly and Powell (eds), *Clubs and societies in eighteenth-century Ireland*, pp 89–108 for an attempt to trace the development of relief; Karen Sonnelitter, *Charity movements in eighteenth-century Ireland: philanthrophy and improvement* (Woodbridge, 2016).

institutions, to pave the way for the effective (re)categorization of food rioting as 'plundering provisions' and for the less accommodating attitude that was a feature of the 1840s.

ENFORCING THE LAW

Policing food protest, 1729–1800

Though they would not have conceived of themselves as strict, and still less repressive, the first impulse of the authorities when they encountered food protest in the early eighteenth century was to respond in a forceful manner. This seemed warranted at Cork in February 1729 because the crowd that assembled to protest 'at the transporting of ... oat-meal and corn' did so 'in a tumultuous manner armed with clubs and other instruments of mischief'. Furthermore, when those who assembled did not secure the positive response they sought to their demand that the mayor should prohibit the movement of grain out of the port city they tore down his house and 'the houses of several other persons, ... whom they gave out, were guilty of sending away the corn from hence'. Determined to regain control, the municipal authorities requested military support. An imposing force of 'two regiments march'd out to quash' the riot, and the fact that 'three or four persons were killed' and 'an estimated eighty or ninety people desperately wounded' in the 'terrible fray' that ensued indicates that little quarter was given. Moreover, the municipal authorities assured the garrison of their unconditional backing by directing the mayor to 'pay the expense of the army, which assisted him and the sheriff in quelling the said mob and guarding this city'.[4] These actions, and the undertaking entered into by Waterford Corporation in March to 'endemnifye' that port town's garrison should it be called upon to suppress 'rioters', were consistent with this, and with the signals and directions emanating from Dublin Castle favouring a firm response.[5]

Guided by the conclusion that the movement of foodstuffs within the island was vital if the population was to negotiate the crisis conditions that precipitated food protest in 1729, the authorities also approved the transfer of two companies of the King's Own Regiment to Drogheda to respond to further 'disturbances' there in March. The object was to overcome all resistance because the movement of grain northwards was essential 'to relieve the poor' in Ulster where the crisis was then at its most severe.[6] Moreover, they had support in so doing since, as well as the backing of the main arms of the state and major municipalities, the Catholic Church in Dublin produced a statement, which was 'publish'd from the

---

4 *Dublin Intelligence*, 4 Mar. 1729; *Dublin Weekly Journal*, 15 Mar. 1729; *An express from Cork, with an account of a bloody battle*, broadsheet; Nicholas Hussey's *Dublin Post Boy*, 4 Mar. 1729; Caulfield (ed.), *Council book of the Corporation of Cork*, p. 482.   5 Downey, *The story of Waterford*, p. 301; Waterford City Archives, Corporation of Waterford council book, 7 Mar. 1729.   6 *Dublin Gazette*, 29 Mar. 1729; and April–May passim; *Dublin Weekly Journal*, 5 Apr. 1729.

altars of all the Romish chappels' in the city on Sunday 13 April, exhorting Catholics 'on pain of excommunication' not to engage in tumults 'on pretence of discovering corn'. [7] And lest there is any doubting that the respectable deemed severe sanctions appropriate, the expectation, articulated by Lord Egmont's Irish agent, that capital sentences would be delivered to those prosecuted for their role in the Cork food riots indicated that there was no willingness to exculpate food protesters because they were activated by the fear that high food prices were a prelude to shortages and its twin – hunger.[8]

The determination manifested in 1729–30 to treat food protest as first and foremost a law and order issue proved enduring. It was again in evidence during the 1730s when 'the sovereign, burgesses, freemen and ... the Protestant inhab-itants of New Ross' and the 'mayor, sheriffs and citizens' of Waterford each responded to food protest in their jurisdictions with a 'humble memorial' to Dublin Castle seeking military assistance. In the latter instance, officials requested that the army was made available to suppress 'rioters' in Carrick-on-Suir because their refusal to allow foodstuffs to be transported from county Tipperary was a cause of 'great hardships' to 'the poor in about this city', and a 'great discouragement of trade and tillage, and the public good of the nation'. Though the Waterford memorial, which was forwarded on 29 March 1734, man-ifested less disquiet than that emanating from New Ross, which preceded it, the language and content of both suggest that civic leaders in the two locations were disinclined at this moment to distinguish between the activities of those denom-inated food protesters and those denominated 'tories'. Thus the memorial of 'the town of New Ross' maintained that without 'an armed force ready at hand to suppress their disorders', the 'Protestant inhabitants' would be 'utterly defence-less and exposed to the fury and outrage of a disaffected riotous populace'.[9] This was to exaggerate the vulnerability of the Protestant population, as well as the seriousness of the threat posed to law and order every time the 'populace' heaved, yet their unease cannot be dismissed simply as hyperbole.[10] Fear guided the response to food protest as it did the reaction to most issues with perceived implications for the security of the Protestant interest in eighteenth-century Ireland. For some it was an inchoate instinctive feeling, exemplified by the response to the invasion of bakers' shops in Dublin in March 1741: 'These tumults ought to be discouraged, because no one can tell where they will end', it was observed portentously.[11]

7 *Dublin Weekly Journal*, 19 Apr. 1729; Swift, *History of the Dublin bakers*, pp 178–9.   8 Boutler to Cartaret, 8 Mar. 1729 in *Boulter Letters*, i, 228; Taylor to Percival, 30 Mar. 1729 (BL, Egmont Papers, Add. MS 46994 f 88).   9 Waterford City Archives, Corporation of Waterford council books, 29 Mar. 1734; Hore, *History of Wexford*, i, 346–8.   10 For a related consideration, albeit driven by fear of a domestically supported French invasion, of the sense of vulnerability that guided the Protestant population see James Kelly, 'Disappointing the boundless ambitions of France: Irish Protestants and the fear of invasion', *Studia Hibernica*, 37 (2011), 56–70.   11 *Faulkner's Dublin Journal*, 10 Mar. 1741.

There is no reason to conclude that the author of these words shared the sectarian perspective that animated officials in New Ross some years earlier, but the observation of the under-secretary to the lord lieutenant, John Potter, in his response to events in Carrick-on-Suir in 1741, that the town was 'famous for popish rioters', demonstrates that food protest did not operate in a political vacuum.[12] Potter's invocation of the denominational allegiance of the Carrick 'mob' was atypical. The alarm expressed in February 1757 by the mayor, bailiff and magistrates of Wexford at the actions of a 'very audacious and insolent mob', and the request 'for a command of the army to be sent here ... to quell so dangerous a mob, to protect your memorialists lives and properties, and enable the dealers in corn to export the same to Dublin or elsewhere' were more characteristic of the sentiments emanating from the provinces, and of the disquiet food protest raised. It is, for example, also identifiable in the despatches to Dublin Castle penned by George Macartney, the acting sovereign of Belfast, in 1756; by the sovereign, recorder and free burgesses of New Ross in 1758, and by the mayor of Clonmel, John Hayman, in 1766 requesting 'the aid of the military power'. The absence of an overtly sectarian allusion in each appeal is noteworthy, but there is no masking the nervousness that these incidents excited.[13]

While it is demonstrable that some municipal officials appealed reflexively for military support when faced with food protest, the disinclination of the mayor of Kilkenny to take this step until he was convinced by a deputation of flour millers to request 'an officer guard' after three days of rioting in 1766 indicates that others were disposed to regard food protest more sympathetically.[14] Indeed, it is reasonable to conclude, given the readiness of some magistrates to allow riots to run their course, that some were loath to call upon the army. Moreover, garrison commanders were disinclined, given the chequered character of the army's relationship with the public, to assume this policing role unless formally called upon, in which case they were obliged to comply.[15] This may explain why, by comparison with smuggling and illicit distillation, the number of occasions on which the army was called upon to deal with food rioters was small.[16] Furthermore, as

---

12 Potter to Wilmot, 2 July 1741 (PRONI, Wilmot papers, T3019/306). **13** Benn, *History of Belfast*, p. 595; Hore, *History of Wexford*, i, 394–5, v, 398–400; Burke, *History of Clonmel*, p. 126. **14** Colles to Colles, 14 June 1766 (NAI, Prim Collection, no. 89/92). **15** This function is best documented in respect of revenue collection. Revenue officers were authorized by the commissioners to call on the military, and to this end they lobbied the lord lieutenant and lords justices to approve the deployment of parties of soldiers in those parts of the country where their officers encountered resistance: Minutes of the Revenue Commissioners, 5 Sept. 1748, 28 Aug. 1752, 10 Oct. 1754, 26 Mar., 21 Apr., 8, 24 Nov. 1760, 13, 19, 24 Jan., 17 Apr. 1761, 5 May, 26 June 1764 (TNA, CUST1/47 f. 94, 1/51; f. 158; 1/55 f. 24; 1/66 ff 29–30, 35, 76, 151; 1/67 ff 8, 13–4, 148, 151; 1/81, ff 121–2; 1/82 f. 76). **16** See Watt, 'Taxation riots and the culture of popular protest in Ireland, 1714–1740', passim; Aidan Manning, *Donegal poitín: a history* (Letterkenny, 2003), pp 96–132 passim; K.H. Connell, 'Illicit distillation' in Connell, *Irish peasant society* (Oxford, 1968), 1–50; Breandán Mac Suibhne, 'Spirit, spectre, shade: a true story of an Irish haunting or troublesome pasts in the political culture of north-west Ulster 1786–1972', *Field Day Review*, 9 (2013), 154–7.

exemplified by their presence on the streets of Galway in August 1740, this did not invariably result in violent confrontation.[17] The number of food riots that resulted in death and injury was almost certainly exceeded by those that concluded peacefully because of the actions of officials, 'respectable' inhabitants, and, in the mid-nineteenth century, Catholic priests. One may instance incidents such as those at Cork in 1753 when the 'mob' was 'restrained from committing any disorder by the mayor and sheriff ... with the assistance of a guard'; at Carrick-on-Suir in 1791 when the mayor, James Ramsay, 'by prudence and fair words so far succeeded in appeasing the excited people' who had gathered to lay 'an embargo' on the export of potatoes 'that they dispersed'; at Enniskillen in 1817 when 'the prompt interference of the Provost' defused a difficult situation and 'the mob dispersed'; at Galway in November 1845 when three priests 'addressed the people in Irish, and pointed out to them the necessity of peace and good order'; at Broadford, county Clare, in October 1847 when local 'Roman Catholic clergymen ... counselled a more temperate and becoming mode of making known their wants', and by other local eminences at Milford, county Carlow, Macroom, county Cork, and Tralee, county Kerry, in 1846 when famine protest was on the incline.[18] The likelihood of this occurring obviously increased when both protesters and officials eschewed confrontation, but it was only necessary for one side to behave inappropriately for a protest to career out of control. This is what happened in May 1781 when the provost of Ennis Corporation attempted unsuccessfully to dissuade 'the trades people of Ennis to the number of 300' from pursuing and immobilizing a boat 'laden with potatoes and oats' *en route* from Clarecastle to Limerick.[19] No injuries ensued on this occasion, but if February 1729 in Cork demonstrated how easily food protest could become violent, the connection was reinforced in 1740–1 by two incidents, the first of which took place in Dublin in the summer of 1740, the second in Carrick-on-Suir in the spring of 1741.

The lesser of the two incidents occurred in Dublin, where as well as the two rioters that lost their lives as a result of a clash involving separate mobs (referred to above, p. 149), three soldiers 'were desperately wounded' when 'some of the rioters, being taken to Newgate under a military guard, were attempted to be rescued by a mob near the Castle market'. To assist them to restore order, the authorities imposed a curfew, quartered soldiers at strategic points throughout the city, and offered a £20 reward for the apprehension of those involved. This achieved the desired result, following which fourteen men and one woman were

---

17 'The army continued under arms the whole' of the 22 August 1740 to restore order to the streets of Galway when the 'populace rose up on account of the shipping off some biscuit made in the city'; they did so without any violent clashes: *Dublin Newsletter*, 26 Aug. 1740.   18 Kerr, *The Catholic Church and the Famine*, pp 11–13; *Universal Advertiser*, 10 Apr. 1753; Power (ed.), 'A Carrickman's diary, 1787–1809', p. 66; *Freeman's Journal*, 15 Feb. 1817, 5 Oct. 1846; *Nation*, 29 Nov. 1845; Kinsella, 'Milford Mills', pp 327–8; Redington to Kennedy, 20 Oct. 1847 (NAI, OP: Clare, 1847/5/1116).   19 *Hibernian Journal*, 30 May 1781.

prosecuted for rioting and food theft. Five were acquitted, but the fact that four were sentenced to seven years transportation is demonstrative of official resolve to make it known that the courts would not tolerate such behaviour.[20] A still-more stern lesson was handed down at Carrick-on-Suir a year later when an attempt by the 'popish' populace to stop boats laden with grain departing the town resulted in the dispatch of 'a troop of horse and a party of foot', which responded to a shower of stones from a crowd, said to number a thousand, with a fusillade of bullets. As a result, five were killed and an indeterminate number – somewhere between five and eighteen – wounded. It was the largest loss of life incurred in a food protest to that point, and one of the largest ever in Ireland, and it demanded official attention. The lords justices and Privy Council issued a proclamation offering a reward of £30 for the apprehension of 'any person or persons, who was or were concerned in the said assault and riot', while the under-secretary, John Potter, sent a detailed account of the episode to Robert Wilmot, who represented the Irish administration in England, to enable him to answer any questions that came his way.[21]

The attention given events at Carrick-on-Suir in 1741 indicates that confrontations of this order were not presumed or regarded lightly. Yet the failure formally to investigate the episode, or long to ponder the implications of the fact that the eighteen-strong army company was commanded by a sergeant and not a commissioned officer as regulations stipulated, and that the order to fire was given by a justice of the peace, demonstrated that the authorities were instinctively disposed to place the blame on such occasions squarely on the shoulders of the protesters.[22] There was, as this suggests, little sympathy in official, or public, circles for those killed and injured, notwithstanding the fact that their primary offence was to take sixty barrels of oats off a ship freighted for Waterford. Yet the episode was not without impact, for though the frequency with which food protests occurred increased in the decades that followed (Table 2.1), no further fatal clashes involving the army and protesters took place in cases of food rioting for three decades. In May 1772, a military detachment commanded by the mayor, Christopher Carr, fired on the large crowd of protesters that assailed the Lock Mills in Limerick city, as a result of which 'three men' were killed and 'several men and boys wounded'. The authorities contrived in this instance to deflect criticism by pointing out that the army had not fired until the assembled throng – 'some thousands of them' – had broken the mills' windows, and threat-

20 Dickson, *Arctic Ireland*, 27–8; Kingsbury to Price, 31 May 1740 (NLW, Puleston papers, Add. MS 3548D); *Dublin Gazette*, 3, 7 June 1740; *Dublin Newsletter*, 3, 7, 21 June, 5, 8 July 1740; *Dublin Daily Post*, 3, 8 June; *Faulkner's Dublin Journal*, 3, 7 June 1740; Gilbert, ed., *Calendar of ancient records of Dublin*, viii, 374–5. 21 Magennis, 'Food scarcity in 1756–57', pp 197–8; Dickson, *Arctic Ireland*, p. 34; *Dublin Gazette*, 25 Apr. 1741; *Dublin Newsletter*, 25 Apr., 5 May, 6 June 1741; *Pue's Occurrences*, 25 Apr., 6 June 1741; Potter to Wilmot, 2 July 1741 (PRONI, Wilmot papers, T3019/306); Kelly and Lyons (eds), *The proclamations of Ireland*, iii, 291–2; Burke, *History of Clonmel*, p. 126. 22 Potter to Wilmot, 2 July 1741 (PRONI, Wilmot papers, T3019/306); *Dublin Gazette*, 25 Apr. 1741.

ened 'destruction to the building', but the angry response of the local populace indicate that they believed the army had overreacted. They followed the example of urban crowds that responded to perceived miscarriages of justice in capital cases by parading the corpse before the door of the person they believed responsible, by laying the bodies of two of the victims before the house of the mill owner, and shattering his windows. This accomplished, they broke the windows of the mayor's house, and, on the following day, engaged in another altercation with the army when soldiers intervened to prevent the ritualized hanging by a chimney sweep of the mayor in effigy. As a result, three more people – a man and two women – were killed, and several soldiers 'dangerously wounded'.[23]

Though revealing of the closeness of the link between food protest and other forms of purposeful riot, the Limerick incident was exceptional in many respects. Yet less than a year later, 'two or three persons' were killed on the Coomb, Dublin, when soldiers fired on 'a great mob' that had assembled to seize flour, which not only ignored an order to disperse but also 'continued so outrageous as to fire on the soldiers'.[24] It seemed then that events of this kind might be about to become commonplace, but this is not what transpired. There was a strand of opinion, hostile to any disruption of market activity, which could be relied upon to counsel the authorities to take whatever steps were necessary to ensure the free flow of goods, but more prudent counsels generally prevailed.[25] As a result, more people were killed and injured by food protesters than by the security forces during the last two decades of the eighteenth century. The death in Kinsale in March 1784 of a fifteen-year-old boy when the military fired on a crowd resisting the transfer of three rioters taken in the 'terrible tumults' that ensued when local fishermen broke open several warehouses containing potatoes demonstrates that fatalities at the hands of the army continued to take place, but they were irregular and few in number.[26]

Why this was so is less easily explained since altercations between the people and the army over illicit distillation were commonplace.[27] It may be that it mir-

23 *Limerick Chronicle*, 14, 18 May, 12 Oct. 1772; *Hibernian Journal*, 18 May 1772; John Ferrar, *History of Limerick* (Dublin, 1787), p. 132; *Freeman's Journal*, 19, 23 May 1772; *Hoey's Publick Journal*, 20 May 1772; Jim Kemmey, 'The siege of Lock Mills' in idem (ed.), *The Limerick anthology* (Dublin, 1996), p. 236; James Kelly, 'Laying the executed corpse at the prosecutor's door' in Salvador Ryan (ed.), *Death and the Irish: a miscellany* (Dublin, 2016), pp 101–4.   24 *Hibernian Chronicle* (Cork), 30 Aug. 1773; Waller to Macartney, 28 Aug. 1773 in Bartlett (ed.), *Macartney in Ireland*, p. 169.   25 *Finn's Leinster Journal*, 22 Oct. 1774, 1 Feb. 1775; *Hibernian Journal*, 6 Feb. 1775.   26 *Hibernian Journal*, 22 Mar. 1784.   27 In Ulster in 1783 when the army undertook to stamp out illicit distilling on the grounds that it was a wasteful use of scarce grain reserves, a number of fatal confrontations ensued. A row over a still in April resulted in five deaths while, in June, three more people died in a similar confrontation: Kelly, 'Scarcity and poor relief', p. 50.   28 Powell, 'Ireland's urban houghers', pp 231–53; Jim Smyth, *The men of no property: Irish radicals and popular politics in the late eighteenth century* (Dublin, 1992), pp 36–7, 120–39; James Kelly, 'Parliamentary reform in Irish politics: 1760–90' in David Dickson et al. (eds), *The United Irishmen: republicanism, radicalism and rebellion* (Dublin, 1993), pp 84–5; idem, 'Matthew Carey's Irish apprenticeship: editing the *Volunteer's Journal*, 1783–84', *Eire-Ireland*, 49:3 and 4 (2014), 201–43;

rored changes in the relationship of the army and people. The tradition of houghing soldiers, the clashes that occurred in the summer of 1784 in Dublin, the anti-Rightboys activity of the mid-1780s, the militia riots of 1793, and the draconian counter-insurgency measures deployed by the state in the later 1790s are testament to the fact that the last two decades of the eighteenth century were not halcyon days in civilian–military relations.[28] The involvement of the army in putting down food protests in Waterford in 1783, in dispersing 'a riotous mob' at Sallins, and in locating 'riotous … distressed manufacturers' at Dolphin's Barn, county Dublin, in May 1793, illustrate also that the military continued to be called upon to assist the civil authority, but the relative infrequency of such encounters suggests that they were not appealed to regularly.[29] It was not that authorization from on high was an issue. It was reported in the press in May 1793 that the lord lieutenant, the earl of Westmorland, responded to a spate of incidents in Dublin with an instruction 'that the magistrates of the city and county of Dublin should, on application forthwith be accommodated with every possible aid of military force for the purpose of effectually checking such daring and desperate attacks and robberies'.[30] Rather, it seems that local officials chose not to confront food protesters unless matters threatened to get out of hand. It is notable in this context that the magistracy of the city of Waterford was singled out in the public prints for its 'humanity' for not calling upon the army, which was 'drawn up' and at the ready, when the city experienced serious food protest in May 1791.[31] There is a fine line between discretion and misjudgement, of course, and if the mayor of Waterford got in right in the estimation of contemporaries, the officials in Bandon and environs may have got it wrong in 1792 when their failure to intervene in a timely fashion permitted the town mob to embark on a rampage that lasted for three days; in this instance the refusal to engage was no less calculated, but the primary consideration was fear – 'the mob in Bandon was so well armed, … and determined, that had they been opposed by force, the consequence would be dreadful'.[32]

Confrontation was avoided on this and, one presumes, other occasions by comparably calculated decision making. This outcome was certainly facilitated by the fact that in those instances in which the army was involved during the 1780s and 1790s, it was at the invitation of civilian officials, with the result that the decision remained with those whose priority was to avert rather than to engage

Donnelly, 'The Rightboy movement, 1785–8', pp 120–202; Bartlett, 'The end of moral economy', passim; N.J. Curtin, 'The magistracy and counter revolution in Ulster, 1795–1798' in Jim Smyth (ed.), *Revolution, counter-revolution and Union in Ireland in the 1790s* (Cambridge, 2000), pp 39–54. **29** Captain G. Walpole to [ ], 5 July (NAI, Index to departmental letters and papers, 1760–89, ii, 83); *Dublin Evening Post*, 17 June 1783; *Clonmel Gazette*, 25 May 1793. **30** *Freeman's Journal*, 21 May 1793. **31** 'A party of the army were drawn up, in awful preparation to assist the civil power, but it was judged inexpedient to have recourse to so dangerous a remedy, when the disorder promised to subside without any very serious consequence': *Dublin Morning Post*, 19 May 1791. **32** *Hibernian Journal*, 27 Nov. 1792.

in confrontation. This outcome was made more likely by the fact that the military was also deployed in a preventative capacity, which generated fewer life-threatening situations.[33] That local officials chose to avail of the services of various paramilitary forces employing a less confrontational approach is also pertinent. Beginning with the Volunteers, corps of which were called upon on a number of occasions during the highpoints of food rioting in the early 1780s and early 1790s, the civilian authorities could, and did, draw thereafter upon the Militia, the Fencibles and the Yeomanry for assistance. The specific character of each of these bodies differed, but the absence of bloody confrontations, and claims that Fencibles sided with protesters at Killaloe, county Clare, in 1800, is consistent with the conclusion that these paramilitary organizations were less aggressive than the army.[34]

An evolving pattern of more active policing: the early nineteenth century
The desire to eschew confrontation identifiable in the later eighteenth century echoed the responsiveness of certain public and civic bodies to public distress during the 1790s, and for a time afterwards.[35] However, the relationship of those disposed to engage in food protest and those charged with maintaining order was inherently changeable, and it assumed a more security-driven form thereafter. The decision to send 'a representation … to the lord lieutenant' in 1808 to request that steps were taken to prevent a repeat of the incident when the *Anne* of Londonderry was stripped of its sails in Galway was consistent with this.[36] A further pointer was provided in 1812 when, in contrast to what had transpired in 1800–1 and in 1808, the army was called upon to respond to threatening crowds in Belfast, Galway, Drogheda and Carrick-on-Suir; on each occasion the army assisted with the restoration of order, or the populace 'dispersed quietly' following the reading of the Riot Act.[37] This trend was accelerated a year later when the complicity of members of the Bangor Yeomanry in an attempt to intercept cars conveying potatoes for export caused the authorities to summon soldiers from Belfast.[38] As well as the doubts they harboured as to the reliability of the Yeomanry, the authorities were now disposed to pursue a security-driven response in order to put an end to all forms of riotous activity. Moreover, they were encouraged to do so by the fact that they could draw upon an augmented military establishment, which stood at an imposing 33,000 in 1815. This was greatly in excess of its pre-Union level but it was conceived of as the minimum necessary to sustain the 'military government' that the lord lieutenant, Earl Whitworth maintained, Ireland required.[39]

33 *Dublin Evening Post*, 21 June 1783; *Clonmel Gazette*, 23 Feb., 25 May 1793; *Freeman's Journal*, 6 June 1793; *Hibernian Journal*, 1 June 1795.   34 *Dublin Evening Post*, 17 June 1783; *Freeman's Journal*, 22 Apr. 1784; *Dublin Morning Post*, 6 June 1793; *Clonmel Gazette*, 9 Apr. 1794; Wells, 'The Irish famine of 1799–1801', p. 182.   35 Below, pp 199–201.   36 *Freeman's Journal*, 27 Apr. 1808. 37 Cunningham, 'Popular protest and a "moral economy"', p. 36; Cunningham, *Galway, 1790– 1914*, p. 86; *Cork Advertiser*, 5 May 1812; *Belfast News Letter*, 10 July 1812.   38 Cunningham, 'Popular protest and a "moral economy"', p. 37.   39 Virginia Crossman, 'The army and law and

The implication that confrontation and, with it, casualties would inevitably ensue, was heightened by the order of the 1816–17 subsistence crisis, which ensured not only that 1817 was the most prolific year in the annals of food protest in Ireland to that point, but also the most bloody, as fourteen people were killed by the military and police in incidents at or near Carrigaholt, county Clare (3 deaths), Wilkinstown, county Meath (1), Ballina, county Mayo (2), Rathangan, county Kildare (1), Robertstown, county Kildare (2), Loughrea, county Galway (1), Nobber, county Meath (2), and in Limerick city (2).[40] Indeed, it might have been more since shots were fired in a number of other incidents in which the security forces were involved, but the magistrates present contrived to avert more serious outcomes.[41] This is not to imply that magistrates could be relied upon to provide prudent direction. The magistracy of county Meath, for example, was singled out as being particularly disengaged in the commentary accompanying an account of the incident that resulted in two deaths in the environs of the village of Nobber in June:

> Great supineness prevails among the magistracy of the county Meath ... We have not heard of any activity to preserve the peace; and men who are calling for vigorous measures beyond the law, are neglecting to use the means which they have.[42]

It was not as if the army was any more at ease with the role they were expected to perform. The failure of the garrison at Trim in 1817 to quell disturbances in the town because they were not formally invited by the town magistrates (though procedurally correct) was as revealing of the army's attitude as it was of that of the magistrates in the locality.[43] Indicatively, though the provost and magistrates

---

order in the nineteenth century' in Thomas Bartlett and Keith Jeffreys (eds*), A military history of Ireland* (Cambridge, 1996), pp 358–60; Thomas Bartlett, 'Ireland during the Revolutionary and Napoleonic wars, 1793–1815' in James Kelly (ed.), *The Cambridge history of Ireland, vol. 3 – 1730–1880* (forthcoming). **40** O'Neill, 'Clare and Irish poverty, 1815–1851', pp 10–11; Cunningham, 'Popular protest and a "moral economy"', pp 38, 40, 41, 42, 44; Abbott, 'The Downshire estates', pp 38–9; Jordan, *Land and popular politics in Ireland*, pp 94–5; McCabe, 'Law, conflict and social order: county Mayo, 1820–1845', p. 199; *Gentleman's Magazine*, 87 (1817), 619–20; *Freeman's Journal*, 11, 12 June, 2 July 1817. In county Meath, the interception in January 1817 of a convoy of cars carrying grain close to the village of Wilkinstown resulted in one death when the military escort was authorized to fire upon the crowd by the attending magistrate. In county Mayo, a request by the grain merchants of Ballina in February for a military escort to enable them to export grain valued between £30,000 and £40,000 in the teeth of resistance from 'the working and lower classes' reflected acute tension in the area that boiled over when 'a mob consisting of five hundred persons' seized a number of carts laden with meal destined for Sligo town; in the resulting confrontation with the army two rioters lost their lives. **41** *Freeman's Journal*, 15 Jan., 11, 15 Feb. 1817; Military report, Feb. 1817 (TNA, HO/100/192 f. 164); Cunningham, 'Popular protest and a "moral economy"', p. 408. **42** *Freeman's Journal*, 12 June 1817. **43** Mooney, 'The origins of agrarian violence in Meath', p. 58; Crossman, *Politics, law and order*, pp 41–3; Crossman, 'The army and law and order in the nineteenth century', p. 368.

of Ennis felt they had no option but to call upon the army quartered at nearby Clarecastle to assist them to deal with the serious rioting that gripped that town over three days in May 1817, they also drew on the local Yeomanry. No fatalities ensued, and the Yeomanry was applauded for their 'firmness of behaviour, which effectually preserved quiet, but not in the slightest degree going beyond their line of duty'.[44]

If these incidents suggest that the magistracy and the military were still not disposed always to respond forcefully to food protest, the fact that the employment of the military resulted in a record number of fatalities, and that it coincided with pronouncements of the necessity of upholding the law indicates that food protesters were less likely to be afforded clemency. The recorder of Cork was explicit on this point during the trial of food rioters in his court:

> There could be no doubt but the distresses of the poor were very great, but it was most mischievous to allow persons who ought to be governed by the laws of the land, to interfere with those laws, and take them into their own hands. The laws were sufficient to put down all tumult and violence, and the must be strictly executed, even though it may be at the expense of some lives. If riotous proceedings were allowed, and mobs to assemble, there would be no security in society, and the whole frame would be destroyed.[45]

The pronouncement in the proclamation issued by Cork Corporation in 1817 in response to food protest that 'it was their determination in the first place to suppress the rioters', and that only 'when perfect order and tranquillity shall be restored' would 'prompt and efficient measures be adopted to procure supplies of potatoes and meal' echoed this new-found resolve.[46]

The ongoing pattern of food protest indicates this message was not heard by those at whom it was directed, but its public articulation was a harbinger of a less acquiescent, more assertive attitude on the part of the authorities that had the backing of the elite. The reaction of John Alexander, the owner of Milford Mills in county Carlow, is illustrative. Though an entrepreneur and landowner of exceptional benignity, Alexander was so taken aback when he learned that his 'mills and extensive stores' were in 'imminent danger' in the summer of 1817 that he apprehended a reprise of the lawlessness experienced in 1798. 'The state of the country', he advised the attorney general, William Saurin, 'is everyday becoming more alarming ... I always thought there was sufficient food in this country for its wants. I hope I am not yet mistaken, but if it is to be distributed by the mob, [the country] will soon meet their fate, and lie in one heap of indiscriminate ruin'. Like a majority of his peers, Alexander favoured a security-based response – the 'government ... should put the Yeomanry on permanent duty and

44 *Freeman's Journal*, 29 May 1817.   45 *Belfast News Letter*, 13 June 1817.   46 Cork Corporation proclamation reported in *Belfast News Letter*, 13 June 1817.

embody the militia for three months'. His advice was not taken but he remained convinced of its merits.[47] Ten years later, when 'mobs of the most alarming nature' appeared in Carlow and 'threaten[ed] the peaceable inhabitants with destruction if they were not supplied with food', Alexander reiterated his request for more military personnel.[48]

The intermittent nature of food protest at this time meant that the authorities were generally on safe ground when they failed to respond to such requests. Yet the sentiments to which Alexander gave expression were not unique to mill-owners. There was a gathering belief among the elite that it was incumbent on government not only to curb food protest but also to deal with its causes.[49] It was a manifestation, first, of the expectations that were fostered by the growth in the state, and, second, of the easily aroused fears that were an enduring legacy of the rebellion and insurgency that gripped the country between 1793 and 1803.[50] There is an inherent interpretative risk in concluding that the opinion of an interested party, such as John Alexander, reflected the entirety of the social group to which he belonged, but there are reasonable grounds for concluding that his personal trajectory from paternalist intervention to promoting a law and order response was reasonably representative.[51] The observation of a German visitor in 1834 that 'landlords and magistrates ... brought hatred upon themselves' by the manner in which they ran their estates and participated in the administration of the country indicates that some contemporaries were of the opinion that the elite had only themselves to blame, but this was not how they saw it. Be that as it may, the fact that this was a realm where at that date the 'Yeomanry must travel in large numbers through the countryside – otherwise they are in danger of being waylaid and shot down' – suggests that the diminishing tolerance with which food protest was perceived was part of a wider increase in suspicion and fear in society at large.[52]

The intensified interdenominational unease animated during the 1820s by the campaign for Catholic 'emancipation' was critical in this respect because for all the tension that radicalism and insurgency, 1793–1803, generated, it was the emancipation agitation that ensured 'the spirit of co-operation' evident in the response to famine in county Clare in 1822 'had almost disappeared by 1830'.[53] The character of the society that would take its place was still opaque. But the observation of J.G. Kohl in 1835 that mutual suspicion defined the relationship of landowners and commercial farmers on one side and 'poor leaseholders and

---

47 Alexander to Saurin, 4 June 1817 (BL, Peel papers, Add. MS 40211 f. 341), quoted in Kinsella, 'Milford Mills', p. 179.   48 Alexander to lord lieutenant, 15 Mar. 1837 (NAI, SOC papers, 2831/1), quoted in Kinsella, 'Milford Mills', p. 179.   49 Lord Leitrim to Cooper, 25 May 1822 (NLI, Killadoon papers, MS 36064/12; A.P.W. Malcomson (ed.), *The Clements archive* (Dublin, 2010), p. 572).   50 James Patterson, *In the wake of the Great Rebellion: Republicanism, agrarianism and banditry in Ireland after 1798* (Manchester, 2008); James Kelly, *Sir Richard Musgrave, 1746–1818: ultra-Protestant ideologue* (Dublin, 2009).   51 Kinsella, 'Millford Mills', passim.   52 Bourke (ed.), *German travel writers' narratives*, pp 227–8.   53 Enright, 'Terry Alts: the rise and fall of an agrarian society', p. 227.

farm labourers' on the other indicated that antipathy, antagonism and animosity were endemic. By extension, the sense of community required for a 'moral economy' to prosper contracted as the country's economic problems deepened. Indicatively, it was a society in which everyone sought to secure access to firearms. The clandestine importation and the transportation of weaponry by labourers returning from England was not yet a preoccupation of the authorities,[54] but it was already of sufficient concern for the better off to conclude that it was necessary to be armed if they were to protect themselves from those less well circumstanced than themselves, as Kohl noted:

> We found most of the well-to-do leaseholders armed with weapons, shotguns, sabres and pistols. 'We could not do without them', they said. Also the Peelers, policemen armed like soldiers that are to be seen everywhere in Ireland, the farmers said: 'We could not do without them'. These rich leaseholders speak just like the masters and are completely on their side. As middlemen who often have their own subtenants they have as much to fear from them as their landlords.[55]

If the inauguration of a national system of policing (the Police Preservation Force) in 1814, its elaboration in 1822 into the Irish Constabulary (IC), and its reorganization as a national force in 1836 can legitimately be portrayed as a manifestation of the societal transformation that was underway, the availability of an armed police enhanced the capacity of the state to respond to food protest. They were assisted also by legislative changes – notably the strengthening of the law to empower officials to intervene to prevent 'persons from unlawfully assembling' – which permitted the authorities to invoke a broader range of security strategies to deal with this form of protest.[56] The threat in 1817 to put Galway under martial law; the imposition, by mayoral proclamation, also in 1817 of a curfew in Dublin; the proscription in Cork in 1817 of 'all persons from unlawfully assembling in the city and suburbs'; and in Waterford in 1819 of assemblies of more than three people were examples of the new possibilities.[57]

The availability of a constabulary, numbering 8,600 men in 1841, permitted the police to assume the primary responsibility of responding to breaches of the

---

54 NAI, Registered papers, 1845, first division, vols 1–2, 6/20385, 16/19421, 25/19741, 19805, 19819. 55 J.G. Kohl, *Ireland in 1835* in Bourke (ed.), *German travel writers' narratives*, p. 351. Kohl's observation receives some corroboration from the application by 'a respectable farmer' to a petty sessions court in county Wicklow in October 1846 for permission to 'keep arms for the defence of his property as he was every hour in dread of his place being attacked by some of the numerous parties going through the country extorting money etc.': Warburton's report, 25 Oct. 1846 (NAI, OP: Wicklow, 1846/32/29471). 56 S.H. Palmer, *Police and protest in England and Ireland, 1780–1850* (Cambridge, 1988), pp 198–203; Galen Broeker, *Rural disorder and police reform in Ireland, 1812–36* (London, 1970), pp 55–104; Crossman, *Politics, law and order*, pp 37–9, 70–2. 57 Cunningham, *Galway, 1790–1914*, pp 86–7; *Freeman's Journal*, 17, 21 Jan., 12 June 1817; Swift, *History of the Dublin bakers*, p. 204

peace. In statistical terms, the relatively modest number of food protests in the 1820s and the 1830s ensured the constabulary was not overtaxed on this front. Moreover, they were not disposed *a priori* to take a draconian approach. For example, when in 1832 the firing of shots over the heads of a large crowd at Doone, county Mayo, failed to quell the several hundred people who sought to appropriate 'provisions' the police were escorting, the six-person patrol prudently allowed the food to be taken. The superior officer responsible defended their (in)action on the grounds that the crowd posed no threat to the well-being of his men: 'all they wanted was meal'.[58] This was unexpectedly permissive, but it was not unparalleled. The constabulary who responded to a threatened 'riot' at Ennis in 1837 impeded the 'wholesale purchasers' present who sought 'to buy for exportation' and made it clear where their sympathies lay by 'purchasing bags of potatoes, and then retailing them on the spot'. In Wexford, in June 1842, the police declined to intervene when the town mob appropriated potatoes (destined for Liverpool) and sold them at 25 per cent below the current market rate because 'there was no disposition to riot or tumult', while the refusal of the officer in charge to authorize the combined force of soldiers and constabulary that was present 'to fire on the people' was one reason why the well-chronicled riot in Galway on 13 June 1842 concluded without fatalities or serious injuries.[59]

Revealing as these incidents are of the humanity of individual officers, it would be misleading to conclude that the constabulary as an institution looked upon food protest as other than a breach of the law. It is noteworthy, for instance, that the response in county Clare in 1831 to the prospect of food protest was to place mills in Ennis, Tulla, Corofin and Killaloe under police protection. More notably, one person was shot dead at New Quay in the same county in 1830 when a body of some 20 men rushed a police patrol tasked with ensuring that shippers were not impeded, while two policemen in Limerick fired (without inflicting serious injury) on 'the mob of some twenty or thirty persons' that protested the price of potatoes in July 1839.[60] The number of such instances was exceeded by the number of cases in which arrests were made. It may be that it was not always easy to secure the witness cooperation required to ensure that offenders were successfully prosecuted, but the fact that the police did so, and that some at least of those that were apprehended were sentenced to 'hard labour' is a further indication of the inclination to treat food protest in the same fashion as other offences.[61]

It was not possible to respond in a comparable fashion in all instances, of course, which is why when major incidents of food protest took place – at Limerick in 1830 and 1840, Newtownards in 1839 and Ennis and Galway in 1842 – the army was called upon to assist the civil power.[62] Though the presence of a

---

58 O'Neill, 'The Catholic Church and relief of the poor', pp 139.   59 *Tuam Herald*, 15 July 1837; *Nenagh Guardian*, 11 June 1842; *Belfast News Letter*, 21 June 1842.   60 Enright, 'Terry Alts: the rise and fall of an agrarian society', p. 226; *Freeman's Journal*, 4 July 1839.   61 *Belfast News Letter*, 1 Aug. 1837; *Freeman's Journal*, 18 June 1840, 31 May 1842; *Weekly Freeman*, 24 June 1840.   62 *Belfast News Letter*, 25 Jan. 1839; Lee, 'The food riots of 1830 and 1840', pp 56–62; *Nenagh*

military guard is a good guide to the scale and seriousness of an incident, it did not mean that fatalities were likely, still less inevitable. The three men who died in Ennis in 1842 were fired on by the police, and though the incident prompted a barrage of claims to the effect that the protesters had done nothing 'to warrant the deadly fire' and that those responsible deserved to be prosecuted, it did not prompt a change of policy.[63] When John Richards, the justice of the Court of Common Pleas, who heard the case pronounced from the bench at Clare assizes on Monday 4 July, he made it explicitly clear to the grand jurors who were tasked with determining the bills of indictment that violent food protest was contrary to law:

> If a multitude assembles to discuss anything appertaining to their wants or privations, or any subject pertaining to general concerns, so long as they conduct themselves with order and propriety, and without detriment or danger to the public peace, there can be no objection to such an assemblage. But if instead of endeavouring to obtain redress and relief by peace and order, if by force and strong hands persons without regard to the rights of others or the law of the land are to act as they think proper, then such a meeting is illegal and should be treated as an unlawful assembly. If they go farther and are guilty of overt acts, then the persons so offending are unquestionably guilty of a riot.[64]

This was as unambiguous a statement of the legal position as a grand jury, or the general public, could anticipate. Yet it did not herald a legal crackdown; the outcry that followed the 'Ennis massacre' combined with the exceptional severity of the Great Famine to ensure that the response to the surge in food protest during the late 1840s continued in the same vein.

Though the 'readiness' of the army at Galway in November 1845, and the presence of a 'military and police guard' with the convoy of carts that arrived in Clonmel on 30 March 1846 might suggest that the authorities were prepared for any eventuality as the devastation of the potato crop in 1845 struck home, this was not the case.[65] When food protest commenced in earnest in April 1846 with the spectacular descent of several thousand protesters on Clonmel, neither the magistracy, the police nor the army was ready, with the result that the 'mob had it all its own way' initially at a number of locations – Carrick-on-Suir and Clonmel most notably.[66] The situation was not much better elsewhere in the region at that moment, as various crowds pursued a diversity of strategies targeted at carts, boats, corn stores, bakeries and grain mills that animated genuine alarm among the nobility, gentry, officeholders and strong farmers in the bar-

Guardian, 11 June 1842; *Freeman's Journal*, 16 June 1842.   **63** *Freeman's Journal*, 16 June 1842. **64** *Cork Examiner*, 6 July 1842.   **65** *Nation*, 29 Nov. 1846; Pennefeather to Shaw, 29 Mar., Bianconi to Pennefeather, 30 Mar. 1846 (NAI, OP: Tipperary, 1846/27/7897, 7889).   **66** *Kerry Examiner*, 20 Apr. 1846.

onies of south county Tipperary. The absence of a number of reputable resident-
ial magistrates from the region and the refusal of carmen to offer 'any resistance'
when they encountered an angry crowd, or even promptly to report their losses,
suggested momentarily that this primarily rural Munster crowd was embarked on
a campaign more akin to the *guerre de farines* that gripped the Paris basin in 1775
than a typically localized Irish food protest, but the communication by the under-
secretary at Dublin Castle, Thomas Redington, of an instruction to the general
commanding that the army prioritize the protection of property ensured this was
not the case. Redington's instruction, which dovetailed with the additional troops
billeted at appropriate locations (grain mills notably), and the beefing up of the
armed escorts (of soldiers and police) that accompanied the convoys those transporting grain were encouraged to form, indicated that the authorities were determined to regain control.[67] Moreover, the efforts that were made to apprehend
offenders and to recover foodstuffs when they were intercepted sent a clear message that those who engaged in food protest could not assume they would benefit even if they succeeded in making off with suitable comestibles.[68] The
galvanizing of local elites and the admission of 'respectable inhabitants ... as special constables' was also crucial as it not only facilitated the resumption of control in Clonmel and other towns, but also energized the magistracy.[69] The
deployment of additional troops (in response to a flurry of importunate requests)
was also helpful in rallying the elite, and it dovetailed with a variety of other tactics discouraging protest, to ensure that, as was typical of these occasions, order
was largely restored within a few days.[70]

   Though the responsiveness of the security apparatus of the state was the most
important factor, the authorities were grateful for the assistance they received in
the spring of 1846 from the Catholic clergy, who 'denounced [rioting] in the
strongest language'. The 'forbearance' shown by the military was also important.
The army sustained a high level of discipline during the eventful days of the
spring of 1846, and, when they found themselves in confrontational situations,
remained stoic in the face of provocation that in other circumstances might have
elicited a fatal volley of shots.[71] They did not turn a blind eye on food protest,
but whereas the more reactionary among the resident gentry opined that 'destitution' was 'a pretext for an insurrectionary movement of a very dangerous char-

67 Above, p. 65; *Kerry Examiner*, 20 Apr. 1846; County inspector's report, 13 Apr. 1846, Redington
to [ ], 14 Apr. 1846, Pennefeather to [ ], 15 Apr. 1846 (NAI, OP: Tipperary, 1846/27/9025, 8935,
9055); Bouton, *The flour war*, passim.   68 County inspector's report, 13 Apr. 1846 (NAI, OP:
Tipperary, 1846/27/9025); Canon to Redington, 4, 23 Nov. 1846 (NAI, OP: Queen's county,
1846/24/30573, 32619); Kelly to Pennefeather, 16 June 1846 (NAI, OP: King's county,
1846/15/18807).   69 Harvey to Bessborough, 16 Apr. 1846, Glengall to Bessborough, [15] Apr.
1846 (NAI, OP: Tipperary, 1846/27/9091, 9237); *Cork Examiner*, 20 Apr. 1846.   70 *Cork
Examiner*, 1 May 1846; Glengall to [ ], 14 Apr., Resident magistrate to [ ], 16 Apr. 1846, Redmond
to Pennefather, 17 Apr. 1846 (NAI, OP: Tipperary, 1846/27/8929, 9113, 9349).   71 Redmond to
Pennefeather, 19 Apr. 1846 (NAI, OP: Tipperary, 1846/27/9413); *Kerry Examiner*, 21 Apr. 1846;
Cork Examiner, 1 May 1846.

acter, which, if not immediately checked, may be productive of fearful consequences paralysing trade and commerce', the army, magistrates, justices of the
peace, and landed elite were more realistic.[72] The arrest and detention of protesters at Clonmel in April 1846 was not done for effect, however, and if some
had doubts as to the message they sought to convey, they were eased in July
when 77 of the 88 sent for trial at the Clonmel assizes were found guilty.
Furthermore, the presiding judge, Thomas Lefroy, played his part well. He did
not deviate from the official position that 'no amount of distress would excuse
persons from taking food, or other property by force', but he was disposed to
leniency, since having made clear the seriousness of the offence he contrived to
distinguish between degrees of culpability. In pronouncing sentence, he singled
out a number of offenders whose transgressions were 'of a very aggravated
nature' – breaking into stores, attacking boats and cars and the like – for seven
years transportation, but the majority of the 77 who were found guilty were sentenced to prison terms of between four and nine months.[73]

While the seriousness of the condition of the country guided Lefroy in his
actions, his display of leniency was in keeping with the prevailing mood, which
acknowledged the distress that many experienced and that the more judgemental ascribed to 'the dangerous and cruel experiments which have been made by
empirical politicians'.[74] The inclination to respond in a measured manner persisted, moreover, and it was still more evident in the autumn of 1846 when
there was a further surge in food protest. The most striking manifestation of the
authorities' eagerness not to overreact is to be found in the 'forbearance' displayed once more by magistrates and the military. They were assisted to be sure
by the fact that they had a 'large military force' at their disposal, which meant
they were generally in a position to respond to exigent calls for general assistance, and specifically for the military to aid the civil power, emanating from
landowners, magistrates, millers and others engaged in the grain trade then and,
as protest and theft continued, during the winter of 1846–7, and beyond.[75] The
provision of armed escorts certainly facilitated the transfer of flour,
meal and grain by cart from centres of production and manufacture to canal and
river ports *en route* to Dublin and other large conurbations but it did not prevent confrontation.[76]

72 Shaw to Redington, 17 Apr. 1846 (NAI, OP: Tipperary, 1846/27/9325).   73 Pennefeather to [ ],
24 Apr. 1846 (NAI, OP: Tipperary, 1846/27/10203); *Freeman's Journal*, 21, 23 July 1846; *Nenagh
Guardian*, 25 July 1846; *Nation*, 25 July 1846; *Cork Examiner*, 29 July 1846; *Belfast News Letter*, 31
July 1846.   74 *Belfast News Letter*, 17 Apr. 1846.   75 Macken to Redington, 4 Oct. 1846 (NAI,
OP: Cavan, 1846/4/26803); *Freeman's Journal*, 5, 8 Oct. 1846; Whitty to [Redington], 21 Apr.,
Plunkett to [Redington], 28 Apr., RM (Ennis) to Redington, 7, 31 May 1847 (NAI, OP: Clare,
1847/5/376, 398, 523, 613); NAI, Registered papers, 1847, division 1, vol. 1, 4/100, 6/596, 599,
14/17, 32; Routh to Redington, 6 Dec. 1847 (NAI, OP: Kerry, 1847/12/449).   76 Dopping to
Redington, 30 Sept., Joly to Redington, 13 Nov. 1846 (NAI, OP: Kildare, 1846/13/26539, 31797);
NAI, Registered papers, 1847, division 1, vol. 1, 4/19, 15/223; Rosse to Redington, 28 Nov. 1847
(NAI, OP: King's county, 1847/15/610).

One of the most notable took place in late October when 20 carts carrying a large quantity of flour was intercepted *en route* to Shannon Harbour, which was an important loading point for foodstuffs transported from this midlands region via the Grand Canal. The convoy of carts was accompanied by a military escort but they were powerless to inhibit 'the large body' of men and women that descended on them when they declined to use their weapons. There was no masking the embarrassment officials in King's county felt as a result, but they were not alone. This was true also at Cahirciveen, county Kerry, two months later when an angry crowd, three hundred strong, broke into the government provisions depot; yet this was secondary to the sense of relief that the military had taken the best option in the circumstances as 'it was scarcely possible to keep them [the crowd] back ... without a loss of life as ... they stood up to the bayonet saying they might as well be stuck as starved'.[77] The fact that officials accepted this, and were on the alert, where possible, as the magistrates of Carrick-on-Suir demonstrated in September 1846, to take steps to prevent large assemblies was also helpful.[78]

It did not inhibit the ongoing communications to Dublin Castle from here, and elsewhere, seeking military reinforcements well beyond the capacity of what was available to protect the movement of flour, or alarmist pronouncements (doubtlessly genuinely felt) to the effect that the police and army were stretched beyond their capacity, when the reality was that the authorities' control was never seriously at risk.[79] Furthermore, though there was ongoing disorder during the winter of 1846–7, and during 1847, it was not pursued with the same collective intensity as earlier protest. The resulting surge in theft, the killing of animals (sheep and cattle), and assault fostered an environment that, some apprehended,

77 Rosse to Redington, 29 Oct., Browne to Redington, 2 Nov., Berry to McMullen, 29 Oct, McMullan to Labouchere, 2 Nov. 1846 (NAI, OP: King's county, 1846/15/29753, 30075, 30087); Dillon to Redington, 8 Dec., Dillon to Henshaw, 8, 24 Dec. 1846 (NAI, OP: Kerry, 1846/12/34967, 35021, 37191). The endorsement of the action of Johnson, a justice of the peace at Youghal, for refusing to order the army to confront the crowd that 'emptied the bakers' shops of their contents ... so long as they confined their plunder to a few loaves of bread' fits this pattern: Knaresborough to Redington, 22 Sept. 1846 (NAI, OP: Cork, 1846/6/25641).   78 Magistrates of county Tipperary to Labouchere, 28 Sept. 1846 (NAI, OP: Tipperary, 1846/27/22907).   79 NAI, OP: Tipperary, 1846/27/30381, 30673, 37205, 37579; Clare, 1846/5/27463, 29333, 29831; Petition of justices of the peace, 2 Oct., Memorial of William Kelly (miller), 5 Nov., Eager to de Vesci, 9 Dec., Memorial of magistrates, 18 Dec., Memorial of mill owners and corn buyers, 16 Dec. 1846 (NAI, OP: Queen's county, 1846/24/28115, 40867, 36549); Drought to Labouchere, 25 Sept. 1846 (NAI, OP: King's county, 1846/15/25913); Memorial of magistrates, 21 Oct. 1846 (NAI, OP: Monaghan, 23/1846/29467); Memorial from Kilbeggan, 31 Dec. 1846 (NAI, OP: Westmeath, 1846/30/37911); O'Connor to Bessborough, 2 Oct. 1846 (NAI, OP: Sligo, 26/1846/26555); Memorial of the town commissioners for the borough of Ardee, 20 Oct. 1846 (NAI, OP: Louth, 1846/20/30479); Magistrates at Gorey petty session, 11 Dec. 1846 (NAI, OP: Wexford, 1846/31/35795); Merchants, traders and inhabitants of Newport, 20 Oct., Merchants of Westport, 19 Dec. 1846 (NAI, OP: Mayo, 21/29769, 36245); Dopping to Redington, 30 Sept. 1846 (NAI, OP: Kildare, 1846/13/26539); Memorial of magistrates of Butlersbridge, Nov., Memorial of merchants, traders and shopkeepers of Ballyjamesduff, 7 Dec. 1846 (NAI, OP: Cavan, 1846/4/28599, 34267); Justices of the peace, Banbridge, 24 Dec. 1846 (NAI, OP: Down, 1846/8/37013).

was 'fast verging on a frightful state of insubordination and anarchy', but much of what was denominated 'provisions plundering' continued to be conducted within acceptable parameters.[80] This was not invariably the case, of course. There were stand-out incidents – such as the manner in which the crowd of 2,000 that descended on Dennison's mills at O'Brien's Bridge, county Clare, in October 1846 sought to elicit a promise from the mill owner to sell meal at an affordable 2*s*. 8*d*. per stone – that met the definition of orthodox protest, but once the government had embarked on reducing public works in 1847, the deportment of the 'mob' was more confrontational. This impressed on the respectable their dependence on the police and military for protection. It also encouraged calls, such as that made in May 1847, for 'firmness' otherwise 'the peace of any part of the country cannot be maintained'.[81]

The greater responsiveness of the police and military thus mirrored public concern at the increase in lawlessness and criminality as famine intensified in 1847. This fostered a diminution in the tolerance shown food protest that can be highlighted by the increased recourse to reading the Riot Act; by incidents such as that at Ennistymon in April when a police party of six 'repelled' a crowd of some two hundred 'with fixed bayonets', and by intensified efforts to frustrate rioters by recovering grain and other appropriated foodstuffs.[82] In addition, the provision of rewards by bodies, such as the Dublin Steam Packet Company, plying the Grand and Royal Canals dovetailed with and reinforced the message provided by the ongoing pattern of arrests that followed the sequence of urban food rioting in the early months of 1847.[83]

Arrests were not confined to these occasions, of course, but if the intention was to convey the message that food protest would not be accommodated it was vitiated by the pattern of prosecution, which could be selective, and remained disposed to clemency when this offence was at issue. One may instance the response to events in county Waterford in September 1846. A total of fifty-one persons were charged with involvement in the fatal Dungarvan riot on 28 September 1846, of whom 39 were arraigned at the quarter sessions. Since all pleaded guilty and expressed 'contrition for their unwise and unlawful conduct', there was no onus on the court to make examples of those brought to trial, but it is still surprising that 38 were 'liberated' on recognizance, and that only Pat Power, their putative 'leader', was sentenced to twelve months imprisonment.[84]

80 Leyne to Redington, 15 Sept., Kenny to Redington, 21 Oct. 1846 (NAI, OP: Clare, 1846/5/23897, 28843); *Freeman's Journal*, 5 Oct. 1846, 6 Jan. 1847. 81 Ryan to [ ], 29 Oct. 1846 (NAI, OP: Clare, 1846/5/29929); O'Brien to Redington, 12 May 1847 (ibid., Clare, 1847/5/490). 82 Bell to Redington, 29 Jan. 1847, Osborne to Redington, 3 June 1847 (NAI, OP: Cork, 1847/6/199, 902); Police report, 14 Apr. 1847 (NAI, OP: Clare, 1847/5/389); *Tuam Herald*, 9 Oct. 1847. 83 Bayles to Redington, 13, 20 Dec. 1847 (NAI, OP, Kildare, 1847/13, 313, 3220); NAI, Registered papers, 1847, division 1, vol. 1, 15/9–10; *Freeman's Journal*, 11, 12, 16 Jan., 18, 26 June; *Leinster Express*, 16 Jan. 1847; *Cork Examiner*, 15 Jan., 8, 13 Feb., 10 Sept.; *Tralee Chronicle*, 16 Jan., 15 May; *Tuam Herald*, 9 Oct. 1847. 84 *Freeman's Journal*, 30 Oct. 1846; Howley to [Redington], 28 Oct. 1846 (NAI, OP: Waterford, 1846/29/30363).

Contrition was less in evidence five months later when the spring assizes were held at Clonmel, but the sharp decline in the proportion and number of offenders prosecuted for 'plundering provisions' on this occasion and the concomitant surge in the number pursued for, and found guilty of, larceny and allied offences here and in Queen's county was no less revealing of the continuing reluctance to bring the full weight of the law down on those who engaged in food protest than it was of the relative order of both categories of offending.[85]

The reluctance of magistrates to prosecute was another manifestation of the enduring disposition to treat food protest more sympathetically. It is observable in the response of the resident magistrate, W.P. Tracey, at O'Brien's Bridge, in county Clare in October 1846. Having identified *circa* 100 of those who participated in the attack on Dennison's mills, Tracey observed that whereas in ordinary times he would pursue prosecutions he was unwilling to do so on this occasion because of the 'indescribable distress' of the moment and 'the unmistaken sense of doubt as to the expediency of proceeding against such a crowd of misguided men, where imprisonment would be utterly destructive of … families'.[86] The resident magistrate at Tulla, also in county Clare, made a similar observation; his perception that there was 'no willingness to prosecute' those responsible for forcing entry to a meal store in Tuamgraney in November 1846 indicates that as it neared its end, food protest was still capable of generating empathy among those charged with upholding the law.[87]

Be that as it may, the manner in which the authorities responded to food protest then and earlier echoes the conclusion that it was never entirely tolerated or permitted to function outside the normal rules of law. Some additional perspective is cast upon official attitudes by examining the legal and legislative response.

PROCLAIMING FOOD PROTEST

Even more so than acts of parliament, proclamations (royal and municipal) were the legal instrument that best expressed the authorities' disapproval of food rioting. One of the first interventions of this kind, promulgated by the Privy Council on 5 February 1730, alerted the public to the fact that the lord lieutenant had instructed the 'officer … commanding His Majesty's forces' at Clonmel to be at the ready to assist 'the civil magistrates in suppressing riots and tumults' should they be called on.[88] Since local officials were reliant on the army to quell serious outbursts of disorder, this assurance was comforting. It also set a precedent, and

85 Clonmel Spring assizes, 26 Mar. 1847 (NAI, OP: Tipperary, 1847/27/817, 899); List of cases … tried at Borris in Ossory, Maryborough and Carlow Graigue, quarter sessions for Queen's county, Spring, June 1847 (NAI, OP: Queen's county, 1847/24, 188, 262).   86 Tracey to Redington, 5 Nov. 1846 (NAI, OP: Clare, 1846/5/30567).   87 Bailey to [ ], 31 Oct. 1846 (NAI, OP: Clare, 1846/5/39941).   88 *Dublin Gazette*, 17 Feb. 1730; Kelly and Lyons (eds), *The proclamations of Ireland*, iii, 202.

it is a matter of little surprise therefore that the authorities responded to the fatal incidents in Dublin in June 1740 and in Carrick-on-Suir in 1741 with a mayoral proclamation in the former instance and a Privy Council proclamation in the latter offering rewards of £30, £20 and £10 for the apprehension and conviction of those responsible.[89] Since there were no incidents of equivalent seriousness, there were no further proclamations of this kind for a number of decades. Indeed, other than the boarding of the *Happy Return* in Dublin port in 1767, an attack on a sloop in Cork harbour in 1778, and anonymous letters communicated in Waterford in 1768 and 1784, each of which was perceived as a serious transgression, the Privy Council did not pronounce with respect to a food protest episode during the second half of the eighteenth century.[90]

It was not as if the authorities perceived that food protest was not sufficiently serious to merit their attention. The observation in the proclamation issued on 31 March 1778, in response to a sequence of attempts by a 'riotous and tumultuous mob' to prevent 'corn or meal being exported' from Cork, that the lord lieutenant and council abhorred 'all such outrageous and violent proceedings' and were 'fully determined' to bring those responsible 'to speedy and condign punishment' followed legislation enacted in 1771 with this offence in mind.[91] Introduced by Lucius O'Brien, the MP for county Clare, the 1771 act for 'punishing such persons as shall ... hinder the exportation of corn' decreed that 'any person who wilfully and maliciously threw down or otherwise destroy any store house or granary or other place where corn shall be kept' was targeted at promoting the movement and exportation of corn, and not at discouraging food rioting *per se*. Nonetheless, the statute deemed the offence a felony, for which the sanction for a second transgression was five years transportation.[92]

The promulgation of a proclamation in respect of this matter in 1778 indicated that the authorities were prepared, when circumstances warranted, to invoke the 1771 legislation to counter food protest. But the failure to make use of it in 1783–4, though two proclamations were issued proscribing the exportation of foodstuffs, demonstrated that the 1771 measure was insufficiently muscular, and following discussion in the press and on the floor of the House of Commons parliament revisited the matter.[93] Presented to MPs by John Foster, the chancellor of the exchequer designate, on 26 February 1784 and given the royal assent three months later, this new measure sought 'more effectually' to provide for the punishment of food protesters by deeming it 'a felony without

89 Gilbert (ed.), *Calendar of ancient records of Dublin*, viii, 374–5; *Dublin Gazette*, 7 June 1741; Kelly and Lyons (eds), *The proclamations of Ireland*, iii, 291–2. 90 Kelly and Lyons (eds), *The proclamations of Ireland*, iv, 97, 117, 258–60, 407–8; *Dublin Mercury*, 1 Dec. 1768. 91 Kelly and Lyons (eds), *The proclamations of Ireland*, iv, 258–60. 92 11 George III, chap 7: *An act for the punishing such persons as shall do injuries and violences to the persons or properties of his majesty's subjects, with intent to hinder the exportation of corn*. 93 Kelly and Lyons (eds), *The proclamations of Ireland*, iv, 372–3, 387–8; *Volunteer Journal* (Dublin), 6 Feb. 1784; *Freeman's Journal*, 5 Feb. 1784; *Hibernian Journal*, 6 Feb. 1784; *Parl. Reg. (Ire.)*, ii, 347–9, 383.

benefit of clergy' to enter, damage or destroy 'any storehouse, mill, granary, cornstack' where foodstuffs were kept, to incapacitate any 'ship, vessel or boat' used to transport foodstuffs, or to obstruct the 'free passage' of corn, grain, meal, flour, bread, biscuit and potatoes.[94]

The categorization of a host of activities associated with food protest as capital offences meant there was less reason for the Privy Council to concern itself with the practice from that point, and few proclamations appertaining to food protest were promulgated thereafter.[95] Indeed, it is a measure of the extent to which the 1784 enactment shaped attitudes that local officials chose increasingly to invoke the act when they pronounced publicly against food protest. This was a new *modus operandi*. Prior to 1784 the practice was to offer financial inducements to incentivize the apprehension and conviction of rioters. For example, the mayor of Cork issued a proclamation in 1753 offering a £5 reward 'to any person who shall convict anyone who molests or disturbs the country people in bringing in their corn, potatoes or other provisions' to the city. And following on the £20 and £10 offered in 1740, successive mayors of Dublin in 1774 and 1775 promised 20 guineas for the apprehension and successful prosecution of those who compelled the carriers of food to the capital to bring it 'to a crane, lately erected at New-market, in the county of Dublin'.[96] A number of jurisdictions opted for alternative solutions. The most imaginative – inaugurated by Youghal Corporation in 1773–4 in response to the decline in the grain market and the collapse in grain exports from that port – was an attempt to empower 'magistrates' to take swift and firm action (up to and including 'banishing a few of the wanton that may intend to disturb any shippers of corn') to discourage 'riots'. This scheme also involved removing 'all town dues' on oats and meal brought to market to encourage trade; and setting aside a sum of £100 for the purchase of oats for grinding into oatmeal and sale 'to the poor at first cost' when prices were high.[97]

Food riots in 1783 and 1801 demonstrate that Youghal's plan failed to secure a reliable grain supply for the port town, but well before the latter date the 1784 act had a transformative impact on the manner in which municipalities responded to food protest within their jurisdictions.[98] As a result, local proclamations appertaining to food rioting opted increasingly for the verbatim iteration of the relevant clause in the 1784 act describing food protest as a capital offence.[99] This was, as its frequent reiteration attests, the most significant legal weapon in the armoury of the authorities for thirty years though the want of prosecutions suggests it func-

94 24 George III, chap. 20; *An act for the more effectually punishing such persons as shall by violence obstruct the freedom of corn markets and the corn trade* (Dublin, 1784). **95** Interestingly, when they responded to pressure to intervene in 1789, the proclamation that belatedly emerged was hardly publicized: Kelly and Lyons (eds), *The proclamations of Ireland*, iv, 383. **96** Caulfield (ed.), *Corporation book of Cork*, p. 671; *Dublin Mercury*, 7 Jan. 1775; *Dublin Gazette*, 25 Nov. 1775. **97** Caulfield (ed.), *Corporation book of Youghal*, pp 485–7, 490–1; Dickson, *Old world colony*, p. 284. **98** 23 and 24 George III, chap. 20. **99** *Volunteers Journal* (Cork), 30 June 1783, 17 June 1784; Wells, 'The Irish famine of 1799–1801', p. 182; *Freeman's Journal*, 30 May 1795, 20 Mar. 1800; *Cork Advertiser*, 26 Feb. 1801.

tioned more as a threat than as an effective sanction.[100] Be that as it may, it was all that was available until legislative change in 1814 empowered officials to intervene to prevent food rioting by proscribing 'persons from unlawfully assembling', while the parallel invocation of the Riot Act permitted a more structured (and based on the frequency with which it was invoked) more focussed and effective response.[101]

These tactics facilitated the transfer of responsibility for dealing with food protest from the military to the fledging police, though the military remained available to assist in serious cases. In June 1817, for example, the mayor of Kilkenny sought assistance to deal with the poor of the town, who sustained several days of disturbance, and refused to disperse in response to his reading of the Riot Act; order was soon restored, and 'maintained, for a period, by the 16th regiment' which was deployed to the city for that purpose.[102] Subsequently, the development in the 1830s of a more mobile military capacity during the tithe war ensured that cavalry companies (dragoons) frequently assumed the initiative in dealing with aggressive crowds and, as the history of the response to protest in 1846–7 attests, they were integral to the protection that was accorded mill owners and others from still-more mobile crowds.

The posting of official proclamations offering rewards for the apprehension of individuals had less obvious purchase in this context, though the practice of promulgating the 1784 act remained an option. It was the option appealed to by 'the sovereign and magistrates' of the town of Belfast in 1838, when they responded to 'disgraceful and serious rioting' in that place by reminding the public in bold print that it was a 'felony, punishable by death' in advance of a lengthy verbatim extract from the 1784 measure.[103] It was not resorted to subsequently. Yet the fact that the Irish Privy Council did not issue a proclamation during the Great Famine until the autumn of 1846, when it responded to reports from 'various parts of the country' of 'assemblages ... attacking the shops of bakers and the stores of merchants, and interrupting the free traffic in provisions', indicated that as far as officials were concerned the law was sufficient to deal with the issue; the crucial matter was no longer – as was the case for a majority of the eighteenth century – the absence of an appropriate law but its interpretation and application.[104]

PUBLIC OPINION AND FOOD PROTEST

If the maintenance of law and order was the primary reason why officials sought to defuse food protest, they did so in the knowledge that they had the support of

---

100 There are no figures with which to measure its effectiveness, but since the conviction rate for committal for riotous assembly in Ireland stood at a modest 22 per cent (compared to 60 per cent in England), it can safely be concluded that it was ineffectual at that point: Palmer, *Police and protest in England and Ireland, 1780–1850*, pp 196–7. 101 Above, p. 180; *Freeman's Journal*, 12 June 1817. 102 Cunningham, 'Popular protest and "a moral economy"', p. 43. 103 *Belfast News Letter*, 27 Aug. 1838. 104 The proclamation, which was signed by Henry Labouchere, was issued from Dublin Castle on 2 October: *Freeman's Journal*, 6 Oct. 1846.

major societal stakeholders. The broadly consonant approach pursued by local and national officials (addressed above) represents the strongest evidence of this, but it is notable also that they had the backing of the grand juries, commercial interests and the Catholic Church. This was not always publicly articulated, but the pronouncement by the foreman and members of the grand jury of county Dublin in the summer of 1766 that they would 'attend the high sheriff and the justices of the peace of our county as a *posse comitatus*, and come properly armed to assist them in the due execution of their respective offices' was a strong statement of intent.[105] Elsewhere, the 'instruction' in 1766 of the Catholic bishop of Ossory, Thomas Burke (*c*.1709–76), that the clergy of Kilkenny should read at Mass an episcopal letter in which he expressed 'abhorrence of the most pernicious evils perpetrated lately by an unruly mob in this city' echoed an earlier expression of disapproval of food rioting from the same quarter in Dublin in 1729; the 'exhortation … read at the several Romish chapels in the city of Dublin' in the spring of 1757 urging the population to 'humble, peaceful and obedient behaviour'; and anticipated the admonition of Archbishop John Carpenter of Dublin, *c*.1780, to the population of the parish of Ballymore-Eustace and Eadestown 'to avoid all riots and unlawful assemblies'.[106] It is notable that trades guilds were less forthcoming with expressions of disapproval. The £50 reward offered by the Corporation of Coopers for the discovery of those who boarded and damaged the *Happy Return* in Dublin port in 1767 was not emulated by other guilds then or later. Yet the statement issued by 'the principal linen weavers and other working tradesmen of the town of Belfast' in which they expressed their 'abhorrence' of recent rioting in that town in August 1756, indicates that the sympathy for those in distress fell well short of tolerating riotous intervention.[107]

In the course of his strongly worded episcopal letter condemning food rioting in June 1766, Bishop Thomas Burke sought to impress upon the Catholics of Kilkenny that as well as the grievous offence their actions gave 'God and their neighbours', they generated difficulties for themselves and threatened the future prosperity of the region by disrupting the movement of foodstuffs:

> For by discouraging the making of meal [by targeting millers], no meal will be made; and then they must miserably starve in a country sufficiently stored with provisions. Hence the charity so freely, bountifully and plentifully provided for, which lessened the high price of food, will become useless. The consequence has already been that the quantity of

105 *Freeman's Journal*, 18 Oct. 1766. It should be noted that Edward Newenham, the foreman of the grand jury, was personally incentivized to agree such a declaration, not by food rioting, but by disturbances at St Doulagh's well, Belcamp, county Dublin: James Kelly, *Sir Edward Newenham, MP, 1734–1814: defender of the Protestant constitution* (Dublin, 2004), p. 38. **106** Ó Fearghail (ed.), 'Episcopal edicts of the diocese of Ossory', pp 83–4; *Gentleman's Magazine*, 27 (1757), pp 464–5; Curran (ed.), 'Dr Carpenter's admonitions', p. 156; above, p. 42. **107** *Freeman's Journal*, 14 Mar., 4 Apr. 1767; *Belfast News Letter*, 27 Aug. 1756.

corn brought to the market is apparently lessened, and the price risen: and that two classes of buyers in the market, the meal-men, and the starch makers, are already destroyed, the millers discouraged, and no buyers remain but the bakers. The further consequence whereof must be that Kilkenny which was advancing fast to the granary of Leinster to the visible increase of industry and wealth by tillage must become deserted.[108]

Though Burke made it known that he made this point on foot of advice received from the town mayor Barry Colles, his willingness to do so indicated that he shared the broader concern, expressed with varying levels of intensity, at the implications of the disruption for the circulation of goods. This was an unintended consequence of food protest, but it was one of which the authorities and commentators were increasingly aware. It was, for example, very much on the mind of Primate Hugh Boulter when in the spring of 1729 he explained that the 'poor wretches' who had caused such a stir in the city of Cork in February 1729 did not appreciate 'that by their riots the country are deterred from bringing them in provisions, which will make things dearer in those places than the exportation they are so angry at'.[109] Boulter's contention that instead of bringing relief food rioting might exacerbate an already difficult situation did not discourage him from the charitable giving for which he was renowned during his lifetime, but the irony of the situation was not lost on him, or on others subsequently. It was manifest, for example, in Waterford in 1734 in the memorial of the mayor and sheriff appealing to the lord lieutenant to 'suppress' the rioters in Carrick-on-Suir who prevented the transportation of grain from their town on the grounds that, as well as causing 'great hardship' to the 'poor' of Waterford, it was a 'great discouragement of trade and tillage and the publick good of the nation'.[110]

The more frequent articulation of this sentiment during the mid-1750s and 1760s suggests that there was still greater awareness of the negative implications of such activity by mid-century. Indicatively, the response of the Dublin press to an attempt in November 1756 'to force open the warehouses of several merchants in this city in order to carry off corn and meal' was particularly critical: 'No merchant either abroad or at home will venture to have their property exposed to such violent outrages; consequently, the importation of corn will be prevented and farmers will not send to the city for the same reason', according to the commentary in *Pue's Occurrences*.[111] This concern was shared by the political and mercantile communities of Belfast, which apprehended that 'the town must in all probability be starved for none will bring in meal either by land or sea till they can be secured of their property'.[112] Things never deteriorated to such an extent

---

108 Ó Fearghail (ed.), 'Episcopal edicts of the diocese of Ossory', p. 83.   109 Boulter to Newcastle, 13 Mar. 1728/9 in *Boulter letters*, i, 230.   110 Kenneth Milne and Paddy McNally (eds), *The Boulter letters* (Dublin, 2016), pp 67–8; Memorial of the mayor, sheriffs and citizens of Waterford to the duke of Dorset, 29 Mar. 1734 (Waterford Archives, Corporation of Waterford council book).   111 *Pue's Occurrences*, 20 Nov. 1756.   112 Macartney to [ ], 31 July 1756 in Benn's *Belfast*, p. 595.

in either location, but the communication from the partnership of Marsden and Benson of Dublin to Daniel Mussenden, a merchant based in Belfast, in November that they would not dispatch oatmeal 'for fear of the mob' indicates that these sentiments were not simply alarmist, and the impact of the disruption of trade was an important consideration later that same month when it was agreed at a 'general meeting of the associated inhabitants of Belfast' not only to establish 'an association for suppressing riots, and effectually protecting all farmers bringing grain, &c into our markets, and other dealers in provisions', but also to attempt to ensure there was no repeat of the earlier food seizures by offering a reward for the apprehension of 36 named individuals and by placing 'a guard of twenty men … at the Market House' in the town.[113] Confirmation that Marsden and Benson were not alone in declining to fulfil orders in such situations was forthcoming in 1772 when the Cork merchant, Richard Hare, refused to export offal to Liverpool on the grounds that 'it would be hazardous for a merchant to ship any at this time, as he may have his house pulled down'.[114] Hare evidently negotiated this threat to his livelihood, but this was not always possible. The inability of the Quaker merchant, Richard Jacob, to ship oatmeal he had in store in Waterford and the losses he encountered at the hand of 'the mob in Clonmel' early in 1784, precipitated him into bankruptcy. Jacob was one of the unlucky ones, for though his misfortune did not dissuade others from engaging in speculative purchases, which was integral to the profession, it demonstrated that actions such as occurred at Clonmel, and the ability of 'the great mob' that arose at Dungarvan in 1766 to frustrate the movement of 'three hundred barrels of oats' from that town 'for the use of the poor inhabitants' of Waterford disrupted mercantile activity, and that this impacted adversely those who made the movement of foodstuffs possible.[115]

Though few merchants were hit as hard as Richard Jacob, others also experienced loss as well as inconvenience. James Heron, a Dublin merchant who was prevented by mob intervention in 1757 from shipping a cargo of oats, barley, malt and beans to the capital, was obliged as a result not only to bear the cost of repairing his ship but also to petition for the restoration of 1500 barrels of grain that were seized by an overly zealous revenue official.[116] The restoration of the cargo on the direction of the commissioners, who were (as subsequent decisions made clear) eager to encourage the movement of food to the capital, eased

A week earlier, Macartney claimed in similar terms that unless order was restored 'there will be no meal to buy': ibid., p. 594. **113** *Belfast News Letter*, 7, 10 Sept., 26, 30 Nov., 3, 10, 20 Dec. 1756; Marsden and Benson to Mussenden, 25 Nov. 1756 (PRONI, Mussenden papers, D354/170); Magennis, 'Food scarcity', p. 200. **114** Hare to Thomas and Clayton Case esqs., 20 May 1772 in James O'Shea (ed.), *The letterbook of Richard Hare, merchant of Cork, 1771–1772* (Dublin, 2013), p. 244; Dickson, *Old world colony*, p. 141. **115** Mary Jacob to Thomas Greer, 12 Feb. 1784, Richard Jacob to Thomas Greer, 12 Feb. 1784 (PRONI, Greer papers, D1044/ 686, 687a); *Parl. Reg. (Ire.)*, ii, 347; Minutes of Waterford Corporation, 30 June 1766 (Waterford Archives, Corporation of Waterford council book). **116** Minutes of the Revenue Commissioners, 6 May 1757 (TNA, CUST1/60 f. 62v).

Heron's difficulty, but this was not always the case.[117] There was, for example, no masking the seriousness of the implications of the inability of merchants at Dungarvan, Youghal, Cork and Waterford in 1784 to send foodstuffs to the metropolis and northern parts for the economy generally. According to the *Dublin Evening Post*, which was not unsympathetic to those in distress, the negative effects of mob intervention in Waterford, Clonmel and Carrick-on-Suir was keenly felt by Munster farmers, who were prevented from selling their produce at the market premium they anticipated, and by landowners whose rent rolls suffered.[118] Alarmed at what it perceived as the self-interested inclination of the urban 'mob' in certain Munster towns to put its well-being ahead of the legitimate interests of others, and of the larger economy, the paper called upon landowners to take decisive action. It is not known if the author of this commentary perceived that the *Act for the more effectually punishing such persons as shall by violence obstruct the freedom of corn markets and the corn trade* was a solution to this problem, but, if so, it was deemed insufficient a decade later when the ripple effect of food protest, then most acutely felt in Dublin, once again animated concern at the implications of food protest for the free movement of foodstuffs. The target in this instance was the 'numerous mob from the Earl of Meath's Liberty':

> These unfortunate people are much to be pitied, but nothing can excuse such riotous behaviour as they have recently practised. It is to be observed that the equally unfortunate people whom they plunder are not in a much better situation than they are themselves. Farmers are afraid to send their goods to market in consequence; and, to the disgrace of the capital, by these acts of outrage is to be added the distress of the middling ranks of the community, from the scarcity which they occasion in the markets of every necessary article of life. The zeal of the public for their relief is likely to be damped by nothing so much as these sallies of intemperance, tumult, and depredation.[119]

Despite the appreciating realization manifest by commentaries such as this that food protest was not an unqualified benefit even to those it was intended to assist, this argument was not widely articulated until the early nineteenth century when it was presented in a more tangibly ideological manner. Indicatively, a commentary in the *Londonderry Journal* in 1812 drew heavily on the free trade theory of Adam Smith in pointing out the illogicality of food protest because, it argued, of the propensity of 'tumultuous risings' of this kind to 'terminate in the destruction of … the very article of which they [the rioters] stand so much in need'.[120] Five years later, the criticism was still sharper. The condemnation by the *Belfast News Letter* in 1817 of the actions of the Galway 'mob' which sought to prevent

117 Ibid., ff 66, 70, 71.   118 *Dublin Evening Post*, 5 Feb. 1784.   119 *Dublin Morning Post*, 6 June 1793.   120 Cunningham, 'Popular protest and "a moral economy"', pp 26–7.

'a vessel taking in a quantity of oatmeal at that port for Derry' as both 'shameful' and deserving of 'the most severe reprehension' is particularly notable because the paper avowed, in a more explicit manner than previously encountered, that food protest was unjustifiable:

> Would the mob of Galway allow the people of Derry to famish for want rather than permit a ship load of meal to be carried to them. Let them reverse the case, and say how they would feel were they in need, and the people of Derry to refuse a supply to them. The cruelty, the injustice, and the absurdity of such conduct must be obvious to everyone, and can only be accounted for by the ignorance and rashness which generally pervade a tumultuous mob.[121]

The reality of the matter, of course, was that for those paying high prices or faced with the prospect of scarcity there was nothing cruel, unjust or absurd about food rioting. Yet the fact that commentators thought otherwise, and were prepared to say so publicly, suggested that the tolerance shown food protest was weakening. There was no question as yet of society agreeing that food rioters did not deserve to be extended some understanding because, as had been the case since it emerged on the Irish landscape in the early eighteenth century, it was not regarded as an ordinary crime. This was made clear by the reaction to the bloody events at Ennis in 1842, when a conscious effort was made to elicit sympathy for the people that were prompted to protest – 'the gaunt and hungry beings that disturb the calm and quiet stillness of the night; blind men, and mothers of children, with physical strength prostrated, but led by instinct, and the condescension of all senses into one, to the neighbourhood of food'.[122]

Similar sentiments were expressed in July 1842, in the aftermath of the meeting at Clare assizes at which 'three men' were 'found guilty of having, under the pressure of starvation, attacked a boat, and helped themselves to a portion of the property of Messrs Bannatyne', and no prosecutions were pursued against the policemen who had fired on the crowd. The grand jury was aspersed also for affording the 'protection' of property greater priority than the protection of the life of the poor; and for acting 'according to the doctrine laid down by the gentlemen of Clare, [which held that] any policeman may shoot a peasant without orders, or … any policeman may order him to be shot, and neither shall be held responsible'. This was pure hyperbole of course, but it was the antithesis of the sentiment offered by those, disapproving of food protest, who 'strongly denounce[d] those who … [seek] revenge, … who will be satisfied with nothing short of a dread but unwarranted retribution'. This observation was consistent with the official position articulated by Baron Richards in his address to the grand jury, yet the crown prosecution 'declined to call for [the] punishment' of those brought to trial because it served the state better to be seen to demonstrate compassion.[123]

121 *Belfast News Letter*, 17 Jan. 1817.   122 *Cork Examiner*, 13 June 1842.   123 *Freeman's Journal*,

Moreover, this remained the view of the public at large as well as the official position during the early years of the Great Famine, since in addition to the sympathy shown protesters by cart drivers, by elements of the police, and by commentators, who properly acknowledged that the serried ranks seeking relief claiming they were 'starving' were genuine, the severity of the crisis elicited an empathetic response in the press.[124] This was the import of the observation in the *Freeman's Journal* on 3 October 1846 that 'one can hardly call the assemblage of hungry multitude demanding work or bread, a riotous mob'.[125] It was implicit in the commentary carried in the *Belfast News Letter* in response to the outbreak of food protest in Munster earlier in the year:

> The riots which we deplore are traceable to the impatience and irritations fomented by the dangerous and cruel experiments which have been made by empirical politicians on their temper. It is easier, too, to obtain large supplies of food by plunder, than to wait patiently for the restricted modicum which the unfortunate circumstances of the country can afford them.[126]

This empathetic tone was augmented by calls for food and employment emanating with the Roman Catholic clergy and the O'Connellite Loyal National Repeal Association though both were at pains in the autumn of 1846 to urge the population 'to bear yet a little with the evils with which it has pleased an all-wise providence to plunge them'.[127] The responsiveness of various crowds to appeals by priests, clergy and others then and later to be patient in the face of the gathering crisis clearly did not register with the many who engaged in food protest and in the still more thorough disapproval of practices pursued by agrarian protesters, but there was no evading the uncomfortable fact that food protest was disruptive and that 'food riots ... lead to the destruction of great quantities of food'.[128] It was inevitable, in this fraught environment, that criticism of the government increased, and that the prime minister, Lord John Russell, and his 'insane declaration not to interfere' should be the focus of specific criticism; it complemented the mounting sense that the public was being sacrificed to 'the cold-blooded arguments of political economy'.[129] This was more than usually perceptive, but it was to be expected as the reality of hunger exposed the frailty of so many well-intentioned arguments and simplistic analyses of the condition of the country, and the inadequacy, if not always the impotence, of the strategies,

9 July 1842; *Leinster Express*, 18 June 1842; above, pp 56–7.   **124** County inspector's report, 13 Apr. 1846 (NAI, OP: Tipperary, 1846/27/9025).   **125** *Freeman's Journal*, 3 Oct. 1846.   **126** *Belfast News Letter*, 17 Apr. 1846.   **127** Kerr, *The Catholic Church and the Famine*, pp 11–13, 19–20; *Freeman's Journal*, 29 Sept., 5, 7, 15 Oct. 1846.   **128** *Freeman's Journal*, 2, 5, 15, 19, 30 Oct. 1846; 15 May, 18 June 1847; Redington to Kennedy, 20 Oct. 1847 (NAI, OP, Clare, 1847/5/1116).   **129** *Freeman's Journal*, 29 Sept., 15 Oct. 1846. There was even a call for the return of Robert Peel: *Freeman's Journal*, 5 Oct. 1846.

schemes and solutions emanating from all sides. There were forecasts that 'a general system of plunder will be resorted to' if some urgent steps were not taken; others, despairing of the 'mockery' that was the system of public works, opined that 'if it were intended to create riot and disorder of every sort, there could be no better means adopted'; while still others, perceiving 'the sufferings of the poor ... intolerable', called upon the 'gentry and shopkeepers' to supply 'provisions within the [financial] limits of the poor', which was as impractical a solution as systemic food protest.[130]

Yet there were also those, disapproving of food protest, and indeed of protest in general, who shared the official conclusion that those who engaged in food rioting were 'plunderers' or 'mere robbers' and that what they were doing was 'plundering'. The fact that food protest was now designated an 'outrage' – the offence of 'plundering provisions' – fostered the use of such unsympathetic terminology, and it was reinforced, as the severity of the Great Famine crisis intensified, by reports that the internal movement of food had been interrupted, that local markets had been disrupted, and that rioting crowds were responsible for the suspension of the export of grain from Westport, county Mayo, Dungarvan, county Waterford, Youghal, county Cork, Tarbert, county Kerry and other ports.[131] This was not new or unique to the Great Famine, of course, but it was more widespread then, and its negative consequences seemed to register more deeply.

It was inevitable, given the severity of the crisis, that those in need should seek their own solutions, and while it can be concluded that the tradition of agrarian protest exerted a strong influence on the populace in the winter of 1846–7, it is still more noteworthy that those seeking assistance in order that they could provide, and those seeking aid to survive looked increasingly to the state.[132] The way may have been prepared by evolving trends in government and relief in the quarter century leading up to the Famine, but the latter-day reality was captured by the commentary appended to a report of a food protest at Ballinrobe, county Mayo, in May 1847, during which a crowd was dispersed by a bayonet charge. While it was observed in an account of the incident that the preparedness of the people 'to seek death at the point of the bayonet or sabre' exposed the inhumanity of 'political economy', the still-more harsh reality was that it demonstrated the incapacity of food protest.[133] The concern expressed in a number of newspapers in October 1847 that 'we can as yet see no active indications of any intention on the part of government to provide for the coming emergency' cautions against concluding that the population accepted that the government was a more reliable source of relief than traditional protest, but the

130 *Freeman's Journal*, 15 Oct. 1846.   131 Glengall to Redington, 13 Apr., 4 Dec., Phipps to Redington, 18 Apr., Purdy to Pennefeather, 24 Apr. 1846 (NAI, OP: Tipperary, 1846/27/8989, 9425, 10171, 33961); *Connaught Telegraph*, 7 Oct. 1846; *Freeman's Journal*, 7, 9 Oct. 1846; Memorial of magistrates of Newmarket-on-Fergus, 20 Oct. 1846 (NAI, OP: Clare, 1846/5/29333); Cunningham, ""Tis hard to argue starvation into quiet"', pp 17–18.   132 *Freeman's Journal*, 6 Oct. 1846.

fact that it was uttered points to the fact that those in need looked primarily to government sponsored relief.[134] This was not the case in the eighteenth century.

PROVIDING RELIEF

Though it took second place to restoring order, the response of the authorities to the first major episode of food protest in Ireland – in 1729–30 – illustrates that officials accepted that it was incumbent upon them to alleviate the distress that fuelled food rioting. A revealing demonstration was provided by the proposition, presented on 1 March 1729 to Cork Corporation by mayor Millard whose house had been 'torn down' a few weeks earlier, 'importing a subscription for a sum of money for the better providing bread and corn for the use of the city at this time of scarcity', and by the Corporation's undertaking to make good 'whatsoever deficiency may happen'.[135] Since the famine crisis of the late 1720s was within months of its conclusion at this point, it might seem that this intervention was reluctant as well as tardy, whereas it complemented the 'great and extensive charity' pursued at the same time by Peter Browne, the local Church of Ireland bishop.[136] Meanwhile in Drogheda, a similar pattern of responsiveness can be identified; there the mayor and corporation ordered the town's bakers to make a return of the number of barrels of grain they sent to be ground to ensure there was sufficient available 'for the use of the inhabitants', while the mayor took possession of the keys of the town grain stores to the same end. The charitably minded also contributed; in Drogheda the most active figure was James Scholes, a merchant, who undertook to re-land two cargoes of barley, oats and oatmeal if he was remitted the duty he had 'already paid on their export'.[137]

These local interventions were equalled on the national stage by the attempt, instigated by Primate Hugh Boulter in March, to import '2,400 quarters of rye' from England. A still more significant initiative pursued by the lords justices sought at the same time to convince the British Privy Council to prohibit grain exports 'for a month or two' in order to 'ease the minds of the people, and incline them [the people of Munster] more readily to submit to the sending corn to their countrymen in the north'.[138] The Privy Council did not deem this approriate and the opposition of councillors, following their earlier refusal to

133 *Connaught Telegraph*, 12 May; *Tuam Herald*, 15 May 1847.   134 *Tuam Herald*, 9 Oct. 1847; *Kerry Examiner*, 12 Oct. 1847.   135 Caulfield (ed.), *Council book of the Corporation of Cork*, p. 482; Boulter to Newcastle, 13 Mar. 1729 in *Boulter letters*, i, 229; *An express from Cork with an account of a bloody battle*, p. 1.   136 Caulfield (ed.), *Corporation book of Cork*, p. 485; C.A. Webster, *The diocese of Cork* (Cork, 1920), p. 311.   137 Thomas Gogarty (ed.), *Council book of the Corporation of Drogheda: vol. 1 from 1649 to 1734* (Dundalk, 1988), p. 392; *Faulkner's Dublin Journal*, 8 Mar. 1729; Minutes of the Revenue Commissioners, 7 Mar. 1729 (TNA, CUST1/21 f. 82).   138 Boulter to Cartaret, 20 July 1727, Boulter to Newcastle, 13 Mar. 1729 in *Boulter letters*, i, 151–2, 231; [Rye], *Considerations on agriculture*, introduction; Minutes of British Privy Council, 26 Mar. 1729 (TNA, PC2/90 f. 458).

agree a 5 per cent tillage quota, did nothing to persuade the 'poor' that direct action was not more effective, especially as the intervention of the Cork populace was publicly credited with causing the price of a gallon of potatoes and a peck of oatmeal to fall by 55 per cent and 66 per cent respectively, and with saving 'a thousand families' from perishing.[139]

Whatever the truth of the matter, the impact of charitable relief was not inconsequential in 1729–30, and it was still more important when the country was plunged into a serious famine in 1740–1.[140] Then the efforts of national, municipal and private interests was pursued against a backdrop that was so undeniably dire that the Irish Privy Council had no hesitation in imposing an embargo, on 19 January 1740, on 'the exportation of all manner of grain or meal'.[141] It was insufficient to prevent a sharp rise in prices and thereby to discourage food protest, and, in keeping with the level of distress, the relief effort that food protest incentivised was larger, more ambitious and more varied than any previously undertaken. As a focal point of the country's grain trade, Drogheda was a benchmark, and it lived up to its reputation as one of the country's more responsive municipalities when the magistrates of the town responded to the attempt to prevent a ship laden with oatmeal departing the port for Scotland by agreeing a 'resolution … not to allow any more food to be exported', and James Scholes, who was now an alderman, 'let the poor have several tons of meal in small quantities at 9s. per cwt.'.[142] It was a testament to the civic responsibility the wealthy felt towards those in distress, and it is noteworthy that other urban locations responded with comparable initiatives. The single-most expansive, and expensive, scheme was pursued by the Corporation of Waterford, which in November 1840 authorized its mayor 'to take up any sum not exceeding two thousand pounds upon the city seal at interest for eight months, the same to be imploy'd or laid out in buying corn for the relief of the poor'.[143] This was ambitious, but it was impelled by the same urgency that prompted the mayor of Belfast in June to require a number of merchants, who were hoarding grain in anticipation of still higher prices, to make the foodstuffs in their possession available to the public, and the mayor of Cork to order that 300 barrels of corn located on board a French ship in Cork harbour be sold at the much reduced price of 6s. a barrel.[144]

139 *An express from Cork with an account of a bloody battle*, p. 1; Giblin (ed.), 'Catalogue of Nunziatura di Fiandra, pt. 5', 13. Oatmeal fell from 15p to 5p a peck; potatoes from 4p to 1.5p a gallon. 140 Kelly, 'Harvests and hardship', pp 87–9; idem, 'Combatting distress: the famine of 1740–41', passim; Dickson, *Arctic Ireland*, pp 16–19, 35–43. 141 *Dublin Newsletter*, 26 Jan. 1740; Kelly and Lyons (eds), *The proclamations of Ireland*, iii, 282–3. 142 Kelly and Lyons (eds), *The proclamations of Ireland*, iii, 282–3; *Faulkner's Dublin Journal*, 22 Apr. 1740. 143 Minutes of Waterford Corporation, 26 Nov. 1740 (Waterford Archives, Corporation of Waterford council book). It may be observed that this decision was not without negative consequence; it contributed to raise the levels of anxiety in Carrick-on-Suir which culminated in rioting in April 1741. 144 *Dublin Newsletter*, 24 June 1740, 25 Apr., 5 May 1741. A week previously, wheat from France sold at 31s. a barrel.

A more traditional, but possibly more effective, response, employed by the lord mayor of Dublin, Daniel Falkiner, in the wake of major riots in the metropolis in May–June 1740, was to enforce the various regulations that governed the sale of goods, in order to discourage forestalling, hoarding and fraud. Mayor Falkiner issued a proclamation in June alerting farmers, millers, bakers and mealmen to the regulations targeted at preventing forestalling and regrating and ensuring the market in bread ran smoothly. He also instructed the church wardens of the city's seven parishes to investigate if there were corn or grain reserves in their parishes so that they might be brought to market 'to prevent the disturbances that arise from people concealing corn'. Falkiner's decision to revisit this matter in September when he issued a further mayoral proclamation against 'forestallers, regraters and ingrossers', and targeted below weight bread and corn for seizure indicated just how difficult it was to eradicate abuses in these sectors. But no less than the admonition to farmers 'to send their grain to market', these interventions were a further demonstration of the fact that public stability as well as philanthropic concern required those in office to intervene to ease the plight of those in distress.[145]

It is not merely coincidental therefore that calls were also issued in Dublin in 1741 for a scheme of public works to provide for the deserving poor, or that the Corporation of Waterford, one of the most energetic municipal authorities in the country, established a high ranking committee 'to consider of ways and means for relieveing the poor of this city, and imploying them'. Another, even more far-seeing proposition that acquired traction as a potential solution to scarcity and, therefore, food protest, favoured the establishment of a network of public granaries.[146] Like the calls for public works initiatives, this was beyond the capacity of municipalities to deliver, but its suggestion was indicative of the recognition that food protest was a manifestation of a real and serious problem, and not simply an emotional response by an irrational 'mob' to the manipulative actions of 'meal mongers', 'ingrossers', 'farmers', and other 'county people' – deemed 'cruel oppressors' by one correspondent – who sought to 'take advantage of circumstances' by profiteering.[147]

One consequence of this was the preparedness of municipal officials, in Dublin and Cork, during the 1740s and 1750s to take an active stand against forestalling, ingrossing, regrating, price fixing and other fraudulent and frequently reported

145 *Faulkner's Dublin Journal*, 3, 7, 17 June, 16 Sept., 4 Oct. 1740; *Dublin Newsletter*, 7, 17 June 1740. **146** Minutes of Waterford Corporation, 10 Mar. 1741 (Waterford Archives, Corporation of Waterford council book); *Faulkner's Dublin Journal*, 7 June 1740, 16 June 1741; for the wider debate on establishing a network of granaries see Philip Skelton, *Necessity of tillage and granaries* (Dublin, 1741), pp 41–2; Thomas Prior, *A proposal to prevent the price of corn from rising too high, or falling too low, by the means of granaries* ([Dublin], 1741), 3, 6; *The groans of Ireland: in a letter to a member of parliament* (Dublin, 1741), p. 11; Gordon Rees, '"The most miserable scene of universal distress": Irish pamphleteers and the subsistence crisis of the early 1740s', *Studia Hibernica*, 41 (2015), 99–102; Engler et al., 'The Irish famine of 1740–1741', 1169, 1174. **147** *Faulkner's Dublin Journal*, 6 Dec. 1740; *Universal Advertiser*, 5 May 1753.

'publick abuses' in the supply and pricing of food. It was a well-intended but ultimately insufficiently developed strategy. The presumption of officials was that if they could successfully combat forestallers, ingrossers, hoarders, meal-mongers and others, the supply of food was assured, and that there would be no grounds for food rioting. Interventions to this end may have served on occasions, such as the spring of 1753 and 1758, to de-incentivize potential food protesters, but since it was grounded on a misplaced confidence in the efficacy of the existing market system, it did not relieve officials from the responsibility to interpose in a more direct fashion.[148] Thus in the spring of 1746, the mayor and common council of Drogheda responded to the attack on several Scottish vessels taking corn on board by causing 'the several stores in that town to be opened, and the grain [therein] to be sold in small quantities to the poor'.[149] In 1753, in Cork city, the mayor and sheriffs responded to the unsuccessful attempt by the 'mob' to 'force open some cellars' by directing that 'some meal ... was sent to the market house to keep down that article, which, with all other provisions, is at a high rate'; while in October 1765, having previously directed that 133 bags of oatmeal on board a lighter should be 'brought back to be sold at market', the then mayor, Will Parkes, responded to the first sign of unrest prompted by a scarcity of provisions in the city by giving notice that if any 'were shipped for exportation he would "cause the same to be unladen and sold in the public market"'. A year later, 'the mayor, sheriffs and common council' went one better; they ordered 'that a premium of two shillings the quarter [should] be paid on the first 3000 quarters of wheat ... imported from foreign parts'.[150] Waterford Corporation was hardly less active. It responded to the deterioration in conditions in 1757, first by instructing in January that 'the saving on account of entertainments' should be made available to the mayor 'to purchase oatmeal for the use of the poor', and subsequently, in April, by ordering that 60 tons of grain appropriated from a mill near the town was sold at an affordable 1½d. per pottle.[151]

A still more ambitious and structured response was instituted in Belfast in 1756. This was consistent with the order of food protest in that town in that year, but it was also indicative of a greater willingness, once steps had been taken to apprehend the leading offenders, to conceive an ambitious 'scheme for the relief of the poor inhabitants'. Approved at a 'general meeting of the associated inhabitants' on 8 December, it was overseen and administered by a committee of twenty directors, whose number included the earl of Donegall as well as the sovereign and burgesses of the town. The 'scheme' involved dividing the town into 'ten wards or districts', each of which was assigned to two overseers, to whom was delegated the task of identifying those who were in a position to provide

148 See *Pue's Occurrences*, 2 May 1747, 29 July 1758; *Munster Journal*, 19 Nov. 1750; *Universal Advertiser*, 10, 17 Apr. 1753, 2 Sept. 1755. **149** *Dublin Courant*, 25 Mar. 1746. **150** *Universal Advertiser*, 10 Apr. 1753; *Freeman's Journal*, 19 Oct. 1764; Gibson, *City of Cork*, ii, 211; Tuckey's *Cork remembrancer*, pp 144, 146. **151** Minutes of Waterford, Corporation, 13 Jan. 1757 (Waterford Archives, Corporation of Waterford council book); *Pue's Occurrences*, 19 Apr. 1757.

charity, those who 'are only able to support themselves' and those who were 'real and suitable objects of charity'. Since those in the first category, who were assigned to eight classes according to their ability to maintain a monthly payment (ranging from 6*d.* to £1 2*s.* 9*d.*), were expected to provide the funds upon which the scheme depended, the explicit affirmation that existing charitable arrangements would function as normal offered some assurance that the demand would be kept within bounds, but this hardly detracted from the ambition of what was proposed.[152] It was a demonstration of a sophisticated vision of civil society in operation, and it echoed the ambitions signalled by the foundation, four years previously, of the Belfast Charitable Society, and the broader societal and political preparedness to support the deserving poor that was taking shape at this time throughout the country.[153]

This charitable endeavour was reliant on the generosity of a broad range of social groups who conceived of food protest as a spur to action. It can, for example, be perceived in the willingness of merchants such as Mr Lucas at Kinsale to accept that the potatoes taken off a sloop in the harbour 'should be disposed of at the market price'. The efforts of the association of gentry and clergy to provide grain at market price, and to distribute aid to the poor of Navan, county Meath, and its environs in 1756 attests to the involvement of members of the gentry. Meanwhile, local initiatives to discourage the employment of grain in distilling; and the willingness manifest at Youghal in 1751 and 1771 to relax the 'custom' usually levied to 'encourage … potatoes being brought to market' illustrates there was a more general societal acceptance of the merit of relieving those in distress.[154] The underlying empathetic capacity, of which this combination of gestures and actions was a manifestation, was vividly articulated in Belfast at the height of the riots in the summer of 1756 by a body of linen weavers in the town who, having made clear their disapproval of the actions of food protesters, drew attention to 'the distress to which many of the poor [a]re reduced by the cruelty and oppression of the hucksters, regraters and forestallers of the markets'.[155] These expressions of concern were not unmotivated, of course, but they reflected an outlook that caused the Irish Privy Council to embargo the export 'of all manner of corn, grain and meal whatsoever' on 9 November 1756 (reaffirmed on 13 December), and the lord lieutenant to assign a substantial sum (said to be £10,000) to the importation of grain.[156] The authorization by parliament in 1759

---

152 *Belfast News Letter*, 10 Dec. 1756; Bardon, *Belfast: an illustrated history*, p. 33; David Dickson, 'In search of the old Irish poor law' in Rosalind Mitchison and Peter Roebuck (eds), *Economy and society in Scotland and Ireland* (Edinburgh, 1988), p. 154.   **153** Kelly, 'Charitable societies: their genesis and development, 1720–1800', pp 91–8; R.W.M. Strain, *Belfast and its Charitable Society: a study of urban social development* (Oxford, 1961).   **154** *Dublin Weekly Journal*, 4 June 1748; Caulfield (ed.), *Corporation book of Kinsale*, pp 280–1; Magennis, 'Food scarcity in 1756–57', pp 201–2; Caulfield (ed.), *Corporation book of Youghal*, pp 453, 482.   **155** *Belfast News Letter*, 27 Aug. 1756.   **156** Kelly and Lyons (eds), *The proclamations of Ireland*, iii, 463–5; Magennis, 'Food scarcity in 1756–57', p. 204. In addition, the lord lieutenant reputedly advanced £500 in 1766 to permit the Corporation of Kinsale purchase provisions: Caulfield (ed.), *Corporation book of Kinsale*, p. 279;

of a bounty scheme to encourage the transportation of grain from the provinces to Dublin was another significant intervention. It did not, as has been claimed, banish 'the fear of food riots in the capital', but it diminished both their frequency and their severity for several decades.[157]

Yet there was a limit to the willingness of parliament to act to ensure a ready supply of food, and, by extension, to pursue policies aimed at discouraging food protest. This was made clear in 1765 when a protest was entered in the House of Lords against an amendment introduced into an Irish bill at the British council board that would have allowed the British as well as the Irish Privy Councils to suspend relevant provisions in a measure appertaining to the exportation of corn.[158] Difficulties were also encountered in securing parliamentary authorization for a network of houses of industry because of the additional costs that grand juries would incur and, once the legislation was agreed in 1774, in securing its implementation though the establishment of such a network was integral to the capacity of the state to respond to the distress of which food protest was another manifestation.[159]

If the elaboration of a response to food protest in the quarter century between the famine of 1740–1 and the mid-1760s is best characterized as *ad hoc*, it also explains why relief was not a visible feature of the response to the pattern of low-intensity food protest that prevailed between the 1766 and 1783–4 subsistence crises. This is not to suggest that the steps that were taken in response were without effect. Limerick in 1772 is a case in point. Following the dramatic attack in May 1772, the Lock Mills Company not only advertised flour and meal for sale at competitive prices but also affirmed its standing commitment 'never ... [to] manufacture any oatmeal for sale' and undertook not 'to send any more of our stocks to Dublin, or to any place whatsoever from this city, whilst any scarcity continues'. Further, the mayor, George Roche, issued a proclamation in October affirming his resolve to enforce the 1738 regulation which stipulated that potatoes at market must be sold by 'weight and not by measure or in any other way'.[160] Six years later, in 1778, when Dublin teetered on the edge of potentially serious unrest, the generous support for a subscription initiated at 'a very numerous meeting of ... inhabitants' and the appointment of a committee 'to purchase and distribute provisions' proved helpful to 'the poor manufacturers in the Liberty', who numbered an estimated 10,000 and who 'were nearly perishing for want of ...; the necessaries of life'.[161] One cannot conclude that this was the dom-

above, p. 39.   **157** *An act for better supplying the city of Dublin with corn and flour*: 31 George II, chap. 3; Dickson, 'In search of the old Irish poor law', p. 154.   **158** *A collection of protests of the Lords of Ireland* (Dublin, 1772), pp 101–7; James Kelly, *Poynings' Law and the making of law in Ireland, 1660–1800* (Dublin, 2007), p. 303.   **159** See James Kelly, 'Defending the established order: Richard Woodward, bishop of Cloyne (1726–94)' in James Kelly et al. (eds), *Parliament and politics in seventeenth- and eighteenth-century Ireland* (Dublin, 2009), pp 150–4; Cousins, 'The Irish parliament and the relief of the poor: the 1772 legislation establishing houses of industry', pp 95–115.   **160** *Limerick Chronicle*, 14 May, 29 Oct. 1772; 11 George II, chap.11.   **161** *Dublin Evening Journal*, 12, 14 May 1778.

inant sentiment, however. Reports of individuals dying on the streets of Dublin in 1772 'for want of the common necessaries of life' encouraged a sympathetic response, but there were sceptics.[162]

One theme raised during these years was that of 'artificial' (as opposed to 'real') scarcity, and the suggestion that some food protest was contrived. Concerns expressed in 1772 that unregulated exportation might create the illusion of scarcity were intensified a decade later, as the implications of 'the badness of our harvest' elicited some worried commentary to the effect that 'farmers' might 'keep up their corn in expectation of … an exorbitant price'.[163] Others, who acknowledged the order of the difficulty of ensuring an affordable supply of food applauded the ongoing, if only ever partially successful, efforts by local officials to combat fore-stalling, fraud, inflated pricing and other enduring and inventive abuses.[164] They concurred with the commentator from Kilkenny, who was prompted by the inter-ception of carts carrying oatmeal in 1778, to observe that 'the people seldom rise without cause'.[165] They certainly had cause in the summer of 1783, when a sharp rise in food prices prompted the authorities to issue a proclamation discouraging exportation and incentivizing importation. Though the lord lieutenant was obliged to justify this strategy, because it necessitated the temporary suspension of the 1782 corn act which had been introduced to encourage grain exports, others con-cluded that both this action and the 'compact' agreed by the bakers and magis-trates of the city of Dublin to protect the assize of bread from the effects of high grain prices were well judged and helpful.[166] There was plenty of protest, both politically and economically motivated, in favour of protective duties; there was also food rioting in various southern and midlands towns, but Dublin remained free of disturbances then and during the difficult winter of 1783–4 when the House of Industry and various parish committees oversaw a system of indoor and outdoor relief, comparable to, but on a larger scale, than that delivered in Belfast in 1756.[167] The response elsewhere was more variegated. The activities of the Belfast Charitable Society was helpful in defusing tension in that city; the decision of Cork Corporation on 12 February 1784 to assign £500 for the purchase and sale of oatmeal at cost was also significant since the absence of comparable measures elsewhere in Munster unleashed the traditional fears that fuelled food rioting in Carrick-on-Suir, Waterford, Kinsale, Clonmel and Youghal.[168]

If, as has been argued, the combined impact of state intervention and local relief kept excess mortality within bounds in 1783–4, it also helped to ensure

162 *Limerick Chronicle*, 19 Nov. 1772.   163 *Hibernian Chronicle*, 23 May 1778, 4 Nov. 1782. 164 *Limerick Chronicle*, 18 May, 13 Aug. 1772; *Independent Journal*, 6 Apr. 1775; *Hibernian Morning Post*, 27 Apr. 1775; *Dublin Evening Journal*, 19 Feb., 7 May 1778.   165 *Finn's Leinster Journal*, 23 May 1778.   166 Kelly, 'Scarcity and poor relief in eighteenth-century Ireland', pp 49–50; Kelly and Lyons (eds), *The proclamations of Ireland*, iv, 372–3; *Volunteer Journal* (Cork), 15 May, 30 June 1783; *Dublin Evening Post*. 17 June, 19 Aug. 1783.   167 Kelly, 'Scarcity and poor relief in eigh-teenth-century Ireland', pp 56–60.   168 Caulfield, (ed.), *Corporation book of … Cork*, p. 989; Kelly, 'Scarcity and poor relief in eighteenth-century Ireland', pp 58–9; *Freeman's Journal*, 14 Feb., 22 Mar. 1784; *Volunteer Journal* (Dublin), 22 Mar. 1784; above, pp 43–4.

there were fewer food riots during this two-phase crisis than might otherwise have been the case. The capacity of this dual approach was further demonstrated in the early 1790s, for though food rioting was not impelled then by subsistence crisis or by famine, the localized nature of protest demanded more of the municipal authorities. Indeed, by comparison with 1783–4, when the Privy Council intervened twice, and in 1789 when a precautionary embargo was instituted, the lord lieutenant and council were more reserved.[169] This was most obvious in the early winter of 1792 when, following major riots in Cork and Bandon, Cork Corporation applied 'to government for an embargo on wheat, oats, flour, oatmeal and potatoes'. Unwilling to be seen to take the matter other than seriously (though his 'cabinet' of closest advisors 'were generally of opinion that it was unnecessary'), the lord lieutenant, the earl of Westmorland, chose to bring the matter to the Privy Council, but the conviction that there was 'enough corn' in the country ensured that an embargo was not imposed.[170] Approximately a year-and-a-half later, in April 1794, when Dublin city was in the throes of serious food protest, the Privy Council again rejected an application, this time from Dublin Corporation, 'for the importation of British and foreign wheat', for though the bounties provided by parliament on the land carriage of grain to Dublin were not working as desired at that moment, the prices nationally were not sufficiently elevated to justify suspending the law prescribing importation when the domestic price was less than 34s. a barrel.[171]

In the absence of government relief, the onus lay with the municipalities, and some at least of those with a tradition of food protest identified locally appropriate solutions. These varied in approach and emphasis, but they shared certain common foci. The public subscription was now a favoured strategy. In Waterford, for example, it was initiated in November 1792 at a meeting of 'merchants and inhabitants' convened by the mayor, and it proved an efficient means of 'furnishing provisions at a moderate rate for the poor of that city'. In Cork, the Corporation gave an equivalent initiative its *imprimatur* by assigning one hundred pounds 'in aid of the collection for the relief of the poor' and a further hundred pounds for the purchase of coals and the prevention of forestalling. Parallel efforts in both cities to persuade merchants not to export provisions also served to exert a downwards pressure on prices, and, effectively, to enable the two locations to negotiate what seemed destined at the outset to be a particularly trying winter.[172]

169 Kelly and Lyons (eds), *The proclamations of Ireland*, iv, 372–3, 387–8, 483; Northington to Sydney, 26 Jan. 1784 (Yale University, Beinecke Library, Osborn Collection, Northington letterbook, ff 104–5); Trumbull to Alex and James Robertson, 19 Aug. 1789 (New York Public Library, Trumbull papers, letterbook 1). 170 Westmorland to [ ], 28 Nov. 1792 (NLI, Lords lieutenant union correspondence, MS 886 ff 17–19); *Clonmel Gazette*, 24 Nov., 1 Dec. 1792; *Hibernian Journal*, 28 Nov. 1792; *Dublin Chronicle*, 1 Dec. 1792; *Freeman's Journal*, 4 Dec. 1792. 171 *Hibernian Journal*, 11 Apr. 1794; Gilbert (ed.), *Calendar of ancient records of Dublin*, xiv, 351–2. 172 *Dublin Chronicle*, 17 Nov. 1792; Burtchaell, 'The *Waterford Herald* for 1792–3', p. 12; *Cork Gazette*, 17 Nov. 1792; Dickson, *Old world colony*, p. 384; Caulfield (ed.), *Corporation book of Cork*, p. 1082; *Hibernian Journal*, 28 Nov. 1792.

In Dublin, meanwhile, the economic challenges that served to make the early 1790s such difficult years prompted a more familiar regulatory response building on the initiatives taken in the late 1780s when the opening of Smithfield market and the Cornmarket was signalled 'by [the] ring of a bell'. Its purpose was 'to preclude forestallers', while bakers who sold bread 'materially deficient in weight' were threatened with public shaming by having their names published.[173] Another response was to police fraud. This was embarked upon in the summer of 1791 by the 'market juries of the Liberties of St Sepulchre and Donore', which seized underweight bread.[174] The exacerbation of the plight of the poor and marginalized in the years that followed elicited calls for officials to enforce the regulations against forestallers, regraters, salesmasters, butchers, bakers, coal-factors and others, but there was no relaxation of the expressions of disapproval of food rioting. Responding in 1794 to 'a marauding excursion' by 'a party of manufacturers' in the Liberties, the *Dublin Morning Post* observed unequivocally that 'no circumstances can justify so flagrant a violation of the laws as this'.[175] These views did not impress the then chief secretary, Thomas Pelham, who ensured that berths were secured in March 1796 to enable the potato boats in Dublin Bay to land their cargo, but while the majority of the respectable remained disposed to conclude that those who were hungry were deserving of support there was a diminishing tolerance of food rioting in Dublin at least. This encouraged different responses. Whereas the lord mayor of Dublin, Richard Montcrieffe, issued a proclamation in May 1795 advising would-be protestors that food rioting was a capital crime, the mayor of Waterford, James Moore, responded to the forcible entry of the stores of Messrs Cherry and Sykes and the boarding of two ships in Waterford harbour in 1784 by authorizing a 'subscription' to supply oatmeal 'at a reasonable rate' to 'the lower class of the people'.[176]

The response of mayor Montcrieffe in 1795 notwithstanding, it was not possible for the metropolitan authorities to pursue a primarily law and order approach in 1799–1801. Indeed, the approval by the Privy Council of six proclamations in the three-month period spanning 30 December 1800 to 17 March 1801 prohibiting the use of grain in making alcohol, urging economy in the consumption of corn, grain and potatoes, admitting flour duty free, and facilitating the importation of rice and Indian corn constituted an unprecedented demonstration of the recognition by the national authorities that they were bounden to intervene.[177] This set the tone, and metropolitan officials sought to complement these macroeconomic initiatives by working energetically 'to prevent the impositions and extortions of forestallers', and to detect and penalize fraud by intercepting underweight bread. This did not mean they neglected to remind the public that food rioting was a capital offence, which they did in March 1800.[178]

173 *Ramsey's Waterford Chronicle*, 16 Oct. 1787.   174 *Hibernian Journal*, 22 July 1791. 175 *Freeman's Journal*, 13 June 1793; *Dublin Morning Post*, 3 Apr. 1794.   176 *Clonmel Gazette*, 9 Apr. 1794; *Freeman's Journal*, 30 May 1795.   177 Kelly and Lyons (eds), *The proclamations of Ireland*, v, 318–23; *Ennis Chronicle*, 26 Jan. 1801.   178 *Freeman's Journal*, 30 May 1799, 20 Mar.,

However, when the 1799–1801 crisis was at its deepest during the winter of 1800–1, Dublin followed Waterford, Limerick, Cork, Ennis and Drogheda in inaugurating a subscription to raise funds for the relief of the poor.[179]

Though by then an acknowledged feature of famine and poor relief across the British Isles, subscriptions to raise funds for the provision of cash payments and subsidised foodstuffs to those in need were particularly closely identified with food protest. The origins of such initiatives in the desire manifest at Cork in 1729 to discourage food protest assumed a more structured form with the inauguration of the Mansion House Committee also in Cork in 1801. Established 'for the purpose of devising a plan to enable the lower orders of people to meet the high prices of the market', the committee sought to make it known to those who were tempted to protest 'that it is only by observing a peaceable line of conduct, they can expect to participate in the relief which their fellow citizens are anxious to procure for them'. And lest there was any ambiguity, the mayor, Philip Allen, reinforced this message with a 'very spirited proclamation' that included the relevant text from the 1784 act.[180] His was not a lone voice, moreover. The observation in the *Cork Advertizer* of 28 February 1801, when 'every public symptom of discontent among the lower classes in this city' had eased, that violence would only 'increase ten-fold the hardships of their situation', echoed the mayoral message, and represented a further step on the road towards a situation wherein, instead of incentivizing the respectable to provide relief, officials signalled that relief would not be forthcoming until protest had ceased.[181] This was not yet the accepted position, but the enunciation of sentiments to this effect signalled that the sympathy for food protesters expressed in the 1790s and earlier had begun to ebb away. This change in attitude revealed itself in various ways. On the face of it, the communication conveyed on 11 March 1801 from Dublin Castle to the mayors of towns where subscriptions had been raised that the lord lieutenant (the benign Marquis Cornwallis) 'much approves of the charitable exertions which have been made in Cork city, for relieving the distresses of the poor', and that he would authorize an additional sum, 'not exceeding a third of the subscription', to be added to the amount raised locally, might have seemed an endorsement of the existing approach whereas it echoed the emerging attitude that it was poverty and not food protest that merited redress.[182]

This perception fuelled criticism of food protest in the early nineteenth century and, indeed, of the various responses and solutions it spawned. Most of the strictures voiced echoed those that were already in the public domain, but they now possessed more purchase. It is noteworthy, for example, that the disapprobation expressed by a number of magistrates of the 'ill-disposed and misguided persons' who intercepted and robbed cars 'conveying meal and other articles through the town' of Antrim in 1812 was endorsed by the *Belfast News Letter*.

21 Oct. 1800.   **179** *Cork Advertizer*, 27 Dec. 1800, 26 Feb. 1801; Ó Dalaigh, *Corporation book of Ennis*, pp 314–15; *Ennis Chronicle*, 26 Mar. 1801.   **180** *Cork Advertizer*, 24, 26 Feb. 1801; above, pp 182–3.   **181** *Cork Advertizer*, 26, 28 Feb., 3 Mar., 26 Apr. 1801.   **182** *Ennis Chronicle*, 26 Mar. 1801.

The paper condemned 'the giddy and thoughtless multitude who engage in these turbulent measures', and, having called upon the poor 'to behave peaceably', appealed to the paternalist sensibility implicit in so much commentary on poverty by lauding the 'benevolent intentions of the rich to relieve the distresses of the industrious poor'. Subscriptions to provide food 'gratis' or 'at a rate much below the market price' were specifically instanced as a demonstration of this benevolence in action and pointedly contrasted with the tendency of food rioters 'to destroy the very provisions which are so essentially necessary'.[183] The equally familiar, and equally exaggerated criticism that food protest generated 'artificial scarcity' by dissuading 'farmers from bringing provisions' to market was also invoked in support of the argument that rioting was a wholly inappropriate response to the interrelated problems of poverty, unemployment and hunger that the more sophisticated analysis of Ireland's deepening economic travails now encouraged, and that over time achieved ascendancy in the public sphere.[184]

The commentary that accompanied the account of the major food riot that took place in Limerick in 1840 articulated this increasingly negative outlook with particular lucidity:

> We cannot but express, in the strongest terms, our disapprobation of the conduct of the people in this respect, as we deplore the cause that led to it. To be sure low wages, and in many cases, no employment a tall [*sic*], [and the] high price of provisions, are powerful incentives to disorganise society; but we must say, and we tell the people, that, though they be justified in uniting to express their dissent from the shameful practice of the unwarrantable rise of provisions brought about by schemers; yet, to proceed to acts of violence is not the best way to obviate their difficulties. We frequently forewarned that the nefarious practice of forestalling would tend to this end. Prompt measures should have been, 'ere now, put in force, and followed up by the civic authorities, to keep the market prices of provisions within the reach of the working classes.[185]

The confidence in the capacity of the market when it was not distorted by self-interest and weak regulation, implicit in this reaction to a major urban food protest, was not new of course. It echoed similar sentiments expressed at different points in the eighteenth century. However, it now enjoyed increasing intellectual ascendancy. This is detectible in the readiness in 1817 of William Parnell, the author and liberal MP for county Wicklow, to criticize the use of subscriptions to make foodstuffs available 'at a reduced price', and to do so 'too early'. Though he required no persuading that 'properly directed' relief 'would prevent most of the evils of extreme scarcity', Parnell insisted that it was in the self-inter-

183 *Belfast News Letter*, 10 July 1812.   **184** *Freeman's Journal*, 11 Feb. 1817; R.D. Collison Black, *Economic thought and the Irish question, 1817–1870* (Cambridge, 1960).   **185** Lee, 'The food riots of 1830 and 1840', p. 64, quoting the *Limerick Reporter and Tipperary Vindicator*, 2 June 1840.

est of the 'lower orders' to 'retain as long as possible the valuable habit of look-ing to their own industry to provide against want':

> It is always advisable to delay giving charitable assistance as long as pos-sible, since every interference which may accustom the labouring classes to look for support to any means but their own industry and economy, diminishes their providence and in some degree degrades their character. Experience proves that where the labouring classes are most in the habit of receiving charitable assistance, they exert themselves less; and their cir-cumstances are proportionably worse, since benevolence can never supply the means of subsistence so steadily as is done by individual industry and economy. Thence it follows that charitable contributions, though highly creditable to the feelings of the rich, must be regarded ultimately as an evil to the lower orders, and should be had recourse to very tardily, except in an extreme case of scarcity like the present.[186]

Parnell's concluding additional contention that 'assistance should proceed from private individuals rather than from government' was in keeping with the indi-vidual self-reliance he and the emerging liberal political and economic consensus favoured.[187] But the fact that one of the more thoughtful voices of Irish liberal-ism ventured such a viewpoint is testament to the shift in opinion that had taken place since the 1790s, and to the intellectual appeal of the self-reliance classical liberalism fostered.

Yet William Parnell's positive reference to the 'zeal displayed by the upper ranks in relieving the distresses of the necessitous' in 1817 indicates that he did not object either in principle or in practice to the use of subscriptions to garner money for distribution in cash or in kind to those in need, and the number and scale of the subscriptions that were launched at parish, county and national level in 1816–17 attest to its continuing strength as a means of galvanizing relief.[188] Such initiatives were not immune to criticism however. Indeed, it is observable that the endorsement of 'the late handsome collection in the city of Cork for the relief of the poor' published in the *Cork Advertizer* in May 1812 was conditional, since its author contended that the money raised would be best employed if it was assigned, not to the traditional purpose of subsidizing the purchase of provisions, but in sup-porting the establishment of 'soup houses', which were, he contended, 'one of the most effectual' means 'of affording subsistence to a greater number of people'.[189] This writer was, in other words, at one with the expanding chorus of voices advo-cating a broader policy response to poor relief than that articulated by those who were spurred into action by the activities of food protesters.

186 William Parnell, 'Hints towards relieving the present scarcity' in *Freeman's Journal*, 19 June 1817.   187 Parnell, 'Hints towards relieving the present scarcity'.   188 Ibid.; *Freeman's Journal*, 3, 7, 9, 10, 14, 21, 31 Dec. 1816, 7 Dec. 1817; *Ramsey's Waterford Chronicle*, 8 Nov. 1817.   189 *Cork Advertizer*, 7 May 1812.

Another suggestion regarded with increased favour as a solution to distress was a scheme of public works, which dovetailed with the appreciating realization that under- and unemployment was a root cause of food protest. One may, in this context, instance the call issued in Galway in 1822 for a public works programme, which both mirrored the increased expectations the public had of government and the dawning realization of subscription committees that, useful though they might be in the short term, they provided no more than a temporary solution to the indivisible problems of which food protest was merely a symptom – poverty, unemployment and access to food.[190] The fact that the Mansion House, or General Poor Fund Committee to give it its correct title, which raised £10,000 in short order in Dublin in the winter of 1816–17, advocated a more structured approach to relief – specifically 'procuring employment for the poor' – was indicative.[191] Moreover, the Mansion House Committee was not a lone voice. The committee established in Waterford to 'solicit subscriptions and to consider the best mode of affording relief to the poor' in that city was also concerned to encourage employment, while its Cork equivalent, the Poor Fund Committee, sought to promote the domestic production and wearing of clothing 'of Cork manufacture'. Significantly, the Irish chief secretary, Robert Peel, was won over. In June 1817, when food rioting was endemic, he made it known to the then lord lieutenant, Earl Whitworth, that should it be necessary he (Peel) would introduce legislation empowering a relief 'commission' to authorize 'the employment of persons at low wages ... on the roads or in other measures'. The ratification in 1817 of the poor employment act was thus an important demonstration of intent, though the distribution of 'food and fuel' trumped this object in the short term.[192] Moreover, the fact that the initiation of relief preceded food protest in Drogheda, Dublin and Cork was indicative of the declining importance of food protest as a stimulus of relief.[193]

Its medium to long-term impact notwithstanding, the changing attitude towards food protest detectible in the early nineteenth century did not, as the case of Waterford in 1817 attests, cause a dramatic shift in the response either to food rioting or in the relief that was provided at those moments of acute distress when food prices, the demand for access to food, and food rioting invariably peaked. For example, subscriptions were raised and administered in an essentially traditional way at Lurgan in 1808, and in Cork, Waterford and Galway in 1812 in order to

---

190 *Freeman's Journal*, 9 May 1822. Ireland, in this respect, mirrored England where the emphasis was also on employment as a form of poor relief: Jones, 'Swing, Speenhamland and rural social relations', p. 278, and the references there cited.   191 *Freeman's Journal*, 8, 15 Jan. 1817; O'Neill, 'Clare and Irish poverty, 1815–1851', pp 12–13.   192 57 George III, chap. 34: the object of the act was limited; its purpose was 'to authorise the issue of exchequer bills and the advance of money out of the Consolidated Fund, to a limited amount, for the carrying on of public works and fisheries in the United Kingdom and Employment of the Poor in Great Britain', but it set a precedent that culminated, fourteen years later, in the Board of Works.   193 *Freeman's Journal*, 14, 16, 21, 22 Jan. 1817; Peel to Whitworth, 13 June 1817, quoted in O'Neill, 'Clare and Irish poverty, 1815–1851', p. 12.

make staple foodstuffs available to the 'labouring poor' at an affordable price.[194] Subscriptions were also raised in 1817 at Galway, Waterford, Cork and Limerick; in 1822 at Galway and Skibbereen, and in the barony of Inchiquin, county Clare, while the initiation of subscriptions in response to major food riots in Limerick in 1830 and 1840, and in Ennis and Galway in 1842 captured its enduring usefulness as a means of raising and distributing money (£2,343 was raised in Limerick in 1830) in urban spaces for as long as food protest endured.[195] Other familiar strategies also continued; the decision of a merchant at Athlone to sell 'potatoes to the poor people at 4*d.* per stone' in 1817 indicated that the tradition of mercantile philanthropy also persisted, and that the owners of some stores and retail outlets still responded to attacks on their premises by making their contents available at a reduced price.[196] However, its diminished visibility suggests it occupied a less prominent role then than it had previously. If so, this trend was accented by the shift in the geographical focus of food protest from the towns on the eastern and southern seaboards inland and towards the west where there was less of a tradition both of organized relief and of food protest.

The role of the government is appropriately more complex. As the promulgation in June 1817 of a proclamation calling on members of the elite not to consume potatoes and to reduce their consumption of oats attests, the Irish Privy Council maintained the tradition, which can be traced back to the embargo it instituted in 1709 prohibiting the exportation of grain and meal, of seeking to pre-empt food protest by maintaining the domestic supply of food.[197] It emulated the British Privy Council, which approved prohibitions on grain exportation on no fewer than 23 occasions between 1698 and 1800.[198] The problem, in Ireland at least, was that this can hardly be described as other than moderately successful. Nevertheless, the involvement of government expanded greatly in the early nineteenth century. The assignment by parliament in 1817 of £150,000 for the relief of Irish distress, and Sir Robert Peel's willingness to 'assist ... local subscriptions with advances from public funds' was an important pointer in that respect.[199]

The cost of responding to the 1822 famine was still larger, in keeping with the greater severity of the crisis. Of the £300,000 voted by parliament, an estimated £175,000 was dispensed to local relief committees, and a programme of public works was inaugurated commensurate with the increasing role government assumed in the funding of relief as the scale and visibility of Irish poverty mounted.[200] This did not immunize the government against criticism from the

194 Cunningham, 'Popular protest and a "moral economy"', pp 31, 36; Cunningham, *Galway, 1790–1814*, p. 86; *Cork Advertizer*, 7 May 1812. **195** Cunningham, 'Popular protest and a "moral economy"', pp 40, 42; Cunningham, *Galway, 1790–1814*, pp 86–7, 89, 91; O'Connor, *Labour history of Waterford*, p. 18; *Freeman's Journal*, 26 Apr., 9, 15 May, 19 June 1822; Lee, The food riots of 1830 and 1840', pp 59, 65; Power, *A history of Clarecastle*, p. 416. **196** Cunningham, 'Popular protest and a "moral economy"', p. 40. **197** Kelly and Lyons (eds), *The proclamations of Ireland*, ii, 623–4, v, 536. **198** Bohstedt, 'The moral economy and the discipline of historical context', 273. **199** Cunningham, 'Popular protest and a "moral economy"', p. 42; O'Neill, 'Clare and Irish poverty, 1815–1851', 11–12. **200** McNamara, 'This wretched people: the famine of 1822', pp

likes of Nathaniel, second earl of Leitrim, who perceived that they were 'very remiss' in not doing more; it was Leitrim's perception then that it was incumbent on government to intervene as landlords' rents were so depleted they were ill-positioned to assist their own poor.[201]

The increasing expectation that landowners harboured of government was still more in evidence in 1830–1, when Dominick Browne, the MP for county Mayo, requested the advancement of £200,000 'to employ the needy on public works', and the chancellor of the exchequer was sharply criticized when he stipulated that the £50,000 proposed 'for purposes of local and temporary relief' should be repaid.[202] Despite this, expectations remained high, and they were manifested once more in 1837 when 'the alarming state of distress among the lower orders' in Limerick prompted further calls for public 'employments' in order to quieten 'the apprehensions of the citizens, and allaying the present excited state of the poorer classes'.[203] The advancement of this proposition in this manner at this time did not imply that the country's landed and urban elites sought to withdraw from the provision of relief. The establishment of a committee at Ennis in 1831 'for the purpose of devising the means of relief for the distressed portion of the people of our county [of Clare]'; the launch of a public subscription in Limerick in 1840 to purchase potatoes from Scotland; in Galway, also in 1840, to provide potatoes at a reduced price; in Ennis in 1842 to provide employment, and in Galway, also in 1842, to enable a 'Committee of Thirteen' to facilitate access to provisions at a more affordable price, attest to the importance of local initiatives, subscriptions particularly, as a means of gathering money and harnessing local public spiritedness.[204] But there was a growing realization too that the continuing deterioration in denominational relations, which had the effect of encouraging 'many Protestant families … to emigrate', diminished the pool of potential philanthropists.[205]

The consequences of this were not lost on the higher echelons of the Irish administration during the Great Famine. Acknowledging the seriousness of the impact of the destruction of the potato crop and the obligation to provide 'employment and food' for the poor in the wake of the spate of food riots in April 1846, the under-secretary, Thomas Redington, advocated the establishment of relief committees composed of those 'possessed of property' on the grounds that it was 'their duty … to make exertions to provide against the evil [of distress] and [to] contribute in proportion to their means'.[206] On foot of this admo-

20–3; O'Neill, 'Clare and Irish poverty, 1815–1851', 15–18; *Transactions of the central relief committee of the Society of Friends during the Famine in Ireland in 1846 and 1847* (London, 1852), p. 26. **201** Leitrim to Cooper, 25 May 1822 (NLI, Killadoon papers, MS 36064/12). **202** *Chute's Western Herald*, 24 Feb. 1832; *Kerry Evening Post*, 6 Apr. 1831. In practice, £40,000 was advanced by government: *Transactions of the … Society of Friends*, p. 29. **203** *Freeman's Journal*, 12 June 1837. **204** *Kerry Evening Post*, 16 Apr. 1831; Lee, 'The food riots of 1830 and 1840', p. 65; Power, *A history of Clarecastle*, p. 417; Cunningham, *Galway, 1790–1814*, pp 90, 91–2. **205** See *Kerry Evening Post*, 12 April 1831, which announced the departure of Richard John Stacpoole of Edenvale, county Clare. **206** Redington to Donoughmore, 15 Apr., Redington to Glengall, 16 Apr. 1846, Draft response to Harvey to Bessborough, post 16 Apr. 1846 (NAI, OP: Tipperary, 1846/27/8945, 8989, 9091).

nition, and the recognition that it was in their interest to do so, relief commit-tees were established in Clonmel, Carrick-on-Suir and Cashel in the South Riding of county Tipperary, while the animation of a similar body in Tullamore, where 'the labouring classes' suffered 'in silence', suggests that this pattern was emulated elsewhere. In practice, the committees were of varying effectiveness. The Clonmel committee, which was operational within days, perambulated the town 'raising subscriptions' (totalling £1200), and adopting measures 'for giving the poor employment'. In Carrick-on-Suir, '300 poor' were reported 'employed' on 17 April, and, though it took longer, a comparably positive report was forth-coming from Cashel a fortnight later.[207]

It is not possible to assay precisely the effectiveness of such initiatives, but the decline in food protest in the summer of 1846 suggests that they dovetailed with the state's public work schemes, and the private importation of maize, to assist the populace to negotiate the summer months. The problem, once the potato failed again in 1846, was that the available relief was insufficient to calm popular fears. Some landlords responded by expanding their relief initiatives. But as the attack on Lord Stuart de Decies in county Waterford and the assault of Hugh Hickman in county Clare indicated, this did not secure landowners against violence, with the result that sentiment oscillated within their ranks between those who perceived that this was 'the time for charity' and those who appre-hended 'an universal practical rebellion of starvation against property' that would cause 'the gentry [to] abandon their houses and seek protection elsewhere'.[208] As a result, further subscriptions were initiated by relief committees in the autumn of 1846.[209] The problem now was that food protest was (as it had seldom previ-ously been) a 'rebellion of the belly', and that the number of people that were 'starving' so far exceeded what individuals and local interests could do to relieve the needy that attention focussed on the public works schemes and the increas-ingly clamorous calls that the daily stipend was increased in order to keep pace with prices.[210] Few relief committees were in any position to comply, but the effort devoted to the cause, and the concentration on public works were mani-festations of the fact that the focus had shifted inexorably and irreversibly during the winter of 1846–7 to state-mediated relief. It was a logical consequence of the fact that the government alone (as Daniel O'Connell correctly pointed out) pos-sessed the resources required to rise to the challenge. It was not the sole provider of relief, of course, then or thereafter, but the complex of community interests that had traditionally responded to the call for relief implicit in many (but not

207 Redmond to Pennefeather, 17 Apr., RM to Pennefeather, 16, 24 Apr., James [ ] to [Redington], 30 Apr. 1846 (NAI, OP: Tipperary, 1846/27/9349, 9113, 10203, 10735); *Cork Examiner*, 20 Apr. 1846; *Freeman's Journal*, 30 Apr. 1846.   208 *Freeman's Journal*, 19 Oct. 1846; Bagwell to [Redington], 23 Apr., Kenny to Redington, 21 Oct. 1846 (NAI, OP: Clare, 1846/5/10185, 28843). 209 *Nenagh Guardian*, 7 Oct. 1846; *Freeman's Journal*, 28 Sept., 8, 9, 15 Oct. 1846; *Nation*, 10 Oct. 1846 refers to subscriptions at Youghal, Ardmore, Newport and Galway.   210 *Freeman's Journal*, 6, 16 Oct. 1846, 6 Jan. 1847; Pollock to [Redington], 4 Oct. 1846 (NAI, OP: Tipperary, 1846/27/26769).

all) food riots was no longer in a position to mount a response capable of redressing the problem.

This left the onus squarely on the state, and, as events were to reveal, its preoccupation with cost, and its disdain both for Irish poverty and the Irish landed elite, ensured it failed badly to rise to the greatest relief challenge in Irish history.[211] The death of 885,000 people is a grim testament to its deficiencies, but it was not as if the 'old Irish poor law', which had functioned for more than a century and which depended in times of difficulty on the combination of self-help that was food rioting and relief from within the community, could have coped either.[212] The Great Famine not just posed a challenge of an order beyond the capacity of relief from whatever quarter it came; it exposed and shattered what remained of the communitarian reciprocity upon which food protest relied. Perceived from this vantage point, the unprecedented scale of the food protest identifiable of 1846–7 constituted the final desperate kick of a unique form of protest that required a particular set of circumstances to function effectively.

211 Kinealy, *This great calamity*, passim; Peter Gray, *Famine, land, and politics: British government and Irish society, 1843–1850* (Dublin, 1999); K. Theodore Hoppen, *Governing Hibernia: British politicians and Ireland, 1800–1921* (Oxford, 2016), chapter 5: Oliver McDonagh, *The emancipist: Daniel O'Connell, 1830–1847* (London, [1989]), pp 312–13.   212 Dickson, 'In search of the old Irish poor law', pp 149–59; Cormac Ó Gráda and Phelim P. Boyle, 'Fertility trends, excess mortality, and the Great Irish Famine', *Demography*, 23:4 (1986), 543–62.

Was there an Irish 'moral economy'?

INTRODUCTION

The identification of an active tradition of food protest means it is no longer possible to sustain the conclusion that 'in Ireland food riots did not "work" … because there was no political space (as in England) within which the plebs could exert pressure on their rulers'.[1] Indeed, one could contend that Ireland sustained a pattern of food rioting comparable to that of England and France since, like the latter jurisdictions, 'the basic contours of the food riot remained in place for more than a century'.[2] A number of caveats can be entered, however, first, because one cannot simply conclude that the way in which food protest was pursued in Ireland conforms to the model of 'the communal consensus proponents', which is concerned with how effective food riots were in rallying 'public collective agreement … in the face of changing structures within preindustrial society', since Ireland (unlike England and France) did not experience an industrial revolution. Second, since food protest was pursued for far longer in the latter jurisdictions than it was in Ireland, it may be that it did not penetrate as deeply spatially and socially. In his comprehensive study of food rioting in England, John Bohstedt has tracked the 'genesis' of 'provision politics' to the late sixteenth century; Buchanan Sharp and others have identified a pattern of protest in England, 'displaying many of the characteristic of later disturbances', still earlier.[3] The origins and evolution of food protest in France is more opaque, but it may have followed a comparable trajectory until a point was arrived at in the mid-seventeenth century when 'the particular behaviour associated with *taxation populaire*' assumed a recognizably modern form.[4]

Viewed from a purely statistical perspective it is evident that food protest was pursued more actively in France and England than it was in Ireland until the Great Famine. Jean Nicolas has calculated that food rioting was the second-most popular form of protest (behind tax riots) in France between the conclusion of

---

1 Thompson, 'The moral economy reviewed', p. 296. 2 Bouton, *The flour war*, pp 22–4. The quotes are from p. 23. 3 Sharp, 'The food riots of 1347 and the medieval moral economy' in Randall and Charlesworth (eds), *Moral economy and popular protest*, chapter 2; Buchanan Sharp, *Famine and scarcity in late medieval and early modern England: the regulation of grain marketing, 1256–1631* (Cambridge, 2016), chapters 3, 5, 8; Bohstedt, *The politics of provisions*, pp 21, 23; Bohstedt, 'The moral economy and the discipline of historical context', 276–7; Wood, *Riot and popular politics in early modern England*, pp 95–100. 4 Bouton, *The flour war*, p. 6; Bouton, 'Provisioning, power and popular protest …', pp 80–4.

the Fronde (1653) and the outbreak of the French Revolution (1789), accounting for 17.6 per cent (1,497) of locatable riots (8,528).[5] Since there were 317 incidents in the Paris basin alone in the space of three weeks during the 'flour war' of 1775, these figures are not unanticipated though much depends on how they are categorized. One cannot pronounce definitively that France was more prone to food protest than England, though John Bohstedt's comprehensive 'sample' ('700 plus') is less than half the size of that assembled by Nicolas.[6] One can certainly enter a caution with respect to the tabulated samples of incidents located for Ireland for the period 1710–1845 on the grounds that one is seeking to establish a temporal perspective from a serendipitous corpus of reports. But because individual English episodes were capable of generating more than a hundred incidents – 105 in 1756–7, 131 in 1766 and 170 in 1795–6 – when one did not have to reach double figures to generate a spike in Ireland in the eighteenth century (Table 2.1) and the total sample of cases for the period 1710–1845 is fewer than three hundred, one may justifiably conclude that prior to the Great Famine food protest was conducted on a smaller scale there than it was in its two largest European neighbours.[7] Yet it may be that these are not the most appropriate comparators; it is notable also that food protest was more prevalent in Ireland than it was in Scotland and Germany. K.J. Logue's identification of 42 incidents in Scotland between 1780 and 1815 is half (50.6 per cent) the number (83) located in Ireland for the same period (Tables 2.1, 2.2), while Manfred Gailus contends that 'the onset of far-reaching food riots' in Germany did not occur until 'the crisis years of the 1790s, especially 1795–6'.[8]

FOOD RIOTING IN IRELAND IN CONTEXT

In any event, purposeful food protest was pursued in Ireland for a sustained period, even if it emerged more slowly there than it did in England and France. This can be attributed at least in part to the particular history of the island, in the sixteenth and seventeenth centuries most notably, but the primarily urban location

5 Jean Nicolas, *La Rébellion française, mouvements populaires et conscience sociale (1661–1789)* (Paris, 2002), chapter 1. It is also notable that food rioting was not only 'a general feature of the popular experience' but increasingly commonplace since (according to Guy Lemarchand) the number of disturbances in the period 1760–89 was four times greater than that in the thirty years 1690–1720: Guy Lemarchand, 'Troubles populaires au XVIIIe siècle et conscience de classe: une préface à la Révolution Francaise', *Annales historiques de la Révolution Française*, 279 (1990), 34; Bouton, *The flour war*, pp 6–7, 215. 6 Bohstedt, *The politics of provisions*, pp 2, 261; Bohstedt, 'Riot censuses' at http://?web.utk.edu/~bohstedt/. The statistical limitations of Bohstedt's sampling techniques are suggested by the difference between his 'sample' for the years 1790–1810, which is 240 (*Riots and community politics*, p. 14), and that of Roger Wells, which runs to c.400 (*Wretched faces: famine in wartime England, 1793–1810* (Gloucester, 1988), pp 420–40). 7 Bohstedt, *The politics of provisions*, pp 55, 96, 133, 178; Table 1. 8 Kenneth J. Logue, *Popular disturbances in Scotland, 1780–1815* (Edinburgh, 1979), p. 23; Gailus, 'Food riots in Germany in the late 1840s', pp 160–1.

of protest during its early phases suggests that the absence of the phenomenon prior to the eighteenth century is bound up still more closely with the under-urbanized character of Irish society, and the under-commercialized state of the Irish economy.[9] It is at least arguable in this context, if one takes on board Bohstedt's point that the 1690s in England witnessed the completion of the transformation from the 'enclosure riot', which was pursued during the sixteenth century, to the 'grain riot' that was 'the characteristic form of artisan unrest' in the eighteenth century, that Ireland was but a generation in arrear of its nearest and most influential neighbour in the latter respect.[10] Ireland may not have experienced food protest (targeted at inhibiting the 'export' of grain) equivalent to that identifiable in England in the 1690s, but it is hardly coincidental that the protest that took place in Cork in the winter of 1709–10 is coeval with a spike in comparable protest in England, or that the 'serious rioting' that took place in Cornwall in 1727–8, when 'giant crowds of tinners armed with clubs repeatedly marched into the market-port towns to plunder granaries and cellars', anticipated the first major episode of food protest in Ireland.[11] Furthermore, the manner in which rioting was conducted in both jurisdictions thereafter bears comparison, as 'seizure' rather than 'market place negotiation' was the preferred *modus operandi* in each.[12] Viewed from the particular perspective of food protest, it can be argued that Ireland was sufficiently firmly integrated into the Atlantic commercial world by the early eighteenth century to support a food protest culture, and for that to emerge as a distinct and definable phenomenon during the crisis years of the late 1720s.

Classic food rioting differed from other forms of riotous protest in that it was not perceived as a simple law and order issue either by its practitioners or those tasked with combatting civil disobedience pretty much wherever it was pursued. The authorities in Ireland prioritized a law and order response, but the fact that they did not do so consistently implies that if the 'space' required by food protesters to exert 'pressure' was less commodious there than it was in England, it was sufficiently capacious to permit food rioting to grow, and for it to acquire its distinctive character. Why this should be has been a subject of lively debate. It was Charles Tilly's and Louise Tilly's contention that the 'dynamic structural framework' required to explain food protest is to 'be found in the working out of two processes: the development of capitalism and the rise of centralized nation states'. This makes partial sense in the Irish instance since one can identify the former in 'the expansion of market systems, the increasing division of labor, and proletarianization' to which the Tillys allude in the 'sevenfold rise [in exports] between the 1660s and the 1790s' and in the urbanization that took place during

9 See Raymond Gillespie, 'Explorers, exploiters and entrepreneurs: early modern Ireland and its context, 1500–1700' in Brian Graham and L.J., Proudfoot (eds), *An historical geography of Ireland* (London, 1993), pp 123–57, for an excellent introduction to societal and economic development. 10 Bohstedt, *The politics of provisions*, p. 98. 11 Above, pp 32–5; Bohstedt, *The politics of provisions*, pp 100–1; Malcolmson, 'A set of ungovernable people: the Kingswood colliers in the eighteenth century', pp 93, 116. 12 Bohstedt, *The politics of provisions*, p. 102.

the same period.[13] The perception that food rioting in early modern Europe, and in England and France in particular, was a response to the disruptive impact of embryonic capitalism rather than 'the national states increasing penetration of social life' has many champions; E.P. Thompson's concept of the moral economy is one of the more sophisticated versions of this thesis. Yet the allied contention that it was a manifestation of collective communal determination – a 'popular consensus' – 'to defend traditional rights or customs' has less obvious purchase as an explanatory paradigm in Ireland.[14] In the sixteenth and early seventeenth centuries, when the regulatory environment that gave rise to the *Book of [dearth] Orders* was operative in England, Ireland experienced war, conquest, economic dislocation, and a revolution in the management and ownership of land that left a bitter legacy in the form of the strongly contested memories of the 1641 Rebellion, the Commonwealth (1649–60), the Jacobite parliament (1689) and the Williamite War (1690–1).[15] In addition, there was little by way of revered customary practices, still less a 'golden past' on which food rioters could draw.

Ireland, in other words, pursued a markedly different pattern of development than England, which necessarily complicates, possibly even invalidates, any attempt to establish a common origin for food rioting in a (Thompsonian) world of customary practice and 'traditional rights'. Yet because tradition can be invented as well as handed down, and one cannot rule out its introduction as part of the process of intensified Anglicization that was a consequence of migration into Ireland in the seventeenth century, it would be injudicious to assume *a priori* that those who engaged in food protest in Ireland did not perceive that they possessed customary rights worthy of defending.[16] The percipient Charles O'Hara, for example, believed that this instinct was deeply rooted in Ireland, opining that though 'all men are in some degree fond of old customs, ours are singularly so'. O'Hara did not conceive of this as a virtuous state; quite the opposite, he described it as a manifestation of 'the ignorance of the people', as a barrier in the way of 'industry', and an obstacle to innovation.[17] Yet, the instinct to protect and defend established ways ought not to be airily dismissed when it comes to explaining food protest in Ireland since it can safely be surmised not only that many among those who engaged in the practice in Ireland drew on a common English tradition but also that they shared a common inclination to invoke comparable rules against forestalling, combination and extortion and other market

---

13 Tilly, 'Food entitlement, famine and conflict', p. 143; Geoff Ely, *A crooked line: from cultural history to the history of society* (Ann Arbor, *c.*2005), pp 46–7; Cormac Ó Gráda, 'Irish agricultural history: recent research', *Agricultural History Review*, 38:2 (1990), 166. 14 Thompson, 'The moral economy of the English crowd', 78. 15 Nicholas Canny, *Making Ireland British, 1580–1650* (Oxford, 2001), passim; Colm Lennon, *Sixteenth-century Ireland; the incomplete conquest* (rev. ed., Dublin, 2005); Raymond Gillespie, *Seventeenth-century Ireland: making Ireland modern* (Dublin, 2005); John Gibney, *The shadow of a year: the 1641 Rebellion in Irish history and memory* (Madison, WI, and London, 2013), passim; Vincent Morley, *The popular mind in eighteenth-century Ireland* (Cork, 2017). 16 Terence Ranger (ed.), *The invention of tradition* (Cambridge, 1993). 17 Dickson and Fleming (eds), 'Charles O'Hara's observations on county Sligo', 95.

manipulations as a justification for food protest. This impulse was certainly prominent in the calculations of the populace of Dublin in the early 1770s when it targeted carriers, merchants and retailers; in the early 1790s when the failure to enforce 'the laws against ... forestallers and regraters of provisions, salesmasters, butchers, bakers, coal-factors etc' was identified as a specific grievance; and in the 1830s and early 1840s when it informed various assertions that food protest could be ascribed to the activities of forestallers. There are many specific examples of the latter, but the suggestion by the *Clare Journal* in 1842 that successive rises in the price of potatoes due to 'forestalling' prompted the protest that produced the 'Ennis massacre' is particularly noteworthy.[18] This is not how Thompson envisioned the commitment to defend customary practices, of course, but it does suggest that this was not entirely an irrelevance in Ireland and it echoes, albeit in a modified way, the fundamental insight that food protest was intrinsically a conservative phenomenon.

The same reservation can be entered, *mutatis mutandis*, in respect of Thompson's location of the rights and customs that food protesters in eighteenth-century England sought to defend within a 'paternalist model of the marketing and manufacturing process'.[19] This 'paternalist model' was enshrined in a body of law (statute as well as common), regulations (municipal and urban ordinances, decrees and regulations), and 'traditional rights or customs' that may never have been observed in Ireland outside of a tiny handful of Old English urban spaces if at all.[20] Moreover, the assumption, enshrined in the nationalist narrative of Irish history, and in the interpretative model embraced by those who are guided by a Marxist paradigm, that the relationship of ruler and ruled, landlord and tenant, did not permit paternalism to function in Ireland, encouraged, when it did not mandate, such an interpretation. The tradition of agrarian protest, which was sustained for two-thirds of the life span of food protest, has been invoked in support of this claim, but it accords insufficient weight to the fact that this form of protest was regional, rural and discontinuous.[21] Moreover, it is important not to assume that the pattern of confrontation that characterized the post-Great Famine phase of landlordism in Ireland was a constant before that event, when this plainly was not the case.[22] Indeed, the absence of structured

---

18 Above, pp 41, 45, 56–7; *Freeman's Journal*, 13 June 1793; *Tralee Mercury*, 17 May 1837; Lee, 'The food riots of 1830 and 1840', p. 65; *Connaught Telegraph*, 8 June 1842; Ó Murchadha, *Sable wings over the land*, p. 14; Power, *A history of Clarecastle*, p. 414. 19 Thompson, 'The moral economy of the English crowd', 83. 20 Ibid., 78, 106–7, 108–11, 132; Randall and Charlesworth, 'The moral economy: riot, markets and social conflict', p. 1. This observation is necessarily tentative in respect of Ireland as the thin evidential record, and the consequently thinner volume of historical work in this area, means there is little upon which one might build a more positive statement. 21 Connolly, 'The houghers: agrarian protest in early eighteenth century Connacht', pp 139–62; Clark and Donnelly (eds), *Irish peasants: violence and political unrest, 1780–1914*, passim; Michael Beames, *Peasants and power: the Whiteboy movements and their control in pre-famine Ireland* (London, 1983). 22 See Michael Kelly, *Struggle and strife on a Mayo estate, 1833–1903: the Logans of Logboy and their tenants* (Dublin, 2014); Samuel Clark, *Social origins of the Irish land war* (Princeton, 1979);

214 *Food rioting in Ireland in the eighteenth and nineteenth centuries*

agrarian protest in the interval between the Houghers (1712–14) and the Whiteboys (1760–5), and the ostensible pacificity of the country for much of the eighteenth century has encouraged some to claim that a benign paternalism defined social relations until at least the 1790s, while more recent work on landed estates in the nineteenth century, even that focussed on 'the limits of landlord paternalism', testifies to its continuing existence well beyond that point.[23] The paternalist pulse may never have beat as strongly in Ireland as it did in England, but it beat nonetheless, and it guided and informed attitudes that, for all the demonstrable layers of suspicion that were characteristic of Ireland's *ancien regime*, were not invariably shaped by hostility or preclusive of empathy.[24]

Further, there was a tradition of local government that presumed it was the authorities' responsibility to combat fraudulent practices in order to ensure the availability of foodstuffs. Extant corporation records reveal that they pursued this function from the mid-seventeenth century; the Corporation of Youghal, for example, approved proclamations against regraters and forestallers in 1646, 1647 and 1652; the Corporation of the borough of Ardee directed in 1683 that the measures used in respect to bere, barley, oats, malt were examined to ensure they were 'exact' weight'. The Corporation of Carrickfergus did likewise in 1740. Yet the long intervals that passed between interventions suggest it was not a pressing priority.[25] The most sophisticated, continuous and, in the capital at least, the most effective of these measures was the assize of bread – white, wheaten and household – which was set weekly according to the 'middle [market] price' of the grains (wheat, oats, barley, bere and rye) used. Tabulated to assist with its application, and printed for easy reference (initially as a broadsheet), it was subsequently promulgated widely via the Dublin and provincial press.

Though recourse to an assize of bread has been traced to the thirteenth century in England, the history of its application in Ireland is opaque.[26] It is appar-

M.W. Dowling, *Tenant right and agrarian society in Ulster, 1600–1870* (Dublin, 1999).   **23** S.J. Connolly, 'Violence and order in the eighteenth century' in Paul Ferguson, Patrick O'Flanagan and Kevin Whelan (eds), *Rural Ireland, 1600–1900: modernisation and change* (Cork, 1987), pp 42–61; idem, *Religion, law and power: the making of Protestant Ireland 1660–1760* (Oxford, 1992), pp 136–9; Bartlett, 'The end of moral economy', 42–4; McNamara, 'This wretched people: the famine of 1822', pp 26–33; Brian Casey, 'Land, politics and religion on the Clancarty estate, east Galway, 1851–1914' (PhD, Maynooth University, 2011).   **24** T.C. Barnard, 'The uses of 23 October 1641 and Irish Protestant celebrations', *EHR*, 106 (1991), 889–920; Kelly, 'Disappointing the boundless ambitions of France: Irish protestants and the fear of invasion', 27–105, passim; James Kelly (ed.), *Proceedings of the Irish House of Lords* (3 vols, Dublin, 2008), ii, 359–85, iii, 219–60; S.J. Connolly, '"Ag deanamh commanding": elite responses to popular culture, 1660–1850' in K.A. Miller and J.S. Donnelly (eds), *Irish popular culture, 1650–1850* (Dublin, 1998), pp 1–31.   **25** Caulfield (ed.), *Corporation book of Youghal*, pp 258, 269–79, 297–8; Assembly of Corporation of Ardee, 16 Jan. 1680, 18 Feb. 1683 (County Louth Archives Service, Corporation of Ardee minute book, 1661–87, pp 35, 43); Records of Carrickfergus Corporation, 8 Sept. 1740 (PRONI, T707/1 p. 120); Gogarty (ed.), *Council book of the Corporation of Drogheda*, passim.   **26** Sidney and Beatrice Webb, 'The assize of bread', *Economic Journal*, 14 (1904), 332–42; Wendy Thwaites, 'The assize of bread in eighteenth-century Oxfordshire, *Oxoniensia*, 51 (1986), 171–81; Thompson, 'The moral economy of

ent that the mayor of Youghal and and portrieve of Ardee possessed the authority in the seventeenth century to intervene to fix the price of bread 'according to
the rising and falling of the price of corn in the markets', and that they did so
on occasions.[27] A comparable 'assize' was fixed by the mayor of Drogheda in the
mid-1720s, but these passing encounters are not inconsistent with the conclusion
that it was applied erratically since parliament directed in 1728, when the country was in the throes of a harvest crisis, that magistrates should set an assize of
bread for two years according to an approved table of grain prices. Though the
act providing for this quickly required amendment to increase the allowance permitted bakers, the assize of bread was a compelling matter, and while interventions by successive mayors to address abuses suggest it was difficult to police, it
had the capacity, when properly enforced, to protect the population of large
towns against a price free-for-all that would otherwise have left consumers at the
mercy of those producers, retailers and others who sought to profiteer.[28] The
'compact' entered into by bakers and officials in Dublin to keep the assize of
bread artificially high in 1783 is an illustration of just how effective a centralized
system could be in diluting the impact of high prices during moments of crisis.
Yet the continuing ease with which mayors looking for favourable headlines
could locate underweight bread suggests that it may have been laxly enforced
otherwise.[29] More might have been done, certainly.

The decision of the market juries of the Liberties of St Sepulchre and Donore
in Dublin to 'perambulate their respective bounds' on 19 July 1791, when 'in the
course of three hours, [they] seized 287 six penny and 94 twelve-penny loaves,
many of which were scandalously deficient in weight', is indicative of the abuses
that were possible in one small area.[30] The problem was that the will to do more
was absent. This was implicitly acknowledged by the suggestion, floated in the

the English crowd', 84.   **27** Caulfield (ed.), *Corporation book of Youghal*, pp 14–5, 20, 270–1;
Assembly of Corporation of Ardee, 16 Oct. 1785 (County Louth Archives Service, Corporation of
Ardee minute book, 1661–87, p. 47).   **28** Gogarty (ed.), *Council book of the Corporation of Drogheda*,
pp 376–7; 1 George II, chap.16: An Act for regulating the price and assize of bread, and the markets; Eoin Magennis, 'Regulating the market: parliament, corn and bread in eighteenth-century
Ireland' in Michael Brown and Sean Patrick Donlon (eds), *The law and other legalities of Ireland,
1689–1850* (Farnham, 2011), pp 211–12, 217–23.   **29** Above, pp 194–5, 202; Kelly, 'Scarcity and
poor relief', 49. One may compare the Dublin situation with that in Oxford; the assize 'may have
marginally raised the price of bread ... in normal years', Wendy Thwaites has argued, but it acted
as a restraint in times of dearth, and it acted as a general reassurance: 'The assize of bread in eighteenth-century Oxfordshire, 176–81; Thompson, 'Moral economy reviewed', 290; Thompson, 'The
moral economy of the English crowd', 106.   **30** *Hibernian Journal*, 22 July 1791. It is not possible,
at present, even to guess how many locations had active 'market juries'. The decision of
Carrickfergus Corporation in 1740 to instruct the clerk of the market court in that town to
'summon ... 24 good and lawful men' to ensure weights and measures conformed to standard is
indicative, but it is not clear how frequently this was done, or if a similar summons was issued to
ensure foodstuffs were of the proper weight: Records of Carrickfergus Corporation, 1569–1801
(PRONI, T/707/1 p. 119).

same report as that commending market juries, that 'the lord mayor might order both bakers and hucksters to affix a printed copy of the weekly table of assize in some conspicuous place in their shops, that the ignorant who have few opportunities of information, may know what they get for their money, when they see their bread weighed before they pay'.[31] Moreover, this was a symptom of a still-larger problem. Newspaper claims that 'illegal' practices were 'permitted to pass unnoticed and [go] unpunished' because 'the laws against them remain dead letters in the statute book' are consistent with the conclusion that the law was widely ignored.[32] Yet, the regulations, and the aspirations of which they were an expression, are still noteworthy. They served by their very existence to give legitimacy to food protest by enabling those who engaged to impute that they aspired to bring equilibrium to a system that had been rendered dysfunctional by those (forestallers especially) who created 'artificial scarcity' in 'time of plenty'; by affirming the value of a regulated marketplace, and by conveying a message to those in authority that food rioting was entitled to be treated differently.[33]

The perception that because food was a 'primary necessity' there was a moral if not a legal *droit de subsistence* also helped to ensure that the law was not applied with the same force against food protest as other forms of riot, and allied offences such as disorderliness, theft, destruction of property and violence against the person.[34] This understanding might extend so far, on occasion, as to absolve those taken up for participating in food protest. This was the case at Drogheda assizes in 1746, when the grand jury threw out bills of indictment presented 'against several persons for riotously cutting down the rigging of some ships freighted with corn ... for Scotland', but this only happened because the vessels that were targeted 'were destined ... for the rebels'.[35] A century later, at the height of the Great Famine, comparable indulgence was manifested when 'clemency' was extended to those involved in food protest in counties Clare and Tipperary.[36] In most instances, due process was followed, and if the absence of a specific offence prior to 1784, and the unwillingness of magistrates to engage in mass arrest thereafter, ensured that the number prosecuted was significantly in arrear of the number of participants, Ireland was little different to England in that respect.[37]

This did not mean that the ruling elite in Ireland accepted that it was their responsibility to ensure the populace access to appropriate foodstuffs, either in quantity or in quality, but it did amount to a conditional acknowledgement that all should have the opportunity to acquire sufficient food to survive. There was, as this suggests, an implicit moral aspect to the efforts that were made to increase the supply of food in the wake of a food riot, though this did not extend so far as to ensure that people were adequately nourished (in so far as this was under-

---

31 *Hibernian Journal*, 22 July 1791.   32 *Freeman's Journal*, 25 May, 13 June 1793.   33 *Freeman's Journal*, 25 May 1793; see Thompson, 'The moral economy of the English crowd', 83–8.   34 Bouton, *The flour war*, p. 8.   35 *Dublin Courant*, 25 Mar. 1746.   36 Above, pp 177–8, 180–1.   37 Bohstedt, *The politics of provisions*, pp 245–6; above, pp 183–4.

stood) or did not go hungry. It did not even extend to the identification of a 'just price', the assize of bread notwithstanding, since the concept of price control was not compatible with the understanding of how the economy optimally functioned, or, indeed, with the concept of a 'just price' as it might be understood today. In Ireland, as elsewhere in western Europe, the just price was, de Roover pointed out more than half a century ago, 'simply the current market price, with this important reservation: in the case of collusion or emergency, the public authorities retained the right to interfere and impose a fair price'.[38] This is why, though price was a crucial factor,[39] one cannot identify a price point (either an absolute or a percentage of the 'normal' price) at which food rioting was likely to commence, since populations could and did (routinely) pay high prices for food in Ireland without feeling impelled to riot in protest. Indeed, stable prices, even if high, tended to be accepted; by contrast, sudden increases which fuelled the suspicion that they were artificial, fixed or contrived by interested parties – farmers, carters, merchants, millers, forestallers, shippers or others – were more reliable triggers.

One cannot conclude from this that food protesters in Ireland were motivated by principled opposition to the increasingly commercialized economy in which they lived. Much of the power of E.P. Thompson's original articulation of the concept of 'the moral economy of the poor' in eighteenth-century England derived from his contention that it existed 'in dialectic tension' with the fast emerging 'market economy'. Viewed from this perspective, the 'repertoire of crowd actions' that constituted food protest – 'price-fixing in the market place; the compulsion of farmers to bring food to the marketplace; the stoppage of foodstuffs in transit; and the seizure and/or destruction of foodstuffs' – can be interpreted as expressions of ideological opposition to the commercial economy and a manifestation of class struggle. By extension, food riots were not simply a response to price inflation or to scarcity; rather they were a response to 'illicit market manipulation'.[40] Its ideological coherence, notwithstanding, this reading of food protest has been much criticized in England – the jurisdiction in which it originated and to which it is reputedly tailored.[41] Its applicability in Ireland is still more problematical, first and foremost because it is difficult, given the close connection that existed between food protest and food crisis, to conclude that the targeting by protesters of farmers, carriers, merchants, shippers and others was other than a reaction to rising prices and the prospect or reality of diminished

---

38 Bouton, *The flour war*, p.8–9, quoting Raymond de Roover, 'The concept of the just price: theory and economic politics', *Journal of Economic History*, 18 (1958), 421.   39 As well as the evidence identified above see Booker to Trumbull, 15 Dec. 1800, 1 Apr. 1812 (NYPL, Trumbull papers, box 1).   40 Thompson, 'The moral economy of the English crowd', passim; Randall and Charlesworth, 'The moral economy: riot, markets and social conflict', pp 2–3.   41 The most comprehensive (though not always fair) guide to Thompson's critics is Thompson, 'The moral economy reviewed', passim; for a less partisan perspective see Randall and Charlesworth, 'The moral economy: riot, markets and social conflict', pp 1–32. Bohstedt's opinions have continued to evolve: see *The politics of provisions*, pp 7–15 and passim.

access to food, and that the object was to redress these problems. In other words, attention was directed at those engaged in the production, movement and sale of foodstuffs because they were the most visible sources of supply rather than because of the roles they performed in a commercial economy. The fact that those involved in the trade in food were not targeted at other times, even though they were always on the lookout for opportunity – in the expectation, the Dublin merchant Nathaniel Trumbull observed, that 'a speculation might answer'[42] – is also striking because it implies that food rioters did not object to the market *per se*. This is not to deny that food rioters entertained reservations – implicit as well as explicit – with the way things were; indeed, it may even imply that their acceptance, perhaps even their engagement with the market, was conditional as well as partial, in keeping with its still emerging, and necessarily imperfect, form. Yet, as the geographically fluid and intermittent nature of protest intimates, when food was available in appropriate quantity at an affordable price the residents of a food producing area or food *entrepôt* were unconcerned if foodstuffs were traded elsewhere. By contrast, when conditions were challenging, food was expensive and its supply was not secure, local communities were prepared to take direct action to enhance its availability at an affordable price.

There can be little doubt but that in Ireland, as well as France and England, the emergence of the market economy was disruptive. But there is no compelling reason to conclude (following Thompson and Louise Tilly) that because 'the sea change beneath the riotous eighteenth century is the movement from pre-industrial society with its protections against privation to the *laissez-faire* policies of an emerging commercial and industrial capitalist society' that food rioting was *ipso facto* a protest against this emerging economy.[43] Indeed, the contrary might be argued since the 'pre-industrial' society that obtained in Ireland manifestly failed to protect the population against death and distress in 1729, 1740–1, 1756–7, 1766, 1783–4, 1800–1, 1817, 1822, 1830–1, 1840, 1842 and, most of all, in 1846–8. In other words, food protest in Ireland fits maybe more easily the pragmatic interpretation offered by John Stevenson, Buchanan Sharp, R.B Rose and John Bohstedt than the ideological readings of Thompson or the Tillys. This is not to deny the insights that both, but Thompson especially, have brought to bear – which meant that food protest is best understood as an essentially logical, disciplined and explicable response (in contrast to the irrational, sporadic and emotional surge of anger which is how it was long conceived) to one of the most acute crisis the human being can experience – the prospect or reality of hunger.

Food rioting was a product of communities whose horizon was quintessentially local. In addition to identifying its mutable geographical and spatial distribution, the mapping of the phenomenon that has been pursued in England,

42 Trumbull to Messrs Lockwood, Russell and Parkinson, 11 July 1789, Trumbull to O'Farrell, 16 July, Trumbull to Cruise, 16 July (NYPL, Trumbull papers, Letterbook 1).   43 Walton and Seddon, *Free markets and food riots*, p. 27; see also Palmer, *Police and protest in England and Ireland*, p. 51.

France, and now Ireland, has highlighted this. Determining the demographic, economic, commercial and other forces that shaped the activity at a given time in an identifiable place is more elusive, but the key to its emergence was the dependence of the *menu peuple* of the port and market towns where is was most actively pursued upon purchased food. Consistent with this, the food riot footprint grew and expanded (see Maps 1–2) in tandem with the geographical expansion of commercialization, till by the end of the eighteenth and the beginning of the nineteenth century (Map 3) it embraced virtually all of the country. It was never evenly distributed regionally of course, not only because commercial activity did not impact the country evenly and because the poor, land poor and precariously located that engaged in food protest were concentrated in different urban and rural pockets at any given time, and because there were other considerations at play.

Urbanization was, it is clear, crucial to the emergence and evolution of food protest. That Ireland had far fewer urban centres than England is thus important in explaining why, the years 1846–7 excepted, the geographical and temporal distribution of food rioting was thinner in Ireland than in England.[44] It is also pertinent in any explanation as to why the history of food rioting in Dublin differs from that of London. Dublin did not experience the number of food protests commensurate with its commanding economic position. It bears comparison with London in this respect, but whereas it is possible ('the unique food riot of September 1800 and the Corn Law rioting in 1815 aside') to argue that London 'had no real tradition of food riots', one cannot sustain this claim with respect to Ireland's capital. The bounties introduced in 1758 in order to encourage the movement of foodstuffs to Dublin interrupted the pattern of protest that had obtained in the city for a generation. In addition, Dublin, like London, developed an elaborate system of public and private poor relief during the second half of the eighteenth century. Neither were pursued with quite the same efficiency in Dublin, however, and their inability to insulate the *lumpenproletariat* from the fear of hunger was an important factor in the resumption of food rioting in the 1790s and, though it was intermittent thereafter, in ensuring that it survived into the mid-1840s.[45]

Food rioting was a learned behaviour, of course. Once adopted by a community, the codes and patterns of food rioting were sufficiently enduring and empowering to sustain what Terence Ranger has termed a 'mobilizing myth' – a fund of memories, experiences and lore transmissible across and between generations 'via oral traditions and networks of sociability' – that people could 'draw [upon] and adapt to respond to present crises'.[46] The Kingswood colliers and var-

44 Bohstedt, *The politics of provisions*, p. 272.   45 Bohstedt, *The politics of provisions*, pp 204–5, 253; Bohstedt, *Riots and community politics in England and Wales, 1790–1810*, pp 208–9; Stevenson, *Popular disturbances in England, 1700–1870*, pp 99–100; Kelly, 'Charitable societies: their genesis and development, 1720–1800', pp 89–108.   46 Bohstedt, 'The moral economy and the discipline of historical context', 270; Bouton, *The flour war*, p. 3 citing Terence Ranger, 'Peasant

ious communities of Cornish tinners maintained a tradition of activity in England that few Irish interests emulated, but the capacity of the Claddagh fishermen to sustain food protest in Galway for at least half a century, and other groups to do likewise, albeit for shorter periods, in Youghal, Dublin and elsewhere was in keeping with this international pattern.[47] However, tradition alone cannot explain the evolving pattern of food protest, or why a predominantly port phenomenon (in contrast to what is observable of England and France) should over time become increasingly rural, when the countryside possessed its own distinctive form of purposeful disaffection – agrarian protest.

FOOD RIOTING AND AGRARIAN PROTEST

The relationship of agrarian protest and food protest was neither straightforward nor unchanging; but they were less antithetical than it is assumed.[48] It is notable, for example, that both have been portrayed as manifestations of unease with the nature and implications of commercialization and economic modernization. Indeed, since the Houghers in the 1710s resisted the attempt to promote pastoral agriculture at the expense of tillage, and the Whiteboys in the 1760s opposed the enclosure of commons, it could be argued that agrarian protesters and food protesters were at one in their uneasiness with the implications of economic modernization.[49] A more certain case can be made that both were products of demographic expansion as, no less than the growth of towns, the embarkation of the country's rural population on a sharp upwards curve in the second half of the eighteenth century was an essential precondition for agrarian protest.[50] Furthermore, there was a spatial correlation in the early nineteenth century between the parts of the country that experienced agrarian protest and food protest.[51]

Yet the contrasts are more striking, and more compelling. The first and most obvious is the manner in which they behaved. In Ireland, as elsewhere in Europe, food protesters pursued short-lived interventions to draw attention to their plight

consciousness: culture and conflict in Zimbabwe' in T. Shannin (ed.), *Peasants and peasant societies: selected readings* (2nd ed., Oxford, 1987), p. 313.   **47** Bohstedt, *The politics of provisions*, pp 118, 134–7, 151–2, 177–80, 182–3, 186–7; above, pp 91, 143.   **48** Beames, *Peasants and power*, pp 89–101; James S. Donnelly, 'The social composition of agrarian rebellions in early nineteenth-century Ireland: the case of the Carders and Caravats, 1813–16' in P.J. Corish (ed.), *Radicals, rebels and establishments* (Belfast, 1985), pp 151 69; Huggins, *Social conflict in pre-Famine Ireland*, chapter 6 and 7.   **49** Connolly, 'The Houghers: agrarian protest in early eighteenth-century Connacht', passim; Donnelly, 'The Whiteboys, 1751–65', passim; idem, 'The Rightboy movement, 1785–8', passim.   **50** Devine, 'Unrest and stability in rural Ireland and Scotland 1760–1840', p. 131; Dickson, Ó Gráda and Daultrey, 'Hearth tax, household size and Irish population change, 1672–1821', 155–6.   **51** One may instance the activities of the Threshers (1806) in north Connaught and the north midlands, the Shanavests and Caravats (1813–16) in the midlands and north Munster, the Rockites (1821–4) in North and west Munster, and the Terry Alts (1831) in county Clare.

rather than to impose a solution. By comparison, agrarian protest was prolonged; most forms of agrarian protest were pursued over a period of years in keeping with the fact that agrarian protesters aspired to effect more fundamental change. Neither aimed to change the structures of society, but an intervention that aspired to alter the manner in which people were taxed or to modify the terms on which land was managed and occupied was of a different order to one that sought immediate relief when prices were rising and scarcity apprehended. Both operated outside the law, of course, but the authorities perceived that agrarian protest presented a more serious challenge not only to law and order but also to the existing confessional and political system. This was something defenders of the *status quo* felt particularly keenly in the 1780s in their response to the Rightboys; then they embarked on the development of an ideology of 'Protestant ascendancy' that informed resistance to the admission of Catholics to the political process for forty years.[52] Food rioting, by contrast, as all sober analysts acknowledged, posed no threat to the political structures of the state. Some alarmists were prone to conclude that the interruption of the movement of grain and foodstuffs challenged the economic foundations upon which society was built, but their protestations were rarely taken seriously by those in power. In the eighteenth century, merchants might find their liberty to trade curtailed by concern that their properties might be ransacked and their goods appropriated, or by the zeal of a local official ordering them to unload a cargo or sell the contents of a store, but these interruptions rarely lasted for more than a few days, and they were of lesser impact than the embargoes imposed by the mercantilist state at times of war or the quarantines introduced to combat the fear of plague. This is not to suggest that the isolated interventions by food protesters did not have financial implications for merchants and dealers in provisions, but other than a few individuals who were precipitated into bankruptcy, most seem to have taken the setbacks in their stride.

Sustained periods of disruption such as occurred in 1783–4 and 1846–7 were a different matter, however, and a notably larger number of merchants then either looked to the authorities for protection or altered their purchasing strategies in an attempt to hedge against losses they might incur at the hands of the crowd. This was particularly striking in the autumn of 1846. Moreover, there are sufficient examples of millers, merchants and retailers voicing concern to conclude that it may well have had the effect of disrupting the existing supply chain. One may instance W.B. Armstrong of Garrycastle House, who ran a mill at Banagher, King's county; he was loath 'to import Indian corn and other foods' in October 1846 for fear they would be appropriated. The merchants and traders

---

52 Kelly, 'Defending the established order: Richard Woodward, bishop of Cloyne (1726–94)', pp 159–62; idem, 'The genesis of Protestant ascendancy: the Rightboy disturbances of the 1780s and their impact upon Protestant opinion' in Gerard O'Brien (ed.), *Parliament, politics and people: essays in eighteenth-century Irish history* (Dublin, 1989), pp 93–127; idem, *Sir Richard Musgrave, 1746–1818: ultra-Protestant ideologue*, passim; Thomas Bartlett, *The fall and rise of the Irish nation: the Catholic question, 1690–1830* (Dublin, 1992).

of Newport, county Mayo, expressed the same apprehension some weeks later; they maintained that they were 'afraid to import or otherwise risque their capital' in the absence of military 'protection'.[53] Rush and Palmer were one of a number of undertakings embracing millers, distillers and carriers in Galway that called for the deployment of a troop of Dragoons in that town in the autumn of 1846 when trading was 'suspended by the mob preventing the exit of either flour or meal'. John Mosse of Ballyconra, then 'the largest flour miller in county Kilkenny', and James Swanton of Skibbereen Mills did likewise; Swanton threatened in September 'to ship all our stock' and 'close' his and John Gould's multiple 'concerns' in west Cork, and Mosse, in December, undertook to run down his business unless a military guard was stationed in nearby Ballyragget to secure his mill against invasion. Meanwhile, the firm of Goodbody and Sons, of Clara, warned of the 'dangers' that could ensue if the movement of foodstuffs was disrupted because of 'outrages ... committed on carts drawing flour from their mills' in county Westmeath, while Thomas Bulfin reported from north county Donegal in December that traders there only bought 'a sufficient quantity for one week's consumption' in order to minimize the losses they would incur if they were targeted. Comparable reports from merchants and traders at Tarbert, county Kerry, and Rathbeg, King's county, also dating from the autumn of 1846, to the effect that they 'feared' to purchase food because it could not be transmitted safely 'from any part of the country to another' were compounded by the decision of some poor relief committees to do likewise, and by the fear and beleaguerment that gripped elements of the civic minded as well as merchants then and later.[54]

Moreover, these concerns were not only reiterated but felt more acutely in 1847 when protest peaked once more. In May 1847, for example, a justice of the peace based at Charleville, county Cork, informed Under-secretary Redington that 'stocks are in general exhausted' in north county Cork because 'the mills which draw their supplies from Cork and Limerick as well as the retailers are ceasing to purchase' because they could not move grain safely, while in March Samuel Bell of Ahascragh in east county Galway responded to the assembly of 'a mob of nearly 1000 persons' by threatening 'to close my mills for the season as

53 Armstrong to [Labouchere], 17, 21 Oct., Richardson to [ ], 31 Oct. 1846 (NAI, OP: King's county, 1846/15/288821, 28823, 30105); Merchants, traders and inhabitants of Newport, 20 Oct. 1846 (NAI, OP: Mayo, 1846/21/29769).   54 Rush and Palmer to [ ], 5 Oct., Burke to Bessborough, 7 Oct., Memorial of carriers, 7 Oct. 1846 (NAI, OP: Galway, 1846/11/26995, 27165); Bulfin to Labouchere, 28 Dec. 1846 (NAI, OP: Donegal, 1846/7/37821); Creagh to Godley, 1 Oct., Memorial of relief committee, 28 Dec. 1846 (NAI, OP: Kerry, 1846/12/26573, 37645); Swanton to Bessborough, 3 Sept. 1846 (NAI, OP: Cork, 1846/6/23565); Goodbody to Browne, 14 Oct., Browne to Redington, 16 Oct. 1846 (NAI, OP: Westmeath, 1846/30/28117); Mosse to Labouchere, 11 Dec., Mosse to [ ], 26 Dec. 1846 (NAI, OP: Kilkenny, 1846/14/34973). Saliently, Mosse was in business a year later when a crowd of 'men, women and boys' seized flour *en route* to Mountmellick canal harbour: Cannon to Redington, 19 Dec. 1847 (NAI, OP: Queen's county, 1846/24/384).

no profit would compensate for the state of mind I am continually kept in' unless 'a party of the military were placed here'. Some certainly had good reason to cease trading because, as Bell's worried communication attests, the losses incurred were not only financial. The 'dealer', Daniel McEvoy of Slieve Ardagh, county Tipperary, advised Dublin Castle early in 1847 of his intention to 'give up the business' because he feared for his life following a second assault.[55]

Both food protest and agrarian protest challenged the capacity of state and local officials to maintain law and order, to be sure, but the nature and seriousness of the threat differed. In keeping with its reactive and, ostensibly, impulsive character, the interruption to the rule of law caused by food rioting was usually transient and generally geographically confined, though this was not always how the authorities were disposed to perceive it. Moreover, they had cause on occasion, and not only in 1846, as food protest had a long history of disrupting regular commercial activity. The interruption of the movement of grain from Munster, and Drogheda to Ulster at a number of moments in the mid-eighteenth century, for example, was regarded very seriously by mercantile interests as well as those in power. Crowd interventions during the Great Famine likewise animated unease, since they too may have 'increas[ed] … distress' if the concerns expressed in county Waterford at the interruption of the supply of Indian meal destined for the Ardmore Relief Committee in mid-September and the fears articulated in the wake of the Dungarvan riots in late September 1846 that 'food would be scarcer and dearer than ever' are not categorized simply as alarmist. There was less ambiguity in county Tipperary earlier in the year when it was reported that 'no flour can stir from any of the mills'; in county Cork in September 1846, when farmers were 'threatened with destruction … should they attempt to send in corn to market; in county Cavan where the sale and movement of potatoes was discouraged; and in Limerick in October when 'the intimidation exercised in the county of Clare' ensured that 'no corn' was conveyed to the city from that quarter.[56] Comparable reports at other times from other locations, and reports of thin markets in 1839 and 1842 attest to the disruptive capacity of protest then and to the seriousness with which it was viewed locally as well as nationally.[57] Yet, the authorities were able to maintain control, and even in those instances where their command was compromised, as in South Tipperary in April 1846, it tended to be for a short interval – generally for no more than a small number of days when protest was at its peak. It may be, if one accepts the claims of the acting sovereign of Belfast in 1756 that the authorities lost control for longer

55 Clanohy to Redington, 12 May 1847 (NAI, OP: Cork, 1847/6/773); Bell to [Redington], 14 Mar. 1847 (NAI, OP: Galway, 1847/11/291); McEvoy to [Dublin Castle], 3 Feb. 1847 (NAI, OP: Tipperary, 1847/27/489).   56 *Freeman's Journal*, 19, 30 Oct. 1846; Glengall to Redington, 13 Apr. 1846 (NAI, OP: Tipperary, 1847/27/8989); Knaresborough to Redington, 29 Sept. 1846 (NAI, OP: Cork, 1846/6/26407); Martin to Pennefeather, 14 May 1846 (NAI, OP: Cavan, 1846/11659); de Decies to [Labouchere], 22 Sept., Petition of merchants of Dungarvan, 1 Oct. 1846 (NAI, OP: Waterford, 1846/29/25731, 26755).   57 *Freeman's Journal*, 4 July 1839, 9 Oct. 1846; Cunningham, *Galway, 1790–1914*, p. 91; Leyne to Redington, 11 Nov. 1846 (NAI, OP: Clare, 1846/5/31485).

there than elsewhere, but prudence dictates that some discount is applied in respect of George Macartney's panicky missives.[58] Magistrates were empowered to call on the military, and while some hesitated, there were few, if any, occasions when the combination of civil and military force failed to restore order within a short compass. This did not prevent fatal clashes on occasion, but the number of such instances was small, certainly smaller than was the case in agrarian protest, and the number of casualties dramatically fewer. Indicatively, food protest was never on a scale that demanded the formal deployment of the army as was the case, for instance, in 1786 when Lord Carhampton was tasked with restoring order in Munster arising out of the activities of the Rightboys.[59] The closest comparison that can be drawn is the Great Famine. The assignment of mobile companies of soldiers to deal with the exceptional surge in food protest in south Tipperary in April 1846, and subsequently to assist with the escort of convoys of grain- and flour-bearing carts attests to the dependence on the army to restore order when serious lawlessness threatened. It was matched by the psychological dependence of the Anglo-Irish elite on the military for their security as well as their expectation that their calls for its deployment would be answered.[60]

Food protest was, to reiterate, inherently less violent and less disruptive than agrarian protest. Saliently, unlike agrarian protesters who generally operated under cover of darkness, food protesters typically conducted their business by day, and, other than during the Great Famine and in those contexts in which it was intertwined with agrarian protest, they rarely administered punitive punishments. Moreover, they maintained this *modus operandi*. As a result, though the trend was upwards, the number of casualties attributable to rioters was in arrear of the number that died at the hands of the army and police, and it was much smaller than in the case of agrarian protest, which became progressively more retributive, violent and confrontational. The perception that early nineteenth-century Ireland was an especially violent society has recently been queried (and a focus on the homicide rate does sustain this conclusion),[61] but there is no evading the fact that, because attacks on the person as well as property was integral, agrarian protest was inherently violent. This was a consequence at least in part of the grievances for which it sought redress, and to its expanding ambition as, in contrast to food protest which focussed on accessing foodstuffs, agrarian protest evolved from resisting the enclosure of commons (1760s), advocating tithe commutation and seeking the moderation of the dues paid the Catholic clergy (1780s), to demanding, a Rockite banner asserted in 1821, 'no taxes, no tithes, [and] 60 per cent reduction in rents'. In addition, agrarian movements were typically assertive in their interactions with landlords and their agents, and still more

58 Macartney to [Waite], 22, 31 July 1756 in Benn, *History of Belfast*, pp 593–5; above, pp 60, 99.
59 Donnelly, 'The Rightboy movement, 1785–8', 190–1.   60 Barton to Donoughmore, 17 Apr., Phipps to Redington, 18 Apr., Minute by Richard Pennefeather, 22 Apr., Merchants of Carrick-on-Suir, 29 Sept. 1846 (NAI, OP: Tipperary, 1846/27/9641, 9425, 10159, 26547).   61 Richard McMahon, *Homicide in pre-Famine and Famine Ireland* (Liverpool, 2013).

so with those of their own or related social interests that dared to oppose the sectional, and occasionally economically irrational, demands they contrived to mandate.[62] The determination of 'the Kildare people ... to prevent ... labourers from the west of Ireland from working at the harvest' in 1821 was reflective of a hostility to outsiders that echoed the resolve of some food crowds to prevent the movement of foodstuffs to or from towns; the difference was that the former resulted in 'much bloodshed' compared to the modest effusions that ensued when food protesters imposed blockades.[63] Indicatively, at the very moment that these events were being played out in county Kildare, the Rockites, were embarked on a campaign of agrarian protest that was to result in the death of nearly 100 people in north Munster between 1821 and 1824, while 'several hundred' may have died in clashes between the Caravats and Shanavests in east Munster between 1806 and 1811.[64]

As the more aggressive, more persistent and more aspirational of the two forms of protest, it was inevitable, when the two intersected in the nineteenth century, that the boundaries between the two activities should break down. The pursuit by agrarian protesters of an improved food supply illustrates the impact of the latter on the former, for though a distinctive pattern of food protest was sustained (in port and market towns most notably), the manner in which it was conducted in the countryside ensured food protest acquired a more obviously rural character. This was a consequence of the adoption by the fast-expanding rural poor, which was as vulnerable to economic crisis as the urban practitioners of food rioting, of elements of the *modus operandi* of the latter. It can be seen in the actions of crowds of countrymen descending in large bodies on towns and ports, mills, rivers, canals and roads in pursuit of food; it can be seen in the efforts of agrarian protesters to disrupt fairs and markets; and it was seen, during the Great Famine particularly, in the manner in which cottiers and labourers combined in an attempt to impose their will on commercial farmers. One of the consequences of this was an increase in the tension that one can identify in early and mid-nineteenth-century Ireland between urban dwellers and rural crowds and between commercial farmers and labourers. In the case of the latter, 'small farmers and labourers ... formed a combination to intimidate ... the rich farmers from disposing of their corn' in county Clare in 1846 in an attempt to safeguard their access to food stocks and to secure themselves against price increases.[65] It is hardly a surprise, therefore, as they also had 'no work' since

---

62 Maura Cronin, *Agrarian protest in Ireland, 1750–1960* (Dundalk, 2012), chapter 1; Huggins, *Social conflict in pre-Famine Ireland*, p. 189; and as note 49 above.   63 Daniel Toler, chief constable, Kilcock, to [ ], 4 Sept. 1821 (NAI, RP/SC/1821/1127). In a further example, elements of the populace in county Roscommon in 1846 objected to the presence of individuals from county Longford (NAI, OP: Roscommon, 1846/25).   64 J.S. Donnelly, *Captain Rock: the Irish agrarian rebellion of 1821–1824* (Cork, 2009); P.E.W. Roberts, 'Caravats and Shanavests: Whiteboyism and faction fighting in east Munster, 1801–11' in Donnelly and Clark (ed.), *Irish peasants: violence and political unrest*, pp 64–101.   65 See above, pp 120–4; Leyne to [Redington], 20, 21, 22, 23 Sept. 1846 (NAI, OP: Clare, 1846/5/25309, 25727, 25629, 25631); Martin to Redington, 14 May 1846

farmers declined to employ labourers, that this served (it was remarked upon in county Kilkenny) to exacerbate the plight of the land poor (labourers and cottiers), who were deprived of the facility, evident 'in former years of scarcity of getting potatoes from … neighbours'.[66] This notwithstanding, food protest retained its identifying features, and did so until the end.

FOOD RIOTING AS A FORM OF POLITICAL EXPRESSION

Like agrarian protest, food rioting has been categorized as 'apolitical' or 'pre-political'. Interestingly, this tendency has its champions on the right and left of the ideological spectrum; both Yves-Marie Bercé's studies on 'peasant revolts' in early modern France, which may be said to view matters from the political right, and George Rudé, whose vantage point was firmly from the left, have contended that the mobs that engaged in food rioting were either 'bereft of political implications' (Bercé) or politically innocent (Rudé).[67] Other authors have extended them some grudging recognition. Despite his characterization of the 'mob' as 'a pre-political phenomenon', Eric Hobsbawm insisted this did 'not mean that it had no implicit or explicit ideas about politics', and, though they are not formed from the same ideological or historiographical mould, both E.M. Thompson and John Bohstedt are in agreement on this. For Thompson, food rioting was neither 'political in any advanced sense … [nor] unpolitical' either 'since it supposed definite, and passionately held notions of the common weal'.[68] Bohstedt's conception of community politics in action is more permissive, but food protesters were, in his estimation, possessed of a limited vision since they did not 'challenge the arrangement of local power' in the localities in which they operated.[69]

The fact that food and most other riotous protesters in England and Ireland did not seek to change the structures of power came as a relief to those in the corridors of power, but it does not mean that those who assembled were apolitical. Bohstedt is of the opinion that the crowds that gathered to protest in England and Wales in the late eighteenth to early nineteenth centuries were political, and if one accepts that 'political' is not predicated on 'class consciousness', on national awareness such as became commonplace in the nineteenth-century kind, or on a capacity for structured political organization, it is difficult to deny.[70] It is, to be

(NAI, OP: Cavan, 1846/4/11659).   **66** Roberts to Labouchere, 24 Sept. 1846 (NAI, OP: Kilkenny, 1846/14/25789); Magistrates at Calahane petty session to Redington, Sept. 1846 (NAI, OP: Waterford, 1846/28/25307); Niall Ó Ciosáin, *Ireland in official print culture, 1800–1850: a new reading of the Poor Inquiry* (Oxford, 2014), pp 79–84.   **67** The framework for the discussion of politicisation that follows is indebted to Bouton, *The flour war*, pp 25–36. For this point see pp 25–6; Yves-Marie Bercé, *Revolt and revolution in early modern Europe: an essay on the history of political violence* (New York, 1987); George Rudé, *The crowd in history: a study of popular disturbances in France and England, 1730–1848* (New York, 1964), p. 31.   **68** Hobsbawm, *Primitive rebels*, p. 110; Thompson, 'The moral economy of the English crowd', p. 79.   **69** Bohstedt, *Riots and community politics*, passim; Bouton, *The flour war*, p. 31.

sure, a perspective that does not have much purchase in Ireland where the prevailing view, articulated most consistently with respect to successive agrarian movements, is that the inherent conservativism of their aspirations precludes them being labelled 'political'. This argument is not without purchase since a majority of these movements were reactive, reliant on violence, and disinclined to use either print or the public sphere to organize or to present a public message. It was not true of all, however. Both the Defenders of the 1790s and the Ribbonmen in the early nineteenth century possessed an explicitly political agenda. Moreover, the decision of the Whiteboys in the 1760s to swathe themselves in white – which was the Jacobite colour as well as symbolic of justice – suggests, at the least, that they too cannot be perceived as wholly apolitical. And if the point is acknowledged in respect of the latter, the firm distinction that is drawn between the ostensibly reactive projects of the Whiteboys, Rightboys, Rockites and Molly Maguires, to cite a number of examples, and the more obviously structured, identity-conscious politics that was played out in the public sphere by populist organizations, such as the United Irishmen, the Orange Order and the Catholic Association, breaks down. It may be it is necessary in any event to adopt a more liberal and encompassing definition of what constituted political activity.[71] And if this is done, it is difficult to conceive how a model of food protest that locates it in local or community politics might not also be embraced within a political sphere that was larger, more inclusive and more accommodating of those who do not satisfy the definition of political awareness that Bercé, Hobsbawm, Thompson and even Bohstedt invoke. In that event, Louise Tilly's arresting avowal that 'popular violence' was 'the political tool of powerless people' gives an additional register to Hobsbawm's beguiling insight that 'collective bargaining by riot was ... probably *more* effective than any other means available' to suggest that food rioting and agrarian protest might helpfully be located on the spectrum of plebeian political behaviour.[72] John Walter is certainly persuaded that 'early modern protests' in England were political, and that the 're-conceptualization of the political in social theory as concerned with how power was constituted and contested in social spaces from the family outwards' provides a legitimate basis for this conclusion in respect of food protest in the seventeenth century.[73]

70 Bohstedt, *Riots and community politics*, chapter 9. **71** Thomas Bartlett, 'Defenders and defenderism in 1795', *IHS*, 24 (1985), 373–94; Tom Garvin, 'Defenders, Ribbonmen and others: underground political networks in pre-Famine Ireland', *Past and Present*, 96 (1982), 133–55; Donnelly, 'The Whiteboys, 1760–65', passim; idem, 'The Rightboy movements, 1785–8', passim; idem, *Captain Rock*, passim; Vincent Morley, 'The continuity of disaffection in eighteenth-century Ireland', *Eighteenth-Century Ireland*, 22 (2007), 189–205; idem, *The popular mind in eighteenth-century Ireland*, passim. **72** Eric Hobsbawm, 'The machine breakers' in idem, *Labouring men: studies in the history of labour* (London, 1964), pp 7, 16; Louise Tilly, 'The food riot as a form of political conflict in France', *Journal of Interdisciplinary History*, 2:1 (1971), 57; Bouton, *The flour war*, p. 27. Bohstedt's contention that 'at the end of the eighteenth century, riots were the most common and effective form of popular politics' evidently echoes Hobsbawm and Tilly: Bohstedt, *Riots and community politics*, p. 202. **73** Walter, 'The politics of protest, p. 58; idem, *Crowds and popular politics*

Ireland pursued a different pattern of development of course. Yet it is undeniable that the authorities in eighteenth-century Ireland perceived that agrarian violence was possessed of political motivation, and the urgency with which it was discussed by them whenever it transpired was an unmistakeable manifestation of this. One might instance the apprehension articulated by the dean of Killaloe in 1765 that the Whiteboys posed a threat 'not only [to] the ecclesiastical, but even the civil constitution',[74] but the emergence and articulation of the concept of 'Protestant ascendancy' in response to the challenge presented the established church by the Rightboys twenty years later is still more striking. Moreover, the animated paper war that ensued indicates that this was the assessment not only of Protestant opinion but also of participating Catholic and Presbyterian spokesmen and opinion formers.[75] In any event, more consideration should be afforded William Reddy's contention that it is fruitless as well as confusing to apply categories such as economic and political to the behaviours of people 'who did not neatly separate out such dimensions in their own experience and behaviour', and that class and national identity-based analyses developed in the nineteenth century are inherently fallible when applied anachronistically since the protest groups in an earlier era were populated by communities guided by more traditional sentiments.[76] Indeed, it may be that we should accept that any example of what Colin Lucas has termed 'a purposive crowd' – defined as a crowd assembled for a specific purpose during the *ancien régime* – was political. By this definition, food rioting was a politicized activity. Just how politicized it was at a given moment is open to debate since food protest took different forms at different times and in different locations, but simply to acknowledge that protesting is inherently political is a significant first step.[77] Based on his perception that 'all protests carried within them a potential critique of the obligations attendant upon the exercise of power and possession of

in early modern England (Manchester, 2006).   **74** Henry to Secker, 2 Nov. 1765 in R.G. Ingram (ed.), '"Popish cut-throats against us": papists, protestants and the problem of allegiance in eighteenth-century Ireland' in Melanie Barber et al. (eds), *From the reformation to the permissive society: a miscellany* (Church of England Record Society, vol. 18: Woodbridge, 2010), p. 189.   **75** Kelly, 'The genesis of Protestant ascendancy: the Rightboy disturbances of the 1780s and their impact upon Protestant opinion', pp 93–127; idem, 'Presbyterians and Protestants: relations between the Church of Ireland and the Presbyterian church in late eighteenth-century Ireland', *Eire-Ireland*, 23 (1988), 38–56; idem, 'Inter-denominational relations and religious toleration in late eighteenth century Ireland', *Eighteenth-Century Ireland*, 3 (1988), 39–68.   **76** W.M. Reddy, 'The textile trade and the language of the crowd at Rouen, 1752–1871', *Past and Present*, (1977), 62–89; idem, *Money and liberty in modern Europe: a critique of historical understanding* (Cambridge, 1987). Charles Tilly likewise was unwilling to define eighteenth-century protest as 'prepolitical' or traditional, and later protest as 'political' and 'modern' on the grounds that repertoires of protest are specific to the prevailing political environment, and thus to time and space: *Contentious performances* (New York, 2008). Elsewhere, he maintained (with Louise and Richard Tilly) that 'collective violence [was] a by-product of the political process': Charles, Louise and Richard Tilly, *The rebellious century, 1830–1930* (Cambridge, MA, 1975), p. 288.   **77** Colin Lucas, 'Crowd and politics between *ancien regime* and revolution in France', *Journal of Modern History*, 60 (1988), 421–57; Bouton, *The flour war*, p. 32.

property', John Walter is in no doubt that this was the case with food protest in seventeenth-century England; a similar case can be made in respect of Ireland in the eighteenth and nineteenth centuries.[78]

To take this a step further, one may invoke the capacity for organization that Irish food and agrarian crowds displayed as a manifestation of plebeian politics in operation. The sounding of horns and bells and the sending out of bellmen to gather crowds together is well attested. The use of 'signal fires' is less so, but it was deployed to such effect in counties Waterford and Cork in September 1846 that 'a great extent of country' around Dungarvan and from Youghal to Lismore, and on towards Fermoy was 'lighted up as far as the eye could reach'.[79] The more extensive use of notices and placards – most of which were 'anonymous' and many 'of a threatening character' – as a means of 'calling on the people to assemble' in 1846 and 1847 indicates that the populace capitalized on the growth in literacy in English as they employed the (English) printed word to communicate and to bring 'the labouring and other [poorer] classes' together.[80] Moreover, their notices were not limited to sloganizing, as the printed statement announcing the cancellation of the meeting of 'distressed farmers and labourers' planned for Cork Mountain in August 1846 attests (Fig. 2).[81] This event was conceived of, and advertised, as a public gathering; those meetings convened in response to anonymous hand-written notices were more select and private affairs, and can be frustratingly opaque as a result. Were they fora where tactics and strategy were deliberated, or were they occasions where the leader/s (the so-called 'village lawyers' or 'village politicians' referred to in other parts of the country)[82] within the community instructed those who assembled on how they should act. The notices posed in the parish of Bodyke in east county Clare in October, and on the gate of the chapel at Lady's Bridge, county Cork, in September 1847 certainly suggest that they combined instruction and compulsion as well as consultation, and that the former had the upper hand:

Take Notice

That all persons in this parish are required and requested to collect and meet in the neighbourhood of Ballinahinch on Tuesday the 19th instant without any disappointment at a hill commonly called Bohera in order that they shall consult with each other their distress. Let no person fail them at their peril, and let no person have an assurance of pulling this down for eight and forty hours.[83]

78 Walter, 'The politics of protest', p. 77.   79 Howley to [Redington], 14, 18 Sept., de Decies to [Labouchere], 22 Sept. 1846 (NAI, OP: Waterford, 1846/29/23895, 24081, 25731); *Kerry Evening Post*, 19, 23 Sept. 1846; *Freeman's Journal*, 24 Sept. 1846; Fraher, 'The Dungarvan disturbances', p. 138. 80 Kelly to [ ], 3 Sept. 1846 (NAI, OP: Tipperary, 1846/27/23299); RN (Ennis) to Redington, 11 May 1847 (NAI, OP: Clare, 1847/5/484); *Freeman's Journal*, 5 Oct. 1846.   81 Above, p. 118; Kelly to [Redington], 3 Sept. 1846 (NAI, OP: Tipperary, 1846/27/23299); Memorial of magistrates, 20 Oct. 1846 (NAI, OP: Clare, 1846/5/29333).   82 Warburton to Labouchere, 14 Oct. 1846 (NAI, OP: Wicklow, 1846/32/28015); Gary Owens, '"A moral insurrection": faction fighters, public demonstrators and the O'Connellite campaign, 1828', *IHS*, 30 (1996–7), 534.   83 Plunkett to [Redington], 21

> To the men of Ladies Bridge, stop and read:
> Fellow countrymen: on Monday next the parishioners of Ballymacoda
> intend to meet in the town of Castlemartyr, and we hope to meet our
> fellow sufferers of Ladysbridge for the express purpose of marching legally
> and constitutionally into the Midleton Union Workhouse in order to
> obtain relief.[84]

A fuller perspective on the aspirations and intentions of those behind such notices
can be gleaned from the report provided in the *Southern Reporter* following the
posting on the chapel at Carrigtwohill, county Cork, of a comparable notice 'calling on all the labouring classes of that and the surrounding district to assemble ...
to consider their present state and prospects'. Having made the ostensibly obvious
point 'that there was a famine in the parish', the notice went on to warn

> all those that did not attend [the meeting] that they should be marked;
> and complained that the labouring classes were only paid one shilling a
> day wages when they should be paid 1s. 6d., and that if it rained for half
> an hour that they were broken or put back in their wages a quarter day
> during those famishing times, and that they would not be satisfied unless
> they got 1s. 6d. a day wages.[85]

As well as the organization and co-ordinating intelligence to which notices of this
ilk attest, the discipline that food protesting crowds could bring to bear, exemplified by their capacity to assemble large crowds (comparable on occasion to the
'mass demonstrations' in counties Clare, Tipperary and Limerick in the late
summer of 1828), and to engage in targeted violence or no violence at all, are
indicative of more than organizational efficiency; they point to agreed tactics as
well as shared goals. Their capacity for political strategizing is more elusive but
it is hinted at in the 'regulations' presented by 'Lame Pat' Power to a 2,000
strong crowd in county Waterford in September 1846.

   Impelled by the need to alleviate the plight of smallholders who were strug-
gling to survive as a result of the failure of the potato crop, Power's direction to
those present to pursue the reimbursement of 'all money paid for conacre land'
from the farmers to whom they were beholden was only the most arresting of a
number of 'regulations', two of which directly echoed the concerns of food protesters. These called, specifically, upon 'farmers ... not to thresh or send out any
corn to market' and for milk, normally fed to pigs, to be 'kept and given to the
labourers without any charge'.[86] The pronouncement, also in October, by the tenants of the marquis of Bath and E.J. Shirley, in county Monaghan, that they

Oct. 1847 (NAI, OP: Clare, 1847/5/1150).   **84** Bell to Somerville, 28 Sept. 1847 (NAI, OP: Cork,
1847/6/1233).   **85** Quoted in *Freeman's Journal*, 5 Oct. 1846.   **86** Owens, '"A moral insurection"',
513–41; Fraher, 'Dungarvan disturbances', p. 140; *Connaught Telegraph*, 7 Oct. 1846. These regulations were enforced utilizing the methods of agrarian protest: see de Decies to Labouchere, 26
Sept., 3, 4 Oct. 1846 (NAI, OP: Waterford, 1846/29/26359, 27091, 26761).

were entitled 'to a remission of the present year's rent, and a reduction for the future proportionate to the people's ability to pay' indicates that the populace of county Waterford was not alone in thinking in this (political) fashion.[87] The moment was hardly opportune, of course, to progress schemes of this nature or, indeed, the issue of tenant right which went on to achieve a broader airing in 1848. Be that as it may, the nature and sophistication of these and other pronouncements is consistent with the conclusion that it is the definition of politicization that is at issue if food and allied purposive protest continued to be regarded as apolitical. In any event, it will be helpful to pursue an approach that is not beholden to a school of thought (Marxism) that holds that class consciousness is a prerequisite for politicization, or to the (bourgeois) view that assumes that politicization presumes a recognizably modernist agenda and a focus on representative institutions.

RECIPROCITY AND COMMUNITY

The enduring appeal of E.P. Thompson's concept of a 'moral economy' rests on a number of foundations, one of the most significant of which was the acceptance by those in authority of their obligation to respond to protest by doing what they could to ease the plight of those on the margins. This did not, as the response to riotous activity reveals, extend so far as to tolerate food rioting. It did not, in other words, mean that food protesters could act with impunity; the figures for dead rioters are the most striking testament to this. But they were permitted greater liberty than other forms of riotousness, even those perpetrated by other 'purposive crowds', not least because most episodes of food protest were short lived. The implication that food protesters sought to convey a message to those in charge is now sufficiently commonplace that various commentators have endorsed Hobsbawm's description of food rioting as 'collective bargaining by riot'. These include John Cunningham, who has offered this assessment of the situation in early nineteenth-century Ireland when it might be suggested that the evidence is more complex and the situation more ambiguous.[88]

It is demonstrable, however, that local officials in Ireland turned a blind eye on occasion or were complicit in the appropriation by riotous crowds of foodstuffs and their sale at a reduced price; one may instance the party of constabulary that responded to a food riot near Ennis in 1837 by 'purchasing bags of potatoes and then retailing them on the spot'; local officials also pushed the enve-

---

87 Barry to French, 4 Oct. 1846 (NAI, OP: Monaghan, 23/1846/26971). 88 Above, note 72; the concept has been invoked by Bohstedt, *Riots and community*, p. 68; idem, 'Food riots and the politics of provisions in world history', p. 6; Walton and Seddon, *Free markets and food riots*, p. 25; and Bouton, *The flour war*, p. 31. It has also been adopted in the Irish context by Cunningham, *Galway, 1790–1914*, p. 86, and by Lee who refers to 'violence as a form of negotiation between social classes in pre-Famine Ireland (Lee, 'The food riots of 1830 and 1840', p. 60).

lope of power available to them to its limit on occasion to prevent the transportation of food out of a region, as at Waterford in September–October 1846,
and took actions that might, in other contexts, have been criticized as complicit
with food rioters.[89] Furthermore, they were consistently to the fore in the late
eighteenth and early nineteenth century organizing subscriptions and gathering
funds to purchase food for distribution. Merchants, meanwhile, occasionally sold
the contents of stores and ships' holds at cost, and held back foodstuffs scheduled for transportation to another location either in the country or abroad. And
at a national level, officials not only incrementally increased the powers to which
they could appeal, they extended their entitlement to interfere in the market at
the expense of private property rights by acts of parliament.[90]

These powers were not lightly invoked or these actions taken easily.
Moreover, the evidence suggests that they were resorted to in respect of an inde-
terminable minority of food protests, and only when the authorities were satisfied that they had cause. There were, in short, many occasions – particularly
when the island was not subject to famine or subsistence crisis – when the
authorities refused to initiate relief, and the riotous were left with the choice
either of intensifying their protest, or accepting that the circumstances that
spurred them to riot were insufficiently grave to prompt the reciprocity that gave
food protest legitimacy. In other words, while it may be that one can conceive of
food rioting as a feature of an ongoing negotiation between 'patricians' and 'ple-
beians', this was a 'negotiation' that often concluded without a result or with a
negative outcome for those for whom protest was their defining activity. This
was an inevitable consequence of the fact that this not a 'negotiation' involving
equal parties.

Moreover, this was the case for the duration of the phenomenon. Though one
can readily identify occasions when subscriptions were inaugurated pursuant to
food protest, examples of *taxation populaire*, and incidents in which ships were
incapacitated to prevent them from departing port, and so on from the late 1720s
to the late 1840s, the context was ever evolving. The most striking change,
because it went to the heart of what the moral economy represented, was the
attenuation of the local/community world in which it functioned, and upon
which it was dependent. Food rioting flourished in Ireland, England and France
in the eighteenth century when the economic horizon of those who rioted was
primarily local. A locally produced surplus might be conveyed out of an area
during a good year without objection, but since the perception of the population
of a locality was that they possessed a prior entitlement to food produced in their
space the *menu peuple* felt justified in obstructing the movement of foodstuffs
when they were in short supply. This position was less easily sustained in the
case of traded commodities, but need trumped logic and consistency, with the
result that port dwellers and urban communities had little difficulty rationalizing

89 *Tuam Herald*, 15 July 1837; *Connaught Telegraph*, 7 Oct. 1846.   90 Above, pp 182–3.

their efforts both to prevent the movement of food, and to effect its appropriation when circumstances demanded. Calculations such as these, which might be termed a *droit de subsistence manqué*, sustained food rioting into the nineteenth century when the community was redefined, as the 'concerns of the rural poor ceased to be exclusively agrarian, and agitations became "supra-local"'. As a result, 'community norms were gradually ... replaced by horizontal consociations, as landowners and farmers attempted to respond to change through "private gain at the expense of the community"'.[91] This was not, as might be expected, the outcome of a single trend or tendency. Many factors – economic, social and, even, political – contributed, as the impact of economic growth, an expanded transport network (embracing canals as well as roads), greater demographic mobility (embracing seasonal migration as well as emigration) and fiscal and commercial integration (which was accelerated by the Act of Union) meant not only that more foreign goods were available to purchase but also that more foodstuffs were exported.[92] Moreover, the consequences were distinctive. Ireland did not experience the degree of class-based conflict that, in the early nineteenth century, shattered the foundations of reciprocity in England, which may have given food rioting popular legitimacy in the eighteenth.[93] It was, however, subjected to stresses and strains of a different nature as the legacy of the insurgency of the 1790s, the 1798 Rebellion and the incompatible political visions of the proponents of Protestant ascendancy and Catholic emancipation resulted in the attenuation of the deference and empathy that had once bound the populace and the elite in a working, if untrusting relationship. At the same time, the embrace of a 'less indulgent and more market orient[ed]' culture among the elite accented the 'estrangement of the upper classes from popular culture'.[94] This development impacted the pattern of food protest in Ireland more slowly than the emerging class-based divisions registered in industrializing England, but the cumulative effect, when combined with rapid demographic growth and fundamental economic challenges following the conclusion of the Napoleonic war time boom, was to accelerate changes in the manner in which food protest was pursued.

91 Huggins, *Social conflict in pre-Famine Ireland*, pp 189, 190. The concept of the 'supra-local' deployed by Huggins was conceived of by James W. O'Neill, 'Popular culture and peasant rebellion in pre-Famine Ireland' (PhD, University of Minnesota, 1984). **92** Cullen, *An economic history of Ireland since 1660*, chapter 5; Ó Gráda, *Ireland: a new economic history, 1780–1939*, part one; Patrick Lynch and John Vaizey, *Guinness's brewery in the Irish economy, 1759–1876* (Cambridge, 1960); Ruth Delany, *The Grand Canal of Ireland* (Newton Abbot, 1973); David Fitzpatrick, *Irish emigration, 1801–1921* (Dundalk, 1984); Bruce S. Elliott, *Irish migrants in the Canadas: a new approach* (Belfast, 1988); Anne O'Dowd, *Spalpeens and tattie hokers: history and folklore of the Irish migratory agricultural worker in Ireland and Britain* (Dublin, 1991). **93** Appropriately, E.P. Thompson's *The making of the English working class* (London, 1963) remains a key statement; but see also Boyd Hilton, *A mad, bad and dangerous people? England, 1783–1846* (Oxford, 2008) for a broader analysis. **94** Kelly, *Sir Richard Musgrave, 1746–1818: ultra-Protestant ideologue*, p. 90 ff; Bartlett, *The fall and rise of the Irish nation: the Catholic question, 1690–1830*, chapters 13 and 14; Huggins, *Social conflict in pre-Famine Ireland*, pp 177, 192; Paul Bew, *Ireland: the politics of enmity, 1789–2006* (Oxford, 2007), part 1.

There are various indices of this, most notably the emergence of the rural food crowd, but one must also recognize the surge in poverty-induced crime, in lieu of food protest, that occurred at the height of the 1817 subsistence crisis, in 1826 and again in 1847–8. It was particularly pronounced in certain areas; there was, for example, a spate of food theft by individuals and small groups seeking potatoes and bread, and attacks on farm animals – cows and sheep – in mid-Ulster; and by armed gangs in Limerick in 1817; and in county Tipperary in 1826.[95] This is noteworthy because those who engaged in food protest, even when it involved cutting the banks of the Royal Canal, were disposed to insist they were not 'guilty of any crime'.[96]

These underlying changes contributed to the diminution in the responsiveness to food rioting that can be identified in the 1820s and 1830s. The parallel contraction in the sense of community both facilitated and encouraged the greater assumption by the state of the responsibility for providing relief, and the disengagement by the elite. Taking the latter first; the diminishing role played by the elite is brought into striking view when one compares the response to the famine crisis of 1822 with that to the subsistence crisis of 1817, and its predecessors in 1799–1801 and 1783–4. During the eighteenth century, the effectiveness of the relief provided those in distress depended on a combination of individual, local, institutional and national initiatives. While the growth in capacity then can be ascribed in large part to the lattice of charitable, sociable, masonic and allied philanthropically minded organizations that were brought into being, this expansion in civil society could not have occurred without the active involvement of the elite.[97] It was they who orchestrated the public appeals, charity sermons, door-to-door collections and other fund-raising initiatives that provided the money upon which various charitable societies, parish committees and, from the 1770s, houses of industry and allied bodies and organizations, depended. They also provided relief in cash and kind, funded soup kitchens, and sustained other practical means by which the poor and undernourished were assisted to negotiate periods of particular difficulty.[98] In a valuable expansion of this model in the late 1810s, the lord mayor of Dublin established a Mansion House Committee, which assigned the impressive sum of £10,000 collected in the run up to Christmas in 1816 to the provision of oatmeal and other foodstuffs at a reduced price to the

95 *Freeman's Journal*, 30 May, 11, 12, 19 June 1817, 23 Aug. 1826; *Gentleman's Magazine*, 87 (1817), p. 620.   **96** Cunningham, 'Popular protest and a "moral economy"', p. 41.   **97** Dickson, 'In search of the old Irish poor law', pp 149–59; Kelly, 'Charitable societies: their genesis and development', pp 89–108; Petri Mirala, 'Masonic sociability and its limitations: the case of Ireland' in Kelly and Powell (eds), *Clubs and societies in eighteenth-century Ireland*, pp 315–31; Ciarán McCabe, 'The early years of the Strangers' Friend Society, Dublin: 1790–1845', *Bulletin of the Methodist Historical Society of Ireland*, 90 (2014), 65–92; Deirdre Lindsay, *Dublin's oldest charity: the Sick and Indigent Roomkeepers Association, 1790–1990* (Dublin, 1990).   **98** Dickson, 'In search of the old Irish poor law', passim; Kelly, 'Charitable societies', pp 89–108; idem, 'Combatting distress: the famine of 1740–41', 99–122; idem, 'Scarcity and poor relief in eighteenth-century Ireland: the subsistence crisis of 1782–4', 38–62.

poor. In Belfast, meanwhile, a soup kitchen was opened to respond to a similar need; in Armagh, 1,500 families received weekly relief from their local committee, while across the country, a variety of local relief committees and individuals were no less active. Lord Charleville gave £50 to the poor in Tullamore; the lord mayor of Dublin donated £1,000. The government, too, contributed, as we have seen, but the most striking feature of the 1817 episode is that the bulk of the £300,000 collected and distributed by the various relief committees probably came from non-governmental sources.[99]

Set against this backdrop, 'the decline of the traditional paternal role of the gentry' in evidence during the regional crisis of 1822 might seem sudden. There was no single reason for this. The challenge posed the authority of the landowner in the locality by 'the growing influence of [Daniel] O' Connell's constitutional crusade' has been cited, but since the Catholic Association did not exist at this point, it is improbable. It is more likely that the combination of the contraction of landed rentals as a result of the economic crisis of the post-Napoleonic war era; the strengthening appeal of ideological conservatism as politics fractured along increasingly sectarian lines; and the expansion of the role of the state to embrace relief as well as policing had already set society firmly in this direction. The course of events in 1822 in the west certainly demonstrated, McNamara has observed, 'the limits of landlord paternalism', and if this was still only the beginning of what was to be a prolonged process, the preparedness of newspaper editors openly to accuse the landholding elite of failing to serve the interests of the people, and of landowners to call for governmental intervention indicated that the paternalist bond that is identifiable in the eighteenth century was already fractured.[100] It was, to be sure, never as strong in Ireland as it was in England, but the exposure of ancient suspicions and easily aroused animosities, largely occluded or discouraged for several generations, combined with the growth of the state, and other forces, certainly weakened the local identification that operative food protest required. Moreover, it was destined to continue, as the evolution of the Police Preservation Force into the Irish Constabulary resulted in more barracks and more policemen, while the state moved to fill the welfare space vacated by landowners, by assuming the initiative in providing relief, culminating in the inauguration of the workhouse system authorized by the Poor Law Act of 1838.[101]

99 O'Neill, 'Clare and Irish poverty 1815–51', 12–13; *Freeman's Journal*, 7 Jan., 7 Mar. 1817; M.A. Trant, 'Government policy and Irish distress, 1816–19' (MA, UCD, 1965), passim; above, pp 204–6. **100** McNamara, 'This wretched people: the famine of 1822 in the west of Ireland', pp 26–30. **101** While certain changes and initiatives pursued in the eighteenth century provided the legal antecedents for the involvement of the state in relief, their engagement then was narrow by comparison with what became normative in the nineteenth century. Paradoxically, if it can be argued that the relief provided then was less successful than that provided in the eighteenth century it is likely that this was not because the relief was narrower and less freely given but because demand was greater. It was, of course, increasingly buffeted by ideological argumentation as free trade economics achieved increasing moral ascendancy: see Dickson, 'In search of the old Irish poor law', pp 149–59; Virginia Crossman, *Politics, pauperism and power in late nineteenth-century Ireland*

If, this reading of early nineteenth-century social, governmental and institutional trends suggests, the reason to engage in food protest in Ireland declined from the beginning of the third decade of the nineteenth century, the implication is that prior to this point Ireland possessed a robust 'moral economy'. John Cunningham is in no doubt. In his most explicit statement on the subject he has concluded, based upon his detailed analysis of the early nineteenth century, that 'the events of 1812 are indicative of a widespread moral economic tradition', and he cites a range of features in support of this conclusion:

> firstly, popular mobilizations occurred in all four provinces; secondly, there was variety in the objectives of crowds – most of them came together to prevent exports, but there was price fixing also, and some anti-forestalling measures. This suggests a developed tradition ... as does the response of the authorities, which was so mild in instances as to be almost complicit in the efforts of regulation.[102]

The implication, that food rioting worked and that Ireland possessed a 'moral economy' which relieved those in need, echoes the conclusion arrived at by Walton and Seddon, who close their summary of inquiry into the subject in England with the observation that protest served 'frequently ... in bringing immediate relief, if not the reversal of deeper causal currents'.[103] This dovetails with the considered opinion of E.P. Thompson, who confidently invoked the findings of John Walter and Keith Wrightson in respect of the seventeenth century and John Bohstedt for the eighteenth and early nineteenth, in support of his contention that food rioting was 'invariably successful in stimulating authoritative action to alleviate grievances'.[104] Support for this conclusion is also forthcoming from those who have studied the practice on the Continent. Charles Tilley's observation, based upon a survey of the position in early modern Europe, that food protest 'often worked in the short run; crowd action brought prices down, forced stored grain into the public domain, and impelled the authorities to greater efforts towards assuring the food supply' anticipated positive conclusions by Cynthia Bouton with respect to France in the eighteenth century, and Manfred Gailus of Germany in the 1840s.[105] A comparably positive conclusion might be advanced in respect of Ireland where identifiable examples of 'popular mobilization', price fixing (*taxation populaire*), the prevention of the internal movement and exportation of foodstuffs, and of the official indulgence of food

---

(Manchester, 2006).   **102** Cunningham, 'Popular protest and a "moral economy"', p. 37. **103** Walton and Seddon, *Free markets and food riots*, p. 30.   **104** Thompson, 'Moral economy reviewed', p. 292, citing John Walter and Keith Wrightson, 'Dearth and social order in early modern England', *Past and Present*, 71 (1976), 41; also Bohstedt, *Riots and community politics*, passim.   **105** Charles Tilly, 'Food supply and public order in early modern Europe' in idem (ed.), *The formation of national states in Europe* (Princeton, 1975), p. 386; Bouton, *The flour war*, p. 25; Gailus, 'Food riots in German in the late 1840s', 192.

protest can be seen, and shown to have had a positive local impact. There were, in addition, cases of the appropriation of the content of food stores, mills, bakeries and shops, and the interception of convoys of carts ferrying foodstuffs to ports and towns of which a comparable observation might be made. In 1842, for example, when 'a number of persons ... reduced to the greatest destitution' unloaded potatoes from on board two steamers in Wexford harbour 'and brought them from thence to the town market where they were sold at 25 per cent below the market price', the police declined to intervene 'as there was no disposition to riot or tumult'.[106] This was a remarkable demonstration of empathy with the populace, and it is identifiable also during the Great Famine in the refusal of some carters to offer any opposition to the crowds that sought to intercept their cargoes, in the attitude adopted on occasion by the police, and in the relief initiatives undertaken by local communities in response to crowd interventions.[107] These heartening demonstrations of solicitude notwithstanding, the general atmosphere was less accommodating then than it had been a generation earlier. It was, it is reasonable to assume, only to be expected that judges on assize would state the official position, which was that riot and the disruption of the free market would not be tolerated, but the frequency with which the religious authorities, and specifically Catholic priests, enjoined the public patiently to await the provision of relief indicated that officialdom had support in quarters that were especially influential with the populace.[108] Moreover, though one can identify comparable instances across the time span of food protest, its inclusion in the category of 'plundering provisions' and the greater emphasis in the 1840s on the recovery of 'stolen' foodstuffs indicates that the 'moral economy' continued to retreat in the face of a more clinical political economy. There are sufficient recoverable manifestations of empathy with the needy in 1846–7 to demonstrate that the convictions that sustained a 'moral' approach to distress were not without credit to the end, but it operated then in a world that was less accommodating than that which preceded.

CONCLUSION: IRELAND'S MORAL ECONOMY

The decline in food rioting in Ireland mirrored an international trend that is also identifiable in nineteenth-century England and France. Various reasons have been suggested: addressing 'the decline and disappearance of the classical food riot in France' a generation ago, Louise Tilly ascribed it to a combination of powerful forces that included 'increased productivity, the development of modern communication and transportation networks, and the renegotiation of access to food for

---

106 *Nenagh Guardian*, 11 June 1842.   107 Above, pp 65, 155, 177–8.   108 See *Freeman's Journal*, 5, 6, 7, 8, 15, 20 Oct. 1846, 15 May, 18 June 1847; Kerr, *The Catholic Church and the Famine*, pp 11–3, 19–20; Glengall to Bessborough, [15] Apr. 1846, Redmond to Pennefeather, 19 Apr. 1846 (NAI, OP: Tipperary, 1846/27/9327, 9413).

those previously made vulnerable'.[109] E.P. Thompson perceived the transition in comparable but larger terms. Though peripheral to his primary purpose, which was to explain why the defence of 'traditional rights or customs' was the *raison d'etre* of food protest, Thompson implicitly attributed its demise to the rise of a modern, competitive, profit-oriented market economy.[110] Charles Tilly was more precise; he identified it as a victim of the transition 'from older forms of protest – such as food riots, tax rebellions, and *charivaris* (or 'rough music')' – to 'industrial strikes, public demonstrations and associated social movements'. Based upon his analysis of 'popular contention in Great Britain' between 1758 and 1834, Tilly contended that the manner in which protest was pursued shifted from the 'parochial' and the 'particular' to the 'cosmopolitan' and broad-based form that was possessed of a more outward and national character and outlook.[111] While not disagreeing with this, John Bohstedt highlights the changing nature of the community that underpinned the phenomenon in the eighteenth century: 'community politics gave way to class', making wages and not food the primary battleground; as a consequence 'reciprocity now took shape in bitter battles rather than pragmatic bargaining'. There is no gainsaying that English politics was more confrontational in the early nineteenth century, and that this, and the wholesale economic and societal changes that are encompassed under the umbrella of the industrial revolution, pushed food rioting out of the 'middle-sized county and market towns' that had long been its anchorage, towards the periphery, where it eked out a marginal and declining existence.[112] Ireland also underwent major change of course, but because Ireland in the early nineteenth century was embarked on an economic journey that culminated in the Great Famine – which is distinguished by the single-greatest episode of food protest in Irish history, and an allied if less disciplined phase of agrarian protest and famine induced crime – any explanation of the decline of food protest there must – no less than its rise and *floruit* – take cognizance of the particular history of that island.[113]

Food rioting prospered in eighteenth-century Ireland because it mirrored the state of economic development, and a sufficiently consensual approach to key issues of hunger and alimentation, and poor relief, which required not only that the communities that engaged in food rioting could anticipate a sympathetic response, but also that those in positions of power accepted that it was their responsibility to seek to alleviate distress. It is essential that this is kept in per-

109 Bouton, *The flour war*, p. 6 note 17; Louise Tilly, 'The decline and disappearance of the classical food riot in France', New School for Social Research, Working paper 147 (1992). **110** Thompson, 'The moral economy of the English crowd', 78 and passim.   **111** C. Tilly, *Popular contention in Great Britain, 1758–1834* (Cambridge, MA, 1995), pp 43–6; idem, *Contentious performances*, passim; see Ely, *A crooked line: from cultural history to the history of society*, p. 46. **112** Bohstedt, *The politics of provisions*, pp 245–60; Bohstedt, *Riots and community politics*, pp 26, 202–3 and passim; Stevenson, 'Bread or blood', p. 34; Walton and Seddon, *Free markets and food politics*, pp 32–3.   **113** See Cullen, *An economic history of Ireland since 1660*, chapter 5; Cormac Ó Gráda, *Ireland: a new economic history, 1780–1939* (Oxford, 1994), part one.

spective. Based upon the number of food protests that took place, and their regional and temporal distribution, it can reasonably be argued that the strong community politics integral to food protest in England did not function to the same degree in Ireland. By the same token, and using numbers again as the criterion, it may be that the Irish populace was also less restive, or less volatile, than its French equivalent.[114] Yet the trajectory of food rioting that has been traced indicates that, for all the particularities of the economic, commercial and political systems obtaining in England, France and Ireland, each was at a stage of development that sustained a tradition of protest. The fact that in Ireland (as in France) this coincides with a still-more vibrant tradition of agrarian protest, and a less thoroughly explored tradition of artisanal combination, certainly cautions against assessing food protest in isolation, though no definitive judgement can yet be advanced.

There is, in any event, no single causal explanation for the decline in food rioting in Ireland. The nineteenth century witnessed major societal changes that diminished the rationale for protest of this kind, and deprived it of the opportunity it had long been afforded. These include the emergence of a more vigorous state that assumed responsibility for the care of the poor, and in particular for providing poor relief at moments of crisis. In so doing, the state not only liberated those who had previously shouldered this responsibility but also transformed the social relationships between the poor and vulnerable and the elite that had underpinned food protest. Second, the surge in suspicion manifest in the greater tension visible in the country as landowners distanced themselves from their teeming tenantry, and relations between farmers, who pursued an increasingly commercial agenda, and cottiers and labourers dis-improved meant that suspicion exerted a more formative influence on social relations. And third, arising out of the latter, as food protest borrowed from its more aggressive agrarian equivalent, it became less distinct and less distinguishable, with the result that landowners drew increasingly, both metaphorically and literally, behind the shelter of the demesne walls they constructed as a protection against the threat of assault and assassination.[115]

This was significant, because both the manner in which it was pursued by the populace, and the manner in which the authorities responded demonstrate that food rioting was long conceived of differently to other practices in which rioting crowds were normative – one may instance smuggling, illicit distillation, agrarian protest, urban factions, and opposition to the heart tax, tithe and other imposts.[116] This was the case, moreover, from the 1720s. Then the relief afforded thousands

---

114 See above, pp 209–10. 115 Michael Beames, 'Rural conflict in pre-Famine Ireland: peasant assassinations in Tipperary, 1837–1847, *Past and Present*, 81 (1978), 75–9. 116 See, inter alia, Watt, 'Taxation riots and the culture of popular protest in Ireland, 1714–1740', 1418–38; Patrick O'Donoghue, 'Opposition to tithe payments in 1830–31', *Studia Hibernica*, 6 (1966), 69–98; Kelly, *The Liberty and Ormond boys*, passim; David Fitzpatrick, 'Class, family and rural unrest in nineteenth-century Ireland' in P.J. Drudy (ed.), *Irish Studies, 2: Ireland: land, politics and people* (Cambridge, 1982), pp 37–75; Donnelly, *Captain Rock*, passim.

in Cork as a result of the sharp reduction in food prices that followed the major food riot there in February 1729 demonstrated its potential, and, once the foundations were laid, they remained firmly in place for nearly a century. One of the defining features of this period was the assumption by those who engaged in food protest that they would secure early relief as a result of their actions, though this was not always the case. Indeed, the intervention of the crowd served on occasions to exacerbate issues of supply as farmers responded by holding onto stocks in the expectation of increased profits, or merchants were discouraged from engaging in normal trading for fear of the wrath of the crowd, with the result that, as occurred in Ennis May 1817, markets might be left entirely bare.[117] However, the outcome was sufficiently heartening, both in terms of the immediate reliefs secured by the appropriation and distribution of food, by the enforcement of *taxation populaire*, and by the insistence on the primacy of the public marketplace to induce the crowd to persist in the practice. Moreover, the combined effect of the unwillingness of merchants, dealers and millers to defy the 'mob', and of generations of officials to inaugurate public subscriptions for the relief and easement of those whose circumstances, real or psychological,[118] prompted them to engage in food rioting, is further testament to its moral authority.

There was, of course, an identifiable strand of opinion which believed, with Edmund Burke, that the market was by some measure the best way to ensure that 'the balance of wants is settled'.[119] From this vantage point, food rioting amounted to a dangerous, and damaging intervention in the workings of an efficient economic system. Though it was largely muffled during the eighteenth and early nineteenth centuries by belief in the merit of allaying the concerns that fuelled food protest, it is not difficult to locate this sentiment.[120] It gathered strength thereafter as the values of respectability, evangelicalism, the appreciating power of the state, free trade economics and classical liberalism acquired increased ascendancy in public discourse. As a result, the essentially pragmatic considerations that once guided official and public attitudes to food protest, and the paternalist impulse that informed the reciprocity that was intrinsic to the concept of a 'moral economy' were pushed towards the margins. This might suggest that the interpretation favoured here echoes Bohstedt's model of a pragmatic

---

117 *Universal Advertiser*, 5 May 1753; Cunningham, *Galway, 1790–1814*, p. 91; above, pp 33–4; *Freeman's Journal*, 29 May 1817. This chimes with Thompson's observation in 1971 that 'in the short-term it would seem probable that riot and price-setting defeated their own objects': Thompson, 'The moral economy of the English crowd', p. 121. For further observations see idem, 'The moral economy reviewed', pp 289–90, 291–2. 118 The terms 'subsistence mentality' and 'the psychosis of scarcity' were coined by Steven Kaplan and Yves-Marie Bercé respectively: Kaplan, *Bread, politics and political economy in the reign of Louis XV* (2 vols, The Hague, 1976), i, 200; Yves-Marie Bercé, *Revolt and revolution in early modern Europe*, p.102; see Bouton, *The flour war*, p. 15. 119 Edmund Burke, 'Thoughts and details on scarcity', 1795 in Works (1801), vii, pp 348–51, cited in Thompson, 'The moral economy reviewed', p. 273. 120 According to Bouton, *The flour war*, p. 21, 'These actions reflected popular assumptions about the public nature of food wherever it was found that overrode considerations of private ownership and control'.

as opposed to a 'moral economy'. There is much that can be said in favour of this perspective, but there is also much about the manner in which Irish food protesters conducted themselves, and the ameliorative response that many local and municipal interests undertook that echoes Thompson's thesis. If this is seen to wish to have it both ways, this is not the object. Both Thompson and Bohstedt developed interpretative models that seek to explain food rioting as it was practised by the English crowd. Irish society differed from that of England, and indeed of France, and if there is one thing we have learned from the diversity of studies of food rioting is that the attempts to apply the concept of a 'moral economy' as it was originally conceptualized seldom succeed. Yet, it is a testament to its utility that it possesses sufficient elements to permit its application to contexts that differ signally from England. In Ireland, food rioting was less about the defence of a traditional paternalist economy in the face of an emerging capitalist economy than it was about securing access to food.

Epilogue: the subsistence crisis of 1861–2

1861 was an exceptionally challenging year in a sequence of difficult years between 1859 and 1864.[1] The weather was so inclement – with an 'almost unprecedented concentration of rainfall in the crucial months of July through September – crops failed to mature, cattle did not thrive and turf was not harvestable in some locations. The severity of the impact of these difficulties on the population varied inevitably, but the reports pouring into newsrooms in the early winter was sufficiently portentous to cause the *Freeman's Journal* to invoke 1846 and to call upon 'the government' to 'take instant steps ... to give employment during the ensuing year'.[2] A 'special correspondent' reported from Portumna, county Galway, in mid-November 'that the failure of the potato crop, the deficiency of the harvest generally, and above all the want of fuel, are of sufficient extent to justify the prevalent opinion that this winter will be one of severe distress and privation'. Another report from the same town anticipated 'the prospect of very sad and severe distress among the small farmers and labouring population'.[3] Both were confident that there would not be a repeat of 'the appalling privation of 1847'. But there was no masking public anxiety as news filtered through of the impact of the 'continued over-flowings of the [river] Shannon'; of the 'destruction of ... cattle arising from the want of pasture and loss of hay'; of the 'want of fuel' because horses and carts could not access bogs or because turf failed to dry; of the 'scanty return of oats'; the 'bad' crop of barley; the 'inferior' quality of wheat; 'the under productiveness of the turnip crop'; and the depletion of the potato harvest by between one-third and one-half.[4] Conditions were most ominous along the western seaboard – counties Galway, Mayo, Clare and Limerick particularly – but difficulties were not confined to this region. In Drogheda, where 'large groups of trades-people [we]re to be found daily standing idle at our courthouse and different corners, unable to procure employment', the board of guardians provided outdoor relief in December to 36 per cent more

1 See James S. Donnelly, jr, 'The Irish agricultural depression of 1859–64', *Irish Economic and Social History*, 3 (1976), 33–54 for a fine contextualized analysis of the year. 2 *Freeman's Journal*, 8, 14 Nov. 1861. 3 *Freeman's Journal*, 21, 25 Nov. 1861. 4 *Freeman's Journal*, 7, 14, 21, 25 Nov. 1861. According to the tabulation of 'crop yields' nationally assembled by Donnelly, the potato crop in 1861 was the worst in the six years 1859–64. Using the average yields of 1856–8 as his base line, Donnelly has calculated the potato crop return in 1861 at 42 per cent; wheat 69 per cent; barley 83 per cent; oats 88 per cent; turnips 80 per cent. The clergy and gentry of Connemara, meeting in Clifden in late October, claimed two-thirds of the potato crop was 'totally lost': Donnelly, 'The Irish agricultural depression of 1859–64', 37, 46.

recipients than was the case a year earlier.[5] In Dublin, the suspension of 'outdoor labour' in November following the premature onset of winter, and 'the high price of provisions and fuel' increased the number of 'applications for relief from the sick, the naked and the hungering' beyond the capacity of 'the public charities of the city'.[6]

In short, conditions seemed tailor-made for a repeat of the large-scale food protest that had taken place in 1846–7, or, should it be of a more select nature, of the kind common in the eighteenth century. This was the expectation certainly, as concern at the 'scarcity of fuel' ceded as the winter closed in to disturbing reports of people dying of hunger in Athlone, of 'the poor ... dropping dead from positive want of food in Limerick', and of references to 'hunger' in Headford, Oughterard, Tuam and Galway in county Galway, and Swinford, Ballinrobe and Castlebar in county Mayo.[7] Indicatively, nine magistrates contacted the local police inspector in Galway in December to warn him 'that an outbreak on the part of the unemployed may occur at any time'. The magistrates blamed 'agitators' who advised the populace 'that they should not allow themselves to die of cold and hunger'.[8] They were certainly persuaded that the number of police was insufficient to maintain law and order should the much diminished population engage in food rioting of the kind last experienced in the city in 1857, and, following the example of previous urban crowds, seek to alleviate distress by appropriating food from storage places in the city and ships in port. With the prevention of this in mind they concluded that prudence demanded that the forces of law and order should be augmented. The RIC inspector to whom the communication was addressed was not convinced. But, in deference to his appellants and the sensitivity of the request, he ordered its transmission to Dublin Castle. No reinforcements were conveyed, and because no riot ensued the magistrates' appeal soon faded into memory.

Dublin Castle's unwillingness to order police or military reinforcements to Galway was consistent with the low-key character of their response to events during the winter of 1861–2. In the absence of the lord lieutenant, the tenth earl of Carlisle, who was not in the country, the chief secretary, Sir Robert Peel, 3rd bart. (who visited north Connacht in November), responded to the concerns expressed by a deputation from Dublin Corporation with an assurance 'that the workhouses would be sufficient to meet the pressure of pauperism'.[9] Peel's belief that the existing machinery of relief was adequate contrasted with that of Sir John Grey, the proprietor of the *Freeman's Journal*, and others on Dublin Corporation, who called upon the lord mayor, Richard Atkinson, to convene a

5 *Freeman's Journal*, 11 Dec. 1861. 6 *Freeman's Journal*, 19 Nov. 1861. 7 *Freeman's Journal*, 6, 7, 9, 10, 11, 13, 20 Dec. 1861. 8 Cunningham, *Galway, 1790–1914*, p. 97; NAI, RP, 1860–61/100052. 9 *ODNB, sub nomine*; Gerard Moran, *The Mayo evictions of 1860* (Westport, 1986), p. 111; *Freeman's Journal*, 20 Dec. 1861. The response to the lord mayor was in keeping with the government's determination that relief would be 'provided ... wholly through the ordinary machinery of the ... poor law': Donnelly, 'The Irish agricultural depression of 1859–64', 47–8.

Mansion House Committee, as his predecessors had done previously on similar occasions.[10] Grey ultimately had his way, and the establishment shortly afterwards of a Mansion House Committee attested to the enduring value of structured civic philanthropy.[11] This was still more obviously the case in Connaught, where conditions were much worse, but what was more striking was the prominence of the Catholic clergy in the orchestration, representation and delivery of relief. The presence of Archbishop Cullen of Dublin on the Mansion House Committee was the most obvious symbolic manifestation of the Catholic clergy's increasing prominence, though the archbishop's membership was less important in practice than the active engagement of clerics in the provision of relief. Priests and bishops did not act in isolation, of course. They both supported, and were supported in turn by landowners, and professional men, but the leadership of John MacEvilly, bishop of Galway, John Derry, bishop of Clonfert, and Laurence Gillooly, bishop of Elphin, and the example provided locally by parish priests – Peter Daly in Galway city, Patrick Lavelle in Partry, Peter Conway in Headford, Patrick Lyons in Spiddal, Patrick MacManus in Clifden, and M.A. Kavanagh of Oughterard – was testimony to the temporal as well as spiritual ascendancy they now exerted in the communities in which they lived, and to the fact that this was at the expense of the landed elite.[12] Saliently, they made less reference now in their sermons, public speeches and pronouncements to the virtues of patience, to which they (and others) had appealed both before and during the Great Famine, but apart from outspoken individuals like Patrick Lavelle they did not encourage defiance.[13] Rather, they offered themselves as the spokesman of their communities, and they had the satisfaction of knowing – in contrast to the situation previously – that their message would be heard because, like their clergy, a majority of the Catholic population was eager to be seen to espouse the virtues and values of respectability.

The extent to which this provided the standard by which the public determined what was proper was highlighted by a public letter to the board of Guardians of Tuam Union from Peter Conway, the parish priest of Headford, in December 1861 in which he declined to provide the name of a local woman, 'once in very comfortable circumstances', who had died of 'starvation and cold' lest 'it might be hurtful to the feelings of any of her respectable relations'.[14] This was not incompatible with the expectation that it was incumbent on the state to provide relief, and bishops and priests encouraged their flocks both to look to government and to defer to the structures of power (the workhouses excepted).[15] It is notable

---

10 Report of proceedings of a 'special meeting' of Dublin Corporation, 19 Dec. 1861, *Freeman's Journal*, 20 Dec. 1862.   11 *Freeman's Journal*, 25 Feb. 1862.   12 *Freeman's Journal*, 25 Nov., 7, 11, 13 Dec. 1861, 5, 17 Jan. 1862; K. Theodore Hoppen, *Elections, politics, and society in Ireland, 1832–1885* (Oxford, 1984); Emmet Larkin, *The pastoral role of the Roman Catholic Church in pre-famine Ireland, 1750–1850* (Dublin, 2006).   13 Gerard Moran, *A radical priest in Mayo, Fr Patrick Lavelle* (Dublin, 1994).   14 *Freeman's Journal*, 11 Dec. 1861.   15 See the public letter of Bishop MacEvilly to Archbishop Cullen, 23 Feb. 1862 in *Freeman's Journal*, 25 Feb. 1862.

that the memorial presented by the delegation from Sligo, Roscommon and Galway, headed by Bishop Gillooly of Elphin, which met the earl of Carlisle in January 1816 prioritized public works and additional funding 'for the more distressed [poor law] unions'.[16] Indeed, once the Catholic Church was assured that the crisis would not be seized upon by religious evangelicals as an opportunity to proselytize,[17] it worked closely with the state, and it was willing, in return for support and co-operation, to inculcate and to promote a culture of deference and acquiescence that was far removed from the assertiveness that traditionally fuelled food protest. This was consistent with its definition of what made a good Catholic and the modern Ireland it was seeking earnestly to create, and it was one that possessed increasing purchase with the Catholic rank and file.

The result was demonstrated vividly on Christmas day in Galway city, when, instead of enforcing *taxation populaire* or preventing the movement of foodstuffs out of the city, thousands gathered in church in a collective demonstration of deference, as the report in the *Galway Vindicator* made clear:

> Christmas Day in Galway – The joyous festival of Christmas was celebrated with great splendour in the various Catholic churches and chapels in this city ... The altars were beautifully decorated for the occasion, and the ceremonies of religion were performed with the imposing grandeur which peculiarly belong[s] to the Catholic church. There were crowded congregations at all the masses, and the most intense piety was displayed by the ... people. At the parish church there was a grand pontifical high mass ... The spacious church was crowded to excess, and the sermon preached ... was eloquent and affecting. The offertory on the occasion was for the Lord Bishop, and we are glad to know that the amount received was far above what had been collected on any year ...[18]

Food rioting was not a religious matter of course. But in the context of a time when religious conviction was appreciating, the religious disposition of the population mattered, and the post Great Famine Catholic population was quite different to its pre-Famine predecessor since as well as food rioting it no longer sustained agrarian protest. This can be ascribed in part to the percolation and embrace of the mores and customs of the middling sort, but it was still more manifestly a product of the transformation of the structure of the population by the combination of death and emigration, which meant that the critical mass of labouring and land poor that was long the primary engine of food protest was no more. Having reached its highest recorded level of 8.175 million in 1841, the 6.552 million recorded in 1851 revealed the devastating demographic impact of the Great Famine. Furthermore, it established a trend. By 1861 when the population stood at 5.798 million the demographic impetus for agrarian as well as food

---

16 *Freeman's Journal*, 14 Jan. 1862.   17 See Archbishop MacHale on distress, *Freeman's Journal*, 25 Nov. 1861.   18 *Galway Vindicator*, reported in *Freeman's Journal*, 30 Dec. 1861.

protest had all but disappeared, while the fatalistic resignation that the Great Famine left in its wake discouraged defiance.[19] In addition, the creation of 'sophisticated networks of wholesaling, retailing and credit' in Ireland, as in England and in France, meant that the labouring and land poor were less likely to experience crisis when conditions deteriorated. This meant, a confident correspondent informed the *Freeman's Journal* in 1861, that 'the increased resources of the country at large would enable us to deal effectually with distress of a more aggravated character than any which we are likely to encounter'.[20] There was, as a result, a tangible decline in the number of subsistence crises in the second half of the nineteenth century.[21] It is not clear if the Irish administration anticipated this in 1861–2. The reiteration by the lord lieutenant that 'the government had reason to believe that the distress would not be so formidable as had been apprehended' when he met with the a delegation from counties Sligo, Roscommon and Galway on 13 January 1862 suggests that his horizon was shorter.[22] Be that as it may, the absence of any reference to food protest in the memorial presented by the delegation as well as in the lord lieutenant's reply serves as fully as the absence of any food rioting during the winter of 1861–2 to demonstrate that the era of food rioting in Ireland was over.

19 Timothy Guinnane, *The vanishing Irish: households, migration, and the rural economy in Ireland, 1850–1914* (Princeton, 1997); Cormac Ó Gráda, *Black '47 and beyond: the Great Irish Famine in history, economy and memory* (Princeton, 2000).   2 Donnelly, 'The Irish agricultural depression of 1859–64', 49; *Freeman's Journal*, 25 Nov. 1861.   21 T.P. O'Neill, 'The famine crises of the 1890s' in Crawford (ed.), *Famine: the Irish experience*, pp 176–97.   22 *Freeman's Journal*, 14 Jan. 1862.

Bibliography

PRIMARY SOURCES

I. MANUSCRIPTS

American Philosophical Society, Philadelphia
Franklin papers

British Library, London
Egmont papers, Add. MSS 46978, 46994

County Louth Archives Service, Dundalk
Corporation of Ardee minute book, 1661–87

The National Archives, Kew
Foreign Office papers, Portugal (FO/63)
Home Office papers (HO/100)
Minutes of the Revenue Commissioners, 1729–64 (CUST/1/21–70)
Privy Council registers (PC2)

National Archives of Ireland
Chief Secretary's Office, ICR/1, *Return of outrages reported to the Constabulary Office … 1848, 1849, 1850, 1851, 1852, 1853, 1854, 1855* (Dublin, 1849–56)
Chief Secretary's Office, Official papers, 1839–46
Chief Secretary's Office, Outrage papers (OP), 1846–9: /1 (Antrim); /2 (Armagh); /3 Carlow; /4 (Cavan); /5 (Clare); /6 (Cork); /7 Donegal; /8 (Down); /9 (Dublin); /10 (Fermanagh); /11 (Galway); /12 (Kerry); /13 (Kildare); /14 (Kilkenny); /15 (King's county); /16 (Leitrim); /17 (Limerick); /18 Londonderry; /19 (Longford); /20 (Louth); /21 (Mayo); /22 (Meath); /23 (Monaghan); /24 (Queen's county); /25 (Roscommon); /26 (Sligo); /27 (Tipperary); /28 (Tyrone); /29 (Waterford); /30 (Westmeath); /31 (Wexford); /32 (Wicklow)
Chief Secretary's Office, Rebellion papers (RP), 1822
Chief Secretary's Office, Registered papers, first division registers, 1840–50, 1860–1
Chief Secretary's Office, State of the country papers (SC) 1821
Index of departmental letters and papers, 1760–89 (volumes 1 and 2)
Isabel Grubb's notes from petitions in Public Record Office of Ireland, 1915
Pembroke estate papers, 97/46/1/2/4
Prim Collection

National Library of Ireland
Bellew papers, MS 27126
Killadoon papers, MS 36064
Lords lieutenant union correspondence, MS 886

National Library of Wales
Puleston papers, MS 3548D

New York Public Library
Trumbull papers

Public Record Office of Northern Ireland, Belfast
Carrickfergus Corporation records, 1569–1801 (T/707/1)
Greer papers (D/1044)
Mussenden papers (D/354)
Wilmot papers (T/3019)

Waterford City Archives,
Corporation of Waterford council books, 1701–70

Yale University, Beinecke Library
Osborn Collection, Northington letterbook

2. PRINTED PRIMARY MATERIAL

Altamont: 'Lord Altamont's letters to Lord Lucan about the Act of Union', ed. Brigid
    Clesham, *Journal of the Galway Archaeological and Historical Society*, 54 (2002), 25–34.
Bath: HMC, *Manuscripts of the marquess of Bath*, iii (London, 1908).
Bedford: *The correspondence of John, fourth, duke of Bedford*, ed. Lord John Russell (3 vols,
    London, 1842–6).
Boulter: *Letters written by Hugh Boulter, lord primate of all Ireland*, ed. Ambrose Phillips (2
    vols, Dublin, 1770).
Boulter: *The Boulter letters*, ed. Kenneth Milne and Paddy McNally (Dublin, 2016).
Carpenter: 'Instructions, admonitions etc of Archbishop Carpenter,' ed. M.J. Curran,
    Reportorium Novum, 2:1 (1957–8), 148–71.
Carrick-on-Suir: 'A Carrickman [James Ryan]'s diary, 1787–1809', ed. Patrick Power, *Journal of
    the Waterford and South-East of Ireland Archaeological Society*, 15 (1912), 39–7, 62–70, 124–37.
Catholics: *Catholics in the eighteenth-century press*, ed. John Brady (Maynooth, 1966).
Census: *A census of Ireland, circa 1659: with supplementary material from the poll money ordi-
    nances (1660–1661)*, ed. Seamus Pender (Dublin, 1939, 2002).
Cork: *Council book of the Corporation of Cork from 1609 to 1643 and from 1690 to 1800*, ed.
    Richard Caulfield (Guilford, 1876).
Cork: *The history of the county and city of Cork* by C.B. Gibson (2 vols, Cork, 1861).
Drennan: *The Drennan–McTier letters* ed. Jean Agnew (3 vols, Dublin, 1998–9).
Drogheda: *Council book of the Corporation of Drogheda: vol. 1 from 1649 to 1734*, ed. Thomas
    Gogarty (Drogheda, 1915; rpt. Dundalk, 1988).
Dublin: *Calendar of ancient records of Dublin*, ed. Sir John and Lady Gilbert (19 vols, Dublin,
    1889–1944).
Ennis: *Corporation book of Ennis*, ed. Brian Ó Dalaigh (Dublin, 1990).
German: *'Poor green Erin': German travel writers' narratives on Ireland from before the 1798
    Rising to after the Great Famine*, ed. Eoin Bourke (Frankfurt, 2013).
Kinsale: *The council book of the Corporation of Kinsale from 1652 to 1800*, ed. Richard Caulfield
    (Guilford, 1879).

Hare: *The letterbook of Richard Hare, merchant of Cork, 1771–1772*, ed. James O'Shea (Dublin, 2013).

Henry-Secker letters: R.G. Ingram (ed.), '"Popish cut-throats against us"': papists, protestants and the problem of allegiance in eighteenth-century Ireland' in Melanie Barber et al. (eds), *From the reformation to the permissive society: a miscellany* (Church of England Record Society, vol. 18: Woodbridge, 2010), pp 151–210.

Higgins: *Revolutionary Dublin, 1795–1801: the letters of Francis Higgins to Dublin Castle*, ed. Thomas Bartlett (Dublin, 2004).

Macartney: *Macartney in Ireland, 1768–1772*, ed. Thomas Bartlett (Belfast, [1979]).

Nunziatura: 'Catalogue of Nunziatura di Fiandra, pt 5', ed. Cathaldus Giblin, *Collectanea Hibernica*, 9 (1966), 7–70.

O'Conor: *The letters of Charles O'Conor*, eds R.E. Ward and C.C. Ward (2 vols, Ann Arbor, 1980).

O'Hara: 'Charles O'Hara's Observations on county Sligo, 1752–73', ed. David Dickson and D.F. Fleming, *Analecta Hibernica*, 46 (2015), 85–119.

Ossory: 'Episcopal edicts of the diocese of Ossory', ed. Feargus Ó Fearghail, *Ossory, Laois and Leinster*, 2 (2006), 65–95.

Proclamations: *The proclamations of Ireland, 1660–1820*, ed. James Kelly with Mary-Ann Lyons (5 vols, Dublin, 2014).

Russell: *The journals of Thomas Russell*, ed. C.J. Woods (Dublin, 1991).

Varley: *The unfortunate husbandman: to which is prefaced a short account of Charles Varley's life and times*, ed. Desmond Clarke (London, 1964).

Walpole: Horace Walpole, *Memoirs of the reign of George II*, ed. John Brooke (3 vols, New Haven and London, 1985).

Washington: *The papers of George Washington: presidential series*, ed. W.W. Abbot (4 vols, Charlottesville, 1976–9).

Waterford: *Council books of the Corporation of Waterford, 1662–1700*, ed. Seamus Pender (Dublin, 1964).

Waterford: 'A bundle of Waterford papers, being news items from Ramsey's *Waterford Chronicle* for 1791', ed. Patrick Power, *Journal of the Waterford and South-East of Ireland Archaeological Society*, 10 (1907), 159–60.

Wesley: *The journal of the Rev. John Wesley* (4 vols, London, 1827).

Wexford: *History of the town and county of Wexford* by P.H. Hore (6 vols, Dublin, 1900–11).

Youghal: *The council book of the Corporation of Youghal from 1610 to 1659, from 1666 to 1687, and from 1690 to 1800*, ed. Richard Caulfield (Guilford, 1878).

3. PAMPHLETS AND OTHER CONTEMPORARY PUBLICATIONS

[Anon.], *A collection of protests of the Lords of Ireland* (Dublin, 1772).

[Anon.], *An express from Cork, with an account of a bloody battle fought between the mob of that city and the standing army; in a letter from a person there to his friend here in Dublin* (Dublin, [1729]).

[Anon.], *The groans of Ireland: in a letter to a member of parliament* (Dublin, 1741).

[Anon.], *Transactions of the central relief committee of the Society of Friends during the Famine in Ireland in 1846 and 1847* (London, 1852).

Barker, Francis, and John Cheyne, *An account of the rise, progress and decline of fever lately epidemical in Ireland* (2 vols, Dublin, 1821).

Ferrar, John, *History of Limerick* (Dublin, 1787).

Hall, James, *Tour through Ireland particularly the interior* … (2 vols, London, 1813).

O'Conor, Charles, *The Protestant interest considered, relative to the operation of the popery acts in Ireland* (Dublin, 1757).

Prior, Thomas, *A proposal to prevent the price of corn from rising too high, or falling too low, by the means of granaries* ([Dublin], 1741).

Reid, Thomas, *Travels in Ireland in 1822* (London, 1823).

[Rye, George], *Considerations on agriculture treating of the several methods practised in different parts of the kingdom of Ireland, with remarks thereon* (Dublin, 1730).

Skelton, Philip, *Necessity of tillage and granaries* (Dublin, 1741).

Trotter, J.B., *Walks through Ireland in 1812, 1814 and 1817* (London, 1823).

Tuckey, Francis H., *The county and city of Cork remembrancer, or annals of the county and city of Cork* (Cork, 1837).

4. NEWSPAPERS AND PERIODICALS

Anglo-Celt, 1846–7
Belfast News Letter, 1756, 1808, 1812–47
Chute's Western Herald, 1831
Clonmel Gazette, 1792–4
Connaught Telegraph, 1831, 1839–47
Cork Advertizer, 1800–1, 1812
Cork Examiner, 1842, 1846–7
Cork Gazette, 1792
Dublin Chronicle, 1792–3
Dublin Courant, 1746
Dublin Daily Post, 1740
Dublin Evening Journal, 1778
Dublin Evening Post, 1783–4, 1796
Dublin Gazette or Weekly Courant, 1729
Dublin Gazette, 1729, 1730, 1740–1, 1775
Dublin Intelligence, 1729
Dublin Mercury, 1766, 1768, 1775
Dublin Morning Post, 1791–4
Dublin Newsletter, 1740–1
Dublin Post Boy (Nicholas Hussey's), 1729
Dublin Weekly Journal, 1729, 1748
Ennis Chronicle, 1790–5, 1800–1, 1816
Faulkner's Dublin Journal, 1729, 1740–1
Finn's Leinster Journal, 1766–78, 1787, 1789
Freeman's Journal, 1764–78, 1784, 1790, 1792–1808, 1812–47, 1861–2
Gentleman's Magazine, 27 (1757), 87 (1817)
Hibernian Chronicle (Cork), 1773
Hibernian Journal, 1772–84, 1791–5
Hibernian Morning Post (Cork), 1775

Hoey's Publick Journal, 1772–3
Hume's Dublin Gazette and Weekly Courant, 1729
Illustrated London News, 1842
Independent Journal or Chronicle of Liberty (Cork), 1775
Kerry Evening Post, 1831, 1842, 1846
Kerry Examiner, 1842, 1846–7
Leinster Express, 1842, 1846–7
Limerick Chronicle, 1772
Limerick Reporter and Tipperary Vindicator, 1840
London Evening Post, 1757, 1767
Munster Journal, 1750
Nation, 1845–7
Nenagh Guardian, 1842, 1846–7
Public Gazetteer, 1753, 1759–68
Pue's Occurrences, 1740–1, 1756–9, 1767, 1769
Ramsey's Waterford Chronicle, 1787–9, 1817
Saunders' News-Letter, 1817
Tralee Chronicle and Killarney Echo, 1846–7
Tralee Mercury, 1837
Tuam Herald, 1837, 1842, 1846–8
Universal Advertiser, 1753–7
Volunteer Evening Post, 1784
Volunteer Journal (Cork), 1783–84
Volunteer Journal (Dublin), 1784
Walker's Hibernian Magazine, 1795, 1796
Weekly Freeman, 1840

5. PARLIAMENTARY PROCEEDINGS, JOURNALS, STATUTES

An act for the more effectually punishing such persons as shall by violence obstruct the freedom of corn markets and the corn trade (Dublin, 1784).

Bullingbrooke, Edward and Jonathan Belcher, *An abridgement of the statutes of Ireland ... to the end of the 25 years of the reign of ... King George II* (Dublin, 1754).
Journal of the House of Commons of the kingdom of Ireland (21 vols, Dublin, 1796–1803).
Proceedings of the Irish House of Lords, 1771–1800, ed. James Kelly (3 vols, Dublin, 2008).
Statutes of the realm ed. A. Luders (11 vols in 12, London, 1810–28).
The parliamentary register or history of the proceedings and debates of the Irish parliament (17 vols, Dublin, 1782–1801).
The statutes at large passed in the parliaments held in Ireland 1310–1800 (20 vols, Dublin, 1789–1800).

6. IRISH HISTORIC TOWNS ATLAS

Irish historic towns atlas, volume I: Kildare, Carrickfergus, Bandon, Kells, Mullingar, Athlone (Dublin, 1996).
Irish historic towns atlas, volume II: Maynooth, Downpatrick, Bray, Kilkenny, Fethard, Trim (Dublin, 2005).
Irish historic towns atlas, volume III: Derry-Londonderry, Dundalk, Armagh, Tuam, Limerick (Dublin, 2012).
Gallagher, Fiona, *Irish historic towns atlas, no. 24: Sligo* (Dublin, 2012).
Gearty, Sarah, Martin Morris and Fergus O'Ferrall, *Irish historic towns atlas, no. 22: Longford* (Dublin, 2010).
Gillespie, Raymond and Stephen Royle, *Irish historic towns atlas, no. 12: Belfast, part 1* (Dublin, 2003).
Lennon, Colm, *Irish historic towns atlas, no. 19: Dublin, part 2, 1610 to 1756* (Dublin, 2008).
Ó Dalaigh, Brian, *Irish historic towns atlas, no. 25: Ennis* (Dublin, 2012).
Prunty, Jacinta and Paul Walsh, *Irish historic towns atlas, no. 28: Galway* (Dublin, 2016).

SECONDARY SOURCES

1. PUBLISHED WORKS

Almquist, E.L., 'Labour specialization and the Irish economy in 1841: an aggregate occupational analysis', *Economic History Review*, 2nd series, 36 (1983), 506–17.
Bardon, Jonathan, *Belfast: an illustrated history* (Belfast, 1982).
Barnard, T.C., 'The uses of 23 October 1641 and Irish Protestant celebrations', *EHR*, 106 (1991), 889–920.
Barnard, Toby, *A new anatomy of Ireland: the Irish Protestants, 1649–1770* (London, 2003).
Bartlett, Thomas, 'The end of moral economy: the Irish militia disturbances of 1793', *Past and Present*, 91 (1983), 41–64.
Bartlett, Thomas, 'Defenders and defenderism in 1975', *IHS*, 24 (1985), 373–94.
Bartlett, Thomas, *The fall and rise of the Irish nation: the Catholic question, 1690–1830* (Dublin, 1992).
Bartlett, Thomas, 'Ireland during the Revolutionary and Napoleonic wars, 1793–1815' in James Kelly (ed.), *The Cambridge history of Ireland, vol. 3, 1730–1880* (forthcoming).
Beames, Michael, 'Rural conflict in pre-Famine Ireland: peasant assassinations in Tipperary, 1837–1847', *Past and Present*, 81 (1978), 75–91.
Beames, Michael, 'The ribbon societies: lower-class nationalism in pre-Famine Ireland', *Past and Present*, 97 (1982), 128–43.

Beames, Michael, *Peasants and power: the Whiteboy movements and their control in pre-famine Ireland* (London, 1983).

Benn, George, *A history of the town of Belfast from the earliest times to the close of the eighteenth century* (Belfast, 1877).

Benson, Charles, 'The Dublin book trade' in J.H. Murphy (ed.), *History of the Irish book, volume 4: the nineteenth century* (Oxford, 2011), pp 27–46.

Berce, Yves-Marie, *Revolt and revolution in early modern Europe: an essay on the history of political violence* (New York, 1987).

Bew, Paul, *Ireland: the politics of enmity, 1789–2006* (Oxford, 2007).

Black, R.D. C., *Economic thought and the Irish question, 1817–1870* (Cambridge, 1960).

Bohstedt, John, *Riots and community politics in England and Wales, 1790–1810* (Cambridge, MA, 1983).

Bohstedt, John, 'Gender, household and community politics: women in English riots, 1790–1810', *Past and Present*, 120 (1988), 88–122.

Bohstedt, John, 'The myth of the feminine food riot: women as proto citizens in English community politics, 1790–1810' in Darline G. Levy and H.G. Applewhite (eds), *Women and politics in the age of the democratic revolution* (Ann Arbor, 1990), pp 21–60.

Bohstedt, John, 'The moral economy and the discipline of historical context', *Journal of Social History*, 26 (1992), 265–84.

Bohstedt, John, 'The pragmatic economy, the politics of provisions and the "invention" of the food riot tradition in 1740' in Adrian Randall and Andrew Charlesworth (eds), *Moral economy and popular protest: crowds, conflict and authority* (Basingstoke, 2000), pp 55–92.

Bohstedt, John, *The politics of provisions: food riots, moral economy and the market transition in England, c.1550–1850* (Farnham, 2010).

Bohstedt, John, 'Food riots and the politics of provisions in world history'. Institute of Development Studies Working Paper, volume 2014, 444 (Brighton, 2014).

Bohstedt, John, 'Food riots and the politics of provisions in early-modern England and France, the Irish Famine and World War I' in M.T. Davis (ed.), *Crowd actions in Britain and France from the Middle Ages to the modern world* (Basingstoke, 2015), pp 101–23.

Bourke, Austin, *The visitation of God: the potato and the Great Irish Famine*, ed. Jacqueline Hill and Cormac Ó Gráda (Dublin, 1993).

Bouton, C.A., *The flour war: gender, class and community in late ancien régime French society* (Philadelphia, 1993).

Bouton, C.A., 'Provisioning, power and popular protest from the seventeenth century to the French Revolution and beyond' in M.T. Davis (ed.), *Crowd actions in Britain and France from the middle ages to the modern world* (Basingstoke, 2015), pp 80–100.

Broeker, Galen, *Rural disorder and police reform in Ireland, 1812–36* (London, 1970).

Burke, William P., *History of Clonmel* (rept., Kilkenny, 1983).

Burns, R.E., *Irish parliamentary politics in the eighteenth century, 1714–60* (2 vols, Washington, 1989–90).

Burtchaell, Jack, 'The *Waterford Herald* for 1792–3', *Decies*, 47 (1993), 3–16.

Canny, Nicholas, 'Migration and opportunity', *Irish Economic and Social History*, 12 (1985), pp 7–32;

Canny, Nicholas, 'A reply [to Raymond Gillespie]', *Irish Economic and Social History*, 13 (1986), 96–100.

Canny, Nicholas, *Making Ireland British, 1580–1650* (Oxford, 2001).

Clark, Samuel, and J.S. Donnelly (eds), *Irish peasants: violence and political unrest, 1780–1914* (Manchester, 1983).

Clark, Samuel, *Social origins of the Irish land war* (Princeton, 1979).

Clark Smith, Barbara, 'Food rioters and the American Revolution' in Daniel Pope (ed.), *American radicalism* (Oxford, 2001), pp 18–41.

Collins, Brenda, 'Proto-industrialization and pre-Famine emigration', *Social History*, 7 (1982), 127–46.

Connell, K.H., 'Illicit distillation' in idem, *Irish peasant society: four historical essays* (Oxford, 1968), pp 1–50.

Connolly, S.J., 'Albion's fatal twigs: justice and law in the eighteenth century' in Rosalind Mitchison and Peter Roebuck (eds), *Economy and society in Scotland and Ireland, 1500–1939* (Edinburgh, 1988), pp 117–25.

Connolly, S.J., 'Violence and order in the eighteenth century' in Paul Ferguson, Patrick O'Flanagan and Kevin Whelan (eds), *Rural Ireland, 1600–1900: modernisation and change* (Cork, 1987), pp 42–61.

Connolly, S.J., 'The Houghers: agrarian protest in early eighteenth century Connacht' in C.H.E. Philpin (ed.), *Nationalism and popular protest in Ireland* (Cambridge, 1987), pp 139–62.

Connolly, S.J., *Religion, law and power: the making of Protestant Ireland, 1660–1760* (Oxford, 1992).

Connolly, S.J., '"Ag deanamh commanding": elite responses to popular culture, 1660–1850' in K.A. Miller and J.S. Donnelly (eds), *Irish popular culture, 1650–1850* (Dublin, 1998), pp 1–31.

Connolly, S.J., *Divided kingdom: Ireland, 1630–1800* (Oxford, 2008).

Crawford, E.M. (ed.), *Famine: the Irish experience: subsistence crises and famines in Ireland* (Edinburgh, 1989).

Crawford, W.H., *Domestic industry in Ireland: the experience of the linen industry* (Dublin, 1972).

Cronin, Maura, *Agrarian protest in Ireland, 1750–1960* (Dundalk, 2012).

Crossman, Virginia, *Politics, law and order in nineteenth-century Ireland* (Dublin, 1996),

Crossman, Virginia, 'The army and law and order in the nineteenth century' in Thomas Bartlett and Keith Jeffreys (eds), *A military history of Ireland* (Cambridge, 1996), pp 358–78.

Crossman, Virginia, *Politics, pauperism and power in late nineteenth-century Ireland* (Manchester, 2006).

Cullen, Karen J., *Famine in Scotland: the 'ill years' of the 1690s* (Edinburgh, 2010).

Cullen, L.M., *Anglo-Irish trade, 1660–1800* (Manchester, 1968).

Cullen, L.M., *An economic history of Ireland since 1660* (London, 1972).

Cullen, L.M., 'Eighteenth-century flour milling in Ireland', *Irish Economic and Social History*, 4 (1977), 5–25.

Cullen, L.M., 'Population trends in seventeenth-century Ireland', *Economic and Social Review*, 6 (1974–5), 149–65.

Cullen, L.M., *The emergence of modern Ireland, 1600–1900* (London, 1981).

Cullen, L.M., 'Economic development, 1690–1750', 'Economic development, 1750–1800' both in W.E. Vaughan and T.W. Moody (eds), *A new history of Ireland, iv: Eighteenth-century Ireland* (Oxford, 1986), pp 123–58, 159–95.

Cullen, L.M., 'The Irish food crisis of the early 1740s: the economic conjuncture', *Irish Economic and Social History*, 37 (2010), 1–23.

Cullen, L.M., 'Problems in and sources for the study of economic fluctuations 1660–1800', *Irish Economic and Social History*, 41 (2014), 1–19.

Cunningham, John, *'A town tormented by the sea': Galway, 1790–1914* (Dublin, 2004).

Cunningham, John, '"Compelled to their bad acts by hunger": three Irish urban crowds, 1817–45', *Eire-Ireland*, 45 (2010), 128–51.

Cunningham, John, 'Popular protest and a "moral economy" in provincial Ireland in the early nineteenth century' in Francis Devine, Fintan Lane and Niamh Puirséil (eds), *Essays in Irish labour history* (Dublin, 2008), pp 26–48.

Cunningham, John, ""'Tis hard to argue starvation into quiet": protest and resistance, 1846–47' in Enda Delaney and Breandan MacSuibhne (eds), *Ireland's Great Famine and popular politics* (New York and Abingdon, 2016), pp 10–33.

Cunningham, John, 'The mayor/admiral of Claddagh and Galway's moral economy' in Emmet O'Connor and John Cunningham (eds), *Lives on the left: studies in Irish radical leadership* (Manchester, 2016), pp 22–34.

Curtin, Gerard, *West Limerick: crime, popular protest and society, 1820–1845* (Ballynahill, county Limerick, 2008).

Curtin, Nancy J., 'The magistracy and counter revolution in Ulster, 1795–1798' in Jim Smyth (ed.), *Revolution, counter-revolution and Union in Ireland in the 1790s* (Cambridge, 2000), pp 39–54.

Davis, Graham, 'Making history: John Mitchel and the Great Famine' in P. Hyland and Neil Sammels (eds), *Irish writing: exile and subversion* (London, 1991), pp 98–115.

de Roover, Raymond, 'The concept of the just price: theory and economic politics', *Journal of Economic History*, 18 (1958), 418–38.

Delany, Ruth, *The Grand Canal of Ireland* (Newton Abbot, 1973).

Devine, T.M., 'Unrest and stability in rural Ireland and Scotland 1760–1840' in Peter Roebuck and Rosalind Mitchison (eds), *Economy and society in Scotland and Ireland, 1500–1939* (Edinburgh, [1988]), pp 126–39.

Dickson, David, Cormac Ó Gráda, and Stuart Daultrey, 'Hearth tax, household size and Irish population change, 1672–1821', *RIA proc.*, 82C (1982), 125–81.

Dickson, David, 'In search of the old Irish poor law' in Peter Roebuck and Rosalind Mitchison (eds), *Economy and society in Scotland and Ireland, 1500–1939* (Edinburgh, 1988), pp 149–59.

Dickson, David, 'The demographic implications of the growth of Dublin, 1650–1850' in Richard Lawton and Robert Lee (eds), *Urban population development in western Europe from the late-eighteenth to the early-twentieth century* (Liverpool, 1989), pp 178–89.

Dickson, David, 'Paine and Ireland' in David Dickson et al. (eds), *The United Irishmen: republicanism, radicalism and rebellion* (Dublin, 1993), pp 135–50.

Dickson, David, 'The other great Irish famine' in Cathal Póirtéir (ed.), *The Great Irish Famine* (Cork, 1995), pp 50–9.

Dickson, David, *Arctic Ireland: the extraordinary story of the great frost and forgotten famine of 1740–41* (Belfast, 1997).

Dickson, David, *Old world colony: Cork and south Munster, 1630–1830* (Cork, 2005).

Dickson, David, '1740–41 famine' in John Crowley et al. (eds), *Atlas of the Great Irish Famine, 1845–52* (Cork, 2012), pp 23–7.

Dickson, David, *Dublin: the making of a capital city* (London, 2014).

Donnelly, James S., *The land and the people of nineteenth-century Cork: the rural economy and the land question* (London, 1975).

Donnelly, James S., 'The Irish agricultural depression of 1859–64', *Irish Economic and Social History*, 3 (1976), 33–54.

Donnelly, James S., 'The Whiteboys, 1761–65', *IHS*, 21 (1978–9), 20–55.

Donnelly, James S., 'The Rightboy movement 1785–8', *Studia Hibernica*, 17 and 18 (1977–8), 120–202.

Donnelly, James S., 'Irish agrarian rebellion: the Whiteboys of 1769–76', *RIA proc.*, 83C (1983), 293–331.

Donnelly, James S., 'Hearts of Oak: Hearts of Steel', *Studia Hibernica*, 21 (1981), 7–73.

Donnelly, James S., 'The social composition of agrarian rebellions in early nineteenth-century Ireland: the case of the Carders and Caravats, 1813–16' in P.J. Corish (ed.), *Radicals, rebels and establishments* (Belfast, 1985), pp 151–69.

Donnelly, James S., *Captain Rock: the Irish agrarian rebellion of 1821–1824* (Cork, 2009).

Dowling, M.W., *Tenant right and agrarian society in Ulster, 1600–1870* (Dublin, 1999).

Downey, E., *The story of Waterford* (Waterford, 1914).

Drake, Michael, 'The Irish demographic crisis of 1740–41', in T.W. Moody (ed.), *Historical Studies VI* (London, 1968), pp 101–24.

Edelman, Marc, 'E.P. Thompson and moral economies' in Didier Fassin (ed.), *A companion to moral anthropology* (Oxford, 2012), pp 49–66

Eiríksson, Andriès, 'Food supply and food riots' in Cormac Ó Gráda, *Famine 150: commemorative lectures series* (Dublin, 1997), pp 67–94.

Elliott, Bruce S. *Irish migrants in the Canadas: a new approach* (Belfast, 1988).

Ely, Geoff, *A crooked line: from cultural history to the history of society* (Ann Arbor, c.2005).

Engler, Steven, J. Lutenbacher, F. Mauelshagen and J. Werner, 'The Irish famine of 1740–1741: causes and effects', *Climate of the Past*, 9 (2013), 1161–79 [available at: http://www.clim-past-discuss.net/9/1013/2013/cpd-9-1013-2013.pdf].

Enright, Flannan, 'Terry Alts: the rise and fall of an agrarian society' in Matthew Lynch and Patrick Nugent (eds), *Clare: history and society* (Dublin, 2008), pp 219–41.

Fitzgerald, Patrick, 'The great hunger? Irish famine: changing patterns of crisis' in E. Margaret Crawford (ed.), *The hungry stream: essays on emigration and famine* (Belfast, 1997), pp 110–22.

Fitzpatrick, David, 'Class, family and rural unrest in nineteenth-century Ireland' in P.J. Drudy (ed.), *Irish Studies, 2: Ireland: land, politics and people* (Cambridge, 1982), pp 37–75.

Fitzpatrick, David, *Irish emigration, 1801–1921* (Dundalk, 1984).

Fitzpatrick, David, 'Famine, entitlements and seduction: Captain Edward Wynne in Ireland, 1846–1851', *EHR*, 110 (1995), 596–619.

Fraher, William, 'The Dungarvan disturbances of 1846 and sequels' in Des Cowman (ed.), *The Famine in Waterford* (Waterford, 1995), pp 137–52.

Gailus, Manfred, 'Food riots in Germany in the late 1840s', *Past and Present*, 145 (1994), 257–93.

Garvin, Tom, 'Defenders, Ribbonmen and others: underground political networks in pre-Famine Ireland', *Past and Present*, 96 (1982), 133–55.

Gibbons, Stephen Randolph (ed.), *Captain Rock, knight errant: the threatening letters of pre-Famine Ireland, 1801–1845* (Dublin, 2004).

Gibney, John, *The shadow of a year: the 1641 Rebellion in Irish history and memory* (Madison, WI and London, 2013).

Gill, Conrad, *The rise of the Irish linen industry* (Oxford, 1925, 1964).

Gillespie, Raymond, 'Harvest crises in early seventeenth-century Ireland', *Irish Economic and Social History*, 11 (1984), 5–18.

Gillespie, Raymond, 'Migration and opportunity: a comment', *Irish Economic and Social History*, 13 (1986), 90–5.

Gillespie, Raymond, 'The small towns of Ulster, 1600–1799', *Ulster Folklife*, 36 (1990), 23–30.

Gillespie, Raymond, *The transformation of the Irish economy, 1550–1700* (Dundalk, 1991).

Gillespie, Raymond, 'Explorers, exploiters and entrepreneurs: early modern Ireland and its context, 1500–1700', in Brian Graham and L.J. Proudfoot (eds), *An historical geography of Ireland* (London, 1993), pp 123–57.

Gillespie, Raymond, 'Small towns in early modern Ireland' in Peter Clark (ed.), *Small towns in early modern Europe* (Cambridge, 1995), pp 148–65.

Gillespie, Raymond, 'Dublin, 1600–1700: a city and its hinterlands' in Peter Clark and Bernard Lepetit (eds), *Capital cities and their hinterlands in early modern Europe* (Aldershot, 1996), pp 84–101.

Gillespie, Raymond, *Seventeenth-century Ireland: making Ireland modern* (Dublin, 2005).

Gillespie, Raymond, 'Irish agriculture in the seventeenth century' in Margaret Murphy and Matthew Stout (eds), *Agriculture and settlement in Ireland* (Dublin, 2015), pp 119–38.

Gray, Peter, *The Irish famine: new horizons* (London, 1995).

Gray, Peter, *Famine, land, and politics: British government and Irish society, 1843–1850* (Dublin, 1999).

Griffin, Michael, *The people with no name: Ireland's Ulster Scots, America's Scots Irish and the creation of the British Atlantic world, 1689–1764* (Princeton, 2001).

Guinnane, Timothy, *The vanishing Irish: households, migration, and the rural economy in Ireland, 1850–1914* (Princeton, 1997).

Hansard, Joseph, *The history, topography and antiquities … of the county and city of Waterford* (Dungarvan, 1870, Lismore, 1977).

Harrison, Mark, *Crowds and history: mass phenomena in English towns, 1790–1835* (Cambridge, 1988).

Hayton, D.W., James Kelly and John Bergin (eds), *The eighteenth-century composite state: representative institutions in Ireland and Europe, 1689–1800* (Basingstoke, 2010).

Hernon, Joseph, 'A Victorian Cromwell: Sir Charles Trevelyan, the famine and the age of improvement', *Eire-Ireland*, 22 (1987), 15–29.

Higgins-McHugh, Noreen, 'The 1830s Tithe Riots', in William Sheehan and Maura Cronin (eds), *Riotous assemblies: rebels, riots and revolts in Ireland* (Cork, 2011), pp 80–95.

Hilton, Boyd, *A mad, bad and dangerous people? England, 1783–1846* (Oxford, 2008).

Hoban, Brendan, *Tracing the stem: Killala bishops* (Dublin, 2015).

Hobsbawm, Eric, *Primitive rebels* (Manchester, 1959).

Hobsbawm, Eric, 'The machine breakers' in idem, *Labouring men: studies in the history of labour* (London, 1964), pp 5–22.

Hogan, Liam, 'The Limerick Food riot of 1830' at https://medium.com/@Limerick1914/objects-of-a-deeper-interest-part-2 (accessed July 2016).

Hoppen, K. Theodore, *Elections, politics, and society in Ireland, 1832–1885* (Oxford, 1984).

Hoppen, K. Theodore, *Governing Hibernia: British politicians and Ireland, 1800–1921* (Oxford, 2016).

Hufton, Olwen, 'Social conflict and the grain supply in eighteenth-century France', *Journal of Interdisciplinary History*, 15:2 (1983), 303–31.

Hufton, Olwen, 'Women in revolution, 1789–1796', *Past and Present*, 53 (Nov. 1971), 90–108.

Hufton, Olwen, *The poor in eighteenth-century France, 1750–1789* (Oxford, 1974).

Huggins, Michael, *Social conflict in pre-Famine Ireland: the case of county Roscommon* (Dublin, 2007).

Jones, Peter, 'Swing, Speenhamland and rural social relations: the "moral economy" of the English crowd in the nineteenth century', *Social History*, 32 (2007), 271–90.

Jordan, D.E., *Land and popular politics in Ireland: county Mayo* (Cambridge, 1994).

Karandinos, George, L.K. Hart, F.M. Castrillo and Phillipe Bourgeois, 'The moral economy of violence in the US inner city', *Current Anthropology*, 55:1 (2014), 1–22.

Kaye, H.J., and Keith McClelland (eds), *E.P. Thompson: critical perspectives* (Philadelphia, 1990).

Kelly, James, 'Presbyterians and Protestants: relations between the Church of Ireland and the Presbyterian church in late eighteenth-century Ireland', *Eire-Ireland*, 23 (1988), pp 38–56.

Kelly, James, 'Inter-denominational relations and religious toleration in late eighteenth-century Ireland', *Eighteenth-Century Ireland*, 3 (1988), 39–68.

Kelly, James, 'The genesis of Protestant ascendancy: the Rightboy disturbances of the 1780s and their impact upon Protestant opinion' in Gerard O'Brien (ed.), *Parliament, politics and people: essays in eighteenth-century Irish history* (Dublin, 1989), pp 93–127.

Kelly, James, 'Harvests and hardship: famine and scarcity in Ireland in the late 1720s', *Studia Hibernica*, 26 (1991–2), 65–106.

Kelly, James, 'Scarcity and poor relief in eighteenth-century Ireland: the subsistence crisis of 1782–4', *Irish Historical Studies*, 28 (1992–3), 38–62.

Kelly, James, *'That damn'd thing called honour': duelling in Ireland, 1580–1860* (Cork, 1992).

Kelly, James, 'The glorious and immortal memory: commemoration and Protestant identity in Ireland, 1660–1800', *RIA proc.*, 94C (1994), 25–52.

Kelly, James, 'Conservative political thought in late eighteenth-century Ireland' in S.J. Connolly (ed.), *Political ideas in eighteenth-century Ireland* (Dublin, 2000), pp 195–221.

Kelly, James, *Sir Edward Newenham, MP, 1734–1814: defender of the Protestant constitution* (Dublin, 2002).

Kelly, James, 'Political publishing, 1700–1800' in Raymond Gillespie and Andrew Hadfield (eds), *The Oxford history of the book in Ireland, iii: early modern Ireland* (Oxford, 2006), pp 215–33.

Kelly, James, *The Liberty and Ormond boys: factional riot in eighteenth-century Dublin* (Dublin, 2006).

Kelly, James, *Poynings' Law and the making of law in Ireland, 1660–1800* (Dublin, 2007).

Kelly, James, *Sir Richard Musgrave, 1746–1818: ultra-Protestant ideologue* (Dublin, 2009).

Kelly, James 'Defending the established order: Richard Woodward, bishop of Cloyne (1726–94)' in James Kelly et al. (eds), *People, power and politics: essays on Irish history, 1660–1850* (Dublin, 2010), pp 143–74.

Kelly, James, 'Charitable societies: their genesis and development, 1720–1800' in idem and M.J. Powell (eds), *Clubs and societies in eighteenth-century Ireland* (Dublin, 2010), pp 89–108.

Kelly, James, 'The decline of duelling and the emergence of the middle class in Ireland' in Maria Luddy and Fintan Lane (eds), *Politics, society and the middle class in modern Ireland* (Basingstoke, 2010), pp 89–106.

Kelly, James, 'Disappointing the boundless ambitions of France: Irish protestants and the fear of invasion', *Studia Hibernica*, 37 (2011), 27–105.

Kelly, James, 'Introduction: establishing the context' in idem and Ciaran MacMurchaidh (eds), *Irish and English: essays on the linguistic and cultural frontier 1600–1900* (Dublin, 2012), pp 15–42.

Kelly, James, 'Coping with crisis: the response to the famine of 1740–1', *Eighteenth-Century Ireland*, 27 (2012), 99–122.

Kelly, James, 'Matthew Carey's Irish apprenticeship: editing the *Volunteer's Journal*, 1783–84', *Eire-Ireland*, 49:3 and 4 (2014), 201–43.

Kelly, James, *Sport in Ireland, 1600–1840* (Dublin, 2014).

Kelly, James, '"Ravaging houses of ill fame": popular riot and public sanction in eighteenth-century Ireland' in D.W. Hayton and A.R. Holmes (eds), *Ourselves alone?: Religion, society and politics in eighteenth- and nineteenth-century Ireland* (Dublin, 2016), pp 84–103.

Kelly, James, '"This iniquitous traffic"; the kidnapping of children for the American colonies in eighteenth-century Ireland', *Journal of the History of Childhood and Youth*, 9:2 (2016), pp 233–46.

Kelly, James, 'Laying the executed corpse at the prosecutor's door' in Salvador Ryan (ed.), *Death and the Irish: a miscellany* (Dublin, 2016), pp 101–4.

Kelly, Michael, *Struggle and strife on a Mayo estate, 1833–1903: the Logans of Logboy and their tenants* (Dublin, 2014).

Kemmey, Jim, 'The siege of Lock Mills' in idem (ed.), *The Limerick anthology* (Dublin, 1996), p. 236.

Kennedy, Liam, and L.A. Clarkson, 'Birth, death and exile: Irish population history, 1700–1921' in B.J. Graham and L.J. Proudfoot (eds), *An historical geography of Ireland* (London, 1993), pp 158–84.

Kennedy, Liam, 'The rural economy, 1820–1914' in idem and Philip Ollerenshaw (eds), *An economic history of Ulster, 1820–1940* (Manchester, 1985), pp 1–61.

Kennedy, Liam, and M.W. Dowling, 'Prices and wages in Ireland, 1700–1850', *Irish Economic and Social History*, 24 (1997), 62–104.

Kerr, Donal, *The Catholic Church and the Famine* (Dublin, 1996).

Kinealy, Christine, *This great calamity: the Irish Famine, 1845–52* (Dublin, 1994).

Kinealy, Christine and Gerard MacAtasney, *The hidden famine: poverty, hunger and sectarianism in Belfast, 1840–50* (London, 2000).

Kinealy, Christine, *The Great Irish Famine: impact, ideology and rebellion* (Basingstoke, 2002).

King, Peter, 'Edward Thompson's contribution to eighteenth-century studies; the patrician-plebeian model re-examined', *Social History*, 21:2 (1996), 215–28.

Larkin, Emmet, *The pastoral role of the Roman Catholic Church in pre-famine Ireland, 1750–1850* (Dublin, 2006).

Lee, David, 'The food riots of 1830 and 40' in idem and Debbie Jacobs (eds), *Made in Limerick* (2 vols, Limerick, 2003), i, 55–65.

Lemarchand, Guy, 'Troubles populaires au XVIIIe siècle et conscience de classe: une préface à la Révolution Francaise', *Annales historiques de la Révolution Française*, 279 (1990), 32–48.

Lenihan, Padraig, 'War and population, 1649–42', *Irish Economic and Social History*, 24 (1997), 1–21.

Lennon, Colm, *Sixteenth-century Ireland; the incomplete conquest* (rev. ed., Dublin, 2005).

Lindsay, Deirdre, *Dublin's oldest charity: the Sick and Indigent Roomkeepers Society, 1790–1990* (Dublin, 1990).

Logue, Kenneth J., *Popular disturbances in Scotland, 1780–1815* (Edinburgh, 1979).

Lucas, Colin, 'Crowd and politics between *ancien regime* and revolution in France', *Journal of Modern History*, 60 (1988), 421–57.

Lynch, Patrick and John Vaizey, *Guinness's brewery in the Irish economy, 1759–1876* (Cambridge, 1960).

MacGiolla Phadraig, Brian, 'Dr John Carpenter, archbishop of Dublin, 1760–86', *Dublin Historical Record*, 30 (1976–7), 2–25.

MacLochalinn, Alf, 'Social life in county Clare, 1800–1850', *Irish University Review*, 2:1 (1972), 55–78.

Mac Suibhne, Breandán, 'Spirit, spectre, shade: a true story of an Irish haunting or troublesome pasts in the political culture of north-west Ulster 1786–1972', *Field Day Review*, 9 (2013), 149–211.

Mac Suibhne, Breandán, '"Bastard Ribbonism": the Molly Maguires, the uneven failure of entitlement and the politics of post-famine adjustment' in idem and Enda Delany (eds), *Ireland's Great Famine and popular politics* (New York and Abingdon, 2016), pp 186–232.

Magennis, Eoin, 'In search of the "moral economy": food scarcity in 1756–57 and the crowd' in idem and Peter Jupp (eds), *Crowds in Ireland, c.1720–1920* (Basingstoke, 2000), pp 189–211.

Magennis, Eoin, 'Regulating the market: parliament, corn and bread in eighteenth-century Ireland' in Michael Brown and Sean Patrick Donlon (eds), *The law and other legalities of Ireland, 1689–1850* (Farnham, 2011), pp 209–30.

Malcolmson, Robert, 'A set of ungovernable people: the Kingswood colliers in the eighteenth century' in John Brewer and John Styles (eds), *An ungovernable people: the English and their law in the seventeenth and eighteenth centuries* (London, 1980), pp 85–127.

Manning, Aidan, *Donegal poitín: a history* (Letterkenny, 2003).

Díaz Marín, Pedro, 'Crisis de subsistencia y protesta popular: los matines de 1847', *Historia Agraria*, 30 (2003), 31–62 (published in English as 'Subsistence crisis and popular protest in Spain: the *motines* of 1847' in Cormac Ó Gráda et al. (eds), *When the potato failed: causes and effects of the last European subsistence crisis, 1845–1850* (Turnhout, 2007), pp 267–92).

McCabe, Ciarán, 'The early years of the Strangers' Friend Society, Dublin: 1790–1845', *Bulletin of the Methodist Historical Society of Ireland*, 90 (2014), 65–92.

McCabe, Desmond, 'Social order and the ghost of a moral economy in pre-Famine Mayo' in Raymond Gillespie and Gerard Moran (eds), *'A various country': essays in Mayo history, 1500–1900* (Westport, 1987), pp 91–112.

McClelland, Aiken, 'Amyas Griffith', *Irish Booklore*, 2 (1972–6), 6–21.

McMahon, Richard, *Homicide in pre-Famine and Famine Ireland* (Liverpool, 2013).

McNally, Patrick, 'Rural protest and "moral economy": the Rightboy disturbances and parliament' in Allan Blackstock and Eoin Magennis (eds), *Politics and political culture in Britain and Ireland, 1750–1850* (Belfast, 2007), pp 262–82.

McNamara, Conor, 'This wretched people: the famine of 1822 in the west of Ireland' in Carla King and Conor McNamara (eds), *The west of Ireland: new perspectives on the nineteenth century* (Dublin, 2011), pp 13–34.

Meuvret, Jean, *La problème des subsistances à l'époque de Louis XIV* (3 vols, Paris, 1977).

Mirala, Petri, *Freemasonry in Ulster, 1733–1813: a social and political history of the masonic brotherhood in the north of Ireland* (Dublin, 2007).

Mirrala, Petri, 'Masonic sociability and its limitations: the case of Ireland' in James Kelly and M.J. Powell (eds), *Clubs and societies in eighteenth-century Ireland* (Dublin, 2010), pp 315–31.

Mokyr, Joel, and Cormac Ó Gráda, 'Poor and getting poorer? Living standards in Ireland before the Famine', *Economic History Review*, 41:2 (1988), pp 209–35.

Mooney, Desmond, 'The origins of agrarian violence in Meath, 1790–1828', *Ríocht na Midhe*, 8:1 (1987), pp 45–67.

Moran, Gerard, *The Mayo evictions of 1860* (Westport, 1986).

Moran, Gerard, *A radical priest in Mayo, Fr Patrick Lavelle* (Dublin, 1994).

Morineau, Michel, 'Budget populaires en France aux dix-huitième siècle', *Revue d'histoire économique et sociale*, 50 (1972), pp 203–36, 449–81.

Morley, Vincent, *Irish opinion and the American Revolution, 1760–83* (Cambridge, 2002).

Morley, Vincent, 'The continuity of disaffection in eighteenth-century Ireland', *Eighteenth-Century Ireland*, 22 (2007), 189–205.

Morley, Vincent, *The popular mind in eighteenth-century Ireland* (Cork, 2017).

Munter, Robert, *The history of the newspaper in Ireland, 1685–1760* (Cambridge, 1966).

Neeson, J.M., *Commoners: common right, enclosure and social change in England, 1700–1820* (Cambridge, 1996).

Nicolas, Jean, *La Rébellion française, mouvements populaires et conscience sociale (1661–1789)* (Paris, 2002).

Ó Ciosáin, Niall, *Ireland in official print culture 1800–1850: a new reading of the Poor Inquiry* (Oxford, 2014).

O'Connor, Emmet, *A labour history of Waterford* (Waterford, 1989).

O'Connor, Theresa M., 'The embargo on the export of Irish provisions, 1776–1779', *Irish Historical Studies*, 2 (1940–1), 3–11.

O'Donoghue, Patrick, 'Opposition to tithe payments in 1830–31', *Studia Hibernica*, 6 (1966), 69–98.

O'Donovan, John, *An economic history of livestock in Ireland* (Cork, 1940).

O'Dowd, Anne, *Spalpeens and tattie hokers: history and folklore of the Irish migratory agricultural worker in Ireland and Britain* (Dublin, 1991).

Ó Gráda, Cormac, and Phelim P. Boyle, 'Fertility trends, excess mortality, and the Great Irish Famine', *Demography*, 23:4 (1986), 543–62.

Ó Gráda, Cormac, *Ireland before and after the famine: explorations in economic history, 1800–1925* (Manchester, 1988).

Ó Gráda, Cormac, 'Irish agricultural history: recent research', *Agricultural History Review*, 38:2 (1990), 165–73.

Ó Gráda, Cormac, 'The lumper potato and the Famine', *History Ireland*, 1:1 (1993), 22–3.

Ó Gráda, Cormac, *Ireland: a new economic history, 1780–1939* (Oxford, 1994).

Ó Gráda, Cormac, 'Making Irish famine history in 1995', *History Workshop Journal*, 42 (1995/6), 87–104.

Ó Gráda, Cormac, *Black '47 and beyond: the Great Irish Famine in history, economy and memory* (Princeton, 2000).

Ó Gráda, Cormac, and Diarmaid Ó Muirithe, 'The famine of 1740–41: representations in Gaelic poetry', *Éire-Ireland*, 45:3 and 4 (2010), 1–22.

Ó Gráda, Cormac, *Eating people is wrong, and other essays on famine* (Princeton, 2015).

Ó Murchadha, Ciarán, 'The onset of famine: county Clare, 1845–1846', *The Other Clare*, 19 (1995), 25–31.

Ó Murchadha, Ciarán, *Sable wings over the land: Ennis, county Clare, and its wider community during the Great Famine* (Ennis, 1998).

Ó Murchadha, Ciarán, 'The years of the Great Famine' in Matthew Lynch and Patrick Nugent (eds), *Clare: history and society* (Dublin, 2008), pp 243–64.

O'Neill, Timothy P., 'The Catholic Church and relief of the poor, 1815–45', *Archivium Hibernicum*, 31 (1973), 132–45.

O'Neill, Timothy P., 'Clare and Irish poverty, 1815–1851', *Studia Hibernica*, 14 (1974), 7–27.

O'Neill, T.P., 'The famine crises of the 1890s' in Crawford (ed.), *Famine: the Irish experience*, pp 176–97.

O'Rourke, John, *The history of the Great Irish Famine of 1847* (Dublin, 1875).

Ó Tuathaigh, Gearoid, 'An age of distress and reform: 1800 to 1860' in Art Cosgrave (ed.), *Dublin through the ages* (Dublin, 1988), pp 93–112.

Owen, D.J., *History of Belfast* (Belfast, 1921).

Owens, Gary, '"A moral insurrection": faction fighters, public demonstrators and the O'Connellite campaign, 1828', *IHS* 30 (1996–7), 513–41.

Palmer, Stanley H., *Police and protest in England and Ireland, 1780–1850* (Cambridge, 1988).

Palomera, Jaime, and Theodora Vetta, 'Moral economy: rethinking a radical concept', *Anthropological Theory*, 16:4 (2016), 413–43.

Patterson, James G., *In the wake of the Great Rebellion: republicanism, agrarianism and banditry in Ireland after 1798* (Manchester, 2008).

Philpin, C.H.E., (ed.), *Nationalism and popular protest in Ireland* (Cambridge, 1987).

Post, John D., 'Meteorological historiography', *Journal of Interdisciplinary History*, 34 (1973), pp 721–32.

Post, John D., *The last great subsistence crisis in the western world* (Baltimore, 1977).

Post, John D., 'Nutritional status and mortality in eighteenth-century Europe' in L.F. Newman (ed.), *Hunger in history; food shortage, poverty and deprivation* (Oxford, 1990), pp 244–80.

Powell, M.J., 'Moral economy and popular protest in the late eighteenth century' in Michael Brown and Sean Patrick Donlan (eds), *Law and other legalities of Ireland, 1689–1850* (Aldershot, 2010), pp 231–53.

Powell, M.J., *The politics of consumption in eighteenth-century Ireland* (Basingstoke, 2003).

Power, Joseph, *A history of Clarecastle and its environs* (Ennis, 2004).

Power, Thomas, *Law, politics and society in eighteenth-century Tipperary* (Oxford, 1993).

Randall, Adrian, and Andrew Charlesworth, 'The moral economy: riot, markets and social conflict' in idem (eds), *Markets, market culture and popular protest in eighteenth-century Britain and Ireland* (Liverpool, 1996), pp 1–32.

Ranger, Terence (ed.), *The invention of tradition* (Cambridge, 1993).

Ranger, Terence, 'Peasant consciousness: culture and conflict in Zimbabwe, in T. Shannin (ed.), *Peasants and peasant societies: selected readings* (2nd ed., Oxford, 1987), pp 311–28.

Reddy, W.M., 'The textile trade and the language of the crowd at Rouen, 1752–1871', *Past and Present*, 74 (1977), 62–89.

Reddy, W.M., *Money and liberty in modern Europe: a critique of historical understanding* (Cambridge, 1987).

Rees, Gordon, '"The most miserable scene of universal distress": Irish pamphleteers and the subsistence crisis of the early 1740s', *Studia Hibernica* 41 (2015), 87–108.

Robbins, Joseph, *The miasma: epidemic and panic in nineteenth-century Ireland* (Dublin, 1995).

Roberts, P.E.W., 'Caravats and Shavests: Whiteboyism and faction fighting in east Munster, 1801–11' in Donnelly and Clark (eds), *Irish peasants: violence and political unrest*, pp 64–101.

Rowe, Ashley, 'The food riots of the forties in Cornwall', *Royal Cornwall Polytechnic Society*, 10 (1942), 51–67.

Rudé, George, *Protest and punishment: story of the social and political protesters transported to Australia* (Oxford, 1978).

Rudé, George, *The crowd in history: a study of popular disturbances in France and England, 1730–1848* (New York, 1964).

Rudé, George, 'English rural and urban disturbances on the eve of the first reform bill, 1830–31' in H.J. Kaye (ed.), *The face of the crowd: selected essays of George Rudé* (Atlantic Highlands, NJ, 1988), pp 167–82.

Sharp, Buchanan, 'The food riots of 1347 and the medieval moral economy' in Randall and Charlesworth (eds), *Moral economy and popular protest*, pp 33–54.

Sharp, Buchanan, *Famine and scarcity in late medieval and early modern England: the regulation of grain marketing, 1256–1631* (Cambridge, 2016).

Simms, J.G., 'Connacht in the eighteenth century', *IHS*, 11 (1958), 116–33.

Solar, Peter, 'The Great Famine was no ordinary subsistence crisis' in E. Margaret Crawford (ed.), *Famine: the Irish experience: subsistence crises and famines in Ireland* (Edinburgh, 1989), pp 112–33.

Stevenson, John, 'Food riots in England, 1792–1818' in R. Quinault and John Stevenson (eds), *Popular protest and public order: six studies in British history, 1790–1920* (London, 1974), pp 33–74.

Stevenson, John, 'Bread or blood' in G.E. Mingay (ed.), *The unquiet countryside* (London, 1989), pp 23–35.

Stevenson, John, *Popular disturbances in England, 1700–1870* (2nd ed., London, 1992).

Strain, R.W.M., *Belfast and its Charitable Society: a study of urban social development* (Oxford, 1961).

Swift, John, *History of the Dublin bakers and others* ([Dublin], 1948).

Thompson, E.P., *The making of the English working class* (London, 1963).

Thompson, E.P., 'The moral economy of the English crowd in the eighteenth century', *Past and Present*, 50 (1971), 76–136.

Thompson, E.P., 'Patrician society, plebeian culture', *Journal of Social History*, 7 (1974), 382–405.

Thompson, E.P., 'The patricians and the plebs' in idem, *Customs in common* (London, 1991), pp 16–96.

Thompson, E.P., 'Eighteenth-century English society: class struggle without class', *Social History* 3:2 (1978), 133–65.

Thompson, E.P., 'The moral economy reviewed' in idem, *Customs in commons* (London, 1991), pp 259–351.

Thwaites, Wendy, 'The assize of bread in eighteenth-century Oxfordshire', *Oxoniensia*, 51 (1986), 171–81.

Tilly, Charles, 'Food supply and public order in modern Europe' in idem (ed.), *The formation of national states in Europe* (Princeton, 1975), pp 380–455.

Tilly, Charles, Louise and Richard, *The rebellious century, 1830–1930* (Cambridge, MA, 1975).

Tilly, Charles, *Popular contention in Great Britain, 1758–1834* (Cambridge, MA, 1995).

Tilly, Charles, *Contentious performances* (New York, 2008).

Tilly, Louise, 'The food riot as a form of political conflict in France', *Journal of Interdisciplinary History*, 2:1 (1971), 23–57.

Tilly, Louise A., 'Food entitlement, famine and conflict' in R.I. Rotberg and T.K. Rabb (eds), *Hunger and history: the impact of changing food production and consumption patterns on society* (Cambridge, 1985), pp 135–51.

Tilly, Louise, 'The decline and disappearance of the classical food riot in France', New School for Social Research, Working paper 147 (1992).

Townshend, Charles, *Political violence in Ireland: government and resistance since 1848* (Oxford, 1983).

Truxes, Thomas M., *Irish-American trade, 1660–1783* (Cambridge, 1988).

Truxes, T.M., 'Introduction: a connected Irish world' in idem (ed.), *Ireland, France, and the Atlantic in a time of war: reflections on the Bordeaux–Dublin letters, 1757* (London and New York, 2017), pp 1–31.

Walter, John, 'Grain riots and popular attitudes to the law: Maldon and the crisis of 1629' in John Brewer and John Styles (eds), *An ungovernable people: the English and their law in the seventeenth and eighteenth centuries* (London, 1980), pp 48–81.

Walter, John, and Keith Wrightson, 'Dearth and social order in early modern England', *Past and Present*, 71 (1976), 22–42.

Walter, John, *Crowds and popular politics in early modern England* (Manchester, 2006).

Walter, John, 'The politics of protest in seventeenth-century England' in M.T. Davis (ed.), *Crowd actions in Britain and France from the Middle Ages to the modern world* (Basingstoke, 2015), pp 58–79.

Walton, John, and David Seddon, *Free markets and food riots: the politics of global adjustment* (Oxford, 1994).

Watt, Tim, 'The corruption of the law and popular violence: the crisis of order in Dublin, 1729', *IHS*, 39, 153 (May 2014), 1–23.

Watt, Tim, 'Taxation riots and the culture of popular protest in Ireland, 1714–1740', *EHR*, 130 (2015), 1418–38.

Webb, Sidney and Beatrice, 'The assize of bread', *Economic Journal*, 14 (1904), 332–42.

Webster, Charles A., *The diocese of Cork* (Cork, 1920).

Wells, Roger, *Wretched faces: famine in wartime England, 1793–1801* (Gloucester, 1988).

Wells, Roger, 'The Irish famine of 1799–1801: market culture, moral economies and social protest' in Andrew Charlesworth and Adrian Randall (eds), *Markets, market culture and popular protest in eighteenth-century Britain and Ireland* (Liverpool, 1996), pp 163–93.

Whan, Robert, *The Presbyterians of Ulster, 1680–1730* (Woodbridge, 2013).

Whelan, Kevin, *The tree of liberty: radicalism, Catholicism and the construction of Irish identity, 1760–1830* (Cork, 1996).

Wood, Andy, *Riot, rebellion and popular politics in early modern England* (Basingstoke, 2002).

Wood, Andy, *The politics of social conflict: the Peak Country, 1520–1770* (Cambridge, 1999).

Woodham-Smith, Cecil, *The great hunger: Ireland 1845–9* (London, 1962).

Woodward, Donal, 'Irish trade and customs statistics, 1614–1641', *Irish Economic and Social History*, 26 (1999), 54–80.

2. UNPUBLISHED THESES

Abbot, T.M., 'The Downshire estates at Edenderry, 1800–1856' (MA, Maynooth University, 2004).

Casey, Brian, 'Land, politics and religion on the Clancarty estate, east Galway, 1851–1914' (PhD, Maynooth University, 2011).

Conwell, John J., 'Ulick John de Burgh, first marquis of Clanricarde … and his county Galway estate during the Great Famine' (MA, Maynooth University, 2002).

Eiríksson, Andries, 'Crime and popular protest in county Clare, 1815–1852' (PhD, TCD, 1992).

Fleming, D.A., 'The government and politics of provincial Ireland, 1691–1781 (D.Phil., Oxford University, 2005).

Kinsella, Shay, 'Milford Mills and the creation of a gentry powerbase: the Alexanders of county Carlow, 1790–1870' (PhD, St Patrick's College, DCU, 2015).

McCabe, Desmond, 'Law, conflict and social order: county Mayo, 1820–1845' (PhD, UCD, 1991).

MhicGiobúin, M.E., 'Edward Tierney and the development of Kanturk, 1823–56' (MA, Maynooth University, 2002).

Trant, T.A., 'Government policy and Irish distress, 1816–19' (MA, UCD, 1965).

Worthington, P.A., 'Dearth, death and disease: an analysis of mortality crises in five Lagan valley parishes, 1700–1850' (MA, QUB, 1991).

3. DIGITAL RESOURCES

Bohstadt, John, 'Riot censuses# at http://?web.utk.edu/~bohntedt/.:
   Riot Census I: Census of riots — first century (1580–1650);
   Riot Census II: Census of riots – second century (1650–1739);
   Riot Census III: 1740–41 – third century (1740–1850);
   Riot Census IV: 1756–57 riots – third century (1740–1850);
   Riot Census V: 1766–67 riots – third century (1740–1850).
Irish Legislation data base, 1692–1800, at http://www.qub.ac.uk/ild/

4. WORKS OF REFERENCE

Dictionary of Irish biography, ed. James McGuire and James Quinn (9 vols, Cambridge, 2009).

Oxford dictionary of national biography (60 vols, Oxford, 2004).

Oxford English dictionary (2nd ed., 20 vols, Oxford, 1989).

O'Toole, James, *Newsplan: report of the Newsplan project in Ireland* (London, 1992).

Webb, A.J., *Compendium of Irish biography* (Dublin, 1878).

Index